Measurement in the
Social Sciences

METHODOLOGICAL PERSPECTIVES

A series edited by
RICHARD J. HILL
University of Oregon

MEASUREMENT
IN THE
SOCIAL SCIENCES

Theories and Strategies

edited by H. M. BLALOCK, JR.

University of Washington

ALDINE PUBLISHING COMPANY *Chicago*

First published 1974 by
Aldine Publishing Company
529 South Wabash Avenue
Chicago, Illinois 60605

ISBN   0-202-30271-7 clothbound edition
           0-202-30272-5 paperbound edition
Library of Congress Catalog Number 73-89514
Printed in the United States of America

Contents

Measurement in the
Social Sciences

Chapter 1

INTRODUCTION

In a general way, the importance of good measurement is widely accepted and emphasized within the social sciences. It is even stressed in elementary textbooks. Yet with the exception of psychology and economics, there has been surprisingly little systematic attention given to the subject in the social science literature. To be sure, most investigators are concerned about the measurement of the particular variables they are studying. But there has been relatively little effort to extract general principles from these specific instances or to develop specializations that focus primarily on problems of measurement. Few advanced-level courses on measurement appear in graduate curricula, and when they do they are most likely to be concerned with topics developed out of either the psychometric or the econometric literature—topics such as index construction, factor analysis, or scaling theory.

Each of the social sciences, of course, has its own history of development. In sociology, for example, the emphasis on measurement seems to have been episodic rather than continuous. During the late 1940s and early 1950s there was considerable interest in attitude measurement and procedures such as factor analysis, Guttman scaling, and latent-structure analysis, but a period of relative stagnation set in during the later 1950s and early 1960s that seemed to portend a declining interest. Apparently, attitudinal research was believed to be reaching a plateau, or point of diminishing returns. Carefully conceived scales were replaced by rather simple two- or three-item indices in the belief that the latter were almost as good as the former. Since 1965, however, a kind of revival of interest in the measurement field has been apparent in sociology. Just why this revival has taken place is rather difficult to explain. Perhaps the process is a cyclical one in which we tend to place too much faith in the potential of some specific technique and then become disillusioned by the quality of available data. The process may repeat itself with each new generation of social scientists.

Part of the problem may be that of adjusting our aspirations to the

1

available data-collection capabilities. Here it becomes important to distinguish between two different kinds of tasks commonly discussed in
the measurement literature. The first concerns actual data collection,
together with the theoretical conceptualization of variables, the object
being that of improving the quality of our data before we get to the
analysis stage. The second concerns the problem of analyzing data involving imperfectly measured variables. As a general principle it seems
very clear that the more errors that creep into the data-collection stage,
the more complex our analyses must be in order to make allowances
for these errors. In many instances we may discover that there will
simply be too many unknowns and that untested a priori assumptions
must be made before one may proceed with the analysis.

It is thus the data-collection stage that is crucial, and unfortunately
there are many considerations other than strictly methodological ones
that determine data quality. In particular, data collection is usually a
very costly and time-consuming process, so much so that both sponsors
and investigators find it necessary to cut corners. There are also practical limitations on the number and kinds of questions that can be asked
of each respondent, or on the types of behaviors that can be observed;
and ethical considerations may inhibit data collection. Thus the way in
which social scientists are organized to collect data, the policies of fund-
ing agencies, and the necessity of protecting subjects or respondents in
sensitive areas all combine to place limits on the nature of the data we
may collect.

All this implies that our knowledge of methodological principles and
the availability of appropriate mathematical and statistical tools and
models will never, in themselves, be sufficient. To the degree that our
methodological sophistication greatly exceeds our ability to collect adequate data, disillusionment is likely to result. This means that social
scientists must make much more serious efforts to coordinate their
data-collection procedures, to standardize their measurements, and to
organize so as to make it possible to collect data over much longer time
periods than those to which we are accustomed. Methodologists cannot
really address themselves to such problems, except to sensitize members of their professions to the implications of low-quality data and
measurement errors of unknown magnitudes.

If every variable were perfectly measured by a single indicator there
would be few difficulties. But research always consists of a series of
compromises in design, measurement, and analysis. At many points
there will be decisions that, in effect, require one to cut corners in some
respects in order to handle other difficulties more adequately. Obviously, the smaller the scale of the research the more such corners must
be cut. In sociology it has often been the case that quality of measurement has been sacrificed in order to expand the sample size or to in-

clude a large number of additional variables. In some situations this may be a wise decision, but it will always involve a price. If one could easily estimate the magnitudes of all types of errors, these crucial decisions could be made on a rational basis. The less one knows about measurement errors and their implications, the greater one's tendency to favor the other kinds of criteria. If we generally fail to assess the extent of measurement errors in our major studies, and if we pretend that distortions are negligible, we may not discover these defects for a long time. And we run the risk of returning to a phase in the cycle in which quality of measurement is conveniently ignored.

Although the main thrust of the argument for improvement of measurement often comes from social scientists who are variously labeled as "science-oriented," "quantitative," or "hard," there have been similar criticisms from those who are sometimes regarded as emphasizing the opposite approach. In recent years sociology has witnessed an upsurge of subjectivists who have revived arguments to the effect that it is persons' definitions of situations, or the "meanings" they attach to objective events, that constitute the reality with which social scientists must deal. Interestingly enough, this position is compatible with the extensive literature on attitude measurement, scaling, factor analysis, and latent-structure analysis—all of which were designed to help infer postulated internal states (e.g., attitudes, values, perceptions, or abilities) from objective behavior. Both the quantitative and the qualitative thrusts, in this instance, emphasize the *indirectness* of many types of measurement processes. Both react against the naive linking of behavioral responses or objective stimuli in simple one-to-one relationships with postulated properties. Both insist that *theoretical* assumptions are needed to supplement strictly operational procedures.

Thus the issue is not so much qualitative versus quantitative approaches to measurement as the degree of complexity one is willing to admit into the measurement theory. But complexity quickly leads to perplexity, vagueness, and defeatism unless systematic and rational grounds can be established for handling this complexity. What if several indicators of the same concept yield different results? Sometimes, strictly empirical criteria such as sizes of correlation coefficients are invoked. But without a theoretical rationale for linking the several indicators to a construct, it is difficult to see just how one can interpret diverse results in any coherent or convincing manner. One of the consistent themes that runs through those chapters in this book dealing with matters of substantive interpretation is that one needs explicit theories of measurement in order to make rational decisions in data analysis. In general, the more attention given to the data-collection stage of research, the simpler and more plausible these theories can be.

The coverage of this book is far from complete and is deliberately selective. There has first of all been no effort to include discussions of technical subjects such as factor analysis with which social scientists are generally familiar, or of those that are best developed in book-length presentations. Also omitted are many less technical topics, such as Guttman scaling and other scaling procedures, that have been well diffused into the social science literature and therefore need not be drawn to the attention of most audiences. Unfortunately, many other aspects of measurement do not appear to have been studied systematically enough for reasonable statements of their general properties to be made at this time. For example, informal participant observation is a recognized and important method of data collection in several of the social sciences, but rather than having concentrated on measurement per se, discussions of this approach to data collection have concentrated on the practical problems of the observer's role, entry and rapport, and methods for recording and recalling of information. It does not appear, either, that there is an extensive literature on systematic observation bearing directly on issues of measurement, apart from schemes for categorization. One such scheme—the Bales categories—is discussed briefly in the chapter by D'Andrade; otherwise, the subject of systematic observation has been omitted from this volume. Finally, there has been no effort to cover the literature on interviewing techniques or questionnaire construction.

The chapters in this volume fall rather naturally into three types. In Part I the concern is with data collection through the device of asking people questions. The general theme consistently pursued in these five chapters is that of perfectionism and the need to improve existing data-collection procedures. The concern in Part II is basically that of linking data collection with data analysis, namely, the problem of what to do in the presence of fallible measurements. Here the stress is placed on the need for multiple measures of each construct and for a flexible mode of data analysis involving a willingness to analyze data in several ways so that results may be compared. The discussions in this section make it abundantly clear that, to the degree that the data are of poor quality, distinct limitations and ambiguities are produced. Finally, Part III consists of five chapters dealing with the analysis of data assumed to be at the ordinal level, a kind of analysis that is not only necessary, given the poor quality of much of our data, but that has also been the subject of considerable debate and confusion. Thus the general flow of the discussion is from data collection to data analysis, the two kinds of issues that nearly always occur in connection with problems of measurement in the social sciences.

All the chapters in Part I deal with the way we ask questions of respondents, the first three being concerned with scaling procedures developing out of the psychometric literature, and the remaining two introducing major notes of caution concerning memory distortions and measurement errors in sociometric data. In Chapter 2, Long and Wilken discuss Coombs's unfolding technique and use simulated data to evaluate the adequacy of this approach to constructing quasi-interval scales, even in the presence of response errors. In Chapter 3, Hamblin shows how the ratio-scaling approaches of S. S. Stevens and other psychometricians can be applied to diverse kinds of measurement tasks in sociology and political science. Shinn, a political scientist, discusses in Chapter 4 some of the psychometric literature dealing with the precise nature of the functional relationships between different kinds of scales, again showing that many of these same findings can be applied to a much wider range of substantive topics. Chapter 5, by D'Andrade (an anthropologist), shows how memory distortions may be patterned in such a way that investigators may obtain a totally erroneous picture of the interrelationships among behavioral dimensions, even where the memory pertains to very recent events. Finally, in Chapter 6, Holland and Leinhardt show how an inferred sociometric structure is very much dependent upon the way questions are asked and, in particular, on whether or not respondents are given a fixed number of choices to make. Chapters 5 and 6, in effect, call into question the adequacy of almost all findings based on either of these types of research. Presumably, many other chapters could have been written concerning inadequacies of other specific kinds of data-collection techniques.

In Part II there is the general recognition that, since any given measure is likely to be inadequate, there must be a reliance on more than a single measure of each variable. In the opening chapter in this section, Jacobson and Lalu discuss the strategic question of the conditions under which a single indicator, multiple indicators, or a combined index are either advantageous or disadvantageous, and they provide both algebraic results and simulated data to assess this question. The following chapter, by Sullivan, illustrates a number of considerations of strategy in selecting indicators by using a concrete illustration involving an application to political science. Chapter 9, by Werts, Linn, and Jöreskog, is more general and abstract and consists of an overview statement linking the causal approach to multiple indicators, recently developed primarily by sociologists, to the earlier and more traditional psychometric literature involving notions such as reliability and validity, as well as procedures such as factor analysis. The final chapter in Part II, written by Hannan, Rubinson, and Warren, deals with complications that exist in panel designs when there are multiple measures —some of which may involve nonrandom errors—as well as more than two variables in the theoretical system. All these chapters provide insights into the kinds of complications, needed assumptions, and potential ambiguities introduced when data are of relatively low quality or when not all indicators yield the same empirical results.

The final section, Part III, contains five chapters dealing with the problem of analyzing data provided in the form of ordinal scales. Statistical tests and measures appropriate for interval or ratio scales are well developed and familiar to social scientists. Nominal scales can be approached either through the use of dummy variables in a regression framework or through contingency-table procedures that are likewise well developed. But there has been considerable debate and a general uneasiness about data given in ordinal form. The opening chapter in this section, by Wilson, relates the choice of ordinal measures to the nature of one's hypotheses about the substantive relationship between two variables. Chapter 12, by Ploch, and Chapter 13, by Quade, constitute efforts to give ordinal measures the theoretical statistical underpinnings not hitherto brought to the attention of most social scientists. Ploch concentrates on the formal parallels between ordinal procedures and the more familiar regression approach, and Quade discusses the problem of partial correlations among ordinal variables. Reynolds, in Chapter 14, provides a number of empirical results from simulated data designed to evaluate the adequacy of ordinal procedures in testing causal models. And in the final chapter the editor presents a series of weak tests designed to evaluate the possibility that the underlying data could be treated at higher-than-ordinal levels of analysis. All the chapters in Part III are thus concerned with data analysis, given situations in which data-collection procedures have not yielded anything better than ordinal scales, and sometimes data that merely have been grouped into several ordered categories. The conclusions reached are rather optimistic, but the reader will note a much lower level of aspiration and perfectionism than is evident in the chapters of Part I.

The chapters in this book are not highly technical. Yet the issues that lie behind many measurement problems in the social sciences are indeed complex, and most of these require technical discussions for their ultimate justifications. A number of other kinds of problems are not so much technical as substantive in nature. The latter must be addressed by specialists in each substantive field, and they typically involve questions of conceptual clarification, levels of generalization, micro-macro distinctions, and dimensionality. But even where these problems can be satisfactorily resolved, imperfections in our measuring instruments and the necessity of indirect measurement will require that rather complex auxiliary theories be formulated so that we may pass back and forth between our conceptual variables and operational measures with minimal confusion.

Therefore, the serious student who believes that it is possible to avoid technical discussions by relying on common sense and intuition is very likely to reach an impasse, once even a moderate degree of complexity is admitted. Here, as elsewhere, we need a division of labor between those who specialize in substantive areas and those who possess a knowledge of the more technical literature on measurement. But the more successful we are in combining these two sorts of knowledge in the same individuals, the easier the communication process will be. The study of the principles of measurement is especially important in the social sciences, where we seem to lack a clear understanding of the complexities involved. It is of course also important in the more advanced physical sciences, where research operations are often taken for granted until some unusual finding leads to a fundamental overhauling of particular measurement procedures. But in the social sciences, it seems fair to say, we can afford to take few measurement procedures for granted.

I

IMPLICATIONS OF ALTERNATIVE DATA-COLLECTION APPROACHES

Chapter 2

A FULLY NONMETRIC UNFOLDING TECHNIQUE: INTERVAL VALUES FROM ORDINAL DATA

JOHN FREDERICK LONG
PAUL H. WILKEN

John Frederick Long is a Ph.D. candidate in the Department of Sociology, University of North Carolina, Chapel Hill. He has served two years as Lecturer and Acting Assistant Professor at the University of California, Riverside. His areas of interest are methodology, demography, human ecology, and Latin American studies. Paul Wilken is a Ph.D. candidate in the Department of Sociology, University of North Carolina, Chapel Hill. His special interests include social change and development, political sociology, and race relations. He is now working as a research associate with H. M. Blalock, Jr., on a project in race relations at the University of Washington.

Guttman scaling has been used both as a scaling criterion for determining whether a set of items measures a unidimensional concept and as a scaling method for assigning an ordinal value to some attribute of a subject for which there exists only a set of nominal variables. The technique thus provides a convenient summation of questionnaire information and permits the use of ordinal data-analysis techniques rather than the lower-level, nominal techniques.

Many quantitative social scientists believe, however, that the social

We wish to thank Hubert M. Blalock, Jr., David Heise, Lowell Kuehn, and Krishnan Namboodiri for their helpful comments and suggestions on earlier versions of this chapter. We also wish to thank Reginald Golledge for making available to us his and Gerard Rushton's summary paper on the use of nonmetric scaling techniques by geographers.

11

sciences should move in the direction of more extensive use of interval-level data and of measurement techniques that yield such data. Psychologists have developed a scaling technique which, by allowing the assignment of an approximate interval value to some attribute of a subject for which there exists a set of ordinal values, yields an ordered-metric scale.[1] Since such a scaling method could prove useful in various social science applications, we have attempted in this chapter to adapt this technique for use by social scientists other than psychologists. For the moment we might point out the utility of such a method in determining such phenomena as social distance. Bogardus's (1928) method of determining social distance produces an essentially ordinal ranking of ethnic groups. Later, we shall attempt to illustrate that the method to be discussed here could be used to measure the distance between ethnic groups rather than used simply to order them.

Another area of application in sociology is the determination of the interval perceived by individuals for given socioeconomic status (S.E.S.) indicators. Sociologists frequently adopt an interval scale without determining whether the intervals contained in the scale are meaningful for the purposes for which they are to be used. For example, years of education and dollar income have been used as interval-scale measures of S.E.S. This practice has been criticized on the grounds that a $1,000-a-year increment does not have the same significance in terms of S.E.S. for a family with a $3,000-a-year-income as for a family with a $30,000-a-year income (Carter 1971). A similar situation applies in years of schooling, with the further complication that we do not know exactly what effect the "milestone" periods of twelve years, sixteen years, and others have on years of education as a measure of S.E.S. Is the period twelve years closer to eleven or thirteen? We hope that the technique to be discussed will provide the means of shedding some light upon this question.

Although its use as a scaling method provides the most interesting possibilities for the technique, it may prove more useful as a scaling criterion. It has been most widely used in psychology as a criterion for determining whether there is indeed an underlying metric for a set of ordinal variables.

The technique, first developed in the psychometrics literature by Coombs (1952, 1964), is referred to as the *unfolding technique*. Although Coombs emphasizes the unfolding technique's usefulness as a scaling criterion, he does discuss the procedure for using it as a scaling

1. Coombs (1953, p. 478) defines an ordered-metric scale as one in which "it can be said of any triplet of classes that $a > b > c$ and also that for at least some intervals between classes, e.g. the intervals $\overline{ab}$, $\overline{bc}$, ..., $\overline{kj}$, ..., $\overline{kl}$, either $\overline{ij} > \overline{kl}$ or $\overline{kl} > \overline{ij}$ where in general, $\overline{jk}$ signifies the distance from j to k."

method.[2] We have attempted to extend this procedure for use in sociological measurement containing error. The accuracy of this extension is evaluated by means of various simulations of possible error configurations.

In the next few sections we shall present and evaluate an example of the unfolding technique's use in obtaining interval-scale information under the ideal conditions of error-free measurement. We shall next present our evaluation of the effectiveness of the technique under conditions in which error is present in the data. Finally, we shall present suggestions for possible additional applications of the technique.

Coombs's Theory of Data

The unfolding technique is grounded in a more comprehensive "theory of data" (Coombs 1964). Coombs suggests that there are basically four different types of data: preferential choice, single stimulus, stimulus comparison, and similarities. The unfolding technique deals primarily with preferential choice data, and to some extent with similarities data. But before turning to the unfolding technique itself, we shall briefly summarize these different types to show how unfolding fits into the larger conceptual framework.

Preferential Choice Data

Preferential choice data result from subjects' evaluations of stimuli with respect to their ideal points. Thus, they may be asked whether they prefer candidate *A* to candidate *B*, candidate *B* to candidate *C*, and candidate *A* to candidate *C*. An alternative method of obtaining preferential choice data is simply for the subject to rank the three candidates in order of his preference for them. In either case one attempts to produce a ranking of preferences for each subject of the form *A, B, C,* or *C, B, A,* and so forth. The basic assumption is that these preferential judgments are based on the proximity of the candidate's position and the subject's position, called his *ideal point*, on some set of attributes. Thus, the most preferred stimulus is the one that comes closest to the subject's ideal point. Different subjects have different ideal points, and therefore different preferences. They may also make their judgments about the same stimuli on the basis of different attributes and thereby exhibit different preferences. So with preferential choice data the researcher is interested in determining the attribute or attributes in terms of which the stimuli are being judged, how the stimuli relate to these attributes, and how the stimuli relate to the subjects' ideal points.

2. Shepard (1966) has emphasized that the usefulness of the unfolding technique as a scaling method was underestimated by Coombs.

This type of data can be depicted spatially by equating degree of preference with relative distance from a stimulus, as shown in Figure 2.1 for three stimuli in one dimension. From this figure we can conclude that *B* is located closer to the ideal point than either *A* or *C*, and that *A* is located closer to it than *C*, so that the preference ordering for this particular subject is *B, A, C* (which is called the subject's *I* scale).

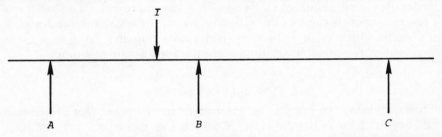

Figure 2.1.   Hypothetical distribution of stimuli and ideal point on underlying dimension of preferential choice data or single stimulus data.

Let us give a sociological example of a case in which we have preferential choice data. In measuring occupational status we might ask the respondent to rank the occupations of businessman, doctor, and lawyer in order of his preference for a vocation. Suppose he ranks the professions in the following order: lawyer, doctor, and businessman. One of several sets of circumstances to which this response might apply is the case, illustrated in Figure 2.1, in which on some scale—perhaps occupational status or prestige—the subject's ideal point is *I*, and stimulus *A* represents the position of doctor, stimulus *B* that of lawyer, and stimulus *C* that of businessman.

However, to reconstruct the underlying distribution of stimuli and subjects' ideal points by means of the unfolding technique, we must use preference information from a large number of subjects, not just the one subject used in Figure 2.1 and in the above example. We shall see later that the unfolding technique provides us with a method of reconstructing the entire "joint space" of subjects and stimuli. This joint space is represented by a joint scale, or *J* scale. From this we can determine the dimension or dimensions on which the stimuli and individuals should be located, the location and spacing of the stimuli, and the location of the subjects' ideal points in relation to these stimuli.

Single Stimulus Data

The second type of data, single stimulus, may result from the same type of distribution of stimuli and subject's ideal point as underlies preferential choice data in Figure 2.1. But single stimulus differ from preferential choice data in that the individual responds to each stimulus separately and makes some type of judgment about it. A positive, or more favorable, response implies that the stimulus is relatively close to his ideal point, while a negative, or less favorable, judgment implies that it is relatively far away. The resulting type of data is like that obtained by most attitudinal questionnaires, in which each question represents a stimulus to which the subject—depending on his ideal point or attitude about the question—replies with varying degrees of approval (e.g., strongly agree, agree, . . . , strongly disagree). Given the distribution of stimuli and the single subject's ideal point shown in Figure 2.1, we expect stimulus B to receive the most-favorable response, and stimulus C the least-favorable response, from our subject.

Continuing with the same sociological example of occupational preference used before, with A, B, and C representing the occupations of doctor, lawyer, and businessman, respectively, we see that this figure could represent responses of a subject to questions asking how he would evaluate each of the three occupations. Figure 2.1 shows that he would most prefer to be a lawyer and least prefer to be a businessman. One of the possible underlying distributions of stimuli and subject's ideal point yielding such a result is that shown in Figure 2.1, where stimulus A represents question 1; stimulus B, question 2; and stimulus C, question 3.

Comparison of Preferential Choice Data and Single Stimulus Data

Although both preferential choice data and single stimulus data may be produced by the same underlying distribution of stimuli and subject's ideal point, they differ in the method of analysis which can be applied to them, and hence in the ability to reconstruct the initial underlying distribution. We have already seen that the method of analysis used with preferential choice data is the unfolding technique. With single stimulus data one of the most widely used methods is Guttman scaling. Both methods require sets of data from numerous subjects for the analysis to be effective.

The major difference between the two methods lies in the amount of information which can be reconstructed and in the type of data used. Guttman scaling used with the appropriate type of data, that is, single stimulus, can reveal whether the data fit a single underlying dimension or not, and, if they do, what the ordering of the stimuli and ideal points is along that dimension. On the other hand, the unfolding technique with its appropriate type of data, that is, preferential choice, can not only determine whether there is a single underlying dimension but can also identify any multiple dimensions that may exist. Moreover, the unfolding technique gives not only the ordering of the stimuli and ideal points along the relevant dimensions but also an ordering of the distances between them. As a result, the unfolding technique allows an almost complete reconstruction of the original distribution of stimuli and ideal points.

Stimulus Comparison and Similarities Data

The types of data we have discussed so far have both dealt with a "joint space" in which both the subjects' ideal points and the stimuli are distributed along some dimension or dimensions. For the remaining two types, stimulus comparison and similarities, interest is restricted to the ordering of stimuli on some dimension. Hence there does not exist a joint space of individuals' ideal points and stimuli, but only a space in which the stimuli alone are ordered in relation to one another. Thurstone's scaling techniques for analyzing data, which are based on the Law of Comparative Judgment, exemplify methods of analysis for constructing scales by means of these types of data. We shall briefly explain these types, although anyone interested in measurement theory should study Coombs's methods of dealing with them (Coombs 1964). The chapters by Hamblin and Shinn in this volume provide other approaches.

Stimulus comparison data result from subjects' judging which stimuli have more and which have less of a certain attribute and then ordering them on that basis. Continuing with our earlier sociological example, we might view Figure 2.2 as illustrating responses to an instruction such as, "Rank the professions of businessman, lawyer, and doctor from most prestigious to least prestigious" where the subjects believe doctors have more prestige than lawyers, and lawyers more than businessmen.

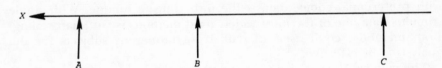

Figure 2.2. Hypothetical distribution of stimuli on underlying dimension of stimulus comparison data or similarities data.

Similarities data result from subjects' judging which stimuli are the most alike, and which the least alike. Similar stimuli are depicted as lying closer to each other than dissimilar stimuli are lying to each other. The same type of distribution of stimuli underlying stimulus comparison data can be thought of as underlying this type of data as well. If we interpret Figure 2.2 as similarities data we see that stimuli A and B are perceived to be more similar than either A and C or B and C, and B and C more similar than A and C. Continuing our example, we see that doctors and lawyers are judged to be more similar than either are to businessmen.

Of the four types of data, the unfolding technique is primarily applicable to preferential choice data, but with only a slight extension it can be used with similarities data as well. We shall discuss only its application to preferential choice data. (For a helpful example of its application to similarities data, see Goldberg and Coombs 1963).

Theoretical Basis of Unfolding Technique

Methods of Data Collection

The preferential choice data on which the unfolding technique is based may be obtained in three ways: (1) the method of rank order, (2) the method of paired comparisons, and (3) the method of triads. Probably the easiest is the method of rank order, in which each subject is simply asked to rank stimuli from most to least preferred. The ranking (e.g., A, B, C, D) is then used as input for the unfolding technique. A problem with the rank-order method is that it may yield erroneous preferential choice data because of its inability to discern intransitivity or inconsistency in the subject's true preferences.

The problem of intransitivity arises when a subject prefers A to B and B to C but prefers C to A. Such data cannot be used to reconstruct the original distribution of stimuli and subjects' ideal points with the method of analysis used by the unfolding technique, at least in the beginning stages. If transitivity is not assumed, it is necessary to identify subjects for which intransitivity occurs so that the data for those subjects will not be used in the reconstruction of the original distribution.

The method of paired comparisons, in which each stimulus is paired with every other stimulus and the subject is asked which member of the pair he prefers, enables one to discover intransitive preferences. If there is transitivity (e.g., the subject prefers stimuli A to B, B to C, C to D, B to D, A to C, and A to D), the resulting scale ($ABCD$ in this case) is used as input for the unfolding technique. If the results for any subject are intransitive, they are not used as any part of the input for the unfolding technique, although once the underlying distribution is obtained an attempt can be made to explain the intransitivity (Coombs 1952, p. 74; 1964, pp. 106-18).

The method of triads can be used to assure consistency as well as transitivity. Consistency obtains when a subject's judgments remain stable over time; as a check for consistency, all possible sets of triads are formed and the subject is asked to indicate his most- and least-preferred stimuli in each set of stimuli. In this manner one gets information equivalent to that obtained by the subject's making a paired-comparison judgment for each pair of stimuli $n - 2$ times, where n equals the number of stimuli. This redundancy of information permits a test for consistency. Subjects with inconsistent or intransitive preferences can be ignored for the time being, and the preference orders of the remaining subjects used to form the preference rankings of the form *ABCD*.

By using the method of triads to obtain preferential choice data one can thus check for both transitivity and consistency. The method of paired comparisons allows testing for transitivity, but not for consistency. Neither a test for consistency nor one for transitivity is possible with the rank-order method. Instead, it imposes both consistency and transitivity on the data. It is the least time-consuming method, however, and may be preferred for that reason (Coombs 1953, pp. 496-513).

Initial Format of Data

All three methods of data collection yield a set of preference orderings, often called *I* scales, or individual scales, of which there is one representing each subject's preference ordering of the stimuli (e.g., subject 1, *BCAD*; subject 2, *DCBA*; subject 3, *ABCD*; etc.). From this set of rank-ordered preferences the underlying distribution of both the stimuli and the subjects' ideal points can be reconstructed by means of the unfolding technique. This underlying distribution is known as the *J* scale, or joint scale, because it includes both stimuli and subjects.

The unfolding technique derives its name from the fact that the reconstruction of the *J* scale can be visualized as the unfolding of the *J* scale from the *I* scales of a number of subjects. Figure 2.3 shows a *J* scale unfolded from one subject's preference ordering for five stimuli. The subject's ideal point is shown as lying closest to his most-preferred stimulus, in this case *C*. The subject ranks *B* second, meaning that as the *J* scale unfolds *B* will be the next closest stimulus to his ideal point. This can be extended to the least-preferred stimulus, *E*, which lies farthest from the subject's ideal point. Thus, the subject's *CBDAE I* scale, or preference ordering, can be unfolded to reveal a *J* scale on which the stimuli lie in *ABCDE* order.

The object of the approach, therefore, is to determine the underlying *J* scale from the *I* scales of a number of subjects and ultimately to estimate distances between stimuli on the *J* scale; thus, an ordered-metric scale is produced. In other words the genotypic *J* scale is inferred from a number of phenotypic *I* scales.

Locating I Scales on the Underlying Scale

Since both subjects and stimuli are to be located on the same scale, each subject's preference ordering, or *I* scale, can be converted into a location on the underlying *J* scale through the following procedure: A preference for one stimulus rather than another is assumed to indicate an ideal point located closer to the preferred stimulus. It will prove useful in determining this preference to locate the point midway be-

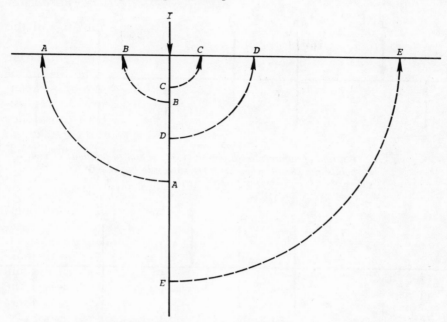

Figure 2.3. Process of unfolding an I scale (in this example, CBDAE onto a J scale (ABCDE).

tween the two stimuli of interest. The ideal point can be represented as lying on the side of this midpoint that is closer to the preferred stimulus. Thus, if a subject prefers stimulus A to stimulus B, he is located on the A side of the AB midpoint.[3] If he prefers stimulus B to stimulus A he is located on the B side of that midpoint. This relatively simple argument can be extended to more stimuli and more preferences. If a subject has the preference ordering ABC, that is, prefers A to B, B to C, and A to C, he is located on the A side of the AB midpoint, the B side of the BC midpoint, and the A side of the AC midpoint, as shown in Figure 2.4, and his I scale is ABC. If he prefers B to A, C to A, and B to C his I scale is BCA, and he is located on the B side of the AB midpoint, the C side of the AC midpoint, and the B side of the BC midpoint, as in Figure 2.5.[4]

Thus, any subject's I scale for the stimuli can be located on the underlying J scale in a segment between two midpoints. These segments, corresponding to I scales, are numbered $I_1, I_2, \ldots, I_n$. Figure 2.6 shows a J scale with four stimuli, the six midpoints between these stimuli, and the seven segments into which the J scale is divided, with each segment

3. Midpoints between two stimuli are represented simply by combining the letters representing the stimuli, for example, AB.

4. We are assuming only one dimension here, and no error in measurement.

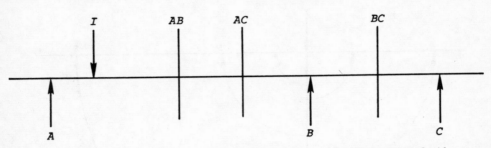

Figure 2.4.   *Position of subject's ideal point* (I) *in relation to positions of mid-points and stimuli when his preference ordering is* ABC.

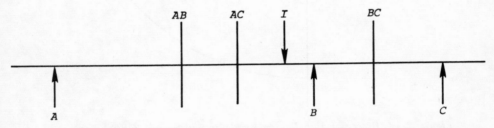

Figure 2.5.   *Position of subject's ideal point* (I) *in relation to positions of mid-points and stimuli when his preference ordering is* BCA.

corresponding to a different *I* scale. As will be seen, the order of the midpoints on this *J* scale is crucial for reaching conclusions about the relative distances between the stimuli on the scale.

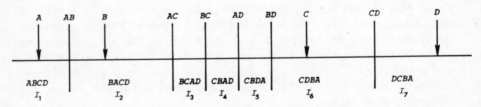

Figure 2.6.   *J scale with stimuli spacing such that midpoint* BC *precedes* AD *and fourth* I *scale is* CBAD.

The *I* scales, and hence the midpoints and stimuli, are in correct order on the *J* scale if, as one moves across the scale in either direction, two and only two letters representing the stimuli reverse their order in adjacent *I* scales. In moving from *I* scale 1 to *I* scale 2 in Figure 2.6, the *AB* midpoint is crossed and *I* scale *ABCD* changes to *I* scale *BACD*, where only the two stimuli *A* and *B* are reversed.

Extraction of Information on Midpoint Ordering from I *Scale Set*

Once the *I* scales are in the correct order, one can determine the relative distances between various stimuli on the *J* scale from the ordering of midpoints. The more stimuli included in the *I* scales, the more such metric information can be obtained. We shall see later that there is a tradeoff here when there is the possibility of measurement error, in the sense that it becomes more difficult to fit the *I* scales to an underlying *J* scale and take advantage of the potential metric information available from more stimuli. For example, with four stimuli, relatively little metric information is obtainable. Given stimuli in the order *ABCD* on the *J* scale, the order of midpoints *AB, AC, BC,* and *CD* is all set. Midpoint *AC* has to be on the right side of *AB*, and *CD* has to be on the right side of *BD*. The ordering of *AD* and *BC* is not determined, however, and Figures 2.6 and 2.7 show the two possible orderings of midpoints. If *BC* precedes *AD*, the order of *I* scales 3, 4, and 5 is *BCAD, CBAD,* and *CBDA*. If *AD* precedes *BC*, the order is *BCAD, BCDA,* and *CBDA*. In the first case the reversing of *BC* prior to the reversing of *AD* indicates that the *BC* midpoint was crossed before the *AD* midpoint, and in the second case the reversing of *AD* prior to the reversing of *BC* indicates that the *AD* midpoint was crossed first. This can be visualized as two possible paths along the *J* scale, one by way of *I* scale *BCDA*, and the other by way of *I* scale *CBAD*. Figure 2.8 illustrates these paths.

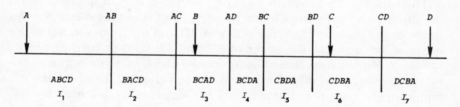

Figure 2.7. J *scale with stimuli spacing such that midpoint* AD *precedes* BC *and fourth* I *scale is* BCDA.

With more stimuli, a smaller number of the midpoint locations is set, and more metric information is obtained. With six stimuli ordered *ABCDEF*, we know that the midpoints between *A* and the other stimuli must be in the order *AB, AC, . . . , AF*, and the same holds for the midpoints between *B* and the succeeding stimuli. We also know that the order of any two midpoints sharing a common stimulus is set by this underlying order. Thus, *AB* must precede *BC*, and *CD* must precede *DE*, and so forth. This ordering is not influenced by the distances between the stimuli.

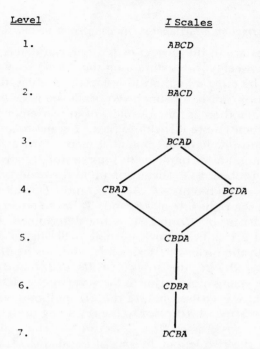

Figure 2.8.   Set of I *scales from four-stimulus* J *scale showing two alternative paths illustrated in Figures 2.6 and 2.7.*

The order of midpoints not sharing common stimuli depends upon the distance between the stimuli, however, and is not set merely by the order of the stimuli. Thus, the order of *AD* and *BC* is not set, nor is the order of *BE* and *CD*, the order of *BF* and *CE*, and so forth. Coombs (1964, p. 89) suggests that all instances in which one line segment envelops another yield metric information. In Figures 2.6 and 2.7 the $\overline{AD}$ line segment (i.e., the distance between stimulus *A* and stimulus *D*)[5] envelops the $\overline{BC}$ line segment, and the order of the midpoints *AD* and *BC* is determined by the relative lengths of the $\overline{AB}$ and $\overline{CD}$ line segments. If $\overline{CD} > \overline{AB}$, that is, if the distance between stimulus *C* and stimulus *D* is greater than that between *A* and *B*, the *BC* midpoint precedes the *AD* midpoint, as in Figure 2.6. If $\overline{AB} > \overline{CD}$, the *AD* midpoint precedes the *BC* midpoint, as seen in Figure 2.7.

Determination of Relative Distances between Stimuli from Midpoints Order

With knowledge of the midpoint order, we can infer line-segment lengths by using the unfolding technique, as follows: If midpoint

5. Line segments between two stimuli are represented by the two stimuli with a bar over them, for example, $\overline{AB}$.

AD precedes *BC*, then $(A + D)/2 < (B + C)/2$; and using the rules for mathematical operations on inequalities, we can show that $(A + D) < (B + C)$ and, further, that $(D - C) < (B - A)$. Converting this last inequality into information about line segments, we see that $\overline{CD} < \overline{AB}$ or, alternatively, $\overline{AB} > \overline{CD}$. Coombs provides a simpler algorithm for making these inferences, which involves combining the first and the second elements of a pair of midpoints to give two new sets of letters. These sets of letters represent line segments, one of which is in alphabetical order. That line segment is the longer of the two. The other segment can be rearranged in alphabetical order as long as it is remembered that it is the shorter of the two segments. Repeating the example we performed above, we note that if midpoint *AD* precedes midpoint *BC*, combining elements gives the new sets of letters *AB* and *DC*. Using the above rule, we note that *AB* is in alphabetical order, and thus line segment $\overline{AB}$ is longer than line segment $\overline{CD}$, that is, $\overline{AB} > \overline{CD}$. This metric information about the relative lengths of various segments of the *J* scale we can eventually transform into an ordered-metric scale by assigning values to these segments, which allows the underlying distribution of stimuli and ideal points (i.e. the entire *J* scale) to be reconstructed.

An Example of the Unfolding Technique with Error-Free Data

To illustrate the unfolding technique we shall switch to a hypothetical numerical example, for which we shall construct data so that we know the underlying *J* scale and can use it to determine how closely the *J* scale reconstructed by the unfolding technique fits the true *J* scale. We shall also construct the data so that there is no measurement error, inconsistency, or intransitivity. Some of these complications will be discussed later, but for now we shall simply see how well the unfolding technique performs under the ideal case.

Simulation of Initial Data

First, it is necessary to construct a set of *I* scales from a specified underlying *J* scale. We begin by simulating this *J* scale, in which randomly selected values were assigned to the six stimuli *A, B, C, D, E*, and *F* in order of increasing magnitude such that $A = 6, B = 10, C = 26, D = 56, E = 66$, and $F = 80$. This, then, constitutes the distribution of stimuli on the true underlying *J* scale and will be the reference for evaluating the effectiveness of the unfolding technique.

Given the distribution of the stimuli values on the true underlying *J* scale, we are able to construct the corresponding *I* scales. The first step is to calculate the numerical values of all possible midpoints between stimuli. For example, midpoint *AB* is $(6 + 10)/2 = 8$, and midpoint *CE* is $(26 + 66)/2 = 46$. The next step is to order these midpoints by means of their calculated numerical values. In our illustration this means that *AB* will precede *CE*. The resulting midpoint order is given in Table 2.1, column 3.

Table 2.1. Ordered I *Scales with Metric Information*
Obtained by Using Coombs's Unfolding Technique on Example
for Error-free Data

I *scale no.* (1)	I *scale* (2)	Lower bounding midpoints (3)	Information-containing Pair (4)	Metric information (5)
1	ABCDEF			
2	BACDEF	AB		
3	BCADEF	AC		
4	CBADEF	BC		
5	CBDAEF	AD	BC, AD	$\overline{CD} > \overline{AB}$
6	CDBAEF	BD		
7	CDBEAF	AE	BD, AE	$\overline{DE} > \overline{AB}$
8	CDEBAF	BE		
9	DCEBAF	CD	BE, CD	$\overline{BC} > \overline{DE}$
10	DCEBFA	AF	CD, AF	$\overline{DF} > \overline{AC}$
11	DCEFBA	BF		
12	DECFBA	CE	BF, CE	$\overline{BC} > \overline{EF}$
13	DEFCBA	CF		
14	EDFCBA	DE	CF, DE	$\overline{CD} > \overline{EF}$
15	EFDCBA	DF		
16	FEDCBA	EF		

To construct the *I* scales, we simply note that the *I* scale for any value less than the value for the midpoint *AB* is *ABCDEF* and that as each midpoint is passed the position of the two stimuli of that midpoint exchange positions in the *I* scale. Thus after the midpoint *AB*, the *I* scale becomes *BACDEF*; after the midpoint *AC* but before the midpoint *BC*, the *I* scale becomes *BCADEF*; and so forth. The ordered *I* scales constructed from our ordered *I* midpoints are shown in Table 2.1, column 2.

Another way of determining the number of a particular *I* scale, and hence of deriving the correct ordering of a set of *I* scales, can also be seen from the set of *I* scales in Table 2.1. Since in moving from one *I* scale to the next, the letters in one pair reverse positions, one of the letters of the *I* scale moves one space to the right and another moves one space to the left. Paying attention only to the movement of letters to the right, one can determine the number of an *I* scale by counting the number of spaces letters have moved to the right from the extreme left position, since each letter moves all the way to the left before moving to the right. So by counting spaces moved to the right one can determine the correct *I* scale number. For example, in *I* scale 8 of Table 2.1, the initial letter, *C*, has not yet started moving to the right; *A* is four spaces to the right of the extreme left position; and *B* is three spaces to the right. Practically, we perform this calculation by noting the letter beginning the *I* scale and counting the number of spaces each letter alphabetically preceding the beginning letter is to the right of the initial letter. Four plus three equals seven, and since the first *I* scale is number 1, this gives us scale number 8. This means of determining the correct number of an *I* scale, though not particularly important with error-free data, will become more important when one works with data containing error.

In our first simulation we select at random thirty numbers from a normal distribution with mean 50 and standard deviation 20. These thirty values, representing thirty subjects' ideal points, are then assigned to the *I* scales within whose ranges they fall by comparing the randomly assigned numbers or scores with the known initial values of the *I* scale. For example the fourth subject has a randomly assigned numerical score of 34. Since this score falls between 33 and 36, the interval for *I* scale number 6, the fourth subject is assigned to *I* scale number 6. The results of this assignment are shown in Table 2.5, below.

Although this procedure is the exact opposite of the normal procedure in using the technique—in which one would have the *I* scales but not the underlying *J* scale or the values for the stimuli on it—by simulating on this basis it is possible to determine later how closely the ordered metric scale obtained by the unfolding technique approximates the true underlying *J* scale.

Extraction of Information on Midpoint Ordering from I *Scale Set*

At this point we have created the information (ordered *I* scales) constituting the input data for Coombs's unfolding technique. From this set of *I* scales we proceed as with any set of data. Coombs's technique will be used to reconstruct the *J* scale, and thus to obtain approximate interval-level measurement values for our stimuli and the subjects' ideal points.

We first extract the midpoint order as described in the previous section. Table 2.1, column 2, shows the *I* scale information; column 3, the information on midpoint ordering. After ordering the midpoints, we note which midpoint orderings are not implied by the natural order. Not all combinations of midpoints must be analyzed according to the algorithm suggested by Coombs; only pairs of midpoints not sharing a common element (stimulus) or pairs in which the stimuli in one pair envelop the stimuli in the other will provide métric information.

In Table 2.1, column 3, we see that midpoints BC and AD constitute such a pair, since AD envelops BC and all four elements are different. The ordering of AD and BD, on the other hand, is implied by the order of stimuli on the underlying J scale, since they both contain the element D. The pairs of midpoints in our example which contain metric information are shown in Table 2.1, column 4, with the lower midpoint listed first.

Determination of Relative Distances between Stimuli from Midpoints Order

Our next step is to extract the metric information from these information-containing pairs. As we have seen, Coombs suggests that metric information can be obtained from these midpoints by combining the first members and the second members of each pair of midpoints to get two new pairs representing line segments. The pair in alphabetical order represents the longer line segments. Using this procedure the midpoints BC, AD yield line segments $\overline{BA}$, $\overline{CD}$, which implies $\overline{CD} > \overline{AB}$; and midpoints BD, AE yield $\overline{BA}$, $\overline{DE}$, which implies $\overline{DE} > \overline{AB}$. The metric information obtained from all our I scales is given in Table 2.1, column 5.

When all possible metric information has been gleaned from the midpoint order, we use this information in constructing a figure giving at least a partial ordering of the line segments. Figure 2.9 shows the partial order constructed from the metric information given in Table 2.1, column 5. This information is represented generally by placing the shorter line segments ($\overline{EF}$ and $\overline{AB}$) at the bottom of this figure and the longer line segments ($\overline{DF}$ and $\overline{AC}$) above them. Specific metric information from Table 2.1 is represented by a line connecting the appropriate line segments. Thus we represent the fact that $\overline{CD} > \overline{AB}$ by putting $\overline{CD}$ above $\overline{AB}$ in the figure and connecting them with a line. On the other hand, $\overline{DE}$ is listed above $\overline{EF}$ in the figure, but since there is no metric information comparing these two line segments from Table 2.1, we do not know whether $\overline{DE}$ is actually larger than $\overline{EF}$; hence we have not connected these two line segments by a line in Figure 2.9.

The resulting partial order in Figure 2.9 illustrates that the technique has captured the relative order of differences in our simulated data. This can be seen in a comparison of the line-segment order in this figure with the relative lengths of line segments between various pairs of the original stimuli ($A = 6, B = 10, C = 26, D = 56, E = 66, F = 80$). It can also be seen in Figure 2.9 that a complete ordering of all line segments has not been obtained. For example, it is not possible to determine $\overline{BC}$'s relationship to $\overline{CD}$, nor is it possible to determine $\overline{AB}$'s relationship to $\overline{EF}$. As we shall show, however, this has little impact on the final scale, at least in the case of perfect data.

It is not quite clear which line segments one should include in this

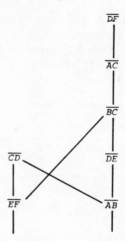

Figure 2.9. *Partial ordering of line segments obtained from metric information in Table 2.1, column 5, with longer line segments positioned above shorter line segments and connected by line.*

partial ordering and which one should omit. For example, in Figure 2.9 one could add $\overline{CF}$ and $\overline{BF}$ above $\overline{DF}$, but too many segments would make the next step in the technique too complicated; so we suggest including only the segments between adjacent stimuli, for example, $\overline{AB}$, $\overline{BC}$, and so forth, and the segments involving stimuli separated by one intervening stimulus, for example, $\overline{AC}$, $\overline{BD}$, $\overline{CE}$, and so forth, for which one can get metric information.

In Figure 2.9 we were able to get all the former and all the latter segments except $\overline{BD}$ and $\overline{CE}$. But since we have no metric information about the relationship of these segments to other segments in the partial order, they can just as well be left out.

Assignment of Metric Values to Stimuli

Once the partial order of line segments has been determined, this order may be used to assign values to the segments. Table 2.2 illustrates this procedure. In column 1 the line segments are listed in the approximate order of their relative lengths. Next we try to design a notational system incorporating all the information about the relative lengths of line segments given in Figure 2.9 into mathematical expressions for each line segment. The notational system we use is that of a series of quantities, $\Delta1$, $\Delta2$, $\Delta3$, and so forth, which are unknown, positive, real numbers.

Using this system, we can assign the short line segments $\overline{AB}$ and $\overline{EF}$ the arbitrary values $\Delta1$ and $\Delta2$, respectively. Since we know from Figure 2.9 that $\overline{CD}$ is larger than $\overline{AB}$, we assign $\overline{CD}$ the value $\Delta1 + \Delta3$.

Table 2.2. Determination of Line-Segment Lengths by Use of Combination of Arbitrary Assignment of Intervals (Δ's) Adjusted to Correspond to Metric Information Contained in Table 2.1, Column 5, Following Coombs's Unfolding Technique

Line segment	Initial assignment of Δ's	Metric information used for adjustments			
		$\overline{DF} = \overline{DE} + \overline{EF}$ $\overline{AC} = \overline{AB} + \overline{BC}$	$\overline{DF} > \overline{AC}$ $\Delta2 > \Delta1 + \Delta5$ $\Delta2 = \Delta1 + \Delta5 + \Delta6$	$\overline{CD} > \overline{EF}$ $\Delta3 > \Delta5 + \Delta6$ $\Delta3 = \Delta5 + \Delta6 + \Delta7$	$\overline{BC} > \overline{EF}$ $\Delta4 > \Delta6$ $\Delta4 = \Delta6 + \Delta8$
(1)	(2)	(3)	(4)	(5)	(6)
$\overline{DF}$		$\Delta1 + \Delta2 + \Delta4$	$2\Delta1 + \Delta4 + \Delta5 + \Delta6$	$2\Delta1 + \Delta4 + \Delta5 + \Delta6$	$2\Delta1 + \Delta5 + 2\Delta6 + \Delta8$
$\overline{AC}$		$2\Delta1 + \Delta4 + \Delta5$	$2\Delta1 + \Delta4 + \Delta5$	$2\Delta1 + \Delta4 + \Delta5$	$2\Delta1 + \Delta5 + \Delta6 + \Delta8$
$\overline{BC}$	$\Delta1 + \Delta4 + \Delta5$	$\Delta1 + \Delta4 + \Delta5$	$\Delta1 + \Delta4 + \Delta5$	$\Delta1 + \Delta4 + \Delta5$	$\Delta1 + \Delta5 + \Delta6 + \Delta8$
$\overline{DE}$	$\Delta1 + \Delta4$	$\Delta1 + \Delta4$	$\Delta1 + \Delta4$	$\Delta1 + \Delta4$	$\Delta1 + \Delta6 + \Delta8$
$\overline{CD}$	$\Delta1 + \Delta3$	$\Delta1 + \Delta3$	$\Delta1 + \Delta3$	$\Delta1 + \Delta5 + \Delta6 + \Delta7$	$\Delta1 + \Delta5 + \Delta6 + \Delta7$
$\overline{EF}$	$\Delta2$	$\Delta2$	$\Delta1 + \Delta5 + \Delta6$	$\Delta1 + \Delta5 + \Delta6$	$\Delta1 + \Delta5 + \Delta6$
$\overline{AB}$	$\Delta1$	$\Delta1$	$\Delta1$	$\Delta1$	$\Delta1$

In like fashion we assign $\overline{DE}$ the value $\Delta1 + \Delta4$. Since $\overline{BC}$ is shown as larger than $\overline{DE}$ in Figure 2.9, we assign $\overline{BC}$ the value $\Delta1 + \Delta4 + \Delta5$. Table 2.2, column 2, shows this initial assignment of Δ's for line segments between adjacent stimuli.

To give a delta assignment to the line segments in Figure 2.9 which are not between adjacent stimuli, we must construct them from their component line segments. Thus $\overline{AC}$ is equal to the sum of line segments $\overline{AB}$ and $\overline{BC}$, which gives a delta assignment of $2\Delta1 + \Delta4 + \Delta5$. Likewise, $\overline{DF} = \overline{DE} + \overline{EF}$, so that its delta assignment is $\Delta1 + \Delta2 + \Delta4$. These results are shown in Table 2.2, column 3.

We now have delta values for each of the line segments in Figure 2.9, but they do not yet contain all the ordered metric information given in that figure. For example, we know from the figure that $\overline{DF} > \overline{AC}$, although this fact is not apparent from the delta representation in Table 2.2, column 3. Note that we should like the delta representation to show that $\overline{DF} > \overline{AC}$, or, in the notation of column 2, that $\Delta1 + \Delta2 + \Delta4 > 2\Delta1 + \Delta4 + \Delta5$. For some possible values of the deltas this is true, but for others it is not. We wish to give a delta representation such that, whatever the values of the deltas, $\overline{DF} > \overline{AC}$. If we simplify the inequality above, we get $\Delta2 > \Delta1 + \Delta5$, which is the same as saying $\Delta2 = \Delta1 + \Delta5 + \Delta6$, where $\Delta6$ is any positive real number. In Table 2.2, column 3, we revise our delta representation such that we substitute the expression $\Delta1 + \Delta5 + \Delta6$ for $\Delta2$. The resulting expressions for $\overline{DF}$ and $\overline{AC}$ are $2\Delta1 + \Delta4 + \Delta5 + \Delta6$ and $2\Delta1 + \Delta4 + \Delta5$, respectively. Thus, whatever the values given to the deltas, $\overline{DF}$ is greater than $\overline{AC}$.

In a similar manner we have changed the delta representations in Table 2.2, columns 5 and 6, to reflect the fact that Figure 2.9 shows $\overline{CD} > \overline{EF}$ and $\overline{BC} > \overline{EF}$. The final delta representation shown in Table 2.2, column 6, is such that, whatever values are used for the deltas, the line segments retain the relative orderings shown in Figure 2.9. Thus all the ordered metric information obtained from Table 2.1 and shown in Figure 2.9 is contained in these delta representations.

We should next like to give numerical values to each of the line segments as a step toward assigning numerical values to the stimuli. To do this we must arbitrarily assign numerical values to each delta quantity used in the representation of Table 2.2, column 6. The first set of deltas we shall use is composed of equal-valued deltas, as suggested by Coombs (1964). For this set $\Delta 1$, $\Delta 5$, $\Delta 6$, $\Delta 7$, and $\Delta 8$ will all be set equal to 5, and the set of delta values will be represented by $[\Delta a]$. Two other sets of arbitrarily selected delta values have been used for purposes of comparison: $[\Delta b]$, where $\Delta 1 = 8$, $\Delta 5 = 3$, $\Delta 6 = 2$, $\Delta 7 = 9$, and $\Delta 8 = 6$; and $[\Delta c]$, where $\Delta 1 = 2$, $\Delta 5 = 8$, $\Delta 6 = 10$, $\Delta 7 = 8$, and $\Delta 8 = 10$.

For each of these sets we calculate the adjacent line segments, $\overline{AB}$, $\overline{BC}$, and so forth. If, further, we make the assumption that stimulus $A = 0$, we can calculate the values of each stimulus for each set of delta values. For example stimulus C would equal $0 + \overline{AB} + \overline{BC}$. The resulting numerical values of the stimuli for the three different delta assignments are given in Table 2.3.

Table 2.3. Comparison of True Stimuli Values with Those Obtained by Using Different Values of Delta in Evaluating Expression for Line Segments in Table 2.2, Column 6

Stimulus	$[\Delta a]$	$[\Delta b]$	$[\Delta c]$	True stimulus values
A	0	0	0	6
B	5	8	2	10
C	25	27	32	26
D	45	49	60	56
E	60	65	82	66
F	75	78	102	80

Assignment of Metric Values to Each Subject's I Scale

Our next step is to reconstruct the metric ordering of the subjects' ideal points on the J scale so as to complete the entire reconstructed J scale. To obtain the subjects' values on the J scale, we must examine the I scale of each subject. To do this it is necessary to use the information about stimuli values obtained in Table 2.3 and calculate the range of values for each I scale corresponding to the appropriate set of deltas, which we accomplish by first calculating the values of the midpoints, BD, BE, and so forth. For example, for the $[\Delta a]$ set of values, $BD = \frac{1}{2}(B + D) = \frac{1}{2}(5 + 45) = 25$, and $AE = \frac{1}{2}(A + E) = \frac{1}{2}(0 + 60) = 30$.

This information, together with the information given in Table 2.1, column 3, is used to give a range for each of the *I* scales. For example, since *I* scale number 6 is bounded by *BD* and *AE*, we know, by using the set of deltas $[\Delta a]$, that its interval is from 25 to 30. The intervals of all the *I* scales for each of the three delta sets are shown in Table 2.4, columns 2, 4, and 6. Having assigned a numerical value to the ideal points corresponding to each *I* scale, we have all the information needed for reconstructing our complete *J* scale. The underlying dimension of the *J* scale is not only delineated by the stimuli values but also by the *I* scale midpoints.

Table 2.4. Range and Midpoints of I *Scale Intervals Reconstructed by Using Each of Three Sets of Midpoint Values Obtained by Applying Stimulus Values of Table 2.3 to* I *Scales of Table 2.1*

I Scale (1)	[Δa] Range (2)	Midpoint (3)	[Δb] Range (4)	Midpoint (5)	[Δc] Range (6)	Midpoint (7)
1	0-2.5	1.25	0-4	2	0-1	0.5
2	2.5-12.5	7.5	4-13.5	8.75	1-16	8.5
3	12.5-15	13.75	13.5-17.5	15.5	16-17	16.5
4	15-22.5	18.75	17.5-24.5	21	17-30	23.5
5	22.5-25	23.75	24.5-28.5	26.5	30-31	30.5
6	25-30	27.5	28.5-32.5	30.5	31-41	36
7	30-32.5	31.25	32.5-36.5	34.5	41-42	41.5
8	32.5-35	33.75	36.5-38	37.25	42-46	44
9	35-37.5	36.25	38-39	38.5	46-51	48.5
10	37.5-40	38.75	39-43	41	51-52	51.5
11	40-42.5	41.25	43-46	44.5	52-57	54.5
12	42.5-50	46.25	46-52.5	49.25	57-67	62
13	50-52.5	51.25	52.5-57	54.75	67-71	69
14	52.5-60	56.25	57-63.5	60.25	71-81	76
15	60-67.5	63.75	63.5-71.5	67.5	81-92	86.5
16	67.5-75	71.25	71.5-78	74.75	92-102	97

We have now reconstructed the order and approximate spacing of the stimuli on the underlying *J* scale. Note that the values for the stimuli vary, depending on the arbitrary choices of the delta values, and, further, that none of the choices of delta values give stimuli values that correspond to the original values. There are, however, a number of similarities between the various sets of reconstructed stimuli values and the original values. First, they all retain the same order, with the value of the stimuli increasing as we go from *A* to *F*. Second, in each set the distances between the stimuli reflect the partial ordering shown in Figure 2.9. For example, the distance between *A* and *B* is less than that between *D* and *E* in each of the three cases. One way of summarizing these similarities is to compute the Pearson product-moment correlation coefficients between the various distributions.

Although just knowing the rank order of the values tells us a lot about the values themselves (r = .9818), the Coombs method not only gives us the ordinal information about the stimuli values; it goes beyond this to give us metric information which improves the correlations—regardless of what our arbitrary choice for the set of delta values is. With our three choices of delta values, the correlations between the calculated stimuli values in Table 2.3 and the original stimuli values are .9948 for $[\Delta a]$, .9975 for $[\Delta b]$, and .9945 for $[\Delta c]$.

The final step in the reconstruction is to assign the subjects the reconstructed metric values corresponding to their I scale numbers. Thus, for each set of delta values we assign each subject the midpoint value of the I scale to which he was assigned in the preceding step. In accordance with our previous example, in which the $[\Delta a]$ values were used, the fourth subject is given the numerical value 27.5, which is the calculated value of the midpoint of I scale number 6. The values assigned to all the thirty simulated subjects for the various sets of delta values are shown in Table 2.5, columns 4, 5, and 6.

Evaluation of Simulation Results

We may now evaluate how well these reconstructed estimates of the subjects' ideal points obtained by means of Coombs's unfolding technique compare with the original values of our subjects shown in Table 2.5, column 2. To do this we calculate the Pearsonian product-moment correlation between the original simulated values and the reconstructed values by using $[\Delta a]$, $[\Delta b]$, and $[\Delta c]$ (shown in Table 2.5, cols. 4, 5, and 6). The correlations we obtain are quite high—.9668, .9676, and .9663, respectively.

That the Coombs unfolding technique is useful in giving us more than the ordinal information readily apparent from Guttman scaling or from ranked I scales can be seen from the correlation between our original data and the I scale number (a value which provides a simple ordinal level of measurement). The correlation coefficient obtained for our example is .9516; hence it appears that, in our example at least, the Coombs technique of getting metric information is something of an improvement over the simple ordinal information obtained in I scales and that this is true no matter which of our choices is used for the set of delta values. Part 1 of Table 2.6 provides a summary of our results, demonstrating that the Coombs' technique provides ordered metric information which represents an improvement over the usual ordinal information obtained from other methods.

To check whether these high values for the correlation coefficient were peculiar to a normal distribution of subjects' ideal points, we repeated the above simulation for a population which was rectangularly distributed over the interval from 0 to 100. We then performed the

*Table 2.5. Simulated Values with Normal Distribution, Mean of 50,
and Standard Deviation of 20, Allocated to Appropriate* I *Scale
and Assigned Midpoint Value Corresponding to Each Set of* I *Scales
from Table 2.4*

			Assigned midpoint value		
Subject No. (1)	Value simulated (2)	Corresponding I scale (3)	[Δa] (4)	[Δb] (5)	[Δc] (6)
1	37.6	7	31.25	34.5	41.5
2	64.4	14	56.25	60.25	76
3	68.4	15	63.75	67.5	86.5
4	34	6	27.5	30.5	36
5	0	1	1.25	2	0.5
6	49	12	46.25	49.25	62
7	39.8	8	33.75	37.25	44
8	62.8	14	56.25	60.25	76
9	56.8	13	51.25	54.75	69
10	24.6	4	18.75	21	23.5
11	52.6	12	46.25	49.25	62
12	90	16	71.25	74.75	97
13	56.6	16	71.25	74.75	97
14	25.6	4	18.75	21	23.5
15	44.4	10	38.75	41	51.5
16	26	4	18.75	21	23.5
17	18.6	4	18.75	21	23.5
18	27.8	4	18.75	21	23.5
19	29.6	4	18.75	21	23.5
20	41.8	9	36.25	38.5	48.5
21	66.4	14	56.25	60.25	76
22	41.8	9	36.25	38.5	48.5
23	32.8	5	23.75	26.5	30.5
24	60.6	13	51.25	54.75	69
25	5	1	1.25	2	0.5
26	46	11	41.25	44.5	54.5
27	48.6	12	46.25	49.25	62
28	63.8	14	56.25	60.25	76
29	78.2	16	71.25	74.75	97
30	89.2	16	71.25	74.75	97

analysis as above. The results of this reanalysis follow essentially the
same pattern as for the normal distribution, with quite high correlations between the original simulated data and our predictions. The resulting correlation coefficients are summarized in Table 2.6, part II.

The conclusion we may draw from this table is that, at least for our
particular scale values under error-free conditions, the reconstruction
of the *J* scale by Coombs's unfolding technique seems to provide a
closer correlation to the original set of data (whether rectangularly or
normally distributed) than could be obtained from knowledge of the
ordinal information in the scale alone. Furthermore, whichever of the

Table 2.6. *Correlations between Known True Values of Subjects' Ideal Points of Underlying* J *Scale and Various Estimates of These Values*

	Correlation coefficient
I. Normal distribution of simulated subjects' ideal points	
A. Estimate using ordinal representation of data (using number of I scale as I scale value)	.9516
B. Estimate using values assigned by Coombs's unfolding technique	
1. $[\Delta] = [\Delta a]$	.9668
2. $[\Delta] = [\Delta b]$	.9676
3. $[\Delta] = [\Delta c]$	.9663
C. Estimate using known midpoint of original scale (not ordinarily known)	.9645
II. Rectangular distribution of simulated subjects' ideal points	
A. Estimate using ordinal representation of data (using number of I scale as I scale value)	.9677
B. Estimate using values assigned by Coombs's unfolding technique	
1. $[\Delta] = [\Delta a]$	.9832
2. $[\Delta] = [\Delta b]$	.9826
3. $[\Delta] = [\Delta c]$	.9832
C. Estimate using known midpoint of original scale (not ordinarily known)	.9876

sets of delta values are used, the correlations obtained with Coombs's technique are quite high, almost equaling those which would be obtained from knowledge of the true scale midpoints.

Use of the Unfolding Technique with Data Containing Error

Admittedly, the previous discussion involves the very unrealistic assumption of error-free data. For this technique to be of use to most social scientists some sort of evaluation must be made of the effect of error on the results. Unfortunately, most of the literature on the unfolding technique deals only with the perfect case. As Torgerson (1960, p. 413) points out, the model itself is an exceedingly stringent one, since no extraneous variation is permitted. Without procedures which can evaluate the degree of approximation of the model to the imperfect data, the unfolding procedure will likely remain of more theoretical than practical interest.

In this section we introduce some procedures for handling data containing error by means of the unfolding technique and then evaluate its effectiveness as a scaling method for data with varying degrees of measurement error. To do this we shall try to reconstruct the original *J* scale from *I* scale data as we did in the preceding section, with the very important difference that the *I* scale for any given subject will be subject to measurement error. Although the main outlines of the technique will remain as in the preceding section, the presence of error will require various additions and changes in our procedure. Following is a list of the steps one follows in using the unfolding technique with preferential choice data containing error.

1. Determination of the dimensionality of the data
2. Determination of the correct ordering of the stimuli (the best ordinal *J* scale)
3. Determination of the correct set of *I* scales for the best ordered-metric *J* scale
4. Assignment of metric values to stimuli and *I* scales
5. Assignment of metric values to all subjects' ideal points

Simulation of Initial Data

As an aid in describing these steps, we present an example in which we assume that our fifty hypothetical subjects must rank six responses to some question in the order in which these responses best match the responses they would give to the question. For example, suppose the question is: As a result of the Watergate scandal, do you believe that President Nixon should be—

A. impeached but not convicted,
B. exonerated of any complicity,
C. reprimanded gently by Congress,
D. impeached and convicted,
E. commended for his handling of the affair, or
F. pressured to resign but not impeached?

By using the responses of fifty subjects to this question we hope to establish an interval scale showing the relative positions of the six responses on a scale of punitiveness of actions regarding the Watergate scandal. We can then use the unfolding technique to obtain values on an ordered metric scale representing the inclination toward punitiveness on Watergate of each of our subjects.

Let us assume that Table 2.7 represents the rank orderings (*I* scales) given by each of our subjects to the six responses. These responses actually represent simulated values formed by selecting six stimuli values at random from a rectangular distribution in the interval from 0 to 100, then randomly selecting a group of fifty subjects' ideal points from a normal distribution with mean 50 and standard deviation 20, and finally computing an *I* scale for each of the subjects. Each *I* scale is calculated so that it is consistent with the relative positions of the subject's ideal point and the original six stimuli values calculated earlier, except that a random error term with a standard deviation of 5 (or 5 percent of the range of the scale) is allowed to operate. We also performed similar simulations using 0, 10, 20, and 40 percent random error terms, but we shall describe only the 5 percent case in detail. Results of the other simulations are reported later in this chapter.

Table 2.7. I Scale Values for Unfolding Example with Simulated Data Containing Measurement Error with Standard Deviation Equal to 5 Percent of Range of Scale with Fifty Subjects Represented

Subject No.	I Scale	Subject No.	I Scale
1	AFDCBE	26	DAFCEB
2	CBEFAD	27	EBCFAD
3	EBCFAD	28	AFBCED
4	AFCBED	29	DAFCEB
5	ECBFAD	30	DAFBCE
6	BECFAD	31	EBCFAD
7	ADFCBE	32	AFCEBD
8	DFACEB	33	DAFBCE
9	DFACBE	34	EBCFAD
10	EBCAFD	35	BECFAD
11	FDCAEB	36	FACBED
12	DFABCE	37	DAFCBE
13	BECFAD	38	BECFAD
14	FCABED	39	CEFBAD
15	EBCFAD	40	DAFBCE
16	DAFCEB	41	DACFBE
17	DAFBEC	42	EBCFAD
18	AFCDBE	43	CFBEAD
19	EBCAFD	44	FACEBD
20	AFCDEB	45	FABDCE
21	ADFCEB	46	BECAFD
22	EBCAFD	47	FDACBE
23	AFDBCE	48	EBCFAD
24	EBCFAD	49	CBEAFD
25	CFBEAD	50	DAFECB

The result of this procedure is a set of *I* scales generally conforming to the underlying *J* scale but with some measurement error. Going back to our example, we note in Table 2.7 that subject 1 most prefers impeachment, but not conviction, then resignation, impeachment and conviction, a reprimand, and exoneration; and least prefers commending the president. We shall return to these data from time to time as a means of illustrating the procedure used in applying the unfolding technique to data containing error. We shall now look at the first step in that procedure.

Step 1: Determination of the Dimensionality of the Data

To determine whether a set of error-free data lies along a one-dimensional scale, one must check to see whether two conditions are met.

These criteria will be modified substantially for a set of data containing error. First, all the *I* scales must end in one of two stimuli. Note that in the example with error-free data shown in Table 2.1, all *I* scales end in either *A* or *F*. Second, there must be one and only one set of mirror-image *I* scales. In the example of Table 2.1 there is only one such set, *ABCDEF* and *FEDCBA*. The two stimuli in which the *I* scales end (*A* and *F* here) represent the ends of the underlying *J* scale, since as Coombs (1964, p. 86) suggests, if one picks up the *J* scale at any point, one or the other of the ends will always be farthest from that point. These two stimuli will also be the ends of the two mirror-image *I* scales, and either of these two scales can serve as the correct ordering of the stimuli on the *J* scale. Of course with other data the mirror-image *I* scales are likely not to be in alphabetical order as they are in the example cited, since we generally will not know the ordering of the stimuli at the time the questionnaire is designed and letters (or numbers) are assigned to the various possible responses. In that case one would want to reletter the correctly ordered stimuli in alphabetical order. For example, if *I* scales *CBDAE* and *EADBC* are the set of mirror-image *I* scales, it is advantageous to relabel stimulus *C* as *A*, let stimulus *B* remain the same, reletter stimulus *D* as *C* and *A* as *D*, and let *E* remain the same so that *CBDAE* is now *ABCDE* and *EADBC* is now *EDCBA*. One would then reletter the other *I* scales accordingly to put them in correct order.[6]

With measurement error present, this first step of determining whether a set of data fits a unidimensional *J* scale is more difficult, because it is not always clear whether the apparent perturbations in the data are due to measurement error or to the fact that the data fall along more than one dimension. Our simulations involving various degrees of error suggest that even if there is only one underlying dimension in the data, mirror-image *I* scales may not appear, or more than one set may appear. On the other hand, more than one set of mirror images may also be evidence for the multidimensional solution. Therefore, we suggest looking at the stimuli ending the *I* scales if measurement error exists. If a large portion of *I* scales end in one or the other of two stimuli, it is likely that they constitute the end stimuli on the *J* scale even though there is no clear evidence from the mirror-image *I* scales. Without this indication to rely on there are $n!/2$ possible underlying *J* scales which would fit the data, where n equals the number of stimuli.[7]

6. Since it does not matter which of the two scales we relabel in alphabetical order (the scale might just as easily run from the positive to the negative end as from the negative to the positive end), we could have chosen to take *EADBC* and relabel the stimuli to make it *ABCDE*.

7. This factorial is divided by 2 because half of the possible combinations will be mirror images of the other half.

If there is error in the data, a set of data otherwise fitting a uni-dimensional *J* scale might have some *I* scales that do not end in the two end stimuli. Table 2.8 shows the proportion of *I* scales in our simulations which ended in one of two stimuli for five- and six-stimulus *I* scales with various degrees of error. We see from this table that with larger and larger degrees of error in our data, the percentage of *I* scales ending in the two stimuli at the extremes of the *J* scale di-minishes. With an error term having a standard deviation of 40 percent of the range of the *J* scale, not much more than a third of the *I* scales end in the correct stimuli for the six-stimulus case, and not much more than half of the *I* scales end in the correct stimuli in the five-stimulus case. One would exclude from the analysis the *I* scales not ending in the two most prevalent end stimuli, either on the assumption that they were the result of error or that they related to a different *J* scale.

Table 2.8. Simulation Results Showing Percentages of I *Scales Ending in One of Two Correct End Stimuli Generally Expected under Varying Degrees of Error, Where Range of Stimulus Values Is from 0 to 100*

Standard deviation of error	Percentage of I scales	
	Five stimuli	*Six stimuli*
1	100	100
5	93	90
10	79	74
20	59	64
40	54	38

Observing our example in Table 2.7, we note that with these data containing error not all the *I* scales end in one of the same two stimuli. However, forty-one of the fifty *I* scales (or 82 percent) do end in either stimulus *D* or stimulus *E*. We conclude at this point that there appears to be a unidimensional *J* scale with the extreme values represented by stimulus *D* at one end and stimulus *E* at the other.[8]

Step 2: Determination of the Correct Ordering of the Stimuli (the Best-fitting Ordinal J *Scale)*

With perfect data, the determination of the correct ordering of the stimuli is accomplished by simply observing the ordering for the mirror-image *I* scales, as discussed earlier. With error in the data, this

8. If the percentage of *I* scales ending in one of the two stimuli drops below 70, we suggest considering the possibility that either the data do not scale or they fit a multi-dimensional *J* scale. A full description of the multidimensional case can be found in Coombs (1964) or Bennett and Hays (1960).

step is much more complicated. Even though, after completing step 1, one may be reasonably certain of the two stimuli which begin and end the *J* scale, there are still $(n - 2)!$ possible ordinal *J* scales which could best accommodate the data.[9] Thus, if *A* and *E* have been chosen as the end stimuli of a five-stimulus scale, the ordinal *J* scale fitting the largest number of *I* scales could be *ABCDE, ABDCE, ADBCE, ADCBE, ACDBE,* or *ACBDE*. As a first step, one might see which of the orders occur as mirror-image *I* scales in the data with which he is working. If one of these appears in the data, it is possible that it is the best ordinal *J* scale; but with error present one can have no assurance of that. If more than one appear, one can either select the pair appearing most often or make a determination in conjunction with the next step in the technique. If none of the orders appears in the data it is likely that a dominant *J* scale cannot be found for the data, and one would probably not continue further.

Table 2.9. Simulation Results Showing Likelihood that Most Frequently Appearing I *Scale Ending in One of Two Correct Stimuli is Actual Underlying Ordinal* J *Scale under Varying Degrees of Error*

Standard deviation of error	Percentage of correct choices of J scale using frequency of appearance as criterion	
	Five stimuli	*Six stimuli*
1	100	100
5	100	70
10	70	70
20	20	40
40	20	10

Table 2.9 shows the proportion of times the correct ordinal *J* scale appeared most frequently in our simulations for different degrees of error. From this we note that the method of step 2—ordering the stimuli by choosing the most frequently appearing *I* scale pair ending in the two extreme stimuli chosen in step 1—is a very crude approximation and should be used only when there is reason to believe there is low error. One should also check to see whether the underlying order chosen in this way makes theoretical sense.

Using this rule of thumb for our example in Table 2.7, we note that nineteen scales have as their first and last letters the stimuli *D* and *E* picked in the preceding step as the most likely extreme stimuli of the underlying *J* scale. We now proceed to determine which pair of

9. Actually, since each scale has a mirror image with the same set of *I* scales, it is only necessary to calculate the number of subjects which fit ½ $(n - 2)!$ of the ordinal *J* scales.

mirror-image *I* scales beginning in *D* or *E* and ending in the other appears most frequently.

The scale *EBCFAD* and its mirror image are the most frequently occurring pair of scales beginning with either stimulus *D* or *E* and ending with the other. Following our rule of thumb, then, we select *EBCFAD* as the underlying ordering of the stimuli on the *J* scale. This means that our Watergate scale runs from response *E* (commending the president) as the least punitive response, through stimulus F (pressing for his resignation) as a middle response, and finally to stimulus *D* (impeachment and conviction) as the most punitive response. Since this fits our expectations, and we have reason to believe that measurement error is not large, we accept this ordering as the underlying ordinal *J* scale and reletter all our *I* scales in Table 2.7 accordingly. Thus stimulus *E* becomes *A*, stimulus *B* remains *B*, stimulus *C* remains *C*, stimulus *F* is relettered *D*, stimulus *A* becomes *E*, and *D* is relettered *F*. The results of this determination and consequent relettering of the fifty *I* scales to fit the underlying order is shown in Table 2.10.

Table 2.10. I *Scale Values for Fifty subjects from Table 2.7 Relettered to Reflect Reconstructed Ordinal* J *Scale*

Subject No.	I *scale*	Subject No.	I *scale*
1	*EDFCBA*	26	*FEDCAB*
2	*CBADEF*	27	*ABCDEF*
3	*ABCDEF*	28	*EDBCAF*
4	*EDCBAF*	29	*FEDCAB*
5	*ACBDEF*	30	*FEDBCA*
6	*BACDEF*	31	*ABCDEF*
7	*EFDCBA*	32	*EDCABF*
8	*FDECAB*	33	*FEDBCA*
9	*FDECBA*	34	*ABCDEF*
10	*ABCEDF*	35	*BACDEF*
11	*DFCEAB*	36	*DECBAF*
12	*FDEBCA*	37	*FEDCBA*
13	*BACDEF*	38	*BACDEF*
14	*DCEBAF*	39	*CADBEF*
15	*ABCDEF*	40	*FEDBCA*
16	*FEDCAB*	41	*FECDBA*
17	*FEDBAC*	42	*ABCDEF*
18	*EDCFBA*	43	*CDBAEF*
19	*ABCEDF*	44	*DECABF*
20	*EDCFAB*	45	*DEBFCA*
21	*EFDCAB*	46	*BACEDF*
22	*ABCEDF*	47	*DFECBA*
23	*EDFBCA*	48	*ABCDEF*
24	*ABCDEF*	49	*CBAEDF*
25	*CDBAEF*	50	*FEDACB*

As we noted, choosing the most frequently appearing *I* scale pairs is very sensitive to large degrees of error, and therefore we could discuss the process of trying all possible combinations of stimuli as an alternative method of obtaining the best-fitting ordinal *J* scale. Because of the complexity of this method, however, we recommend a modified version of this approach. We shall use the information gained earlier in step 1, in which we determined the two extreme stimuli of the *J* scale. Using these two stimuli as a starting point, we need only determine the ordering of the interior stimuli. Thus in the four-stimulus case, had we determined the two end stimuli previously (e.g., *D* and *B*), there would have been only two possible orderings for the qualitative *J* scale (in this case, *DACB* or *DCAB*). For more stimuli the number of possible orderings that must be tried can be similarly reduced. With five stimuli all possible orders of the middle three stimuli only need be tried (six possible orders). All possible orders of the middle four stimuli (twenty-four possible orders) should be tried in the six-stimulus case.

If there are still too many possible orders to be tried, one can modify the procedure still further (although with increasing risk of error) by combining the method of step 1 with this method of comparing various possible orderings of the data. Thus one might use step 1 to limit the possible choices to two or three ordinal *J* scales and then choose the one that best fits the data on the basis of the number of subjects fitting the set of *I* scales associated with each of the possible *J* scales.

Let us illustrate this method by returning to our example of the Watergate scale. For the data of Table 2.7, we concluded in step 1 that the end points of the scale were stimuli *D* and *E*. We could try all possible combinations of the middle four stimuli in order to observe which ordinal *J* scale has the set of *I* scales fitting the maximum number of subjects; however, to reduce the number of computations, we shall use the information on the frequency of mirror-image *I* scale pairs and so reduce the number of combinations we try. Since *I* scale pairs *EBCFAD-DAFCBE*, *ECBFAD-DAFBCE*, and *EBCAFD-DFACBE* appear most often in our data, we shall compare them to see which set of the thirty-two *I* scales associated with each of these three ordinal *J* scales has the largest number of subjects. The set of *I* scales corresponding to the stimulus order *EBCFAD* fits twenty-two of the subjects, whereas the other two ordinal *J* scales, *ECBFAD* and *EBCAFD*, fit only eight and eleven subjects, respectively. The result of this procedure is that we pick *EBCFAD* as the best-fitting underlying *J* scale and reletter all the *I* scales such that *EBCFAD* becomes *ABCDEF*. The results of this assignment agree in this case with what was previously derived by using the most frequently appearing *I* scale pairs, as we have shown in Table 2.10.

Step 3: Determination of the Correct Set of I *Scales for the Best Ordered-Metric* J *Scale*

In the preceding section we determined the underlying ordinal *J* scale. That is to say, we know the ordering of the stimuli on the underlying *J* scale, but we do not yet know the spacing of those stimuli, that is, the underlying ordered-metric *J* scale. To obtain this, we must first determine which set of *I* scales to use in the unfolding technique. This step is a crucial one for moving to the best ordered-metric *J* scale, and undoubtedly the most difficult part of the process. In the previous section we noted that each ordinal *J* scale has a set of *I* scales associated with it. We shall now further note that each ordered-metric *J* scale has a subset of these *I* scales. For example, the four-stimulus ordinal *J* scale *ABCD* has the eight *I* scales shown in Figure 2.8 associated with it. For this ordinal *J* scale, there are two possible ordered-metric *J* scales, depending upon whether the distance from *A* to *B* is greater than or less than the distance from *C* to *D*. Each of these ordered-metric *J* scales has a set of seven *I* scales associated with it, represented by one or the other of the two paths shown in Figure 2.8.

In a like manner the set of *I* scales associated with each possible ordered-metric scale can be shown for scales of more than four stimuli. To represent the sets of *I* scales associated with each possible ordered-metric *J* scale we shall first list all the possible *I* scales associated with an ordinal *J* scale. In Figure 2.10 we have shown the sixteen *I* scales associated with the five-stimulus ordinal *J* scale, *ABCDE*. For each of the possible ordered-metric *J* scales consistent with the given stimulus order, there is associated a subset of eleven of the sixteen *I* scales. Each subset consists of one *I* scale from each of the eleven levels in Figure 2.10.

Not every possible combination of *I* scales from the eleven levels corresponds to an ordered-metric *J* scale, however. Recall that the set of *I* scales associated with an ordered-metric *J* scale must be such that we move from one *I* scale to another by crossing a midpoint between two stimuli. When this occurs two adjacent stimuli in the *I* scale are reversed while the rest of the *I* scale remains the same. Thus in Figure 2.10, an ordered-metric *J* scale which has as one of its *I* scales *CBADE* in level 4 can have *I* scale *CBDAE* in level 5 as another of the scales, since only the adjacent letters *A* and *D* are reversed. On the other hand, there is no ordered-metric *J* scale which has a subset of *I* scales including both *CBADE* in level 4 and *BCDEA* in level 5, since it is not possible to get from one *I* scale to the other simply by reversing two adjacent stimuli.

In Figure 2.10 we have designated the feasible subsets of *I* scales by

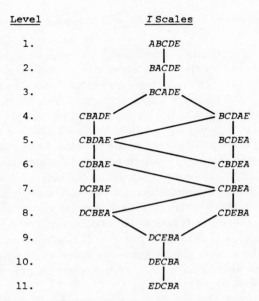

Figure 2.10. Set of I *scales associated with five-stimulus ordinal* J *scale* ABCDE
indicating possible paths followed by various ordered-metric J *scales.*

joining them with lines. Thus, since *CBADE* and *CBDAE* can fit the
same ordered-metric *J* scale, they are connected by a line; *CBADE* and
BCDEA are not. One can find the possible subset of the eleven *I* scales
associated with an ordered-metric *J* scale by choosing one scale from
each level, providing that all the *J* scales so chosen are connected by a
line.[10] This operation will be referred to as *finding the best path*, and it
can be performed with the aid of Figure 2.10 for the five-stimulus case
and of Figure 2.11 for the six-stimulus case.

If we compare Table 2.1, column 2, and Figure 2.11, we can see the
path followed by our simulated *I* scales and the related ordering of
midpoints as shown in Table 2.1, column 3. Since the data lack error,
there is no question which scale to choose at each level. But with measurement error and no clear ordinal *J* scale as discussed above, the situation is much more complex. Not only are there $n!/2$ possible ordinal *J*
scales (if one does not know the end stimuli on the *J* scale), but for *each*
of the ordinal *J* scales there are a large number of possible ordered-
metric *J* scales (or paths). With four stimuli and no indication of the
correct ordinal *J* scale, there are twenty-four different combinations

10. With six stimuli or more it is possible in certain instances that certain paths farther
down in the figure may not be followed because they may contradict the metric information already provided by earlier paths. Since this does not appear to happen often, we
wish only to call the possibility to the reader's attention.

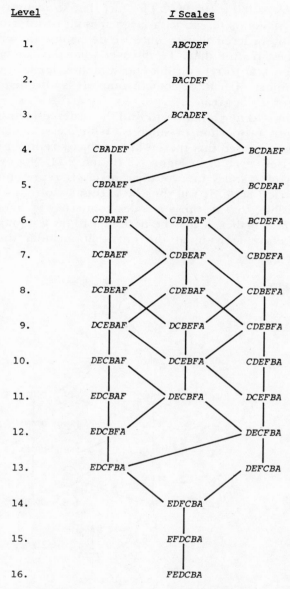

Figure 2.11. Set of thirty-two I scales associated with the six-stimulus ordinal J scale ABCDEF indicating the possible paths followed by the various ordered-metric J scales.

that could be tested: (4!/2) × 2. With five stimuli there are theoretically (5!/2) × 12 = 720 different combinations. With six stimuli the number becomes $(6!/2) \times 286 = 102,960$. The fact that so many combinations are possible allows us to extract a large amount of information about the underlying ordered metric, once we determine the one combination which best fits the data. To discover what this combination is, it becomes important to rely on the end stimuli at least, in order to reduce the number of feasible combinations. It is also helpful if measurement error is not great.

The goal in selecting a path is to find the ordered-metric *J* scale that fits the largest proportion of subjects. With measurement error the probability is increased that there will be subjects representing all the *I* scales at a given level, as in Figures 2.10 and 2.11. Not every possible combination of *I* scales in two adjacent levels represents a possible ordered-metric *J* scale. It will thus be necessary to follow those paths that are feasible, that is, those *I* scales connected by lines in Figures 2.10 and 2.11. Further, it may be necessary to try a number of different paths before arriving at the one that includes the maximum number of subjects.

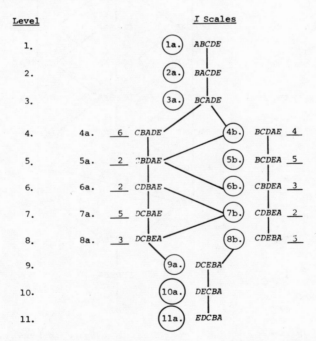

Figure 2.12. Example of distribution of subjects among I scales and selection of path representing best-fitting ordered-metric J scale.

Working with five stimuli, for example, we may represent the *I* scales by the number of subjects shown in Figure 2.12. In this figure, thirty-seven subjects are represented by *I* scales at the intermediate five levels, but clearly not all of them can be fitted to an ordered-metric *J* scale, since all the *I* scales at the intermediate five levels are represented. So it is necessary to find the path that accounts for the largest number of subjects. The path going straight down the left side of the figure (from *CBADE* to *DCBEA*) takes in eighteen subjects; that going straight down the right side (from *BCDAE* to *CDEBA*) includes nineteen. We select the right-hand path as the one with the maximum number of subjects, and hence as the best-fitting path. Could we pick another path that would include more subjects? For example, at level 4 would it not be better to pick *I* scale 4*a* (*CBADE*) instead of *I* scale 4*b* (*BCDAE*), since the former represents more subjects? The difficulty is that *I* scales 4*a* and 5*b* are not compatible with the same ordered-metric *J* scale. Thus in Figure 2.12 these two *I* scales are not connected by a line, and it is impossible to choose a path from *I* scale *CBADE* to *I* scale *BCDEA*. So it is better to skip the six subjects at *CBADE* and choose *BCDAE* even though it represents only four subjects, since it allows picking up the five subjects for *BCDEA*. Once one has started on this path, however, it is impossible to include the five subjects represented by *I* scale *DCBAE*, although the five subjects represented by *CDEBA* can be included. The path down the left-hand side to *DCBAE* includes fifteen subjects through four levels, whereas that down the right-hand side includes fourteen subjects through four levels; but it is not possible to move from *DCBAE* to *CDEBA* to pick up the last five subjects. Thus one must scan both paths entirely to see which will include the most subjects. And with more stimuli and more paths, the process becomes very arduous, particularly if the correct ordinal *J* scale is not known.

To further illustrate this rather complicated process of finding the best-fitting set of *I* scales representing the best-fitting ordered-metric *J* scale, we shall try to find the best path through the sixteen levels of *I* scales in the six-stimulus case illustrated by our example of the Watergate scale, for which we used the data in Table 2.10.

Our first step is to rearrange these data in a figure similar to Figure 2.11. This shows the number of *I* scales from Table 2.10 which correspond to each possible *I* scale represented by the ordering *ABCDEF*. Note, however, that as we have already seen, only twenty-two of the fifty *I* scales fit the set of thirty-two scales representing our chosen ordinal *J* scale, *EBCFAD* (which we relettered *ABCDEF*). Using only twenty-two subjects to fit the best set of sixteen *I* scales results in rather large ambiguity and error, as can be seen by the fact that at levels 3, 5, 7, 8, and 12 there are no *I* scales represented by subjects. Thus a large number of paths fitting the same number of subjects are possible.

One way partially to correct for the problem is to increase the sample size such that more subjects will show up on our figure. Though this might be difficult to do in practice, for our hypothetical example we can easily increase the sample size by simulating 150 more subjects. In

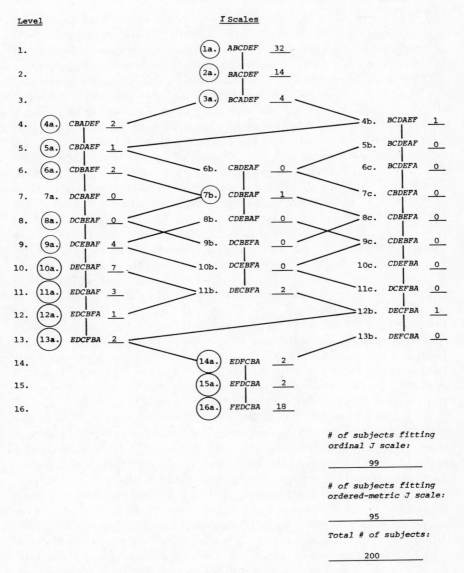

Figure 2.13. Distribution of 200 simulated subjects on thirty-two I scales repre-
senting ordinal J scale ABCDEF and indication of best-fitting set
of sixteen I scales corresponding to underlying ordered-metric J
scale.

Figure 2.13 we see that of the new total of 200 subjects, 99 fit the
thirty-two *I* scales representing the ordinal *J* scale *ABCDEF*. We note
now that the only ambiguity left in determining the path of *I* scales

corresponding to the best-fitting ordered-metric *J* scale is at level 8. The best-fitting path clearly goes through *I* scales 1, 2, 3, 4*a*, 5*a*, 6*a*, 7*b*, 9*a*, 10*a*, 11*a*, 12*a*, 13*a*, 14, 15, and 16. At level 8 we have a choice between *I* scales 8*a* and 8*b* (8*c* does not allow us to get back to *I* scale 9*a* since there is no path between 8*c* and 9*a*). We randomly choose one path, in this case 8*a*. Thus for our example the best-fitting set of sixteen *I* scales is shown by the path indicated in Figure 2.13.

To simplify steps 2 and 3 we suggest first finding the best-fitting ordinal *J* scale and then finding the ordered-metric *J* scale which best fits this ordinal scale. This should give us the best ordered-metric *J* scale in most cases. If, however, one ordinal *J* scale does not clearly accommodate a substantially larger number of subjects than another, (e.g., if one accommodates thirty subjects and another twenty-eight subjects), it is conceivable that the ordinal *J* scale representing the smaller number of subjects nevertheless has a set of *I* scales associated with it that represents a larger proportion of the total subjects than the best ordered-metric *J* scale associated with the better ordinal *J* scale. To alleviate this problem we recommend that when several ordinal *J* scales do about equally well in fitting the data, one should calculate the best-fitting ordered-metric *J* scale for each ordinal *J* scale and then select the ordered-metric *J* scale which fits the most subjects.

Step 4: Assignment of Metric Values to Stimuli and I *Scales*

Once the best-fitting set of *I* scales is found in step 3, the determination of metric values is done exactly as in the case of error-free data. Since the only input for this step of the technique is the set of *I* scales, it does not matter at this point whether it was generated from error-free data and represents all the subjects or generated from data containing error and represents only a portion of the subjects.

For our example of the Watergate scale we have listed in Table 2.11 the sixteen *I* scales selected in Figure 2.13 and have proceeded, as before, to extract the metric information from this set of scales. The metric information is shown in Figure 2.14. The delta intervals are assigned to our example in Table 2.12.

Next we assign numerical values to each of the delta values so that we can evaluate the expressions in Table 2.12, column 6. Here we take advantage of the information gained in our simulation of the error-free case—that the choices of values of delta make little or no difference in the final outcome. We thus pick the simpler, equal-delta solution, set all of our delta values equal to 5, evaluate the expressions for each line segment, and combine line segments to get the resulting stimuli values. We next assign values to the various *I* scales in the same manner as that for the case of error-free data. Table 2.13 shows the reconstructed *I* scale range and midpoints for our Watergate example.

Table 2.11. Ordered Set of Sixteen I *Scales Corresponding to Best-fitting Ordered-Metric* J *Scale for "Watergate" Example as Obtained in Figure 2.13 and Metric Information Obtained from This Set of* I *Scales by Coombs's Unfolding Technique*

I scale no. (1)	I scale (2)	Lower bounding midpoint (3)	Information-containing Pair (4)	Metric information (5)
1	ABCDEF			
2	BACDEF	AB		
3	BCADEF	AC		
4	CBADEF	BC		
5	CBDAEF	AD	BC, AD	$\overline{CD} > \overline{AB}$
6	CDBAEF	BD		
7	CDBEAF	AE	BD, AE	$\overline{DE} > \overline{AB}$
8	DCBEAF	CD	AE, CD	$\overline{AC} > \overline{DE}$
9	DCEBAF	BE	CD, BE	$\overline{DE} > \overline{BC}$
10	DECBAF	CE		
11	EDCBAF	DE		
12	EDCBFA	AF	DE, AF	$\overline{EF} > \overline{AD}$
13	EDCFBA	BF		
14	EDFCBA	CF		
15	EFDCBA	DF		
16	FEDCBA	EF		

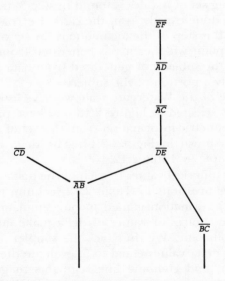

Figure 2.14. Partial ordering of line segments obtained from metric information in Table 2.11, column 5.

Table 2.12. *Determination of Line-Segment Lengths by Use of*
Combination of Arbitrary Assignment of Intervals (Δ's) Adjusted to
Correspond to Metric Information Contained in Table 2.11, Column 5,
Following Unfolding Technique

Line Segments (1)	Initial assignment of Δ's (2)	Metric information used for adjustments			
		$\overline{AC} = \overline{AB} + \overline{BC}$ (3)	$\overline{AD} = \overline{AC} + \overline{CD}$ (4)	$\overline{AC} > \overline{DE}$ $\Delta 3 > \Delta 4$ $\Delta 3 = \Delta 4 + \Delta 6$ (5)	$\overline{DE} > \overline{BC}$ $\Delta 1 > \Delta 6$ $\Delta 1 = \Delta 6 + \Delta 7$ (6)
$\overline{EF}$			$2\Delta 1 + \Delta 2$ $+ \Delta 3 + \Delta 5$	$2\Delta 1 + \Delta 2$ $+ \Delta 4 + \Delta 5 + \Delta 6$	$\Delta 2 + \Delta 4 + \Delta 5$ $+ 3\Delta 6 + 2\Delta 7$
$\overline{AD}$			$2\Delta 1 + \Delta 2 + \Delta 3$	$2\Delta 1 + \Delta 2$ $+ \Delta 4 + \Delta 6$	$\Delta 2 + \Delta 4$ $+ 3\Delta 6 + 2\Delta 7$
$\overline{AC}$		$\Delta 1 + \Delta 3$	$\Delta 1 + \Delta 3$	$\Delta 1 + \Delta 4 + \Delta 6$	$\Delta 4 + 2\Delta 6 + \Delta 7$
$\overline{DE}$	$\Delta 1 + \Delta 4$	$\Delta 1 + \Delta 4$	$\Delta 1 + \Delta 4$	$\Delta 1 + \Delta 4$	$\Delta 4 + \Delta 6 + \Delta 7$
$\overline{CD}$	$\Delta 1 + \Delta 2$	$\Delta 1 + \Delta 2$	$\Delta 1 + \Delta 2$	$\Delta 1 + \Delta 2$	$\Delta 2 + \Delta 6 + \Delta 7$
$\overline{AB}$	$\Delta 1$	$\Delta 1$	$\Delta 1$	$\Delta 1$	$\Delta 6 + \Delta 7$
$\overline{BC}$	$\Delta 3$	$\Delta 3$	$\Delta 3$	$\Delta 4 + \Delta 6$	$\Delta 4 + \Delta 6$

With these values determined our final step in using the unfolding
technique to reconstruct the *J* scale is to give each of our subjects a
value on the *J* scale. In the error-free case this was a simple process of

Table 2.13. *Metric Values for Sixteen I Scales Obtained from*
Knowledge of Stimulus Values

No.	I scale	Range	Midpoint of I scale
1	*ABCDEF*	0-5	2.5
2	*BACDEF*	5-10	7.5
3	*BCADEF*	10-15	12.5
4	*CBADEF*	15-17.5	16.25
5	*CBDAEF*	17.5-22.5	20
6	*CDBAEF*	22.5-25	23.75
7	*CDBEAF*	25-27.5	26.25
8	*DCBEAF*	27.5-30	28.75
9	*DCEBAF*	30-35	32.5
10	*DECBAF*	35-42.5	38.75
11	*EDCBAF*	42.5-45	43.75
12	*EDCBFA*	45-50	47.5
13	*EDCFBA*	50-55	52.5
14	*EDFCBA*	55-62.5	58.75
15	*EFDCBA*	62.5-70	66.25
16	*FEDCBA*	70-100	85

assigning the midpoint value corresponding to each subject's *I* scale. With data containing error, however, this procedure does not work, because some of our subjects have *I* scales that are not consistent with the final ordered-metric *J* scale, and thus their *I* scales are not among the set of *I* scales for which we can determine a numerical value. In our example, of the fifty original subjects only twenty-two had *I* scales consistent with the best-fitting ordered-metric *J* scale. For these subjects we can readily assign the ordered-metric values shown in Table 2.13, but this procedure is not applicable to the other twenty-eight subjects. For a suitable method of dealing with these subjects, we shall go back to the method of determining *I* scale numbers described earlier in this chapter.

Step 5: Assignment of Metric Values to All Subjects' Ideal Points

In the technique of Guttman scaling, each subject is simply given a value equal to the number of items passed, whether or not the subject actually fits the Guttman scale, providing that the data as a whole fit well enough to produce a coefficient of reproducibility of .9. Later in the chapter we shall suggest a criterion analogous to the coefficient of reproducibility, but now we shall merely describe the procedure whereby one can assign *I* scale values to *I* scales that do not exactly fit the best ordered-metric *J* scale. This procedure, assigning each subject the midpoint value of the *I* scale most closely approximating his *I* scale, may be used whenever the criterion indicates that the ordered-metric *J* scale represents the data well enough to be acceptable.

We noted earlier that the correct number of an *I* scale can be determined by counting the numbers of spaces the letters have moved to the right from the extreme left position. By doing this with the *I* scales which do not exactly fit the ordered-metric *J* scale, we can determine which *I* scales the nonfitting *I* scales most closely approximate. For example, subject 28, with *I* scale *EDBCAF* (see Table 2.10) in our simulation, does not fit the ordered-metric *J* scale. However, by counting spaces we see that *A* is four spaces, *B* two spaces, *C* three spaces, and *D* one space to the right of *E*. Since the total is ten spaces, the appropriate place to fit this *I* scale is at level 11. Even though the error in the data has produced an *I* scale impossible to produce with error-free data (i.e., *C* has moved farther to the right than *B*), this method provides for reasonably accurate placement. If *B* and *C* are reversed so that the *I* scale is *EDCBAF*, the total number of spaces moved is still ten, and the *I* scale number remains 11.

One must remember, in using this simple procedure, that each letter must move all the way to the left in an *I* scale before it moves to the right. Thus with subject 28 we count only the spaces moved by *A, B, C,* and *D*. Letter *F* has not yet moved to the left. We determine which letters to count by observing the letter occupying the extreme left position, in this case *E*, and counting only the spaces moved by the letters preceding it in the alphabet. With subject 39 and *I* scale *CADBEF*, one counts only the spaces moved by *A* and *B*. The correct count for this subject is one space for *A*, and three for *B*; and the correct *I* scale number is 5.

Using this method for the twenty-eight subjects that did not fit the ordered-metric *J* scale for our Watergate simulation, we assigned all our subjects the *I* scale numbers and midpoint values shown in Table 2.14. The true values of the subjects are also shown.

Evaluation of Simulation Results

As we did with our error-free data, we may again evaluate how well our subjects' assigned values correspond to their known values by correlating the known values in Table 2.14, column 2, with the assigned values in column 5. Table 2.15 shows the correlations obtained for our simulations involving six stimuli and various degrees of error. It can be seen that with error greater than 5 percentage points the correlations drop below .9, although even with 10 percent error the correlations are not far from .9.

We conclude, then, that with an error term whose standard deviation is equal to 10 percent of the range of the scale, the assignment resulting from the use of the modified unfolding technique provides a good approximation of the original values of the subjects. In almost all research cases, however, one is not aware of the degree of error in his data. Thus it is necessary to use another criterion for determining the adequacy of the ordered-metric *J* scale one has obtained, and this brings us to a reconsideration of the technique as a scaling criterion.

The Unfolding Technique as a Scaling Criterion

Coombs (1964, pp. 81-82) suggests that, because of the unfolding technique's vulnerability to error, it is more suitable as a scaling criterion than as a scaling method. By this he means that it is more feasible to use it to test the hypothesis that a unidimensional metric scale can account for the observed behavior than to construct such a scale from a mass of data. We noted above that, with Guttman scaling, a coefficient of reproducibility of .9 is regarded as evidence of an underlying unidimensional scale. With the unfolding technique we do not have such a coefficient, but on the basis of our simulations we can suggest an analogous criterion—both for deciding whether the assumption that a unidimensional ordered-metric scale underlying the data is reasonable

Table 2.14. True Values for Fifty Subjects of Table 2.10, Simulated I Scale Containing Error for Each Subject, I Scales from Table 2.13 that are Best Approximations, and Assigned Values on J Scale

Subject no. (1)	True value (2)	I scale (3)	No. of Table 2.13 I scale (4)	Assigned midpoint value (5)
1	68.8	EDFCBA	14	58.75
2	42.5	CBADEF	4	16.25
3	29.4	ABCEDF	1	2.5
4	64.2	EDCBAF	11	43.75
5	35.0	ACBDEF	1	2.5
6	33.2	BACDEF	2	7.5
7	72.4	EFDCBA	15	66.25
8	81.9	FDECAB	16	85
9	85.0	FDECBA	16	85
10	23.4	ABCEDF	1	2.5
11	80.0	DFCEAB	10	38.75
12	93.7	FDEBCA	16	85
13	24.5	BACDEF	2	7.5
14	51.1	DCEBAF	9	32.5
15	20.2	ABCDEF	1	2.5
16	95.9	FEDCAB	16	85
17	94.7	FEDBAC	16	85
18	62.3	EDCFBA	13	52.5
19	1.6	ABCEDF	1	2.5
20	66.0	EDCFAB	13	52.5
21	81.0	EFDCAB	15	66.25
22	10.2	ABCEDF	1	2.5
23	61.7	EDFBCA	14	58.75
24	28.8	ABCDEF	1	2.5
25	44.4	CDBAEF	6	23.75

and for determining whether the scale values obtained through use of the technique as a scaling method are acceptable. This criterion involves the percentage of total subjects which fit the final best-fitting ordered-metric *J* scale.

From our simulations we noted that with 10 percent error or less the average correlation between subjects' true values and assigned values was .88, which we feel to be an acceptable correlation when using the technique as a scaling method, and comparable to the Guttman criterion of a .9 coefficient of reproducibility. It is also possible from our simulations to determine what percentage of total subjects are accommodated by the best ordered-metric *J* scale with various degrees of error and thereby to determine what percentage of total subjects should be used as a criterion.

Table 2.14–Continued

Subject no. (1)	True value (2)	I scale (3)	No. of Table 2.13 I scale (4)	Assigned midpoint value (5)
26	97.6	FEDCAB	16	85
27	29.4	ABCDEF	1	2.5
28	59.2	EDBCAF	11	43.75
29	88.0	FEDCAB	16	85
30	99.5	FEDBCA	16	85
31	5.5	ABCDEF	1	2.5
32	59.7	EDCABF	11	43.75
33	70.9	FEDBCA	16	85
34	4.6	ABCDEF	1	2.5
35	30.4	BACDEF	2	7.5
36	48.3	DECBAF	10	38.75
37	82.5	FEDCBA	16	85
38	10.5	BACDEF	2	7.5
39	43.5	CADBEF	4	16.25
40	97.7	FEDBCA	16	85
41	89.8	FECDBA	16	85
42	13.7	ABCDEF	1	2.5
43	45.3	CDBAEF	6	23.75
44	59.0	DECABF	10	38.75
45	69.0	DEBFCA	10	38.75
46	28.9	BACEDF	2	7.5
47	77.7	DFECBA	10	38.75
48	11.6	ABCDEF	1	2.5
49	35.4	CBAEDF	4	16.25
50	76.9	FEDACB	16	85

Tables 2.16 and 2.17 show the percentages of total subjects whose *I* scales were retained as we proceeded toward the best ordered-metric *J*

Table 2.15. Correlations between True Values of Subjects and Assigned Values for Six Stimuli and Various Degrees of Error

Standard deviation of error term as percentage of range of original scale	Correlation (Six stimuli)
0	.97
5	.95
10	.88
20	.77
40	.68

scale for the five- and six-stimulus situations respectively.[11] Row 1 of these tables summarizes the percentages of total subjects whose *I* scales ended in one of the two correct stimuli. Row 2 summarizes the percentages of total subjects whose *I* scales fit the correct ordinal *J* scale, and row 3 summarizes the percentages of total subjects whose *I* scales were included with the best-fitting ordered-metric *J* scale. From this we see that with 10 percent error in the five-stimulus case approximately 50 percent of total subjects were included with the final ordered-metric *J* scale; in the six-stimulus case, approximately 30 percent.

The standard Goldberg and Coombs (1963, p. 110) have suggested for determining whether an ordered-metric *J* scale represents enough subjects to make it an acceptable indicator of unidimensionality is that it should accommodate a majority of subjects. We believe our simulations show, however, that such a rule should be dependent upon the number of stimuli in the scale. The criteria we suggest are that for five and 6 stimuli, 50 and 30 percent of the total subjects should fit the final ordered-metric *J* scale, respectively, to show both the unidimensionality and the acceptability of scale values derived by the method.[12] With more stimuli, which we hope to explore in future simulations, it is likely that degrees of error smaller than 10 percentage points will be neces-

Table 2.16. Summary of Simulations for Five-Stimulus Scale with Varying Degrees of Error, Where Range of Scale Is from 0 to 100

	Standard deviation of error				
	40	20	10	5	1
1. Percentage of subjects with *I* scales ending in one of the two correct stimuli	54	59	79	93	100
2. Percentage of total subjects fitting the correct ordinal *J* scale	17	27	53	74	99
3. Percentage of total subjects fitting the correct ordered-metric *J* scale	14	23	49	70	99

11. Each of the percentages in these tables is the average of several simulations at each degree of error.

12. This, then, is the criterion we would apply before assigning scale values to those *I* scales that do not fit the best ordered-metric *J* scale.

sary to obtain correlations of .9 or better between true values and assigned values, but also that considerably less than a majority of total
subjects fitting the dominant ordered-metric J scale may be adequate to
infer a unidimensional ordered-metric scale.

Applications

To our knowledge the unfolding technique has hardly been used by
social scientists. This is no doubt due partly to a lack of exposure to it,
for which we hope this chapter will compensate, and partly to the difficulty of finding data which will work with the technique, especially data
that can be assumed to have a single underlying dimension with a definite ordered metric. Coombs himself has used the method primarily
with data for which he could be quite sure of the nature of the underlying dimension—grade preferences and preferred risks in gambling
situations (1964, pp. 92-106, 134-38) and preferred number of children and perceived similarities between different numbers of children
(Goldberg and Coombs 1963). The same is true of Cutler's study of
income ideals (Coombs 1952, pp. 69-75). In these situations one can be
quite sure of the ordering of the stimuli on the J scale; the problem is
simply one of determining the metric information.

The only specifically sociological application of the technique with
which we are familiar is Israel's (1959), in which he measured cross-
pressures in a group by comparing the J scales of different actors in a
group situation. In this case, however, he developed his scale values for

*Table 2.17. Summary of Simulations for Six-Stimulus Case with
Varying Degrees of Error, Where Range of Scale is from 0 to 100.*

	Standard deviation of error				
	40	*20*	*10*	*5*	*1*
1. Percentage of subjects with I scales ending in one of the two correct stimuli	38	64	74	90	100
2. Percentage of total subjects fitting the correct ordinal J scale	6	17	35	59	95
3. Percentage of total subjects fitting the correct ordered-metric J scale	5	14	31	55	94

stimuli by means of Thurstonian techniques and used unfolding only to derive the scale values of subjects. Runkel's study of cognitive similarity and communication (Coombs 1964, pp. 122-31) is similar to Israel's in terms of comparing *J* scales. The Dember-Earl study of exploratory behavior (Coombs 1964, pp. 131-34) is an example of its use with data for which the underlying dimension is not evident.

Probably the most extensive development of the technique has been in the area of marketing research (Green and Carmone 1969, 1970). Extension in this area is not surprising, since products represent the type of stimuli for which preferential choice data can be obtained relatively easily. Among the suggested uses for nonmetric scaling techniques in this area are the following: product life-cycle analysis, market segmentation, vendor evaluation, advertising evaluation, test marketing, salesman- and store-image research, brand-switching research, and attitude scaling (Green and Carmone, 1970, pp. 14-19).

The technique has also been used rather extensively in geography,[13] in such projects as: converting distances between points on a map into a configuration, deriving configurations of locational preferences and perceived distances, deriving configurations of migrants' perceptions of destinations, studying consumers' preferences for different shopping areas within a community or in different communities, and deriving configurations of the residential desirability of various states. Some of the more interesting conclusions from such studies are Golledge, Briggs, and Demko's suggestion (1969) that overestimates of interpoint distance reduce the likelihood of interaction between the points, Schwind's (1971) discovery that states known for high rates of inmigration are close to the center of a migrant's perception space, DeTemple's (1971) contention that space-preference structures are more appropriate predictors of spatial interaction than distance-decay functions, and Rushton's (1971) argument that central place theory should be revised to take into account different preference scales. The nature of these studies suggests that the unfolding technique and its offshoots might well be considered by demographers, human ecologists, and urban sociologists. The most complete discussion of the use of nonmetric scaling techniques in geographical research is found in Golledge and Rushton (1972).

In both marketing and geographical research the tendency has been to go beyond the unidimensional situation described here to multidimensional techniques which not only yield a scaling of points on each dimension but also yield configurations of the points on all dimensions (Green and Carmone 1970, p. 35). Coombs's framework, which we have described in this chapter, has provided much of the

---

13. We wish to thank Clyde H. Coombs for calling this to our attention.

basis for these extensions. The various computer programs (Kruskal 1968; Lingoes 1966; Young 1968; Young and Torgerson 1967) developed for these multidimensional nonmetric scaling techniques all involve algorithms which first produce such configurations and then revise them so that high indexes of fit are produced. Since a set of rank orderings of n stimuli can always produce a configuration in $n - 1$ dimensions, the object is to find the smallest number of dimensions that will at the same time retain the rank orderings of the input data (Green and Carmone 1970, pp. 37-40). For the unidimensional situation we have discussed here, one would use one of these programs and specify that his data were unidimensional. In future research we hope to explore these extensions further, particularly to investigate by means of simulations the impact of various degrees of error as we have done in this chapter.

For sociologists, the most feasible area for application of the unfolding technique appears to us to be in the development of ordered-metric scales from micro-level data. It is at this level that one is most likely to get preferential choice or similarities data as well as data that can be represented unidimensionally. We believe there are analogues to both of these types of data at more macro levels, but at these levels one is going to be confronted by a small number of cases and multidimensional situations. It is possible that some of the techniques developed by the marketing and geographical researchers can be adapted to this level, but we feel that the difficulty of getting an adequate number of cases will be a perpetual hindrance. Furthermore, measurement error is likely to be quite high at these levels.

Two areas in which we feel the technique has potential applicability for sociologists are the measurement of social status and the measurement of social distance. An ordered-metric scale for occupational prestige could be derived, for example, by using either preferential choice data or similarities data (asking subjects which occupations they prefer or which occupations are more similar). The major problem here is that one could not handle a very large number of occupations. Perhaps occupations at each decile on the Goode-Hatt scale could be used instead, and occupations lying between those decile points apportioned equally within these intervals.

The use of this technique for measuring social distance appears to us more feasible, because one could work with fewer stimuli. The technique could be used in several ways. First, subjects could be asked to rank ethnic and racial groups for each of the levels typically used in such studies (e.g., "Rank the following groups in order of your preference for them as neighbors: Italians, Negroes, Frenchmen, Puerto Ricans"), and the J scales yielded by this procedure could then be compared to determine the distances between these groups. Second, the J scales derived from different groups of subjects could be compared, in a manner similar to that in Israel's cross-pressures study, to see what differences existed. Third, the ordered-metric scale could be used for correlations with other variables—political attitudes, degree of alienation, and the like.

A third possibility is the use of the technique to gain insights into the relationship between social status and social distance by combining the foregoing two types of stimuli. Subjects could be asked, say, whether they preferred living next to a Negro doctor or a white plumber. This would very likely not yield a unidimensional solution, but it would represent another method for attacking this problem, in addition to the methods used previously (Triandis and Triandis 1960, 1962; Triandis and Davis 1965).

Conclusions

We have shown in this chapter that Coombs's unfolding technique is a feasible means of deriving an ordered-metric scale from ordinal data that yields high correlations with the true values of subjects when certain conditions are met. Coombs has suggested four conditions (1952, pp. 56, 76) under which the technique works best. First, differences between stimuli should be relatively great. Second, the stimuli should be discriminable. Third, each stimulus should have one and only one genotype scale position for all subjects—that is, all subjects should agree on the "location" of the stimuli even though they will have different preferences for them. Fourth, each individual should have one and only one genotypic scale position for all stimuli—that is, he should "locate" the stimuli at only one point.

In addition, we can suggest the following conditions on the basis of our simulations: (1) With five or six stimuli, data should not contain more than 5-10 percent error; with more stimuli the tolerable degree of error will decrease, although we cannot say specifically at this point how much it will decrease. (2) A relatively large number of subjects will be needed if one is attempting to scale many more stimuli than five or six; this factor can be greatly compensated for, however, if one has some idea beforehand regarding both the unidimensionality of his data and the order of stimuli, as would be the case with variables such as grades, income, and years of education. (3) If 50 percent of all subjects fit the best ordered-metric *J* scale with five stimuli, and 30 percent fit the scale with six stimuli, the data can be regarded as unidimensional, and the stimuli values derived are probably very highly correlated with their true values. Furthermore, if 30 percent or more of all subjects fit the best ordered-metric *J* scale for more than six stimuli, we can anticipate that the scale values will correlate very highly with the true values and can consider the data unidimensional.

References

Bennett, J. F., and W. L. Hays
1960. "Multidimensional Unfolding: Determining the Dimensionality of Ranked Preference Data." *Psychometrika* 25:27-43.
Bogardus, E. S.
1928. *Immigration and Race Attitudes*. Boston: Heath.
Carter, Lewis F.
1971. "Inadvertent Sociological Theory." *Social Forces* 50 (September): 12-25.
Coombs, Clyde H.
1950. "Psychological Scaling without a Unit of Measurement." *Psychological Review* 57:145-58.
1952. *A Theory of Psychological Scaling*. Ann Arbor: University of Michigan Press.
1953. "Theory and Methods of Social Measurement." In Leon Festinger and Daniel Katz, eds., *Research Methods in the Behavioral Sciences*. New York: Dryden.
1964. *A Theory of Data*. New York: Wiley.
Coombs, Clyde H., and R. C. Kao
1960 "On a Connection between Factor Analysis and Multidimensional Unfolding." *Psychometrika* 25:219-31.
DeTemple, D. J.
1971. "A Space Preference Approach to the Determination of Individual Contact Fields in the Spatial Diffusion of Innovations." Unpublished manuscript. Terre Haute: Department of Geography, Indiana State University.
Goldberg, David, and Clyde H. Coombs
1963. "Some Applications of Unfolding Theory to Fertility Analysis." In *Emerging Techniques in Population Research*. New York: Milbank Memorial Fund.
Golledge, Reginald G., R. Briggs, and D. Demko
1969. "Configurations of Distance in Intra-urban Space." *Proceedings of the Association of American Geographers* 1:60-65.
Golledge, Reginald G., and Gerard Rushton
1972. "Multidimensional Scaling: Review and Geographical Applications." Technical Paper no. 10. Washington, D.C.: Commission on College Geography, Association of American Geographers.
Green, Paul E., and Frank J. Carmone
1969. "Multidimensional Unfolding: An Introduction and Comparison of Nonmetric Unfolding Techniques." *Journal of Marketing Research* 6 (August): 330-41.
1970. *Multidimensional Scaling and Related Techniques in Marketing Analysis*. Boston: Allyn & Bacon.
Israel, Joachim
1959. "Measurement of Cross-Pressures in Groups by the Unfolding Technique." *Acta Sociologia* 4, no. 1:1-7.
Kruskal, J. B.
1968. "How to Use M-D-SCAL: A Program to do Multidimensional Scaling and Multidimensional Unfolding." Version 4 and 4M of M-D-SCAL (all in FORTRAN IV). Mimeographed. Murray Hill, N.J.: Bell Telephone Laboratories.
Lingoes, J. C.
1966. "An IBM 7090 Program for Guttman-Lingoes Smallest Space Analysis." *Behavioral Science* 11:322-23.

Rushton, Gerard
  1971. "Postulates of Central Place Theory and Properties of Central Place Systems." *Geographical Analysis* 3 (April):140-56.
Schonemann, P. H.
  1969. "On Metric Multidimensional Unfolding." Research Bulletin, RB-69093. Princeton, N.J.: Educational Testing Service.
Schwind, Paul J.
  1971. "Spatial Preferences of Migrants from Regions: The Example of Maine." *Proceedings of the Association of American Geographers* 3:150-56.
Shepard, Roger N.
  1966. "Metric Structures in Ordinal Data." *Journal of Mathematical Psychology* 3 (July):287-315.
Torgerson, Warren S.
  1960. *Theory and Methods of Scaling.* New York: Wiley.
Triandis, Harry C., and Earl E. Davis
  1965. "Race and Belief as Determinants of Behavioral Intentions." *Journal of Personality and Social Psychology* 2 (November):715-25.
Triandis, Harry C., and Leigh Minten Triandis
  1960. "Race, Social Class, Religion, and Nationality as Determinants of Social Distance." *Journal of Abnormal and Social Psychology* 61, no. 1:110-18.
  1962. "A Cross-cultural Study of Social Distance." *Psychological Monographs: General and Applied*, vol. 76, no. 21 (Whole no. 540).
Young, F. W.
  1968. "TORSCA: An IBM Program for Nonmetric Multidimensional Scaling." *Journal of Marketing Research* 5 (August):319-21.
Young, F. W., and W. S. Torgerson
  1967. "TORSCA: A FORTRAN IV Program for Shepard-Kruskal Multidimensional Scaling Analysis." *Behavioral Science* 12:498.

Chapter 3

SOCIAL ATTITUDES: MAGNITUDE MEASUREMENT AND THEORY

ROBERT L. HAMBLIN

*Robert L. Hamblin received his Ph.D. from the University of Michigan in
1955. He is currently Professor and Chairman, Department of Sociology,
University of Arizona, a post to which he was appointed in 1971. His
publications include many articles as well as two recent books,* The
Humanization Processes *(Wiley, 1971), and* A Mathematical Theory
of Social Change *(Wiley, 1973).*

A substantial breakthrough has occurred in psychophysical scaling over
the past twenty years, and that breakthrough has important implications for social science research generally. As Shinn suggests in the next
chapter, a wide range of social science theories deals with attitudes
—how people perceive and react to various aspects of their physical
and social environments. It appears, therefore, that further refinements of those theories must rest largely upon accurate measurement
of attitudes.

Social scientists have used various kinds of categorical scaling procedures for just this purpose. Yet, modern scaling research in
psychophysics has shown that category scaling reflects not magnitude
but a correlated variable: discrimination error. As Shinn suggests, the
relationship between magnitude and discrimination error is not constant; it varies for prothetic and metathetic continua. In contrast, the
newly developed techniques of direct magnitude scaling are relatively
free of problems, and, as previous research illustrates, they have a
strong potential for testing and developing attitudinal theories. The

I wish to thank H. M. Blalock, Lee Rainwater, and Allen Shinn for their helpful comments. Also, I appreciate the released time and other research support by the University
of Arizona, which made this writing possible.

general purpose of this chapter is to introduce the reader to the ways of using and the advantages of using such measures in attitudinal research.

The chapter is divided into three sections. The first reviews the research that resulted in S. S. Stevens's psychophysical law, which in effect says that the magnitude of a psychological sensation increases as a power function of the magnitude of its eliciting physical stimulus. The purpose is to establish a scientific basis for the magnitude-scaling procedures used in the rest of the chapter.

The second section deals with the methodological issues connected with the magnitude measurement of social attitudes. It begins with an illustrative experiment, the methodology of which is evaluated against the dicta developed by Stevens for psychophysical experimentation and against the general standards of mathematical experimentation—the methodology of the mathematical sciences. Involved are the issues of appropriate experimental manipulation, ratio measurement, control by constancy, averaging out measurement error, and fitting equations to data. This section also deals with two issues that have plagued social-attitude research: the multiple stimulus problem and the relationship between attitudes and behavior.

The third section is evaluative. It starts with replies to a number of criticisms of the methodology employed in the attitude experiments reviewed previously, then switches to Pearson's critique of the methodology of the mathematical sciences, which is followed by a countercritique. Since the ultimate evaluation of any methodology is pragmatic, this section concludes with a summary and a discussion of the kind of theory that seems to be coming out of these magnitude-scaling studies of attitudes. The data suggest that one family of equations, bivariate and multivariate power functions, describes a wide range of social-attitude data. This, in turn, suggests a social-attitude law related to the psychophysical law.

Psychophysics

In psychophysical experiments in which he has used various kinds of magnitude scaling, S. S. Stevens (1957, 1960, 1962) has discovered that stimulus-response relationships in man's sensory system are described by a power law,

$$\psi = c\phi^n \, ,$$

where ψ is the magnitude of the sensory response, ϕ is the magnitude of the related physical stimulus, and c and n are empirical parameters.

When the power function is transformed to logarithms the equation becomes linear:

$$\log \psi = \log c + n \log \phi.$$

This means that when the psychophysical data involving magnitude scaling are plotted on logarithmic coordinates they typically yield a linear plot, and the log transformations of the data yield a linear relationship which may be analyzed by the use of standard correlation and regression procedures.

Magnitude Estimation

When making magnitude estimations, judges attempt to match the magnitude of a number to the magnitude of the sensation produced by a stimulus magnitude. Stevens's (1956) first published experiment using this method gave the following instructions to observers:

> The left key presents the standard tone and the right key presents the variable. We are going to call the loudness of the standard 10 and your task is to estimate the loudness of the variable. In other words, the question is: If the standard is called 10, what would you call the variable? Use whatever numbers seem to you appropriate—fractions, decimals, or whole numbers. For example, if the variable sounds seven times as loud as the standard, say 70; if it sounds one-fifth as loud, say 2; if a twentieth as loud, say 0.5, etc.
>
> Try not to worry about being consistent. Try to give the appropriate number to each tone regardless of what you may have called some previous stimulus.
>
> Press the standard key for one or two seconds and listen carefully. Then press the "variable" for one or two seconds and make your judgment. You may repeat this process if you care to before deciding on your estimate.

There were nine sound-variable levels covering a range of 70 db. and spaced as shown by the data points (circles) in Figure 3.1. The data points are the medians for thirty-six estimates, two by each of eighteen observers or judges. The vertical lines mark the interquartile ranges, and the straight lines through the standards are segments of a loudness function determined by Stevens from pooled data of previous fractionation and multiplication experiments. The lower set of data is from a second experiment in which the standard was set at 90 db. and again called "10."

In that first report, Stevens admitted that the foregoing experiments were achieved only after much trial and error in the course of which he at least learned the disadvantages of some steps, as well as the advantages of others. While his procedures have not been subjected to systematic investigation, most are still followed in psychophysical experi-

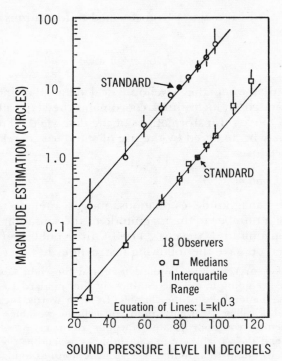

Figure 3.1.   *Magnitude estimations of loudness plotted on logarithmic coordinates as a function of stimulus magnitudes: two experiments.*

ments using magnitude scaling, and most of the points appear to apply as well to social science experiments using magnitude scaling. Consequently, Stevens's dicta are paraphrased here:

1. Use a standard whose level does not impress the observer as being either extremely soft or extremely loud (i.e., use a standard in the middle of the stimulus range).

2. Present variable stimuli that are both above and below the standard.

3. Call the standard by a number like "10" that is easily multiplied and divided.

4. Assign a number to the standard only, and leave the observer completely free to decide what he will call the variable. In particular, do not tell the observer that the faintest variable is to be called "1" or that the loudest is to be called some other number. (If the experimenter assigns numbers to more than one stimulus, he introduces constraints of the sort that forces the observer to make categorical rather than magnitude judgments.)

5. Use only one standard in any experiment, but use various stand-

ards in later replications, for it is risky to decide the form of a magnitude function on the basis of data obtained with only one standard.

6. Randomize the order of presentation. With inexperienced observers, it is well, however, to start with stimuli that are not extreme and are, therefore, easier to judge.

7. Make the experimental session short, about ten minutes.

8. Let the observer present the stimuli to himself. He can then work at his own pace and so is more apt to be attending properly when the stimulus comes on.

9. Since some estimates may depart widely from those of the average observer, it is advisable to use a group of observers large enough to produce a stable median. Groups of twenty to thirty observers are typically used in psychophysical experiments, and these are large enough to obtain parameters which vary plus or minus 5 percentage points.

Stevens's advice to use a median may surprise most social scientists. But magnitude estimations are generally log normally distributed, and the median gives a better measure of central tendency for log normal distributions than the arithmetic mean. (The geometric mean gives a measure comparable to that of the median except when some of the estimates are zero.) Be that as it may, Stevens suggested that these recommendations are probably not equally important. Some may be necessary; some may be merely desirable. For example, he later published good results obtained from experiments in which each observer, in effect, set his own standard (Stevens 1956, pp. 21, 22). That, in fact, has become a preferred way of doing psychophysical experiments, although the lack of a standard bothers many social scientists. The data in Table 3.1 summarize many of the findings in psychophysics. They suggest the variety of phenomena encompassed by Stevens's law, as well as the variability of the exponents obtained.

Cross-Modality Matching

Stevens's numerical magnitude-estimation procedures made some critics rather nervous at first. This nervousness was expressed in a number of ways, but perhaps most aptly by Luce (1959, pp. 81-82): "Using such 'direct' methods as magnitude estimation and production, Stevens and others have accumulated evidence to buttress the empirical generality of a power function. Were it not for the fact that some psychologists are uneasy about these methods, which seem to rest heavily on our experience with the number system, the point would seem to be established."

It was imperative that the magnitude-estimation results be cross-checked by nonnumerical methods of measurement. It occurred to J. C. Stevens, a student and then colleague of S. S. Stevens, that he might do just that by means of cross-modality matching—for example,

Table 3.1. Summary of Exponents for Thirty-two Psychophysical Relationships

Continuum	Conditions	Exponent
Loudness	Binaural	0.60
Loudness	Monaural	0.55
Brightness	5° target-dark adapted eye	0.33
Brightness	Point source—dark adapted eye	0.5
Lightness	Reflectance of gray papers	1.2
Smell	Coffee odor	0.55
Smell	Heptane	0.6
Taste	Saccharine	0.8
Taste	Sucrose	1.3
Taste	Salt	1.3
Temperature	Cold-on-arm	1.0
Temperature	Warm-on-arm	1.6
Vibration	60 c.p.s.—on finger	0.95
Vibration	250 c.p.s.—on finger	0.60
Duration	White-noise stimulus	1.1
Repetition rate	Light, sound, touch and shocks	1.0
Finger span	Thickness of wood blocks	1.3
Pressure on palm	Static force on skin	1.1
Heaviness	Lifted weights	1.45
Force of hand grip	Precision hand dynamometer	1.7
Vocal effort	Sound pressure of vocalization	1.1
Electric shock	60 c.p.s.—through fingers	3.5
Circular velocity	Luminous spot moving in circular track (dia. 24 cm.)	1.1

by having judges match the forces exerted in squeezing a precision hand dynamometer to their estimations of the loudness of a sound (J. C. Stevens and Mack 1959). In this instance, the force measurements could be read off the dynamometer's dial as the experimenter varied the intensity of the sound in an order different for each judge. The judges themselves, then, used no numbers for measurement.

The question is, What type of relationship would obtain in such cross-modality matching experiments? One way to find out, of course, is to run the experiment and to determine the function empirically. Another procedure—deriving the relationship mathematically before determining it empirically—follows Galileo's example. In addition to the elegance of such an approach, it puts the numerical objection to a severe test. If the empirical results are consistent with the derived mathematical results, presumably the assumption, treating the emitted numbers as genuine measurements, is validated. The following is the mathematical derivation, which is slightly more detailed than the original published by S. S. Stevens (1959*b*, p. 202).

We start with two power functions obtained when using numerical

Table 3.1.–Continued

Continuum	Conditions	Exponent
Force of foot pressure	Foot pressed pedal forward while observer sat in chair	1.6
Volume	1,000-cycle tone	0.25
Viscosity	Silicone liquid, shaken or turned in bottle, stirred with rod	0.44
Tactile hardness	Compliant materials compressed between finger and thumb	0.8
Length of line	Lines of light projected one at a time on grey screen in dim room	1.0
Largeness of square	Squares of light projected one at a time on grey screen in dim room	0.67
Taste	Mineral solutions in water	0.92
Distance	Monaural sound source of fixed distance from 0 but variable SPL	−0.7
Density	1,000-cycle tone	0.23
Tactile roughness	Felt diameter of emory grits	1.5

SOURCES: For a similar table giving the first 22 entries, see S. S. Stevens, 1960. The other entries were obtained from the following: Terrace and Stevens 1962; Eisler 1962; Stevens and Harris 1962; Stevens and Guirao 1962; Stevens and Guirao 1963; Eisler and Ottander 1963; Guirao and Stevens 1964; and Harper and Stevens 1964.

estimations in which the intensities of sensations ψ_1 and ψ_2 increase as power functions of the intensities of physical stimuli ϕ_1 and ϕ_2, respectively, and the power exponents are n and m, respectively, as in equations

$$\psi_1 = k_1 \phi_1{}^n ,$$

$$\psi_2 = k_2 \phi_2{}^m .$$

If the intensities of sensations ψ_1 and ψ_2 are matched or equated experimentally by the judges, then

$$\psi_1 = \psi_2 ,$$

and if equals are substituted for equals,

$$k_1 \phi_1{}^n = k_2 \phi_2{}^m .$$

Dividing through by k_1 gives

$$\phi_1{}^n = \frac{k_2 \phi_2{}^m}{k_1} \; ;$$

transforming to logarithms,

$$n \log \phi_1 = \log k_2 - \log k_1 + m \log \phi_2 \; ;$$

dividing through by n,

$$\log \phi_1 = \frac{\log k_2}{n} - \frac{\log k_1}{n} + \frac{m}{n} \log \phi_2 \; ;$$

transforming back to antilogarithms,

$$\phi_1 = \sqrt[n]{(k_2/k_1)} \cdot \phi_2{}^{m/n} \; ;$$

or substituting c for $\sqrt[n]{(k_2/k_1)}$,

$$\phi_1 = c\phi_2{}^{m/n} \; .$$

After Stevens and his associates derived the relationship mathematically, they focused on determining experimentally the extent to which the equal-sensation data are described by a power function and the extent to which the predicted exponent, m/n, fits the measured exponent.

For example, a number of experiments have been conducted in which the force of handgrip was matched to varying stimuli from several other physical continua. The results from nine of these experiments appear in Figure 3.2. Note that each of these equal-sensation plots is described rather nicely by a straight line on logarithmic coordinates, indicating a close fit to the predicted equation.

In Table 3.2, the expected versus the measured exponents (least-squares fit) appear for each of the nine stimulus continua involved in these cross-modality matching experiments. Note that the prediction is not perfect. The range of error is small, however—within plus or minus 5 percentage points. We should expect such variation in exponents from one cross-modality matching experiment to another, just as we should expect it in magnitude-estimation experiments on the same continua or, to a lesser extent, in replications of physical experiments such as Galileo's inclined-plane experiment. Even so, the results of the cross-modality matching experiments thus far appear to provide the

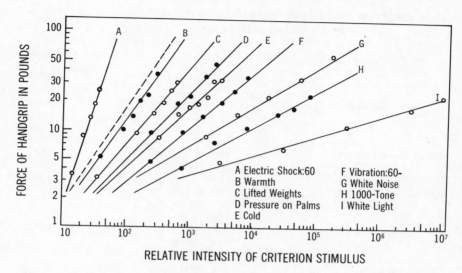

Figure 3.2. Equal-sensation functions obtained by matching force of handgrip to various criterion stimuli. Each point stands for median force exerted by ten or more observers to match apparent intensity of criterion stimulus. The relative position of a function along the abscissa is arbitrary. The dashed line shows a slope of 1.0 in these coordinates (Stevens 1962, p. 34).

"independent measurement operations . . . which do not rest heavily upon experience with numbers," which Luce and others asked for. In fact, the successful derivation of the form of the equal-sensation function and the derivation of the power exponents with reasonable accuracy may go well beyond the requested cross-validation.

Explained Variance

Like Stevens, many scientists who fit equations to data never publish measures of explained variance but rely entirely on visual inspections of the data to gauge the goodness of fit. The reasons are (1) that any plot that looks good to the eye will yield a high r^2; and (2) that measures of explained variance are blind to the gentle curves that to the experienced eye mean an incorrect equation is being fitted to the data, even though r^2 may be .97. Be that as it may, I have calculated r^2's for a number of sets of psychophysical data (some provided by J. C. Stevens), and in most instances the variance explained by the theoretical function is .99+ for data pooled or averaged for ten or more observers, and .95+ for a single set of data for just one observer.

Table 3.2. Exponents (Slopes) of Equal-Sensation Functions as Predicted from Ratio Scales of Subjective Magnitude, and as Obtained by Matching with Force of Handgrip

Continuum	Ratio Scale		Exponents determined by Handgrip	
	Exponent of Power Function (m)	Reference	Predicted Exponent (m/1.7)	Obtained Exponent
Electric shock (60-cycle)	3.5	Stevens, Carton, and Shickman 1958	2.06	2.13
Warmth	1.6	J. C. Stevens and S. S. Stevens 1960	0.94	0.96
Heaviness of lifted weights	1.45	J. C. Stevens and Galanter 1957	0.85	0.79
Pressure on palm..............	1.1	J. C. Stevens and Mack 1959	0.65	0.67
Cold	1.0	J. C. Stevens and S. S. Stevens 1960	0.59	0.60
60-cycle vibration.............	0.95	S. S. Stevens 1959a	0.56	0.56
White noise (SPL)	0.6	J. C. Stevens 1958	0.35	0.41
Loudness (1,000-cycle)	0.6	S. S. Stevens 1955, 1956	0.35	0.35
White light	0.33	S. S. Stevens and Galanter 1957	0.20	0.21

NOTE: This table is an enlarged version of Table 1 in J. C. Stevens, Mack, and S. S. Stevens, 1960, p. 62. The exponents in the last column were determined by least squares. The exponent for force of handgrip obtained using magnitude estimation and production is 1.7 (J. C. Stevens and Mack 1959).

Methodology: The Magnitude Scaling of Attitudes

A Detailed Example

The psychophysical experiments are simple in that they involve but two variables—a physical stimulus, measured as it is varied, and a related sensory or neuroelectric response, also measured. In contrast, most social science phenomena seem to involve multiple causation of various kinds. Even so, some bivariate hypotheses can be tested by rather straightforward adaptations of the psychophysical methodology. Magnitude scaling of social-attitude data is best introduced in such simple experiments. I shall present a detailed example, to give the reader a feel for the methodology, before turning to the more general methodological issues.

Several years ago, I did an experiment (a pretest, primarily of methodological importance) on what Freudians would probably identify as superego reactions or what Meadians would call "me" reactions. I did it to illustrate the broad scientific relevance of psychophysical scaling and methods to extant social theories.

I wanted to find out, at least in a preliminary way, how people might feel if they found themselves violating different societal norms to various degrees. The problematic behavioral continua chosen for investigation varied in seriousness from killing of the enemy in wartime, to becoming angry at one's associates, to drinking and eating in excess. The hypothesis was that people would dislike it if they found themselves doing any of these things beyond a certain point—what we shall call the *relative origin*—even though they might have enjoyed a behavior like drinking or eating up to that point. The general expression of this hypothesis is that, beyond the relative origin, dislike for self increases as a power function of the number, frequency or amount of the behavior in question.

For comparison, disliking estimates were obtained for different amounts of premarital sexual experience of another individual—the subject's wife. Also, because the results of a previous experiment (Hamblin 1971*b*) suggested it, liking estimates were obtained as a cross-check of the disliking estimates. Finally, a positive behavior, earning various amounts of money, was included for methodological purposes.

Method. The judges in this experiment were twenty-one U.S. Navy seamen temporarily assigned to the Naval Medical Research Institute at Bethesda, Maryland, from their regular assignment at Radio School at Bainbridge, Maryland. At the beginning of the day, the judges took part in a simple psychophysical experiment designed to establish their ability to use numbers in magnitude estimation prior to the attitudinal experiment. In the attitudinal experiment the judges were interviewed individually, in accordance with the schedule reproduced here as Table 3.3. The schedule includes spaces for both liking and disliking estimates, obtained in separate series. The instructions for estimating the magnitudes (with no standard set) are as follows:

> You probably like some things that you do more than others. Using numbers, like you did before, I want you to estimate how much you *like* doing the various things I am going to ask you about. Be sure your numbers are proportional to how much *you* would *like* each of these things. You may use whole numbers, fractions, decimals, whichever you feel appropriate, but be consistent. If you feel that you do not like something at all, the appropriate answer is a zero.

Table 3.3. Sample Interviewing Schedule with Medians of Seventeen Magnitude Estimations

1. What if you found that your wife had had sex relations with ___ men before marriage?

	0	2	5	10	18	30
Like	67.0	0	0	0	0	0
Dislike	0	84.5	105	107	122	175

2. What if you found yourself being angry with those around you ___ times each day?

	0	2	5	10	18	30
Like	21	0	0	0	0	0
Dislike	0	30	48	72	92	116

3. What if you ended up earning ___ thousands of dollars per year?

	2	5	9	15	22	30
Like	0	23	49	75	100	119
Dislike	82.33	37.6	0	0	0	0

4. What if you found yourself drinking ___ cocktails, or their equivalents each week?

	0	5	10	18	30	50
Like	2.6	11.5	7.8	0	0	0
Dislike	0	21	33	71	107	121

5. What if you found yourself overweight by ___ pounds?

	0	5	10	20	35	60
Like	62	15	15	0	0	0
Dislike	0	2	18	50	60	111

6. During wartime, what if you found that you were responsible for ___ enemy deaths?

	0	2	40	750	10,000	130,000
Like	0	3	0	0	0	0
Dislike	0	36	59	82	102	139

The liking estimates started with an earnings stimulus, and the following questions were asked:

What if you ended up earning $9,000 per year? How much would you like that? [After receiving an estimate a second question might be asked.] What if you ended up earning $30,000 per year? How much would you like that?

From that juncture on the experimenter skipped from dimension to dimension—for example, from earnings to being angry—usually asking from one to three questions on each dimension before skipping to another. An attempt was made to follow a different random order for each observer.

Once the liking estimates were completed the judges participated in another experiment for about fifteen minutes and were then given instructions similar to but appropriately different from those for liking:

Be sure your numbers are proportioned to how much you dislike each of these things. The more dislike, proportionately bigger the number. If you would not dislike something at all, the appropriate answer is *zero*.

What if you ended up earning $5,000 per year, how much would you dislike that? [Then after obtaining an estimate . . .] What if you ended up earning $9,000 a year, how much would you dislike that?

Again the experimenter proceeded through the stimulus items in a random order, different for each judge.

So that each judge's estimates could be transformed to a standard modulus, the geometric mean of his liking estimates for the three largest salary stimuli was calculated, and the total number of each judge's estimates was multiplied by a number which made his geometric mean equal to 100. The medians of these pooled estimates are given in Table 3.3.

Results. The medians in Table 3.3 show interesting regularities. First, all the stimulus continua except for the maximum yearly earnings represent negative variables. As behavior increases in amount, the negative, or disliking, reaction increases; and the positive, or liking, reaction decreases. For maximum salary, the reactions are exactly reversed; as salary increases, disliking decreases and liking increases.

Second, with the exception of the very extreme continua, there are clear regions of ambivalence where the judges simultaneously dislike and like the behavior in question.

The data were plotted on arithmetic coordinates so that the relative origins could be estimated (a procedure discussed in more detail later). The relative origins for the problematic continua were all zero except for excess eating measured by pounds overweight. In that instance, the dislike-overweight relationship began at four pounds.

The data for the five problematic continua are plotted on logarithmic coordinates in Figures 3.3 and 3.4. These figures indicate that, as expected, all the relationships are described moderately well by power functions; the r^2's are .85, .99, .96, and .98 for the sex, anger, drinking, and weight stimulus-attitude relationships, respectively. Also, the plots show that the more extreme the continuum of behavior in question, the lower the exponent. Thus, the most severe of the behavioral continua, killing the enemy in wartime, resulted in the lowest exponent, .1; the number of the wife's premarital sex partners, .2; the frequency of becoming angry at one's associates, .5; the number of cocktails or equivalents per week, .8; and the number of pounds overweight, 1.0. The data in Table 3.3 clarify the meaning of these exponents. When the exponent is extremely small, as it is for killing the enemy, the growth in disliking increases very rapidly at first, and then at a much lesser rate. At the other extreme, there is a linear increase in dislike of being overweight.

Stevens's Dicta

It may be recalled that, in the above experiment, the judges were allowed to establish their own standards; so five of Stevens's nine methodological dicta do not apply. In each instance, however, I started

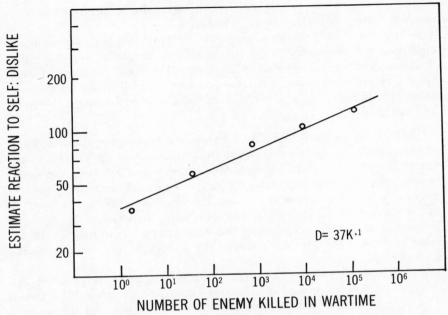

Figure 3.3.   Estimated disliking for self (D) for killing various numbers of the enemy during wartime (K), plotted on logarithmic coordinates. Approximating a straight line, data are described by a power function.

the estimation series with a stimulus in the middle range. The instructions were such that most judges started with a number such as "10" that was easily multiplied and divided. Furthermore, the presentation of the stimuli was randomized in a different order for each judge. The experimental session was short, and broken into two ten-minute periods, and a group of subjects was used to obtain what Stevens calls a stable median, or what sociologists might call a collective representation. In this instance, however, seventeen sets of observations were too few. The data would have been less noisy had there been forty or so measurement series.

The methods in this experiment departed from two of S. S. Stevens's dicta. First, zero was defined as the appropriate response when the judges experienced no feeling, for example, no dislike for a particular stimulus. From my experience, I feel that it is desirable to define zero, to insure that the magnitude scale will be at the ratio level.

Second, I did not let the judges present the stimuli to themselves. Rather, I attempted to be responsive so that each could work at his own pace, because the judges, unlike those in the usual psychophysical experiment, were naïve; that is, they were inexperienced in the use of

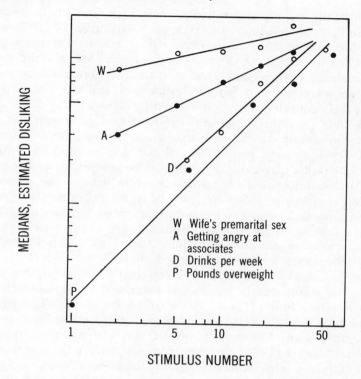

Figure 3.4.   Magnitude estimations of dislike plotted on logarithmic coordinates against four sets of problematic stimuli (in each instance plots approximately linear).

magnitude estimation. I interviewed them myself so that I could monitor the data-gathering process and catch and correct misunderstandings that might appear as they gave their estimates. For example, some judges slip into giving category estimates instead of ratio estimates. If the experimenter suspects this has happened, he can cross-check by using two stimuli and asking the judge to estimate how many times he likes one more than the other. If there is not fair agreement between this ratio and the ratio obtained previously in the magnitude estimations, it is probably appropriate to repeat the instructions and again present all the stimuli, but in a different random order.

This has rarely been necessary in my own work because before an attitudinal experiment I have always trained my judges to use magnitude-estimation procedures in a psychophysical experiment. The psychophysical task is a very simple one. The judges, using an arbitrary unit, estimate the perpendicular distances of a number of dots above a horizontal line. Procedures in that experiment are rather standard except that at the end the experimenter plots the judges' estimates against the stimuli, measured in centimeters, on logarithmic coordinates. The judges are told that the more closely their estimates approximate a straight line when plotted, the more accurate they are; and the approximation is usually very good. Hence, in the psychophysical experience the judges learn to use magnitude estimation, and the success usually bolsters their confidence in their estimating ability.

While this procedure was initially developed to screen out naïve judges who simply could not learn to use the magnitude-estimation procedures accurately, people are seldom that incapacitated. Rather, that simple task apparently trains them to be competent in doing magnitude estimations; hence it assures accurate data in the subsequent attitude experiments. Rainwater (1972), in his experiments, has used an alternative task—that of estimating the areas of circles of different sizes. His samples of adults in the Boston metropolitan area apparently learn how to do magnitude estimation rather quickly with this task, and his attitudinal experiments have turned out to be replicable.

Some investigators who have not given their naive judges this kind of training have apparently conducted successful experiments without it—for example, Shinn (1969a, 1969b) and Sellin and Wolfgang (1964). For the most part, their judges, although naive, were college students, who seem able to follow ratio instructions without great difficulty. Jones and Shorter (1972), however, ran into trouble in their investigation of status. A large number of their Black and Chicano judges apparently made stimulus errors—that is, repeated the stimulus numbers instead of making estimates of their responses—and a large number failed to give complete sets of estimates. Part of the problem may have been that the data gathering was not monitored and the judges used questionnaires distributed for a few minutes during a meeting ostensibly organized for other purposes, and part that the judges simply did not understand how to do ratio estimates (an alternative procedure used by Jones and Shorter). In addition, they may have lacked confidence in their ability to make such estimates accurately and hence aborted the task because of discomfort. The best measurement procedures can only be expected to yield accurate data when they are used knowledgeably and with care.

Mathematical Experimentation

While Stevens's dicta are useful and for that reason were included here, the experiment described above may be analyzed from a more general perspective—that of mathematical experimentation, which was invented by Galileo and ushered in the scientific revolution in physics. Since then, it has become the standard methodology of the physical sciences—physics, chemistry, astronomy—and, more recently, of the biological sciences. Also, experiments in psychophysics and neurophysics are variants of the standard mathematical design.

The elements of mathematical experimentation are (1) the manipulation of one or more independent variables; (2) control by constancy —the effects of all other actual or possible independent variables are held constant during the experiment; (3) periodic multiple and simultaneous ratio measurements of all the variables (dependent and independent) across the entire effective continuum of the independent variables; (4) the averaging out of random measurement error; and (5) the description of the relationships obtaining among the measurements by fitting the appropriate algebraic equation or equations. In sum, the purpose of the mathematical experiment is, first, to measure the functional relationships among empirical variables under carefully controlled conditions, and, second, to translate or decode the measured relationships into the theoretical language of the algebraic equation.

Galileo started his investigations in physics by working in the Aristotelian tradition, which used mathematics as the theoretical language and logic but disclaimed experimental or other empirical tests. Pure logical systems like Euclidean geometry were held to be the scientific ideal. When Galileo invented the mathematical experiment he thereby bridged that gap between the language and logic of mathematics on the one hand and the empirical data on the other. Furthermore, once physicists began checking their mathematical assumptions against empirical data, a fantastic theoretical development occurred. First came the discovery of a large number of empirical laws—data relationships described accurately by particular equations (e.g., Galileo's law of falling bodies, Kepler's laws of planetary motion, and Boyle's law relating the temperature and pressure of gasses in closed containers); then came the attempt to develop theories explaining why these empirical laws should obtain. The first general theory, developed by Newton in his *Principia*, was modified by Einstein so that it accurately described the dynamics and equilibria of both macro (solar) systems and micro (atomic) systems. Even Boyle's law turned out to be derived from basic principles of Newtonian mechanics (see Park 1969 for an interesting summary of that derivation).

A number of sociologists who have viewed these developments in physics (e.g., Lundberg 1964; Dodd 1942; Coleman 1964; Park 1969; Blalock 1969; and White 1970) have suggested that mathematics is the appropriate language and logic for data-based theory in the social sciences. Most of these authors have also accepted, in principle, the importance of mathematical experimentation—and the variant methodology of mathematical correlation (which has all the elements of mathematical experimentation except the first, manipulation).

Yet, many seem uncertain about how procedures of mathematical experimentation and correlation apply to social science phenomena. The discussion below will illustrate how they are used with social-attitude data.

Ratio Measurement

In his classic article, S. S. Stevens (1946) defined ratio measurement in terms of the transformation equation which translates calibrations of alternative ratio scales (x and x', e.g., representing distance measured in inches and distance measured in centimeters, respectively) as follows:

$$x' = cx .$$

This transformation equation differs from that for the next-lower level of measurement, interval scales, by a constant:

$$x' = a + cx .$$

The constant, a, is sometimes erroneously thought of as the amount necessary to adjust x and x' to their true origins. Instead, it is the amount necessary to align the two interval scales to the *same* origin. Be that as it may, a ratio scale eliminates all alignment errors which define interval scales.

Another erroneous impression is that ratio measurement consists of equal calibrations numbered in terms of an absolute zero. Viewed in the context of experimentation, however, ratio measurement consists of calibrations in relation to an origin where *in its effect* the variable in question has *no magnitude*. Thus, if ratio scales were defined in the abstract, in terms of an absolute origin, variables such as time and distance would never have ratio properties, because in the abstract they have no beginnings or origins, only infinite pasts. Either variable may be measured at the ratio level in relation to any relevant origin, however, and that relevant origin in an experiment is always defined as the beginning of the relationship in question.

Galileo intuitively realized this point in his inclined-plane experiment, which set the pattern for mathematical experimentation. Instead of measuring time from some absolute origin, he started his water clock the instant the ball began to move down the inclined plane. The measurement in distance was not taken from some absolute origin, but from the point where the ball began to roll. His average measurements in time were 1, 4, 9, and 16 units from the relative origins which corresponded to the squares of his 1, 2, 3, and 4 units of distance from the relative origin. Hence, his equation, with an appropriate acceleration constant, was

$$d = at^2 .$$

Had he, say, systematically added a unit to every measurement of time by starting his water clock at the beginning instead of at the end of the signal to let the ball roll, the appropriate equation would have been

$$d = a(t - 1)^2.$$

In this hypothetical example, the misalignment of the time measurement with the origin would have been a simple measurement error, and hence the origin correction ("1") might be thought of as a "fudge factor"—something slightly illegal the experimenter added to cover up an earlier error. Not all origin corrections may be thought of as fudge factors, however; rather, some may have important theoretical significance and hence may be appropriate for intensive scientific investigation. For example, the results of two experiments relating satisfaction and dissatisfaction to wages (see Hamblin 1971*b*) apparently illustrate mathematically Merton and Kitt's (1950) theory of relative deprivation.

Satisfaction and dissatisfaction with wages. Involved in these experiments were two samples of subjects—seamen in the U.S. Navy, mostly nineteen to twenty years of age—who were first trained to use magnitude estimation and then were asked to estimate how much they would like earning various amounts of money in summer jobs back home. Subsequently, they were asked to estimate how much they would dislike receiving each of the wages. The data, appropriately averaged, are plotted in Figure 3.5. Note that in both experiments the disliking estimates were high in the lower ranges of wages but decreased at a decelerating rate as wages increased; disliking became zero at $3.25 an hour in one plot, and at $2.75 an hour in the other. In contrast, the liking estimates were zero in the lower ranges but, beginning at $.95 an hour, increased rapidly but at a decelerating rate as wages increased. These origins puzzled me for some time after the first experiment was completed, but they became clear in the second experiment, in which the subjects were interviewed about the wages they and their "significant others"—older brothers and friends—had received in the past.

Although a systematic analysis was not done, the interview data from the second experiment were clear enough to suggest the hypothesis that the origin of the liking function was fixed by the lowest wage received by either the subjects or their significant others, and that the origin for the dislike function was fixed by the highest wage received by either the subjects or their significant others. In other words, a subject appeared to like a wage to the extent that it exceeded his *minimum* expectation, an expectation fixed by his own past experience and by the past experience of his significant others, or reference group. He disliked a wage to the extent that it was lower than his maximum expectation, which again was fixed by his own past experience and that of

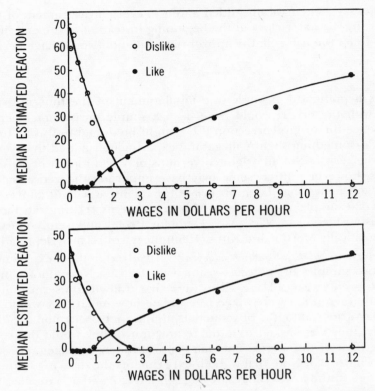

Figure 3.5.   Liking and disliking data for various wages plotted on arithmetic coordinates for two samples of twenty-one seamen, U.S. Navy.

his reference group. This mathematical hypothesis ought to be tested rigorously, but it at least provides a meaningful rationale for the origins in the above experiments. In fact, it should be obvious that, without understanding the origins of satisfaction and dissatisfaction related to wages and how they vary, one would not have an accurate theory of these phenomena.

The social meaning of poverty. A second illustration, an investigation of the social meaning of poverty by Rainwater (in press), also serves to underline the theoretical importance of understanding origins. Rainwater reasoned that the state of poverty is a matter of degree, and that generally, the smaller one's family income, the more poor one is adjudged. But the interesting theoretical question he considered is, Where along the income continuum will a family no longer be adjudged poor at all? Rainwater guessed that it might be the average family income for the population in question. He tested this hypothesis by obtaining magnitude estimations from a probability sample of adult

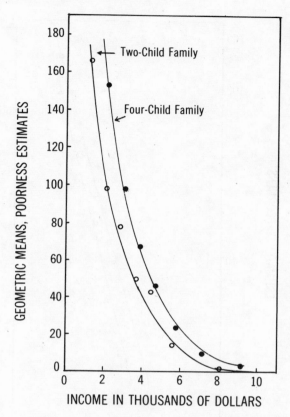

Figure 3.6. Magnitude estimations of poorness and family income plotted on arithmetic coordinates (after Rainwater in press).

housewives in the Boston metropolitan area. The plots of the magnitude estimations of poverty for two- and four-child families are given in Figure 3.6, on arithmetic coordinates. Note that the poverty estimates decreased at a decelerating rate as income increased, until they reached zero at some level greater than $10,000 a year. Rainwater used $12,000 for the median income of families in the Boston metropolitan area (the best estimate available) and therefore defined his income deficit measure, D, by the equation

$$D = 12,000 - I,$$

where I is the family income measured in dollars.

On logarithmic coordinates (see Fig. 3.7), the data show quite clearly that the poverty estimates, P, for two- and for four-child families increased as power functions of income deficit, D. These data, then, in-

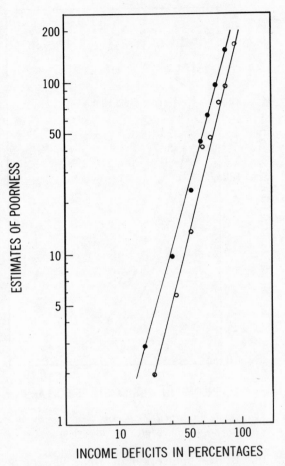

Figure 3.7.   *Magnitude estimations of poorness and family income plotted on
logarithmic coordinates (plots approximate straight lines; hence
data described by power functions) (after Rainwater in press).*

volving r^2's in excess of .99, give astounding confirmation of
Rainwater's theory of the origin and relativity of poverty attitudes.

The origin problem has also been encountered in psychophysics, as
illustrated by S. S. Stevens's (1954) plots for brightness and loudness
functions which, on logarithmic coordinates, were concave downward.
Although Stevens was well aware that such gentle curves signaled that
the wrong equation was being fitted, he rationalized his power function
as being a good first approximation because the fit was excellent over
95 percent of the brightness and loudness continua. Stevens had
expected the absolute psychological threshold to provide the appro-

priate origin; but as it turned out, his origin corrections were too small for sensory mechanisms such as the eye and ear, which make substantial adaptations to extend their ranges of effective operation. Later, Stevens and Stevens (1960) were able to show that with larger origin corrections—what they called the *effective thresholds*—the functions straightened out over the entire range.

A substantial adaptation effect requiring an origin correction occurs in but five or six of the forty or so sensory modalities. Adaptation is much more frequent in social-attitude phenomena however, since expectations, or relative origins, apparently condition easily. Therefore, attitude researchers who do mathematical experimentation must know how to find relative origins in order to preserve the ratio properties of their scales.

Calculating Relative Origins

Unfortunately, there are no simple, rigorous algorithms for determining relative origins when testing for power functions, but in mathematical experiments in which I have used magnitude scaling, I have followed several steps which produce reasonably good results.

1. Plot the data on arithmetic coordinates and, using a ruler or a French curve, draw a line approximating a least-squares fit to the data.

2. Extrapolate that line to a relative origin. This is not particularly easy to do with a power function because its curvature increases substantially as the relative origin is approached. In Figure 3.5 this step is illustrated in four sets of data.

3. On the basis of the extrapolation, estimate the relative origin and use it appropriately in correcting the measurements of the stimulus variable. Next, on logarithmic coordinates, plot the corrected stimulus measurements and, if desired, the uncorrected stimulus measures against the response or attitudinal measures, as in Figure 3.8. Note that for both sets of liking data, the threshold correction is −.90.

4. If the plot of the corrected data approximates a straight line, assume that the estimated origin constant is correct, and that the data may be described by a power function. If the plot still shows a curvature, it is possible that the estimate of the origin is incorrect. Hence, one may wish to attempt a second estimate and repeat step 3. If subsequent estimates of the relative origin, within what seems to be the allowable range on the arithmetic plot, continue to yield a curvature on the subsequent logarithmic plot, one may assume that a power function does not describe the data under consideration. The left-hand set of data in Figure 3.9

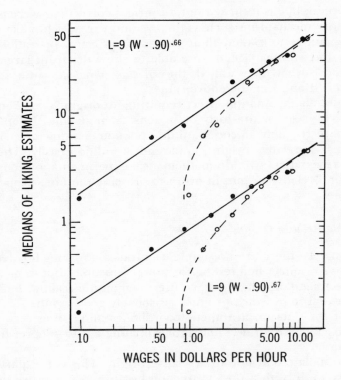

*Figure 3.8.   Medians of liking estimates for various wages plotted on logarith-
mic coordinates for two samples of twenty-one U.S. Navy seamen,
with (filled dots) and without (unfilled dots) threshold corrections.*

straightened up on a second try when a threshold of 3.25 was
tried in place of the original estimate of 2.75.[1]

Shinn (1969*a*, 1969*b*) has suggested that in addition to specific
numerical meaning, any origin should have theoretical meaning.
As we have seen, the origins in the satisfaction-dissatisfaction
experiment and in Rainwater's poverty experiment are understandable in the context of Merton and Kitt's (1950) theory about
reference groups. As suggested above, this reference-group interpretation should be subjected to rigorous empirical testing.
The theory makes sense out of these origins, and it turns what a
skeptic might consider to be a clever equation-fitting device into a
meaningful theoretical problem.

Averaging Out Random Measurement Error

There are those who feel that there is no such thing as random measurement error, but this is an impossible position to maintain for anyone

1. For an alternative method of fitting origins in psychophysical and attitudinal experiments see Ekman (1961).

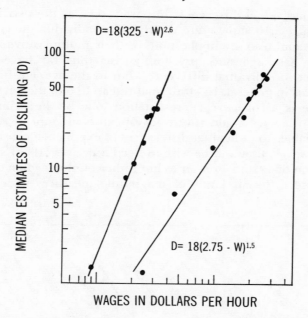

Figure 3.9.   Median disliking estimates for various wages plotted on logarithmic coordinates for two samples of twenty-one subjects (wage data were corrected to threshold).

who has taken multiple measurements. Do the differences between independent measures of the length of a room, for example, mean that the room changes length, or that our measurement procedures are inaccurate or unreliable? It is hard to accept all such differences between measurements as real data reflecting nature; some involve random error which can be eliminated to a large degree.

Galileo did this in his inclined-plane experiment by averaging 100 measurements at each data point. The alternative might have been to devise more accurate measurement devices, as later scientists did. What is interesting in this bit of history, however, is that the later scientists, with their more accurate devices, obtained exactly the same answer obtained by Galileo with his water clock and his 100-measurement series.

So it has been in the mathematical sciences. In fact, Baird (1962), one of the rare physicists who write methodology, has suggested that measurement procedures should always be increased in sensitivity until variability occurs in the measurements. Then, to obtain still greater accuracy, multiple measurements are taken and averaged at each data point. This is the physicist's way of pushing accuracy to the level of the data's determinacy.

It should be noted, however, that when one averages out measurement error in psychophysical and attitudinal experiments, one also averages out individual differences in parameters, as the psychophysical data in Figure 3.10 show quite clearly. The individual plots differ in their slopes and also, by implication, in their multiplicative constants. As Stevens has suggested, psychophysicists thus far have been interested, not in individual differences, but in the average functioning of individuals in general. In attitudinal research, too, this makes sense; the average is a collective representation, one of the prime foci of sociological theory. Should future investigators attempt to relate exogenous variables to individual differences in exponents, constants, and origins, however, they will be wise to heed Stevens's (1966) suggestion to rely not on one estimation series but rather on the median of several, and also use different kinds of magnitude measures in a balanced design.

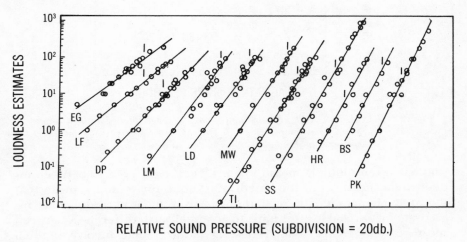

Figure 3.10. Individual loudness functions obtained from eleven observers in first session, in which they both set level of the stimulus and judged loudness. Observers varied greatly in range and number of stimuli they produced and estimated, but all data approximate power functions. Small line above each function indicates level of 80 db. on abscissa (J. C. Stevens and Guirao, 1964).

Control by Constancy

By definition, fixing the values of all but the manipulated independent variables during an experiment effects control by constancy. It has long been a question how this could be done in social experiments, but *control by constancy is approximated by subjecting all participants to all experimental conditions, each in a different random order.* In psychological and in attitudinal experiments it is approximated by having *every* subject respond to *all* the stimulus values in a different random order and by having the other variables constant for all the subjects for the duration of the experiment. Such designs may be inappropriate for many of the theoretical problems of interest to social scientists, but they work well for all experiments involving what Skinner (1953) has called *respondent behavior*. This is a postulated class of behavior which occurs primarily as a function of the stimuli preceding the behavior, and its magnitude is a function of the magnitudes of those stimuli. Psychophysical and attitudinal behavior are apparently subclasses of respondent behavior, which is one of two general classes of behavior. The other general class—*operant*, or *instrumental, behavior*—is, in the long run at least, a function of repetitively reinforcing consequences. Such behavior may be studied in reversal designs, which also use control by constancy. Behavioral data from reversal experiments may also be analyzed mathematically, but those designs and the analysis of the behavioral data they yield are beyond the scope of this chapter (see Hamblin *et al.* 1971).

Early social experimenters such as Chapin (1947) confused control by matching with control by constancy. Control by matching requires that the experimenter know beforehand all the causal variables, that he have near-perfect measures of these causal variables for all his subjects, and that before the experiment he match his experimental and control subjects on all causal variables except the one being manipulated. This, of course, is an impossible task.

In part, Fisher (1950, 1951) has been celebrated because he worked social experimenters out of the control-by-matching box. Fisher's contribution was the method of control by randomization. In social experiments following Fisher's procedures, subjects are more or less matched on a few causal variables and are then assigned by a random process to one of the experimental conditions. Fisher argues that such a process distributes the effects of the unmanipulated causal variables so that they cancel one another out but allow the effects of the manipulated variables to show through. Since random assignment is a stochastic process, Fisher and others in his tradition developed tests to gauge whether the overall difference between experimental conditions is statistically different from zero. They conservatively reasoned that if the probability of an observed difference were small—say, .05 or less —the difference would not be the result of random assignment but would be the causal effect of the experimental manipulation.

While the logic of control by random assignment is acceptable, in practice such controls evidently produce a considerable error variance. In fact, review studies have shown that statistical experiments, the "significant" ones which are published, explain on the average only 10 percent of the total variance (see Hamblin 1971a for a summary of several studies), and—a more serious shortcoming—produce very inconsistent results (see Hamblin 1971a; Stephens 1968; or Hamblin *et al.* 1971).

There may be many reasons for the low explained variance and the inconsistent results of statistical experiments, but a large portion of the difficulties is probably the result of substituting control by matching and randomization for control by constancy.[2]

Control by constancy may seem an impossible ideal for social experiments, but, in contrast to control by matching, it does not require full knowledge of the causal variables. Control by constancy, as it is used in psychophysical, neurophysical, and attitudinal experiments, as well as in experiments in physics *per se* (see Baird 1962), simply requires that every directly manipulable variable in an experiment (including the subjects) remain constant across all experimental conditions. The only exceptions to this rule are the independent variables, which are manipulated and measured systematically, and the *order* of their manipulation and measurement. Ideally, all the participants are subjected to all the experimental manipulations and measurements, each in a different random order, so that order-presentation and measurement effects, which usually are very small, will be canceled out.

It is possible for two or more causal variables to be confounded in experimental manipulation, as in the famous Hawthorne experiment—which, however, was badly designed. True, the subjects were all exposed to all experimental conditions, but all were put through those conditions in the same order. Had they been put through the manipulations in different random orders, as specified in the constancy design, the so-called Hawthorne effect would have been discovered on the second trial. Two other procedures are commonly used to guard against the possibility of compounding manipulations: (1) Clear descriptions of the experimental manipulations are given so that others may detect the possible confounding of two or more variables. (2) Multivariate designs in which the suspected causal variables are manipulated orthogonally to one another are used (these designs will be exemplified below).

Fitting Equations to Data

The final, and in some ways the most difficult, step in mathematical experimentation is fitting an equation which correctly describes the data relationship. Among the many procedures devised for fitting

---

2. Another reason is Fisher's tendency to think of an experiment in terms of an experimental and a control group; so, in effect, only two points on the continuum of the independent variable are represented in the experiment. In general, this results in the investigation of just a small segment of the relationship, and the smaller the segment, the lower the explained variance. No matter how strong a relationship may be over the entire effective continuum, the relationship may be reduced to zero explained variance by picking a small enough segment of the relationship for investigation. One merely has to pick a segment the same width as the range of variability in measurement. This is not a necessary part of Fisherian experiments; as early as the 1930s, in the so-called utility experiments, the effects of the entire practical range of fertilizers were explored in agricultural experiments. Such designs ought to be mandatory in all experiments. (For an example, see Croxton and Cowden 1939, p. 713.)

equations, however, most mathematical scientists use a relatively simple procedure called rectifying the curve, in which curvilinear equations and data relationships are transformed into linear relationships for fitting (see Baird 1962; Ezekiel 1941). Stevens—in fact, all psychophysicists—use this procedure, as do attitude researchers who have been working in the psychophysical tradition. This method has been described and illustrated above. In most psychophysical experiments, as well as in attitude experiments like those described earlier, these equation-fitting procedures work extremely well, giving relatively unambiguous results.

As Stevens (1966) suggests, however, the mathematical scientist never makes hard, fast conclusions about a particular equation describing a data relationship on the basis of *one* experiment, both because almost anything can happen in a given experiment and because most of the characteristics of a relationship—its generality, its variability, and the conditions under which it obtains—can only be ascertained in a *large number of experiments*. Thus, Stevens did not conclude firmly that the magnitude of subjective brightness increases as a power function of the magnitude of luminance until he had done a dozen or so experiments and, ultimately, until he had solved the origin problem associated with the eye's adaptability. Similarly, before Stevens suggested the psychophysical law (1957), he had data from one to a dozen experiments on fourteen psychophysical modalities, all of which were described rather well by power functions. His data were sufficient to suggest the conditions under which the psychophysical law occurred, its generality and variability in fit, and the exponents within and across modalities.

The status investigations. To give the reader a feel for the process of reconciling several sets of data, we shall now turn to an analysis of nine status investigations. The first of these investigations was by Hamblin (1966). In this investigation, his instructions to the judges began:

> In your home town, you probably noticed that some people were looked up to, others were looked down on. In other words, that people were given a different amount of prestige, respect or status. This could be due to many things—income, dress, education, occupation, one's home, one's looks, one's car, etc. Today, however, I want you to estimate the status of a number of individuals on the basis of one item of information—their occupation, their income, or their education. Let us assume that a college graduate has 100 units of status. If another individual has twice as much status in your judgment, give him a 200, a third as much status—give him a 33⅓. In other words, make your number proportional to the amount of status as you see it. You may use whole numbers, fractions, decimals—whatever you need to be accurate. If a man has no status at all, give him a zero, okay?

In Figure 3.11 the pooled estimates of status are shown plotted against their respective income and educational stimuli for two samples, composed of thirty U.S. Navy seamen and twenty-two college stu-

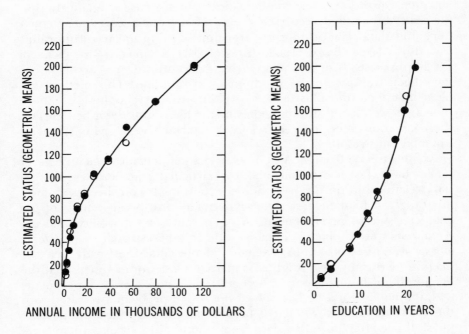

Figure 3.11. Pooled estimates of status plotted against income and education stimuli. Two sets of estimates: from thirty seamen, U.S. Navy (filled dots); from twenty-two college students (unfilled dots). All estimates in relation to same standard: 100 units equals status of college graduate.

dents. Since all judges gave two sets of estimates, the data were based on sixty and forty-four estimates, respectively. Note the high agreement between the samples. Status apparently increases as a decelerating curvilinear function of income, and it increases as an accelerating curvilinear function of education. In general, all the subsequent experiments have confirmed these basic findings (i.e., the general shape of the data relationships), although there has been some ambiguity about the exact equations that describe those relationships.

First, the curves, as drawn in the original analysis (Fig. 3.11), do not go through the origin, where education is zero and income is zero, and the data, plotted on logarithmic coordinates, yielded nonlinear curves without origin corrections. However, the logarithmic plots straightened out when $1,000 was subtracted as an origin correction for the income stimuli and four years were added to the educational stimuli.

The status-income equations and r^2's from the original and the subsequent experiments are given in Table 3.4, and it is evident there that not all the data support this original analysis. For example, in some

Table 3.4. Summary Results: Status-Income Experiments

Experimenter	Sample	Income (I)	S_i	r^2
Hamblin	College students	\$1,500-\$110,000	$.40(I - 1,000)^{.54}$	.994
Hamblin	Navy seamen	\$1,500-\$110,000	$.49(I - 1,000)^{.52}$	.997
Shinn	NROTC students	< \$13,000	$.0089\ I^{1.02}$	.996
		> \$13,000	$.46\ I^{.35}$	.989
Shinn	College students (A)	< \$12,000	$.018\ I^{.93}$	.997
		> \$12,000	$.40\ I^{.60}$	.995
Shinn	College students (B)	\$1,500-\$110,000	$.30\ I^{.63}$	.996
Rainwater	Adults, Boston Area	< \$12,000	$.04\ I^{.84}$	.97
		> \$16,000	$1.03\ I^{.54}$	.91

NOTE: Jones and Shorter (1972) apparently did three status-income experiments but did not report the details of their results, beyond the exponents, .97, .94, and .94.

experiments, the origin correction of \$1,000 apparently improved the fit; in others it did not. In two of Shinn's three investigations, improved results were obtained when the status-income continuum was broken into two segments to which equations were fitted separately. In the Rainwater (1971) investigation in which the range of the income stimuli was extended substantially, the data also suggested such segments.

A skeptic might conclude that ambiguities such as the above are to be expected from an attempt to hypothesize mathematically about anything as indeterminate as human behavior. On the other hand, a more experienced scientist might ask, What can one expect? All the data are described by power functions. The median r^2 is .99. He might also suggest that the variety in the results may be systematic enough to yield interesting refinements in the theory. After all, Einstein's theory of relativity was a refinement of Newton's theory of mechanics which involved a very small improvement at the upper end of the variance continuum. Although the r^2's of the original analysis of the status-income data were .99, we should have no illusions that these data are either as determinate or as accurate as those with which Newton and Einstein worked. However, exploring alternative formulations suggested by systematic deviations has been a fruitful tactic in the mathematical sciences, and I see no reason for not trying it with these data.

In fact, in the analysis of the data from those original experiments, I considered dividing the status-income continuum into two segments, as in Figure 3.12, where the alternative interpretation of those data is pictured together with Shinn's and Rainwater's data, but I chose instead to make the origin correction of \$1,000 because in psychophysics there was ample precedent for origin corrections and no precedent for dividing the continua into segments. Furthermore, with the origin correc-

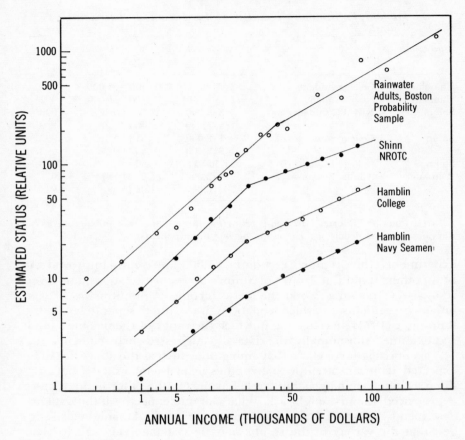

*Figure 3.12.   Magnitude estimates of status (geometric means) plotted on
logarithmic coordinates against their respective income stimuli,
from four investigations (Rainwater 1971; Shinn 1969a; Hamblin 1966, 1971a). Plots in each instance describe two straight-line
segments indicating lower- and upper-income classes in increments
where statuses are earned by quite different rules, that is, are described by different equations.*

tion, the results in terms of explained variance approached .99+, the
limit of the variance explained in psychophysics.

In the subsequent experiments, however, the $1,000 origin correc-
tion did not necessarily improve the fit of the data (see Table 3.5); it
straightened out the plots to some extent, but the segments were still
noticeable. Also, no one has been able to give a theoretical explanation
of the $1,000—at least none as convincing as the explanations sug-
gested above in the satisfaction-dissatisfaction wages experiment and in
Rainwater's poverty-income experiment. All this suggests that the data

be interpreted in terms of two income classes, in which increments in income produce increments in status according to different rules, that is, different structural equations.

The ambiguities in the status-education data are somewhat less striking, but they are, nevertheless, interesting from both a theoretical and a methodological perspective. The summary of the results is given in Table 3.5, together with the equations and the r^2's. Note that in the first six investigations the equations were all power functions with the exponents varying between 2.0 and 2.6. Also, an origin constant of four to six years is added to the educational stimuli. Therefore, the first six experiments yielded data that show relatively high agreement, although this agreement is contradicted by the results of the three investigations by Jones and Shorter (1972). The Jones and Shorter data are described by exponential equations.

Table 3.5. Summary Results: Status Education Experiments

Experimenter	*Sample*	*S*	r^2
Hamblin	College students	$(E + 4)^{2.05}$	.986
Hamblin	Navy seamen	$(E + 4)^{2.14}$	.996
Shinn	NROTC students	$.065(E + 6)^{2.40}$	.995
Shinn	College students (A)	$.067(E + 4)^{2.50}$	.951
Shinn	College students (B)	$.074(E + 4)^{2.46}$	.988
Rainwater	Adults, Boston Area	$.06(E + 6)^{2.6}$	.96
Jones and Shorter	20 Anglo students	$e^{.029+.187E}$	.988
Jones and Shorter	20 Mexican-American students	$e^{.066+.188E}$	.986
Jones and Shorter	9 Afro students	$e^{.275+.195E}$	.974

The discrepant results of the Jones and Shorter investigations could be dismissed on the basis of the methodological difficulties noted above. Why try to interpret a set of measurements that obviously were not taken with the kind of care expected in scientific work? It seems, on the face of it, to be a fruitless enterprise, but even in these faulty data there are more continuities than meet the eye.

In the first place, power functions with exponents ranging from 2.0 to 3.0 describe *j*-curves, as do exponential equations. Jones and Shorter failed to run the appropriate test for a power function (they failed to correct for origin), and most of the other investigators did not attempt to fit exponential equations to their data; so a systematic comparison of the fits of power and exponential equations has not been published. In the various reports, however, enough data are presented, either in the plots or in the tables, to make possible an appropriate test.[3] This I have made. The logarithmic plots (testing for power functions) and semi-

3. With drafting dividers one may recover data plotted in figures fairly accurately. With care the r^2 between the recovered and the original data will be .99.

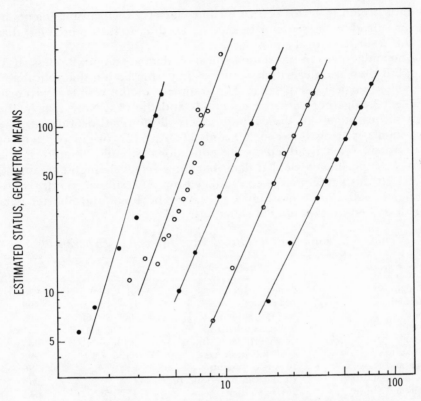

Figure 3.13. Data (with origin corrections: plus six years for first three sets; plus four years for the last two) from five status-education experiments plotted on logarithmic coordinates.

logarithmic plots (testing for exponential equations) are given respectively in Figures 3.13 and 3.14. The Jones and Shorter data and the Rainwater data are evidently ambiguous. They fit power functions (with the six-year origin correction) and exponential equations equally well, or very nearly so. In contrast, the other data, which are much less noisy, are better described by power than by exponential equations. It therefore seems that the power function with the origin correction is more consistent with *all* the data and, hence, is preferred.

Among sets of pooled data from several psychophysical experiments on a given modality, there is usually intersample variation among exponents, averaging about plus or minus 5 percentage points. This is the result of sampling error arising from the considerable variation in the data from individual subjects (see Fig. 3.10). The variation in parameters in the income-status experiments described above is somewhat

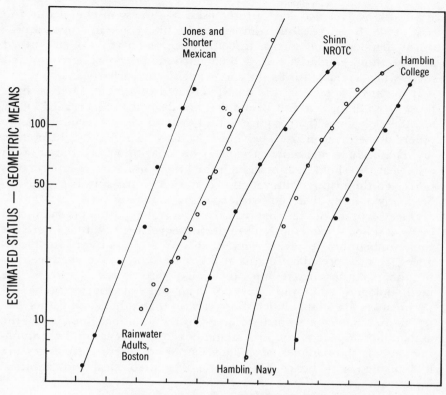

Figure 3.14. Data from five status-education experiments plotted on semilogarithmic coordinates. Two sets approximate straight lines; hence they are described by exponential equations. Three are not. Data standardized so that status of college graduate equals 100 units; data also positioned arbitrarily along ordinate.

greater than this—plus or minus 10 percentage points—as might be expected because attitudinal phenomena, unlike psychophysical phenomena, appear to involve culturally conditioned stimulus-respondent relationships. It should be pointed out, however, that at the present time this variation is unexplained variance.

Even so, Shinn (1969*a*, 1969*b*) and Jones and Shorter (1972) are correct; origin corrections in power functions should not be introduced willy-nilly without being given theoretical interpretation. Rainwater's +6 probably makes more theoretical sense than the +4 used in my status experiments. It turns the education measure into a measure of the number of years of successfully completed, culturally prescribed acculturation. Thus, a child is acculturated during his first six years at home or in preschool, and a certain amount of success in that early acculturation is a necessary prerequisite to success in completing the first grade. By successfully completing the first grade in school, a person is demonstrating success in completing seven years of prescribed acculturation. Similarly, each subsequent year of schooling completed successfully again confirms the success of all the earlier years.

It might be noted that the data from my experiments, and perhaps those from Shinn's A and B samples, are deviant in this regard. They are the only ones that require a four-year origin correction. All the others do better with six. This, however, may be a genuine difference; my data become markedly curvilinear on logarithmic coordinates with a six-year threshold. It is as though the judges used in my experiments perceived the prior acculturation necessary for success in first grade to be that ordinarily achieved by the average four-year-old.

Once again we can see that data from several experiments conducted by several investigators are not in perfect agreement. Rather, there are some ambiguities involving very small differences in explained variances, 1 or 2 percentage points at the upper end of the variance continuum. Those based on invidious differences between the methodologies employed may be dismissed, of course; some experimenters are simply much more careful than others and gather better, more reliable data which deserve greater attention. But some of the ambiguities appear to reflect genuine differences in cultural conditioning among the samples of judges employed; these differences are unexplained and, hence, require intensive theoretical and empirical investigation.

The Multivariate Problem

While the discussion above may not have covered all the methodological issues connected with bivariate attitudinal experiments, most of the important ones have been discussed. Unlike psychophysical sensations, however, attitudes are generally the result of several stimuli. The crucial question is how these stimuli combine to determine attitudes.

The first attempt to use psychophysical methods to study the relationship between an attitude and its multiple stimuli was in the context of the original status experiments (Hamblin 1966, 1971a). It may be recalled that status was defined as feelings of approval, respect, and esteem, or to use Veblen's (1968) term, *moral worth*, and it was suggested that one earns status in competitive contests or in cooperative exchanges between various organizations by demonstrating or providing valued role attributes or valued role behavior (Blau 1955; Homans 1961; Hamblin and Smith 1966). Status in mass society appears to be granted on the basis of indicators of these competitive or cooperative outcomes in organizations. Thus, in our society at least, nearly everyone is enrolled in or competes in an educational organization, and the higher the educational level attained, the greater the individual's validated status. Also, most male adults work in economic organizations within which their statuses are gauged, if only roughly, by how much money they make. And occupations are apparently evaluated, in part, on the basis of the contributions generally made to the welfare of society by persons in those occupations.

It is difficult to know just how many stimuli produce status in mass society, but a first approximation of the multivariate relationships may be diagrammed as shown below.

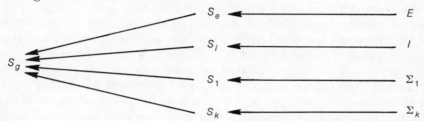

Education (*e*), income (*i*), and occupation (*o*) produce components of status (S_e, S_i, and S_o) and perhaps S_e, S_i, S_o, S_1, ..., S_k (resulting from some other unknown stimuli Σ_1, ..., Σ_k) combine to produce general status, S_g.

In the first series of experiments reviewed above, the bivariate relationships between education and educational status and between income and income status were investigated. We now wish to know how the educational and income components of status, S_e and S_i, and other possible components of status, $S_o, S_i, ..., S_k$, combine into general status, S_g. As suggested in that first report (Hamblin 1966), it would be very simple and convenient if the multivariate version of the stimulus-response function were a direct extension of that bivariate function so that

$$\log S_g = \log c + n_i \log S_i + n_e \log S_e + n_1 \log S_1 + ... + n_k \log S_k$$

or, in antilogs:

$$S_g = c \cdot S_i^{n_i} \cdot S_e^{n_e} \cdot S_1^{n_1} ... S_k^{n_k} .$$

Again, the constants and exponents and the unknown components of status would have to be determined empirically.

As may be recalled, status estimates were obtained in the previous investigations for various levels of education and income as well as for different occupations. Since education, income, and occupation are standard independent variables in the status literature, their respective components of status were used here. The following hypothesis was tested in this experiment:

$$\log S_g = \log c + n_i \log S_i + n_e \log S_e + n_o \log S_o .$$

In the original multivariate experiments and in the replications (Shinn 1969*a*; Rainwater 1972), the judges were presented stimulus "individuals" with three characteristics—occupation, education, and yearly income. For example: "architect, college graduate, $78,000 per year; tenant farmer, fourth grade, $1,500 per year." The full lists have been published and so will not be detailed here. However, each judge estimated the general status of each of fourteen or more individuals. Again the stimuli were presented in a mixed random order.

To test the multivariate hypothesis, the average status estimates obtained previously for each of the occupations (S_o), educational levels (S_e), and income levels (S_i), were used as independent variables to predict averages of general status (S_g) obtained in the multivariate investigations. To be specific, the first stimulus involved an architect who had completed college and had an annual income of $78,000. The average status estimates obtained for each of these stimuli in the above bivariate experiments were used to predict the average general status estimated for this individual in this experiment. So it was with the other stimulus persons. All measures were transformed to logarithms and then appropriately analyzed by means of linear multiple regression-correlation analysis. Thus, the logarithmic version of the hypothesis was tested.

Table 3.6. Summary of Results: General Status (S_g) as a Function of Income Status (S_i), Educational Status (S_e), and Occupational Status (S_o)

Experimenter	Sample	S_g	R^2
Hamblin	Navy seamen	$6.90\ S_i^{.48}S_e^{.36}S_o^{-.02}$	.98
Shinn	NROTC	$.58\ S_i^{.49}S_e^{.24}S_o^{.42}$	.99
Shinn	College students (C)	$.74\ S_i^{.35}S_e^{.42}S_o^{.32}$	.98
Rainwater	Adults, Boston Area	$.71\ S_i^{.69}S_e^{.06}S_o^{.38}$	.96

The results for the five investigations are given in Table 3.6. Note that the variance explained by the multiplicative power function is relatively high in each case—.98, .98, .98, .98, and .96, respectively. The explained variances using the pooled data for the linear additive multivariate equation are .95 and .90, respectively, in the Hamblin and Rainwater investigations. This may not seem much of an improvement, but the difference was statistically significant (Hamblin 1971*a*).

The exponents of the multivariate equations in Table 3.6 are somewhat variable and hence may indicate great differences in subcultural conditioning. This might have been anticipated from the published analysis of the individual data in connection with the first of these experiments (Hamblin 1966, 1971*a*). The multiple regression-correlation analyses of the individual estimates showed considerable variability.

The exponents for occupational status were significantly greater than zero in ten of the individual analyses. Exponents for education and for income were significant for eighteen and twenty-six individuals, respectively. (For most individuals, only two of the three variables predicted significantly.) However, there was essential agreement between the results of the individual analyses and results from the pooled data in that original experiment—only the median exponents for status based on education and income were significantly larger than zero.

A number of other multivariate attitudinal studies show a similar picture—the data are described by multiplicative power functions. For example, Shinn (1969*b*) did a study of international power patterned after the multivariate-status studies discussed above. The judges were graduate students in an international-relations seminar, who used magnitude estimation to measure the power of a number of "nations" characterized by population size, development (as gauged by per capita GNP), and military might (indicated by size of military budget). The average power estimates increased as decelerating functions of population size, per capita GNP, and militarism; and it was found that all these curves were described accurately by power functions.

In the second phase of his investigation, Shinn's judges estimated the total power of nations (P_t), characterized by three variables—size, development, and militarism. He then did an appropriate multivariate analysis of the transformed data, relating total power (P_t) to the components of power: population size (P_s), economic development (P_d), and militarism (P_m). As expected, the multivariate relationship in the data was described accurately by a multiplicative power function. The equation is

$$P_t = .11 P_s^{.50} P_d^{.62} P_m^{.39}$$

The r^2, it should be noted, was .98.

This and the foregoing status investigations were made to determine the form, not necessarily the content, of the equations describing the multivariate relationships in question. That is, there are probably other variables that influence both status and power in extant social systems, but to test for their possible effects it would have been necessary to measure and include them in the analysis. Shinn did this in his last multivariate study of status. He added the variables race and religion to income, education, and occupation. Although they did not explain any variance, that investigation provides a model for investigating alternative substantive hypotheses.

Additive Relationships?

The above investigations suggest that the relationship between an attitude and the multiple stimuli determining it is probably described by a multiplicative power function. Does this mean that there are no additive effects on attitudes? No, in some bivariate relationships the stimulus apparently occurs over and over and has an incremental or additive effect. This is illustrated in what was apparently the first published attempt ever to adapt S. S. Stevens's magnitude-estimation procedures to the study of attitudinal phenomena.

The experiment (Hamblin et al. 1963) was a test of the interference-aggression law. College ROTC students were induced to commit genuine acts of aggression by means of wrong-headed decisions made by their leader in a game. The subjects could advise the leader concerning the strategies of the game, but the leader had final say and so could lose points for the group. The number of points lost by the leader was taken as a measure of interference, and during the game, after each trial, each subject was asked to estimate numerically the degree of dislike for the leader. Before the experiment, in private, the subjects had been told he was a candidate for promotion in ROTC and that after each trial they were to judge his qualities of leadership. In expressing their dislike, the subjects were, therefore, showing aggression against the leader because, to the best of their knowledge, their dislike, to the degree that it was expressed, would injure his chance of promotion.

The results obtained from forty subjects are shown plotted on logarithmic coordinates in Figure 3.15. The plots approximate straight lines, which indicated for the first time that the magnitude of an attitude measured on a ratio scale increases as the power function of the magnitude of the related social stimulus. What is important here is the additivity involved in the stimulus. The measure of interference across trials is simply the accumulative number of points lost by the subjects as a result of the leader's wrong-headed decisions.

It is worth noting that the subjects were also asked after each trial to indicate their dislike for their leader by squeezing a hand dynamometer, and the handgrip-matching data, too, increased as a power function of accumulated interference (Fig. 3.15). The exponent, .30, is what one would expect, from the cross-modality matching studies in psychophysics reported above. The last point, however, is badly out of line and the question is why? Actually, the subjects became extremely angry with the leader during the experiment, so much so that they reached their maximum force of handgrip on the next-to-the-last trial. The last trial is simply within the range of the random variation around that maximum. This study, therefore, suggests that cross-modality matching procedures may be used to cross-check results in attitude experiments. However, the handgrip-matching procedure has its drawback: the reaching of a false plateau because the amount of pressure the subjects can exert on the hand dynamometer is limited.

Even so, this experiment is an important methodological prototype. There are many recurring stimuli in social life—interference, facilita-

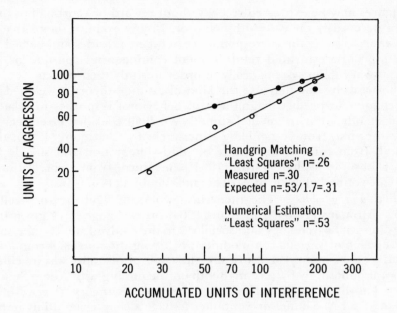

UNITS OF AGGRESSION

ACCUMULATED UNITS OF INTERFERENCE

Handgrip Matching
"Least Squares" n=.26
Measured n=.30
Expected n=.53/1.7=.31

Numerical Estimation
"Least Squares" n=.53

Figure 3.15. Relationship between units of aggression and units of interference plotted on logarithmic coordinates.

tion, and reinforcement stimuli, to mention but three extremely general classes. People's perceptions of one another, their confidence in those perceptions, and their emotional reactions to one another probably vary systematically as power functions, as these stimuli accumulate. Hence, a wide range of investigations could be done, with the above experiment as a paradigm.

Attitudes Versus Behavior

E. A. Ross, L. L. Thurstone, and other pioneer attitude theorists and researchers made the straightforward assumption that attitudes were crucial in mediating the behavioral responses to social and other environmental stimuli. On the surface, this assumption seems to be obviously true, but beginning with LaPiere's (1934) famous study—in which he found that motel owners' actual treatment of orientals did not correspond to their attitudes as previously gauged in a questionnaire through the mail—this mediational assumption has been hard to document. In fact, it is one of the prime foci of a recent anthology edited by Summers (1970). From that work one might judge that the issue is still up in the air in traditional attitude studies.

The essential problem seems to center on the fact that attitudes expressed on questionnaires and behavior expressed in real-life situations are subject to different reinforcement contingencies. Attitudes on questionnaires may be expressed freely without reward or reprisal, but that is not necessarily the case with behavior. In any event, it seems that if one wants to study the correspondence between attitudes and behavior, it is appropriate to hold reinforcement contingencies constant or, at least, to vary them systematically in order to study their effects.

Alternatively, one may use the kind of attitude theory developed in this chapter to predict magnitudes of behavioral responses to related social or other environmental stimuli. We shall consider three sets of data: the first, from a gambling experiment by Clairmont (1969); the second, from correlational study of status integration and suicide by Jack Gibbs and Walter Martin (1964), and third, from a correlational study of voting behavior by Soares and Hamblin (1967).

Utility and gambling. The theoretical works of Thibaut and Kelley (1959), Homans (1961), and Blau (1964) on exchange have given impetus in social psychology and sociology to the study of utility—the subjective value of various commodities (including the universal commodity surrogate—money). Historically, the concept of utility was invented in moral philosophy by Jeremy Bentham. Beginning with Adam Smith, utility has been used extensively in economic theory (e.g., Nobel laureate Paul A. Samuelson continues to have a chapter on utility in his famous introductory text) and in game or gambling theory (Von Neumann and Morgenstern 1947; Edwards 1953, 1954).

The major problem with the concept of utility has been one of measurement, a problem which may have yielded to the new psychophysical measurement procedures (see Figs. 3.5 and 3.8; S. S. Stevens 1959; Clairmont 1969). At any rate, utility implies a mediational theory of behavior which relates objective or social stimuli to mediating attitudinal responses and, finally, to behavioral responses, as diagrammed below for the usual gambling situation. In the diagram the letters represent the utility (U) of the amount of money which might be won (W), the disutility (D) of the amount of money which might be lost, and the ante (A). The subjective probability (P_s) corresponds to the objective probability of winning (P_o). If one chooses not to measure the subjective variables but simply uses them to interpret such gambling decisions as involving a multistimulus response relationship, it follows that the ante the person is willing to wager in such a gambling situation should increase as a multiplicative power function of the amount of money to be won and the objective probability of winning.

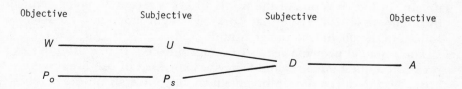

In a series of gambling experiments designed to test this hypothesis, Clairmont (1969) found that samples of lower-class (Job Corps) and middle-class (college) subjects, gamblers and nongamblers, all behaved roughly as anticipated. The following equation represents an average for the four samples:

$$A = .08W^{.8} \cdot P_o^{.65} .$$

Although the explained variance for this equation (.92) was substantially greater than the explained variance for the additive linear model (.41), it was somewhat lower than might be expected. Why? During the gambling experiments, the subjects wagered their own money (earned while participating in a previous experiment). The amounts were relatively small, ranging from three to perhaps eight dollars, but the actual winning and losing over the series of fifty gambles apparently created anxiety which interfered with the subjects' consistent functioning. At least, when they were put into a similar situation and were asked to set what they considered to be fair antes for a variety of bets, similar equations obtained, but the explained variance increased to .96.

The foregoing experiment proves that the multistimuli behavioral-response relationship is in fact described by a multiplicative power function, as would be expected from attitude theory as developed here. Hence, at the very least, that theory serves a heuristic purpose in predicting behavior. Is there any evidence to verify directly the mediational processes attributed to attitudes in the above diagram? The answer is yes.

In a second experiment, with dice used (where the objective probabilities were much less obvious than those in the first experiment, in which gambling cages with dark and light balls were used) the multiplicative equation using perceived probabilities was much more accurate in predicting the amount of money the subjects considered to be a fair ante ($r^2 = .95$) than the equation using objective probabilities ($r^2 = .91$). This appears to be direct evidence that the behavioral response in gambling is in fact mediated by a subjective, or attitudinal, response, postulated in classical attitudinal theory (Ross and Thurstone) and in classical gambling theory (Bernoulli).

Status integration and suicide. Gibbs and Martin's (1964) investigation represents one of the few successful attempts to develop formal theory in sociology. They hypothesize that suicide is essentially a response to role conflict, and they assume, epistemically, that role conflict would be reflected inversely by the degree to which people in various (primarily ascribed) status configurations are concentrated in various achieved statuses. Their data show rather substantial negative rank-order correlations between their various measures of status integration in a vast majority of the 200 or so tests of the theory. The few exceptions seem to involve samples of minority, nonwhite groups, whose movement into and out of the so-called achieved statuses was, in fact, somewhat restricted by discriminatory practices. Even so, role conflict, as measured inversely by status integration, seems to be a stimulus, and suicide, a behavioral response that is mediated by an attitudinal response to the role-conflict stimuli. Consequently, given the attitude theory developed here, one might expect the relationship between the status-integration measures and the suicide rates to be described as a negative power function.

Gibbs and Martin present many sets of data in their book, but I decided to test that expectation with just two sets—obviously the most adequate sets, in that the measurements were taken periodically over a wide stimulus range (Gibbs and Martin 1964, Tables 17, 33). Those data are shown plotted on logarithmic coordinates in Figure 3.16. The plots are approximately linear, as expected. The explained variance is not extremely high, .75 and .70 for 1940 and 1950, respectively, but it is higher than one might expect with multiple causation and no control by constancy. Also, the correlations are higher than those obtained for the least-squares linear equations (.33 and .34, respectively) and for the least-squares exponential equations (.73 and .62, respectively).

Some social scientists may look askance at the theoretical analysis, in terms of a stimulus-response theory mediated by attitudes, of macro phenomena such as these, but Blalock (1971) has wisely called for such analyses. Indeed, they will be necessary if sociology is ever to develop general theory—theory applying equally well to very large and very small social systems. This is not to suggest that all macro theory will be a derivative of the kind of stimulus-response paradigm developed in this chapter, just that some macro theoretical problems—in particular, mass behavioral responses—may reduce themselves into such simple formulations.

Voting for the Radical Left. Soares and Hamblin (1967) have reported a study which relates a number of socioeconomic variables in Chile to the vote for Allende in the Chilean 1952 presidential elections. The results of this investigation are summarized in Table 3.7. Involved are indexes of rather standard sociological variables: class polarization, industrial development, urbanization, and relative deprivation; the variance explained by the least-squares multiplicative power function was .85, whereas that explained by the least-squares linear additive equation was .45.

A number of political scientists have privately expressed their uneasiness about the results of this investigation, particularly the high explained variance. Apparently, the view is that political campaigns are won via charisma, political manipulation, and clever management of

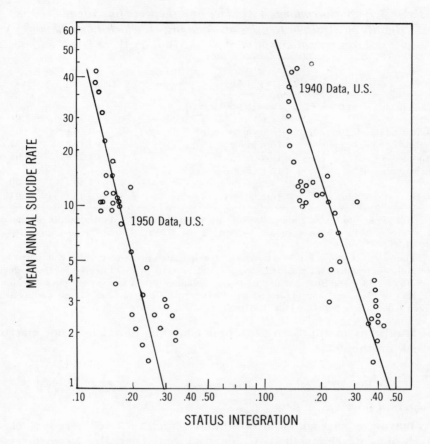

Figure 3.16. *Suicide rates plotted against status-integration measures for forty-four color-age sex-status configurations, about 1950 and 1940, United States. Data from Gibbs and Martin 1964.*

public opinion. These variables obviously do have influence, but it is interesting that, given Allende's charisma, political machinations, and management of public opinion, the subsequent increases in his popular vote and his eventual election as president might have been predicted by the long-term trends in Chile of these macro sociological variables.

Nevertheless, I, too, am uneasy about that report, but for quite different reasons. When the independent variables are highly intercorrelated, as some were in this investigation, it is very easy to draw spurious conclusions about indicators; and the low explained variance (.85 instead of .98) may indicate an incorrect theoretical analysis of the problem. Even so, this and the previous investigations suggest that the mathematical analysis of objective stimulus-response relationships may

Table 3.7. Socioeconomic Variables and the Vote for Allende, 1952:
Results of Multiple Regression Analysis, in which Logarithmic
Transformations of the Various Indexes Were Used

Variable	Index (%)	Type of Index	Regression Coefficient*	t-test
Class polarization (P)	In high school or college	−	−1.33	−3.84
Industrial development (I)	In primary sector	−	+0.45	+2.62
Industrial development (I)	In mining	−	+0.10	+2.34
Anomie (A)	Divorced	+	+1.57	+5.03
Urbanization (U)	In communities 2,000 or more	+	+1.30	+2.49
Relative deprivation (D)	Immigrants	−	−0.46	−1.87

NOTE: The vote for Allende is the vote for the radical left indicating those alienated (V_a) from Chile's socioeconomic system as of 1952. Thus, the equation $V_a = cP^{1.33}I^{-.55}A^{1.57}U^{1.30}D^{.46}$.

*The variables shown survived a stepwise condensation procedure which eliminated all insignificant predictors. Explained variance is 85 percent. With 18 degrees of freedom, a *t*-value of 1.73 is significant at the .05-level, one-tailed test. A linear multiple regression analysis of the same data explained but 45 percent of the variance. These results are taken from Soares and Hamblin (1967), Table 3.

be fruitful as an approach to an understanding of at least some macro social phenomena.

Evaluation

Concerned Questions

As may have been noted, the attitude research reviewed here is a relatively new development, reaching back but ten years. Nevertheless, during that period a number of interesting evaluative questions have been raised which are worthy of comment. We shall start with the more general, or the more philosophical, and work toward the more scientific questions.

Freedom. First, a number of readers have seemed uncomfortable with the suggested automatic or involuntary nature of stimulus-response relationships, whether natural or culturally conditioned, and this discomfort appeared to be exacerbated by the high level of explained variance in the research. It was as though they were finding out that they had much less freedom than they had supposed.

They should remember that because these are averaged data the determinacy is not as high as the r^2's might suggest. Also, as George Herbert Mead observed, we humans, more than any other animals, engage in stimulus management, and we are as free (experientially speaking) as we are good at managing stimuli to produce the "involuntary" responses we desire. A better knowledge of stimulus-response relationships generally may actually increase our experienced freedom by improving our understanding of how our "involuntary" responses may be controlled by ourselves and others.

Self Correlations. There are some who always assume that any high correlation in social science has to involve different indicators of the same thing. Certainly, they would interpret the .99 r^2's that typically obtain for psychophysical relationships as the degree of relationship between an objective indicator and a subjective indicator of the same thing. While it is true that any variable highly related to any other variable may be used as an indicator of that other variable, to say that they are the same thing is quite another matter.

For example, in psychophysical experiments the stimulus is always a physical force measured in objective units; it is something that impinges on the sensory mechanism to produce a neural response experienced as a sensation. Thus, not only are the locales of the stimulus and the response different (outside versus inside the organism), but the stimulus, by operating on the organism, produces or *causes* the psychological response. So, while a direct measure of the physical stimulus may serve as an indirect measure—an indicator—of the related psychological sensation in a normal organism, and vice versa, it is nonsense to call the direct measure of the stimulus and the direct measure of the response indicators of the same thing.

Indeterminacy. Some have questioned why the correlations are never quite perfect—why there is always some error. The specific answer is that in the body's neuroelectric system there is noise—uncontrolled random variation—which means that signals are never transmitted perfectly, that is, without distortion. The more general answer is that in natural phenomena there is always some indeterminacy.

Indeterminacy is that portion of error variance which cannot be reduced by improving the precision of methods or of theory. In some instances, indeterminacy may involve far less than 1 percent of the total variance, but it is, nevertheless, partly responsible for the fact that there is never a *perfect* fit between any scientific theory and the data relationships it purports to describe.

Baird (1962) has noted that the uninitiated might rejoice that he has explained all of the variance when there is no variation in the multiple measurements. As noted earlier, however, to the experienced physicist it is a signal that his measurements are not sensitive enough. Hence, he will develop finer and finer measures of the dependent variable until multiple measurements at given points in the relationship result in, say, a normal distribution, which is taken as a signal that he has reached the limits of the determinacy of the phenomena in question, and that any further improvements in the accuracy of the measurement will not help. By following this procedure in mathematical experiments one may feel confident that the resulting theoretical equations are as precise as the determinacy of the phenomena warrants, sometimes with parameters accurate to several decimals.

In this context, what might be said about the determinacy or indeterminacy of the behavior of the human organism? In neurophysics, where the measurement is done automatically by physical devices calibrated with extreme accuracy, the multiple measurements at given points in the usual relationship are apparently log normally distributed (there is never need for greater accuracy) and, furthermore, the explained variance is generally .98+. In psychophysical and social experiments in which Stevens's measurement procedures are used with care, again the multiple measurements are apparently log normally distributed and the level of explained variance is almost always .98+.

This is not to suggest that the level of determinacy for human behavior is .98+, because the data are aggregated and so obscure much real variation. However, judging from the interexperiment variations in the parameters in the psychophysical and neurophysical equations, determinacy characteristic of stimulus-response relationships may be about 95 percent for pooled data. Determinacy in the raw individual organism, without averaging data, may be about 90 percent.

Pearson: Critique and Countercritique

Karl Pearson, the inventor of least-squares regression, r^2, and χ^2, must be ranked with the great mathematical statisticians of all time, but the scientific methodology he outlined in his *Grammar of Science* is another matter. It is nevertheless of particular interest here because it is a severe criticism of Galileo's and Newton's methodologies. Briefly, Pearson's major points were:

1. There are no cause-and-effect relationships in nature—only perceived contingencies of varying magnitudes.

2. Equations should not be used to describe data relationships, because they imply perfect relationships and there are no perfect relationships in nature.

3. Symmetric measures of degree of contingency or association are the only legitimate tools of science.

While it is probable that few people have read Pearson's treatise on methodology, by indirection it has had a profound impact on the biological and social sciences; his measures of contingency are widely used, and the methodology behind them has dominated research.

Given below are arguments opposing Pearson's major points.

1. As if in reply to Pearson's causal critique, Sir Ronald A. Fisher started a highly influential countermovement in mathematical statistical

theory by developing his statistics of experimentation. His two books, *Statistical Methods for Research Workers* and the *Design of Experiments*, focused on procedures for the direct determination of cause-effect relationships. Like other scientists before and after his time, he was primarily interested in relationships in nature in which one variable could be manipulated indirectly by manipulating one or more other variables directly. Whether or not these are called cause-and-effect relationships is unimportant; they are the heart of science.

2. Mathematical scientists never have pretended that equations describe data perfectly; rather, they view them as representing expected or underlying relationships obtained by averaging large numbers of measurements in experiments or in correlational investigations. Pearson apparently conceded this point, for the criticism was dropped in the second edition. However, it is useful to review the primary rationale of why equations are fitted to data.

Once it has been established that they accurately describe a class of data relationships, equations are given the status of scientific laws. In the history of science, the discovery of one law generally leads to the discovery of other laws, and together they become the building blocks of the marvelously accurate and complex theories that are characteristic of the mathematical sciences. For example, Newton's general theory of mechanics was not created out of a vacuum. Rather, he used Kepler's laws of planetary motion and Galileo's law of falling bodies, among others, as his building blocks.

There have been many in sociology who have tacitly assumed or explicitly suggested that axiomatic theory might be developed from weaker building blocks, that is, theoretical propositions explaining about 10 percent of the variance. However, I agree with Duncan's (1963) original critique of these efforts. He suggested that they would be relatively fruitless unless the correlations were very high. In my experience with equation fitting, I have found that correlations must be about .98 if consistent continuities are to appear across the broad range of data and establish a law. This does not necessarily mean that the determinacy of the phenomena in question need be that high. Historically, mathematical scientists have found that various averaging procedures may be employed to eliminate variation for particular sets of data so that the equation that fits the underlying relationship can be determined unambiguously. Also, as long as the pooled or averaged data yield the requisite fits to equations, the axiomatic derivations will be tolerably accurate. The cross-modality equation in psychophysics is the only derivation included in this chapter, and the accuracy of the predicted exponents is plus or minus 5 percentage points, the same level typically found for psychophysical exponents for a given modality across several experiments (examples of other derivations with a similar level of accuracy for social data are given in Hamblin, Jacobsen, and Miller, 1973.)

3. The most unfortunate part of Pearson's critique was his pushing the use of measures of contingency and correlation, particularly his corollary that in empirical investigations any degree of contingency or correlation is acceptable. It may *seem* reasonable that correlations should not always approach 1.00—that correlations of .10, .50, .70, or even .99 are all natural outcomes which describe reality and therefore should be appreciated equally. But that position allowed Pearson and subsequent workers in his tradition to circumvent what might be called the rule of determinacy, which had guided and still guides the work in the mathematical sciences. Mathematical scientists have always assumed that natural phenomena are completely determined or are very nearly so, that it is always possible to find a correct answer—an equation which accurately describes data relationships under investigation, which explains almost all the variance. Furthermore, they push their investigations until they find such an equation. Since, given their methodology, they have in almost every instance been successful, the rule of determinacy has served them well.[4]

In contrast, Pearson and his followers' circumvention of the rule of determinacy has allowed them to stop whenever they have found some relationship, even if it involved 5 or 10 percent of the variance. Such standards create a wasteland of research; as noted above, the average goodness of fit of even the experimental and correlational data in the best journals in sociology and social psychology is 10 percent of the variance (see Hamblin 1971a; Hamblin et al. 1971). The problem is that such research is destined for early obsolescence. Pearson found this out personally from hard experience. As Galton's protege he spent years gathering data testing Galton's "law" of heredity; the explained variance generally averaged about 40 percent. The jolt came when the reports of Mendel's work reached England; Mendel's laws were very different from Galton's "law"; instead of explaining 40 percent of the variance, they routinely explained nearly 100 percent. As a result they were quickly accepted by the scientific community over Galton's formulation, in spite of Pearson's infamous five-year attack on Mendel's work.

4. There are, of course, phenomena that are not fully determined. I have suggested above, for example, that psychophysical and attitudinal phenomena involve only 90 percent determinacy apparently because of random firings in the nervous system. Another example is the genetic contributions of different ancestors in Fisher's theory of polygenetic inheritance. In those respective instances, however, attempt was made to find empirically the level of determinacy, through comparisons with neurophysical results and using statistical theory and the corresponding genetic results. The point is that without such evidence, the rule of determinacy is appropriate to follow. This should not be construed, however, to suggest that one level of determinacy is better than another; the purpose of scientific theory is simply to mirror the phenomena it describes, including the accuracy inherent in those phenomena—no more, no less.

Later, Fisher developed his theory of polygenetic inheritance, which was consistent with Mendel's laws and accounted for the normal distributions of polygenetic traits—like height and eye color. Fisher's theory, which gave a Mendelian explanation to the data in question in Pearson's attack, was the death blow to Galton's formulation.

In addition to lowering the standards for an acceptable level of explained variance, the neglect of the rule of determinacy has fostered the neglect of a second rule—that of maximum accuracy, which mathematical scientists also appear to follow religiously in their work. The rule of maximum accuracy simply implies that at every juncture in an investigation a scientist is obligated to choose and use the most accurate methods available. Such a rule may seem obvious to most researchers, almost beyond discussion or debate, but the fact is that Pearson and those in his tradition have violated this dictum as often as they have followed it. For example, they obviously follow it in their computations. They would be horrified by published experimental or correlational analyses that were not completely cross-checked to make sure there were no computational errors. Pearson, however, thought nothing of using procedures which introduced huge random errors. For example, he used an ordinal scale—short, medium, and long heads—in his genetic studies, when an accurate ratio scale in centimeters or inches was available. Also, he never took steps to average out random measurement error but chose instead to analyze it as part of the real data. In his correlational studies he always assumed linear additive relationships, ignoring the simple fact that these relationships tend to be extremely scarce in the natural and the social sciences. In the last ten years I have encountered more than five hundred instances in which equations accurately described social data, and almost all of those relationships were obviously curvilinear, multiplicative, or both (see Hamblin, Jacobsen, and Miller 1973).

Substituting nominal, ordinal, or even interval measures for ratio measures, failing to average out random measurement errors, substituting words and common-sense reasoning for mathematics as the language and logic of theory, using control by random assignment instead of control by constancy, using linear additive approximations, and so forth—all these may not seem serious. But these shortcuts are probably responsible for most of the 90 percent error variance typical of the results in sociology—although it may not be possible with the data now available to factor out the effects of each. They are also responsible for the sorry state of axiomatic theory in sociology. As Blalock (1969) has observed, in sociology we have no complex theories which accurately mirror reality and from which may be derived novel or unexpected theorems. These shortcuts, which obviate the rigorous fit of theoretical statement, may be the primary reason why this is so.

Theoretical Implications

One might ask, What do the foregoing studies add up to? What are their theoretical implications? Are they to be taken simply as methodological examples? As noted earlier, I thought of my studies as pretests and did them, essentially, with a view to adapting and evaluating the methodology. However, the replications were excellent—even when a large sample was involved as in the Rainwater experiment. In science, one cannot ignore replications. Nor can one ignore continuities from one substantive investigation to another. Consequently, these mathematical experiments designed to pretest various social-attitude theories have a number of important theoretical implications, both for middle-range theory and for general theory, that are important to consider, since the ultimate test of a methodology is the kind of theory it generates. However, we shall limit the middle-range considerations to one case, that of status judgments.

The Status Experiments. What are the theoretical implications of the status experiments? In the first place, many sociologists have considered status to be a categorical phenomenon involving several social classes—for example, the Lynds (1937) postulated two classes; Hollingshead (1949), five; and Warner, Mecker, and Eells (1949), six. The data obtained in the status experiments described earlier do show that there are two segments of the status-income continuum—each involving a continuous relationship described by a different equation. But if the Lynd-Hollingshead-Warner conception is valid, the magnitude estimates of status plotted against their respective income and educational stimuli on arithmetic coordinates should produce a step function, each step corresponding to a class. There are no hints of such steps; the data are continuous, which proves that the categorical conception is inadequate, as other sociologists (Lenski and Duncan, e.g.) have suggested.

Second, the data show that status in general is a multiplicative power function of status accruing from income, occupation, and possibly education. While the explained variance is not much higher than that obtained by Warner, Mecker, and Eells, or Blau and Duncan, who used a linear additive regression model with categorical data, these results are an improvement, since, as we have seen, they fit the general theory of attitudes that is emerging from this series of investigations.

The present experiments may be criticized because some status stimuli were obviously omitted. That, however, is a criticism of a specific experiment. As noted earlier, Shinn in one of his experiments included religious affiliation and ethnic origin as well as income, occupation, and education. That those added variables were shown to be unimportant is beside the point; it should be possible, using Shinn's strategy, to test the possible status effects of almost any variable.

Finally, from a theoretical point of view, the status experiments might be criticized because the parameters of the equations varied somewhat from one sample to another. This variation has been interpreted, however, as reflecting genuine differences in cultural conditioning. If that is so, it should be possible to discover exogenous variables which explain the variation in the parameters of the status equations. Hence, in future investigations, it may be possible to write equations with those exogenous variables. This criticism, then, involves an important theoretical issue which can be settled only in future research.

Table 3.8. Summary Results: Bivariate Attitude Experiments

Attitude	Social Stimulus	Median n	Median r²	No. of Investigations
Aggression	Decisions leading to losses	0.52	.99	1
Status	Income < 12,000	0.84	.99	5
Status	Income > 12,000	0.48	.99	5
Status	Education	2.46	.98	7
Power	Population size	0.83	.99	1
Power	Per capita military budget	0.72	.99	1
Power	Per capita GNP	0.99	.99	1
Seriousness	Money stolen	0.17	.99	1
Dislike of self	Killing the enemy	0.1	.99	1
Dislike of self	Becoming angry at associates	0.5	.99	1
Dislike of self	Drinks per week	0.8	−.96	1
Dislike of self	Pounds overweight	1.0	.98	1
Dislike of wife	Number of premarital sex partners	0.2	.98	1
Like	Wages	0.66	.99	2
Dislike	Wages	2.05	.98	2
Poverty	Income	−3.8	.99	2
Suicide rate	Status integration	−3.6	.73	2

SOURCES: All of the data come from investigations reported above except for the "seriousness-money stolen" data. Those come from Sellin and Wolfgang 1964.

The General Implications. The data from the bivariate experiments on social-attitude phenomena are summarized in Table 3.8; the findings for fifteen relationships between attitudinal variables and social stimuli are presented there. In every instance, although the investigations were done as pretests, the magnitude of the attitude has turned out to be a power function of the magnitude of the related social stimulus. There was about the same amount of published data (the findings from one to

several experiments on each of fourteen modalities), and about the
same evidence of continuities, when Stevens (1957) suggested his psychophysical law. Consequently, it may not be inappropriate at this juncture to make a similar suggestion: there appears to be a general law
which describes the relationship between the magnitude of an attitude
(A) and the magnitude of its related social stimulus (Σ) as in the
equation

$$A = c\Sigma^n .$$

It must be recognized that this law should be expected to apply only
when the attitudinal variable and the social-stimulus variable are both
measured at the ratio level, that is, from the origin of the relationship.
As noted above, this often implies an origin correction for the stimulus
variable. These origins apparently occur because of cultural conditioning and, hence, need not be constant throughout a large, culturally
heterogenous population. The data also suggest that, for a given attitude, the power exponent may also vary somewhat because of differences in cultural conditioning, or, to put it another way, that parameter
equations must be discovered. In addition, the status-income experiments suggest that a single power function may not hold over the entire continuum of a relationship—that the continuum may be seg-
mented, with each segment described by a different equation.

Also, the data suggest that a given attitude may be conditioned simultaneously to several stimuli. When that happens, the social-attitude law
takes the more general form

$$A = \Sigma_1^{n_1} . \ldots . \Sigma_j^{n_j} .$$

The published evidence for this multiplicative power function is summarized in Table 3.9. While the data are less extensive than those for
the bivariate case, the results have been quite consistent and the R^2's
are quite high. In some instances, the improvement over the R^2 computed by means of a simple linear additive equation has been substantial, 30 or 40 percent explained variance; in others, the improvement
has been small—2 to 5 percent explained variance. But in all the comparisons, the multiplicative power function did better than the linear
additive equation.

The attitude law, then, appears to be useful as a postulate in the
study of behavior. It apparently involves a mediational model, where
the magnitude of a social stimulus determines the magnitude of a related social attitude, which in turn determines the magnitude of a related behavioral response. The empirical evidence, although still not
extensive, uniformly suggests that the relationship between the magnitude of the social stimulus and the behavioral response is described
by a bivariate power function or a multiplicative power function,

Table 3.9. Summary Results of Analyses for Multiplicative Power
Functions: Multivariate Attitude Experiments

Response Variable	Stimulus Variable	Median n	Median R^2	No. of Experiments
General status	Income status	0.48		
	Occupational status	0.38	.98	4
	Educational status	0.35		
General power	Population power	0.50		
	Economic power	0.62	.98	
	Military power	0.39		
Poverty	Income deficit	3.85	.99	1
	Family size	1.19		
Professorial status, local[a]	Merit of teaching	0.65	.97	2
	Professorial demeanor	0.53		
Professorial status, professional	Professional age	0.16		
	Merit of teaching	0.63	.99	1
	Cordiality	−0.47		
	Merit of publication	0.62		
Fair amount to ante	Money to be won	0.98	.96	4
	Probability of winning	0.61		
Money anted	Money to be won	0.80	.92	4
	Probability of winning	0.65		

SOURCES: All of the data are from investigations summarized above except for professional status; see Hamblin and Smith 1966.

whichever is applicable. Furthermore, the level of explained variance for the behavioral equations appears to be as high as the level for the attitudinal equations.

Thus, the biological mechanisms mediating the social stimulus, attitudinal response, and behavioral response can evidently be conditioned with respect to content, to the origin of the relationship on the stimulus continuum, and to one or more social stimuli. This is quite unlike the biological mechanisms mediating the phenomena described by the psychophysical and the neurophysical laws. The relationships involved there are apparently fixed biologically and may not even be modifiable via conditioning. However, the data uniformly suggest that the two sets of mechanisms are similar in one essential respect: their input-output characteristics are apparently the same.

It should be noted that suggesting a law does not establish it. It has to be tested and generally accepted as a law by a wide variety of investigators before it is established. It has taken 120 years in psychophysics to establish the power function as the psychophysical law.

Those of us involved in attitude experiments have had the good fortune to capitalize on Stevens's methodological and theoretical developments, and therefore it should not be surprising that now, after eleven years, we are where Stevens was in 1957—at the suggestion stage. It is also instructive to note that Teghtsoonian (1971) has just recently made the first serious suggestion of an equation to explain the variation of exponents across psychophysical modalities. Hence, it may not be unreasonable to expect such parameter equations for the attitude laws within the next ten years or so.

Even without such parameter equations, the social-attitude laws may have considerable scientific utility as postulates in sociological theory. As propositions, they are of the same order as Homans's (1961) behavior postulates, which he and others have used to develop a wide variety of theories. Although the attitude laws suggested here are more precise than the behavioral postulates (which have yet to be translated into data-based mathematical equations), as propositions they have functioned in the attitudinal research discussed above in much the same way that the behavioral postulates have functioned in behavioral sociology. They allow the derivation of theories for a wide range of social phenomena.

Shinn (1969a) suggested that the magnitude-measurement procedures and the related methodology from psychophysics have great promise for social research. Now, just a few years later, that judgment appears to be too modest. As suggested in my introduction, these methods may have created a breakthrough, not just for attitude theory, but more generally for the refinement of "those social science theories that deal with how people perceive and react to their physical and social environments." We should not be surprised, because such methods—or, more specifically, mathematical experimentation and correlation[5]—have always revolutionized and enlightened any scientific discipline that adopts them.

---

5. I have slighted mathematical correlation in this chapter. For a plethora of examples of its use with macro social data, see Hamblin, Jacobsen and Miller (1973).

References

Baird, D. C.
    1962. *Experimentation: An Introduction to Measurement Theory and Experiment Design.* Englewood Cliffs, N.J.: Prentice-Hall.
Blalock, H. M.
    1969. "Theory Construction." Englewood Cliffs, N.J.: Prentice-Hall.
    1971. "Aggregation and Measurement Error." *Social Forces* 50:151-65.
Blau, P. M.
    1955. *The Dynamics of Bureaucracy: A Study of Interpersonal Relations in Two Government Agencies.* Chicago: University of Chicago Press.
    1964. *Exchange and Power in Social Life.* New York: Wiley.
Chapin, F. Stuart
    1947. *Experimental Designs in Sociological Research,* Rev. ed. New York: Harper.
Clairmont, D. H.
    1969. *An Historical and Experimental Study of Utility.* Ann Arbor, Mich.: University Microfilms, no. 69-22522.
Coleman, J. S.
    1964. *Introduction to Mathematical Sociology.* New York: Free Press.
Croxton, F. E., and D. J. Cowden
    1939. *Applied General Statistics.* New York: Prentice-Hall.
Dodd, Stuart
    1942. *The Dimensions of Society.* New York: Macmillan.
Duncan, Otis Dudley
    1963. "Axioms or Correlations?" *American Sociological Review* 28:452.
Ekman, G.
    1961. "A Simple Method for Fitting Psychophysical Power Functions." *Journal of Psychology* 51:343-350.
Edwards, W.
    1953. "Probability Preferences in Gambling." *American Journal of Psychology* 69.
    1954. "The Theory of Decision Making." *Psychological Bulletin* 51:380-417.
Eisler, H.
    1962. "Subjective Scale of Force for a Large Muscle Group." *Journal of Experimental Psychology* 64:253-257.
Eisler, H., and C. Ottander
    1963. "On the Problem of Hysteresis in Psychophysics." *Journal of Experimental Psychology* 65:530-536.
Ezekial, M.
    1941. *Methods of Correlation Analysis.* New York: Wiley.
Fisher, R. A.
    1950. *Statistical Methods for Research Workers.* Edinburgh: Oliver & Boyd.
    1951. *The Design of Experiments.* Edinburgh: Oliver & Boyd.
Gibbs, J. P., and W. Martin
    1964. *Status Integration and Suicide.* Eugene: University of Oregon Books.
Guirao, Miguelina and S. S. Stevens
    1964. "Measurement of Auditory Density." *The Journal of the Acoustical Society of America* 36:1176-1182.

Hamblin, R. L.
1971*a*. "Mathematical Experimentation and Sociological Theory: A Critical Analysis." *Sociometry* 34, 423-52.
1971*b*. "Ratio Measurement for the Social Sciences." *Social Forces* 50:191-206.
Hamblin, R. L., D. A. Bridger, R. C. Day, and W. L. Yancey
1963. "Interference-Aggression Law?" *Sociometry* 26:190-216.
Hamblin, R. L., D. Buckholdt, D. Ferritor, M. Kozloff, and L. Blackwell
1971. *The Humanization Processes.* New York: Wiley.
Hamblin, R. L., R. B. Jacobsen, and J. L. L. Miller
1973. *A Mathematical Theory of Social Change.* New York: Wiley.
Hamblin, R. L., and C. R. Smith
1966. "Values, Status, and Professors." *Sociometry* 29:183-96.
Harper, R., and S. S. Stevens
1964. "Subjective Hardness of Compliant Materials." *Quarterly Journal of Experimental Psychology* 65:204-15.
Hollingshead, A. B.
1949. *Elmstown's Youth.* New York: Wiley.
Homans, G. C.
1961. *Social Behavior: Its Elementary Forms.* New York: Harcourt, Brace & World.
Jones, Bryan D., and R. Shorter
1972. "The Ratio Measurement of Social Status: Some Cross-cultural Comparisons." *Social Forces* 50:499-511.
LaPiere, R. T.
1934. "Attitude vs. Actions." *Social Forces* 14:230-37.
Luce, R. D.
1959. "On the Possible Psychophysical Laws." *Psychological Review* 66 (March):81-95.
Lundberg, George
1964. *Can Science Save Us?* New York: Longmans, Green.
Lynd, R., and H. Lynd
1937. *Middetown in Transition.* New York: Harcourt, Brace & World.
Merton, R. K., and A. S. Kitt
1950. "Contributions to the Theory of Reference Group Behavior." In R. K. Merton and P. F. Lazarsfeld, eds., *Continuities in Social Research: Studies in the Scope and Method of "The American Soldier."* Glencoe, Ill.: Free Press.
Park, P.
1969 *Sociology Tomorrow.* New York: Pegasus.
Rainwater, Lee
1971. Interim Report on Explorations of Social Status. Mimeo, Harvard University.
In Press. *What Money Can Buy: The Social Meaning of Poverty.* New York: Basic Books.
Sellen, J. T., and M. E. Wolfgang
1964. *The Measurement of Delinquency.* New York: Wiley.
Shinn, Jr., A. M.
1969*a*. "An Application of Psychophysical Scaling Techniques to the Measurement of National Power." *Journal of Politics* 31:932-51.
1969*b*. "The Application of Psychophysical Scaling Techniques to Measurement of Political Variables." Mimeographed. Chapel Hill: Institute for Research in Social Science, University of North Carolina.
Skinner, B. F.
1953. *Science and Human Behavior.* New York: Macmillan.

Soares, G., and R. L. Hamblin
  1967. "Socio-economic Variables and Voting for the Radical Left: Chile, 1952." *American Political Science Review* 61:1053-65.
Stephens, J. M.
  1967. *The Process of Schooling.* New York: Holt, Rinehart & Winston.
Stevens, J. C.
  1958. "Stimulus Spacing and the Judgment of Loudness." *Journal of Experimental Psychology* 56:246-50.
Stevens, J. C., and M. Guirao
  1964. "Individual Loudness Functions." *Journal of the Acoustical Society of America* 36:2210-13.
Stevens, J. C., and J. D. Mack
  1959. "Scales of Apparent Force." *Journal of Experimental Psychology* 58:405-13.
Stevens, J. C., J. D. Mack, and S. S. Stevens
  1960. "Growth of Sensation on Seven Continua as Measured by Force of Handgrip." *Journal of Experimental Psychology* 59:60-67.
Stevens, J. C., and S. S. Stevens
  1960. "Warmth and Cold: Dynamics of Sensory Intensity." *Journal of Experimental Psychology* 60:183-92.
Stevens, S. S.
  1946. "On the Theory of Scales of Measurement." *Science* 103:677.
  1954. "Biological Transducers." *Convention Record, International Radio Engineers,* pt. 9, pp. 27-33.
  1955. "The Measurement of Loudness." *Journal of the Acoustical Society of America* 27:815-829.
  1956. "The Direct Estimation of Sensory Magnitudes: Loudness." *American Journal of Psychology* 69 (March):1-25.
  1957. "On the Psychophysical Law." *Psychological Review* 64:153-81.
  1958. "Some Similarities Between Hearing and Seeing." *Laryngoscope* 68:508-527.
  1959a. "Cross-modality Validation of Subjective Scales for Loudness, Vibration, and Electric Shock." *Journal of Experimental Psychology* 57:201-209.
  1959b. "Tactile Vibration: Dynamics of Sensory Intensity." *Journal of Experimental Psychology* 57:210-18.
  1960. "Ratio Scales, Partition Scales, and Confusion Scales." In H. Gulliksen and S. Messick, eds., *Psychological Scaling: Theory and Applications.* New York: Wiley.
  1962. "The Surprising Simplicity of Sensory Metrics." *American Psychologist* 17:29-39.
  1966. "A Metric for the Social Consensus." *Science* 151:530-41.
  1965. "Matching Functions between Loudness and Other Continua." *Perception and Psychophysics* 1:5-8.
  1970. "Neural Events and the Psychophysical Law." *Science* 170 (December):1043-50.
Stevens, S. S., A. S. Carton and G. M. Shickman
  1958. "A Scale of Apparent Intensity of Electric Shock." *Journal of Experimental Psychology* 56:328-334.
Stevens, S. S., and E. H. Galanter
  1957. "Ratio Scales and Category Scales for a Dozen Perceptual Continua." *Journal of Experimental Psychology* 54:377-411.
Stevens, S. S., and M. Guirao
  1962. "Loudness, Reciprocality, and Partition Scales." *The Journal of the Acoustical Society of America* 34 (September) Part 2:1466-1471.

1963. "Subjective Scaling of Length and Area and the Matching to Loudness and Brightness." *Journal of Experimental Psychology* 66:177-86.

Stevens, S. S. and J. R. Harris
1962. "The Scaling of Subjective Roughness and Smoothness." *Journal of Experimental Psychology* 64:489-494.

Summers, G. F., ed.
1970. *Attitude Measurement*. Chicago: Rand McNally.

Teghtsoonian, R.
1971. "On the Exponents in Stevens' Law and the Constant in Ekman's Law." *Psychological Review* 78, no. 1:71-80.

Terrace, H. S. and S. S. Stevens
1962. "The Quantification of Tonal Volume." *American Journal of Psychology* 75:596-604.

Thibaut, J. W., and H. T. Kelley
1959. *The Social Psychology of Groups*. New York: Wiley.

Veblen, T.
1968. *The Theory of the Leisure Class*. Reprint ed. New York: Viking Press.

Von Neumann, J., and O. Morgenstern
1947. *Theories of Games and Economic Behavior*. Princeton, N.J.: Princeton University Press.

Warner, W. L., M. Meeker, and K. Eells
1949. *Social Class in America*. Chicago: Science Research Associates.

White, Harrison
1970. *Chains of Opportunity: System Models of Mobility in Organizations*. Cambridge, Mass.: Harvard University Press.

Chapter 4

RELATIONS BETWEEN SCALES

ALLEN M. SHINN, JR.

Allen M. Shinn, Jr., received his Ph.D. in Political Science from the University of North Carolina in 1969. He is presently Program Manager with the Division of Social Systems, National Science Foundation, where his responsibilities and interests center on applied social research concerning the impact of telecommunications on society. He has published several other works dealing with problems of measurement in social science.

"Scaling" is an increasingly complex topic, as a casual review of some recent surveys of the field (Ekman and Sjoberg 1965; Zinnes 1969; Pfanzagl 1968) will quickly reveal. It is immediately apparent that the literature is rapidly becoming incomprehensible to all but a relatively small number of specialists, and that the investment in time and effort required to become familiar with it will, for most social scientists, far outweigh the possible gains to be had. Thus it is not surprising that there are few courses in scaling theory in most social science graduate curricula, and correspondingly few social scientists who consider themselves competent to apply the theory of scaling in their own fields of interest.

I think this is unfortunate. To the extent that we build our sciences on theories of human behavior, we must deal with how people perceive and react to various aspects of their environments, and it seems, then, that a wide range of research in the social sciences must rest largely on some measurement of how people perceive. This is what scaling theory is all about, and why I would argue that many social scientists should have at least a casual acquaintance with this field.

The views stated herein are those of the author alone and should not be considered to represent in any way an official position of the National Science Foundation.

121

It is not that we should try to become scaling theorists ourselves; this is a specialist's field, and only those who wish to be specialists in it are likely to have any appreciable impact on it. But unlike many areas of social science, this field is rather well developed, and there exists a body of theory which we have only to accept and make use of. It is entirely a practical matter. If we use this theory and the techniques associated with it, we will be well on the way toward solving some of our more difficult measurement problems; if we continue to ignore it, these problems will remain unsolved, and theoretical development in the affected fields will continue to be slow and uncertain.

The purpose of this chapter is thus fairly simple. I shall attempt to summarize the existing theory in a particular area of scaling, that dealing with the relations to be expected between different scaling techniques. This is important, for the results of different approaches to the scaling problem are not always the same, and if we are to use the methods intelligently we must understand why they differ, and which methods yield the most appropriate results for our purposes. It is the case, I think, that some methods are superior to others for most of our purposes, and also that those methods now most commonly used are often not the best at all. I shall illustrate this theoretical discussion with empirical data drawn for the most part from studies I have conducted, the aim of which has been to apply these methods to real problems in the social sciences, rather than to make further theoretical progress in scaling itself. These illustrations should serve the double purpose of making clear the scaling theory involved and of showing how it can be applied to various problems in the disciplines of political science and sociology. It is hoped that, if these purposes are well served, this work will contribute somewhat to the wider usage of good scaling methods in the relevant areas of social science.

A cautionary note should be added. I am not a psychologist, but a political scientist, and this gives me a particular perspective from which to write. My exposition of psychophysical theory would probably seem inadequate to a specialist in the field. It will be adequate for my purpose, however, if it presents a rough outline of the relevant parts of psychophysics and provides a unified frame of reference in which to place the various scaling methods discussed. Those who wish to investigate the field more deeply will find ample references with which to begin.

A Typology of Scales

We must begin with a typology of scales suggesting what we will and will not cover in this chapter. Following Torgerson (1958, pp. 45-48), we can distinguish between *subject-centered* and *stimulus-centered* scales.

The former are those in which we try to place the respondent, an individual person, on a continuum by means of his responses to a series of items. This class includes nearly all the scales used to measure attitudes and personality characteristics, and thus most of the scales discussed in such standard works as Bonjean, Hill, and McLemore (1967); Robinson, Athanasiou, and Head (1969); and Robinson, Rusk, and Head (1968). Most of these scales are of the Likert type, (Likert 1932; Summers 1970), although other commonly used general types include the semantic differential (Osgood, Suci, and Tannenbaum 1957) when used to measure attitudes, Thurstone's original method of equal-appearing intervals (Thurstone 1928, 1929; Summers 1970), and Guttman's methods (Guttman 1944, 1947; Summers 1970). In a strict sense, Guttman scaling is a cross between the subject-centered and the stimulus-centered approach, and Torgerson terms it a *response* approach because it seeks through the subject's responses to place both the subject and the stimuli on a single continuum. But in most cases social scientists use Guttman scaling to classify subjects rather than stimuli, and thus we shall do no great harm by classing it with the subject-centered methods.

The second class of scales, the concern in the remainder of this chapter, uses respondents only to place a group of stimuli on a continuum. The interest centers as a rule on the stimuli, not on the subjects, although the methods may be used to illuminate how different subjects or, more usually, different groups of subjects perceive the stimuli. But even in the latter case, the information developed places the stimuli, not the subjects, on the continuum of interest.

To illustrate the difference between the two approaches, consider the question of occupational status. Using a stimulus-centered method in asking a group of judges to rate a number of occupations in terms of their statuses, we get information directly bearing upon the occupations, not upon the judges. Of course, we might ask two different groups of judges (say, high- and low-status individuals) to rate the occupations and then compare the ratings in order to illuminate the differences between the two groups' perceptions of this continuum. But we would still have a stimulus-centered scaling project, since only the occupations would be placed on the continuum of status. On the other hand, we might ask an individual a series of questions concerning his attitude toward his occupation. This would be a subject-centered approach, for we would be seeking to place the individual, or a group if we wished to average the responses, on a continuum such as "favorableness toward one's job" rather than seeking to place the *job* on a continuum.

Table 4.1 (adapted from Eisler 1965*b*, p. 284) provides a workable classification of stimulus-centered scaling methods. It suggests a two-

Table 4.1. A Classification of Stimulus-centered Scaling Methods

Method	Perceptual magnitude Scales	Discrimination scales
	(1)	(2)
Direct	Magnitude or ratio (R) scaling (ratio level) Similarity (S) scaling (ratio level)	Category (K) scale (interval level)
	(3)	(4)
Indirect	Thurstonian paired comparisons or successive intervals, Case VI (logarithmic interval level)	Thurstonian paired comparisons or successive intervals, Case V (interval level)

way classification of scales according to whether they are direct or indirect in technique, and according to whether they produce scales of perceptual magnitudes or scales of discriminabilities. These terms will be discussed more fully in the material which follows.

The most important of the scales in cell 1 are those constructed by the methods of magnitude and ratio estimation, methods developed by Stevens (1966 and many other papers) at the Harvard Laboratory of Psychophysics over the past thirty-five years. A great deal of work on these scales has also been done by Eisler, Ekman (see esp. Ekman 1958 on ratio estimation), and others at the Psychological Laboratories of the University of Stockholm. In general these methods yield scales constituting measurement at a ratio level (Stevens 1946, 1957), as the result of procedures in which subjects are presented with stimuli and asked to give direct estimates of their magnitudes on some designated continuum. The estimates may be given in widely varying ways; they may be in the form of numerical estimates or of ratios between pairs of stimuli, or they may be given by matching the stimuli to some other continuum entirely, in which case numbers need not be used by the subject at all. In another variant of the general approach the subject varies the stimuli until their magnitudes or the ratios between them are matched to some other designated continuum or numerical level. These variant procedures, known as magnitude or ratio production, are probably of limited use in social science, since few of the stimuli of interest to social scientists can be easily manipulated.

Good introductions to the use of these methods in the social sciences are still, unfortunately, rather few. Stevens (1966, 1968) provides a fairly complete summary and lists many references. Ekman (1958, 1961) provides two important technical papers. Shinn (1969a, 1969b, 1971a) provides examples of their use in sociology and political science. Sellin and Wolfgang (1964) provide a full-scale application in the area of juvenile delinquency. Hamblin (1971*a*, 1971*b*; also Chapter 3 in this volume) has provided several papers dealing with the theory of these scales and their application in sociology. Finally, Rainwater (1971) has in progress a series of studies which apply the method in the area of social stratification. These studies should make an important contribution, although little has yet appeared in print.

Similarity scaling, also included in scales of this type, has received relatively little attention, although it appears to have promise in social science applications. The work of Eisler (1960) and Ekman, Goude, and Waern (1961) will be discussed below. Briefly, it is a method in which subjects are asked to judge directly the similarity between the magnitudes of pairs of stimuli; this information can then be processed to yield direct measures of the magnitudes of each stimulus. The format is simple, and the judgments appear relatively easy to make.

Category scales, cell 2 in Table 4.1, are the most common of all social science scales; the prototype is the familiar row of boxes with a label on each end to define the continuum, such as "good-bad" or "prejudiced-unprejudiced." Their great advantage is their simplicity; their great disadvantage, the fact that they do not produce estimates of the perceptual magnitudes of the stimuli used, but rather produce estimates of the relative discriminability of the stimuli, which yield, for most purposes, much less useful information. The measurement of these discriminabilities is at an interval level, but there is no simple way to pass from this to interval values for the magnitudes of the stimuli, which is generally what is desired.

The indirect methods, developed by Thurstone (1927; also Torgerson 1958, chaps. 8-10), are generally known as the methods of paired comparisons and of successive intervals. Subjects are asked either to choose which of two stimuli has "more" of a given quality, as in the method of paired comparisons, or to order stimuli with respect to the continuum, as in the method of successive intervals. In the latter case the ordering may be simplified by limiting the number of categories given the subject; the task will then seem quite similar to a category scaling project. The difference is significant, however, for in the method of successive intervals the subject is not expected to provide information of higher than an ordinal level. In either of the two methods, the ordinal data provided by the subject are raised to a higher level of measurement by the application of a set of assumptions concerning the way his judgments must be distributed. These assumptions are not subject to test except in terms of their internal consistency, and conceptually, any number of sets of assumptions might be used. Only two sets are of practical interest: Thurstone's (1927) Case V, and Stevens's (1959*b*, 1961) Case VI. In the former case we get an interval scale, but one in which the scale values represent discriminabilities rather than magnitudes; these are the scales in our cell 4. If we apply Stevens's set of assumptions, Case VI, we get a scale of magnitudes, but the level of measurement is that of a logarithmic interval scale, and this, for reasons we shall discuss in detail below, is of little practical utility.

In spite of what has been said above concerning the results of category scales and of Thurstonian scales when Case V assumptions are applied, we shall see that in a limited number of situations these methods will yield interval-level scales whose values represent true magnitudes rather than discriminabilities. Why this is so will be of some interest, and the fact that this is so will allow us in those situations to use category scales, which are very simple, in lieu of the more complex magnitude-scale methods.

The Relation Between Category and Magnitude Scales

The foregoing discussion and Table 4.1 suggest that there are a number of approaches to the scaling problem, and that we should not expect all of them to give the same results when applied to the same problem. What, then, are the specific relations between the results of the various scaling procedures? This question is an important one, for we shall understand what is going on when we "scale" something only to the extent that we can explain in convincing theoretical terms the differences which result when different approaches to the problem are used.

There is another, more practical reason for concern with this problem. Some approaches to the scaling problem are simpler than others, and some are appropriate in particular research situations where others are not. It is obviously desirable, then, to be able to transform the results of a scale with which data are collected into equivalent forms more useful in data analysis. In practice, this usually means that we should like to be able to use simple category scales in actual research, and then correct the results obtained so that they will be as accurate as they would be had they originally been collected by the more complex techniques of ratio or magnitude estimation. We shall be able to do this, of course, only when we know the theoretical relations between different scale forms.

On most continua, a category scale will stand somewhere between a linear and a logarithmic relation to a magnitude scale of the same variable. The plot is approximately as shown in Figure 4.1 (Stevens 1960; Galanter and Messick 1961; Stevens and Galanter 1957). What this means is that for some reason the category widths increase as we move up the category scale; that is, it takes a greater difference between two stimuli at the top of a scale than at the bottom to produce a perceptual difference of one category-scale unit.

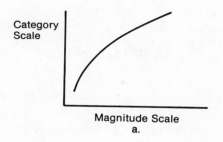
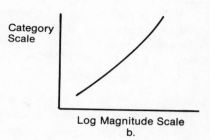

Figure 4.1.

The simplest explanation of this phenomenon is offered by Stevens and Galanter (1957), who argue that it is simply due to the increasing difficulty of distinguishing between two stimuli as their magnitudes increase. Two stimuli close together on the low end of the scale are relatively easily discriminated and hence are assigned different category values, while two stimuli equally close together toward the high end of the continuum are easily confused and hence tend to be assigned the same category value. Two coffee tables differing in length by a foot are easily distinguished, but two city blocks differing by the same amount are not. This explanation seems intuitively reasonable, but some research findings appear to contradict it. For example, Torgerson (1960), in an experiment in which subjects judged pieces of paper with respect to both *lightness* and *darkness*, found that although the effect occurred on both continua, relatively dark stimuli were confused no more often when judged for darkness than when judged for lightness. Thus it does not seem that sheer inability to distinguish between stimuli is at the root of the matter.

Eisler's Equation

Following on Torgerson's experiment, Eisler (1962a) worked out a mathematical proof to show that, under certain conditions, the relation between the two scales must be logarithmic. Torgerson had found—

1. that when lightness and darkness were judged on a category scale, the judgments were complementary, that is, their sum was constant (on a nine-point scale, for example, a stimulus judged "3" for lightness would be judged "7" for darkness, which suggests that the relation judged was one of distance from one end or the other of a scale defined by the poles "light" and "dark");

2. that when the stimuli were judged on magnitude scales, the relation between their scores was one of reciprocality, that is, their product was a constant (consistent judgments, then, might be 100, 1; 50, 2; 25, 4; etc., which suggests that the judgments involved ratios of the stimulus magnitudes, rather than distances).

If, in addition, it can be assumed that the function relating stimulus scores on category and magnitude scales is independent of the direction of measurement—that is, if the function is the same for both lightness and darkness—it can be shown that the relation must be logarithmic. The equation is

$$K = \alpha \log R + \beta ,\tag{1}$$

where K is the category scale score, R is the score of the magnitude scale, and α and β are empirical constants.[1]

Similarity

Equation (1) is very incomplete, from a theoretical point of view, because it does not explain *why* the relations observed by Torgerson should hold. Some work in similarity scaling (Eisler and Ekman 1959; Eisler 1960; Ekman, Goude, and Waern 1961) may provide an insight. Ekman, Goude, and Waern argue that, while magnitudes are directly judged when the magnitude or ratio estimation techniques are used, "similarity, as it is naively conceived" (1961, p. 222), is judged when category techniques are used. They asked subjects to judge the magnitudes of various stimuli and then to estimate the subjective similarity between pairs of stimuli, and were able to show that

$$S_{ij} = \frac{2R_i}{R_i + R_j} \quad (R_i < R_j) ,\tag{2}$$

where S_{ij} is the similarity between stimuli i and j, and R_i and R_j are the magnitudes of the respective stimuli. This is a very simple equation, characterized by Eisler and Ekman (1959) as an empirical equation without empirical constants. It suggests that a subject, in estimating similarity, may be comparing the ratio of the *shared* magnitudes, $2R_i$, of two stimuli to the *total* magnitude, $R_i + R_j$, of the two; or, alternatively, comparing the ratio of the smaller, R_i, to the mean, $(R_i + R_j)/2$. Similarity, then, varies from zero to one (identity).

1. The proof of this statement is contained in Eisler (1962*a*, p. 83). I will not attempt to summarize the mathematical steps necessary to demonstrate the proof, but the reasoning proceeds from the obvious fact that two linearly related variables must both be linearly related to a third variable if either one is. If we assumed, for the moment, that a magnitude scale were linearly related to a category scale of the same variable (e.g., lightness), it would also be linearly related to the category scale for the opposite variable (darkness), since the two category scales are known to be linearly related to each other. If, as we assume, the same relation between the two scale types holds for both lightness and darkness, the two magnitude scales would themselves have to be linearly related; yet we know that in fact they are reciprocally related. It turns out that the only function relating the two scale types which satisfies both the two empirical conditions observed by Torgerson and the assumption that the function is the same for both the variable and its opposite is the logarithmic function.

If it is true that judges subjectively equate similarity in assigning category scale scores, then for adjacent categories in such a scale

$$S_{12} = S_{23} = S_{34} = ... = S_{(n-1)n} \, ,$$

and it follows from equation (2) that

$$R_2/R_1 = R_3/R_2 = R_4/R_3 = ... = R_n/R_{(n-1)} \, , \tag{3}$$

which indicates that equating similarities is the same as equating ratios of stimuli in adjacent categories. This is what Stevens (1959) calls a logarithmic interval scale, and since we don't know what the ratio is, we cannot get from this scale to an ordinary interval or ratio scale without more information.

The fact that ratios seem to be equated suggests that a logarithmic relation is to be expected between category and magnitude scales. As Junge (1960) has shown, however, it is necessary to define the concept of the subjective difference between two stimuli as $d_{ij} = 1 - S_{ij}$, that is, as the complement of the similarity, because similarities, which are ratios, cannot be added. When the stimuli are close together, however, so that their similarities approach one and their differences approach zero, the differences between adjacent stimuli may be added to obtain the difference between two stimuli more widely separated. Since in integration we let the differences between adjacent stimuli approach zero at the limit, we can consider the concept of difference to be additive.

Since if the similarities of stimuli are equated in category scaling their differences as here defined must also be equated, we can write (following Junge 1960):

$$K_j - K_i = \Delta K = k(1 - S_{ij}) \, . \tag{4}$$

If we replace R_i with R and R_j with $R + \Delta R$ in equation (2) and substitute in equation (4), we have

$$\Delta K = k \, \frac{\Delta R}{2R + \Delta R} \, ,$$

or

$$2R\Delta K + \Delta R \Delta K = k\Delta R \, .$$

If ΔK and ΔR approach zero and are replaced by differentials, then

$$2R \, dK + dR \, dK = k \, dR \, .$$

Neglecting the second-order term, since it approaches zero at the limit, and rearranging, we obtain

$$dK = \frac{k}{2} \frac{dR}{R} ,$$

the integral of which is

$$K = \alpha \log R + \beta \quad (\alpha = \frac{k}{2}) , \tag{5}$$

which is identical to equation (1).

The concept of similarity and the empirical work supporting it, then, have led us to the same result as Eisler's more abstract analysis, that is, to the prediction that the relation between the two scale forms will be perfectly logarithmic. But this is not the relation we find empirically; typically, it is close to logarithmic but does not quite make it (Stevens and Galanter 1957). Eisler (1962a) accounts for the discrepancy in the following way: Assume that the subject in a category-scaling task spaces the stimuli such that those in adjacent categories are *equally easy to discriminate*. This seems equivalent to saying that *differences*, as Junge uses the term, are equated, and since $d_{ij} = 1 - S_{ij}$, it would not be possible empirically to distinguish between this point of view and that of Ekman, Goude, and Waern.

Now further assume that discriminability is the inverse of variability of judgment; that is, as the observed variability of estimates increases, discrimination between two stimuli becomes more difficult. We can then write the relation between the category and magnitude scales in the form

$$\Delta K = \Delta R / \sigma_R , \tag{6}$$

where σ_R, the standard deviation of the judgments of magnitude estimation, is the measure of the variability of estimates.

The Weber Function

The standard deviation of these estimates, however, may be expressed as a function of the magnitude of the estimates, the relation between the two being known as the Weber function.[2] If the Weber function is taken to be linear (Fig. 4.2), it may be written

$$\sigma_R = q + kR , \tag{7}$$

2. "Weber's law," after E. H. Weber, was the term originally used to describe the relation between the magnitude of a stimulus and the amount of change in the stimulus that would be just perceptible to an observer. Weber's law stated that the ratio between these two quantities would be constant (Guilford 1954, pp. 23-25). The term has more recently

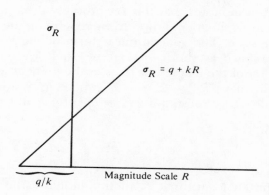

Figure 4.2.

and substituting this expression in equation (6) yields

$$\Delta K = \Delta R/(q + kR).$$

If ΔK and ΔR approach zero and are replaced by differentials, we have

$$dK = dR/(q + kR),\qquad(8)$$

the integral of which is

$$K = \alpha \log (q + kR) + \beta.\qquad(9)$$

This equation indicates that the relation between K and R will be perfectly logarithmic only when $q = 0$.

This relation is at variance, however, with the purely logarithmic relation, which, as we noted at the beginning of this discussion, is implied by the three assumptions given. At least one of the assumptions must be wrong, then, and Eisler suggests that it is the assumption of reciprocality between the scores on the magnitude scale; a close look at

come to be used to describe the relation between the perceived magnitude of a stimulus and the variability of the perception (Eisler 1963c, p. 265). In this usage, Weber's law is said to hold when the variability of perception is directly proportional to the perceptual magnitude. The linear generalization of this law is given by equation (7) and Figure 4.2. There will be a specific Weber function associated with any given scaling method and any subjective continuum. Typical functions empirically found associated with magnitude estimation are strict proportionality (Weber's law), linear increasing (Fig. 4.4) and irregular (Fig. 4.8). The Weber function associated with a category scale is typically constant, and when *pairs* of stimuli are presented and respondents are asked to estimate the ratio between their magnitudes (ratio estimation), or their similarity with respect to some dimension, the Weber function is typically a parabola (Eisler 1963c, p. 269). It will become apparent as the discussion develops that the Weber function associated with a scale type on a given continuum is critically important in determining the form of the relation between that scale type and other scales for the same continuum.

Torgerson's data indicates that this reciprocality does not quite hold. We can correct this situation, however, by redefining the zero point of the magnitude scale. The general linear form of the Weber function may be diagrammed as shown in Figure 4.2. If we now define the "true" zero point of the magnitude scale as the point at which variability vanishes, we have $R' = R + (q/k)$, where R' is the "corrected" magnitude-scale score. Substituting $R' - (q/k)$ for R in equation (9) we have

$$K = \alpha \log R' + \beta , \qquad (10)$$

which is the purely logarithmic relation indicated earlier by equations (1) and (5). In addition, the assumption of reciprocality of magnitude scale scores should hold if these scores are corrected by the addition of the constant q/k (Eisler 1962a, pp. 86-87).[3]

We may conclude from this discussion that it is proper to conceptualize the category-scaling task in terms of equating similarities, differences, or discriminabilities, since all these appear to be different ways of describing the same phenomenon. Whichever conceptualization is adopted, however, we must treat the results of category scaling as at best a logarithmic interval scale, from which it is not possible to proceed through a simple transformation to either a ratio or a conventional interval scale (Stevens 1959a).[4]

We also have a precise expression for the relation between category and magnitude scales. To summarize, we must assume—

1. that a complementary relation holds between category-scale scores for a variable and its inverse;

3. Just how the parameter q/k should be interpreted is not entirely clear, but there is some evidence that it may result from errors in the judgments subjects make of perceptual magnitude, and to be dependent to some extent on method. The importance of this parameter was first pointed out by Eisler (1962a), and the first empirical test of his theory (1962b) suggested that the parameter was independent of experimental conditions, if not of method. His subsequent work, however (1963b, p. 248), seemed to show that the parameter varied with the difficulty of judgments; as they became easier to make, the q/k values decreased. It also seems that the q/k correction is not needed when a ratio-estimation technique is used instead of magnitude estimation (Kuennapas and Wikstroem 1963, p. 620; Jones and Shorter 1972). Finally, it is at least possible that a magnitude-estimation procedure in which there is no standard stimulus to define the unit will result in judgments yielding $q/k = 0$ (Walter H. Corson 1971: personal communication)

4. This is so because we know only that adjacent points on the scale are separated by equal ratios, but we do not know what the ratio is. We are permitted to assume the location of the zero point and *one* other point, and thus establish a unit for the scale, but this will still not allow us to determine scale scores for other points, since we do not know, and under the model used, *cannot* know, the necessary ratio between adjacent points. The use of interval statistics with category-scale data thus appears to be clearly unjustified in a theoretical sense, although ordinal statistics would be appropriate, since an ordinal scale *is* contained in the logarithmic interval scale. Of course it still may be advisable, in practical research, to use interval statistics, but the dangers in so doing should be understood.

2. that the linear generalization of Weber's law holds for the continuum under study, that is, that $\sigma_R = q + kR$; and

3. that a reciprocal relation holds between magnitude-scale scores for a variable and its inverse, when each is corrected by the addition of q/k.

If these assumptions are true, we may expect the relation between the category and magnitude scale scores of a variable to be given by

$$K = \alpha \log [R + (q/k)] + \beta , \tag{11}$$

in which R' has been replaced by $R + (q/k)$.

Empirical Confirmation

In the section that follows we shall present data which appear to confirm the validity of the model described above. This model applies only to situations in which the Weber function is linear, and we will therefore have to modify it somewhat in dealing with situations in which this is not the case.

The first attempt to validate this model was made by Eisler (1962*b*), who compared magnitude and category judgments of the loudness and softness of "white" noise (i.e., noise composed of many mixed frequencies). The results appeared to validate the model convincingly for this continuum, but it could not be assumed that the model would hold for other continua, particularly for continua of interest to social scientists, without a good bit of further testing.

The Importance of Political Offices

As a continuum for a second test of the model we chose "the importance of political offices." Whether or not this continuum is of great theoretical value may be open to question, but for us it seemed appropriate, for it offered the dual advantages of providing clear opposites (importance-unimportance) and of seeming relatively easy to judge. The model should hold for this continuum, then, if it is to hold for any.

Twenty-nine participants in a summer seminar in political science were used as subjects; all were experienced teachers of political science or related subjects, so that all could be assumed to possess the expertise necessary to make judgments of the relative importance of political offices. Of the twenty-nine, three were either uncooperative or gave very inconsistent data and were therefore eliminated.

Stimuli were thirteen political offices, ranging from that of alderman in a small city to that of president; all were generally elective offices, with the exceptions of Supreme Court justice and federal judge.

Subjects were asked to express their judgments by using both a simple nine-point category scale and a variant of magnitude estimation in which, rather than give numerical estimates, the subjects draw lines whose lengths are proportional to the magnitudes involved. Since we know from previous work that the perceived length of a line is proportional to its physical length (Stevens and Galanter 1957; Stevens 1966), we can use the line lengths as direct substitutes for numerical estimates.

Results. The data were summarized by taking the geometric means of the magnitude judgments of "importance" and "unimportance" for each stimulus, and by taking the arithmetic means of the category judgments. The pooled data are presented in Table 4.2.

Table 4.2. Summary of Pooled Estimates of Importance and Unimportance of Thirteen Political Offices on Category and Magnitude Scales

	Importance		Unimportance	
	Magnitude	Category	Magnitude	Category
1. President	138.75	8.88	7.31	1.21
2. Supreme Court justice	111.31	7.77	16.62	2.33
3. U.S. senator	93.13	7.17	23.85	3.09
4. U.S. representative	74.01	6.10	36.35	3.93
5. Federal judge	68.49	5.93	44.46	4.09
6. Mayor of New York City	66.48	6.01	44.61	4.27
7. State governor	63.79	5.83	46.71	4.52
8. State senator*	24.00	4.36	73.54	5.56
9. County judge	19.48	3.35	97.70	6.83
10. Mayor of small city	14.95	3.00	116.29	7.38
11. County sheriff	12.22	2.61	115.85	7.28
12. Justice of the peace	8.55	1.97	135.68	8.02
13. Alderman in small city	8.17	1.97	135.67	8.09

*The office of state senator was chosen as the standard and assigned an arbitrary value of 24.0. All other judgments on the magnitude scales were made relative to this standard.

The model may be tested directly with the data given in Table 4.2, plus information on the amount of variation between individual estimates. As we noted above, Eisler began with three assumptions, which are directly testable. The first of these was that the category scales of a variable (importance) and of its inverse (unimportance) should be complementary, that is, should add to a constant. In Figure 4.3 we have plotted the two category scales against each other, and it is apparent that this assumption holds fairly well. The regression line, fitted by least squares, has a slope of $-.986$, close to the predicted value of -1.0. The correlation is $-.998$, and inspection of the plot shows only random deviations from the regression line.

The second of Eisler's assumptions was that Weber's law would ade-

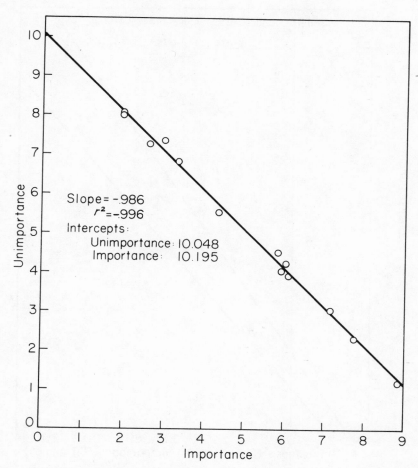

Figure 4.3. Mean judgments of "importance" and "unimportance" of political offices (category scales).

quately describe the relation between the variability of the estimates and the magnitude of the mean estimates; that is, $\sigma_R = q + kR$, where R is the mean response to each stimulus. Figure 4.4 shows the extent to which this is true. The circles indicate mean judgments of importance for each of the thirteen offices, the triangles represent similar judgments of unimportance, and both are plotted against the corresponding standard deviations. The regression lines are fitted by eye and have slightly differing slopes, which indicates that the subjects found unimportance somewhat more difficult to judge than importance, as might be expected. The values for q/k, obtained by dividing the Y intercepts by the slopes, differ correspondingly; they are 18.2 for importance

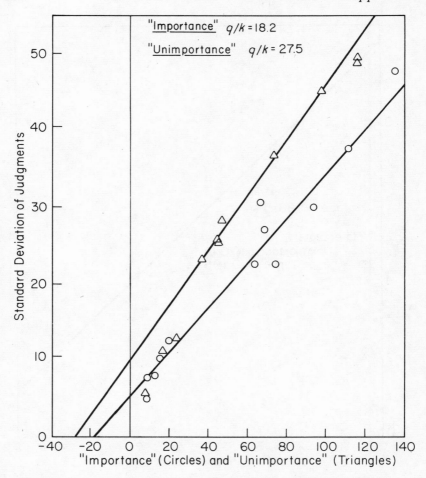

Figure 4.4. Standard deviations of judgments of "importance" and "unimportance" of political offices (magnitude scales) as a function of mean judgments.

judgments and 27.5 for unimportance judgments. The fit of the data to the regression lines, while not perfect, is high enough for us to place reasonable faith in the validity of assumption 2. In calculating the regression lines, the point corresponding to judgments of importance of the office of state senator was eliminated, since this was the reference point and the standard deviation was necessarily zero. For the unimportance curve, only the six points in the middle of the range were used, since the extreme points on both ends of the line were thought to be biased downward as a result of the experimental design.[5]

5. Since paper of a finite size had to be used for the questionnaire, extremely large judgments tended to produce lines as long as the paper was wide. Such lines were easily

To test assumption 3, we plotted, on logarithmic coordinates, the magnitude-scale values for the mean judgments for each office (see Fig. 4.5). Circles in this case indicate the means as calculated, and triangles the values corrected by adding the respective q/k's. The regression line is fitted by eye. Again, the results are not as neat as we might like, but they seem good enough to warrant accepting the validity of assumption 3.

The extent to which the model correctly describes the relation be-

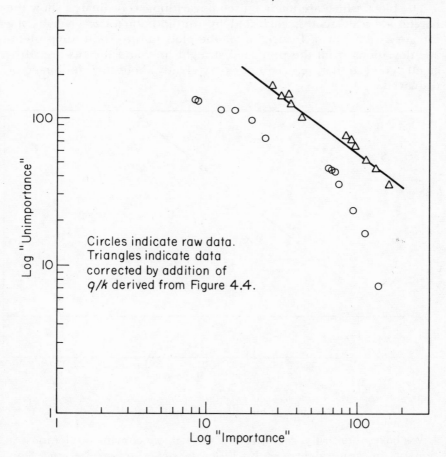

Figure 4.5. Mean judgments of "importance" and "unimportance" of political offices (magnitude scales).

reproduced in subsequent judgments, resulting in lower standard deviations for these judgments than would otherwise have been expected. At the low end of the scale the effect is less marked, and it is almost unnoticeable in the "importance" data. For the "unimportance" data the three lower points seemed obviously to be biased, however, and were therefore ignored in plotting the regression line. A second approach to the problem, described below, confirms this judgment.

tween the two scale types is indicated by Figures 4.6 and 4.7, and by the following equations:

Importance: $K_I = 3.53 \log (R_I + 18.2) - 9.49$,
Unimportance: $K_U = 4.32 \log (R_U + 27.5) - 14.05$,

where K_I = category scale of importance;
                              K_U = category scale of unimportance;
                              R_I = magnitude scale of importance;
                              R_U = magnitude scale of unimportance.

The plots, which are made on semilogarithmic coordinates, show the magnitude-scale scores, corrected by the addition of q/k, versus the category-scale scores. Inspection of the plots fails to show any systematic deviations from the predicted straight line, and the fits are sufficiently good so that we need not worry greatly about the random error displayed.

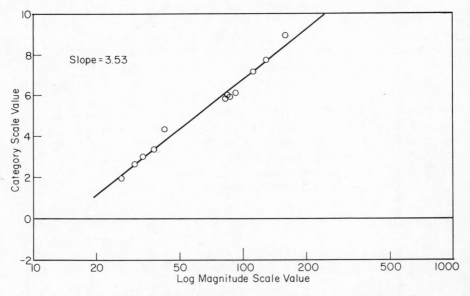

Figure 4.6.   Mean category-scale judgments of "importance" of political offices as function of mean magnitude-scale judgments.

We have, then, what seems to be a reasonably convincing demonstration of the applicability of the Eisler model to a social science continuum. Each of the assumptions necessary was found to hold for the data in question, and the predicted relation between the two scale forms was found to hold to a very good approximation. For this continuum, then, and these stimuli, category-scale scores are a logarithmic function of magnitude-scale scores and thus must be considered to yield either a logarithmic interval scale of the magnitudes of the

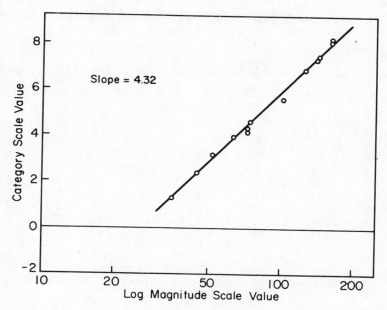

Figure 4.7. Mean category-scale judgments of "unimportance" of political offices as function of mean magnitude-scale judgments.

stimuli, or (Table 4.2) an interval scale of the cumulated differences or discriminabilities of the stimuli.

Determinants of Social Status

Data from another experiment, in which we asked the subjects to estimate the levels of social status attaching to various levels of income and education, provide an opportunity for another test of this model. Judges were asked to give numerical estimates in the magnitude estimation judgments, and were also asked to make judgments using a seven-point category scale. The format of the latter was a variant of the semantic differential, in which the ends of the scale were termed "high status" and "low status," respectively.

Data necessary to test the model of scale relations are presented in Table 4.3. Columns 1-5 are self-explanatory. Column 6 gives corrected standard deviations, "corrected" here meaning that the standard deviations of column 5, computed in the usual way about the arithmetic mean, have been multiplied by the ratios of the geometric to the arithmetic means. This procedure is suggested by Kuennapas and Wikstroem (1963), who argue that this makes the standard deviation more suitable for use with geometric means. While they present no justification for this statement, it seems reasonable, and the procedure seems to

Table 4.3. Summary of Data Relating Income and Education to Status Levels, Used to Test Eisler Model Relating Magnitude and Category Scales

Stimulus* (1)	Magnitude geo. means (2)	Magnitude arith. means (3)	Category arith. means (4)	SD (5)	SD-C (6)	1/SD-C (7)	Fechner integral (8)
A. Income data							
300	3.2	7.2		13.8	6.1	.164	1.00
1,500	22	28	1.59	23.7	18.5	.054	3.05
4,500	55	59	2.75	21.5	20.0	.050	4.77
6,000	74	78	3.24	25.1	23.8	.042	5.64
8,800	89	92	3.93	25.5	24.7	.040	6.26
12,000	123	128	4.55	37.6	36.1	.028	7.41
18,000	155	169	5.33	84	77	.013	8.07
26,000	194	207	5.39	76	71	.014	8.59
38,000	218	238	5.57	95	87	.0115	8.90
54,000	300	345	6.37	186	162	.0062	9.63
78,000	340	410	6.64	235	195	.0051	9.85
110,000	450	530	6.96	290	246	.0041	10.36
B. Education data							
2	7.3	11	1.03	8.8	5.8	.172	1.00
4	13	21	1.41	16.8	10.6	.094	1.76
8	30	37	2.23	19.0	15.4	.065	3.11
12	52	55	3.26	17.9	16.9	.059	4.48
14	79	79	4.45	9.8	9.8	.102	
16	100						
20	235	281	6.04	205	171	.0058	10.43
24	335	393	6.57	237	202	.0049	10.97

*Income in dollars in part A; years of education in part B.

have the effect of smoothing somewhat the relationship between the mean and the standard deviations. The effect, however, is not marked.

Columns 7 and 8 present the reciprocals of these corrected standard deviations and the "Fechner integrals," which we shall discuss in detail later.

Since in this case we do not have data for the inverses of the continua of interest, tests of the first and third of the three assumptions made earlier are not possible. The assumption that Weber's law in its linear generalization will hold may be tested, however, and Figure 4.8 shows the necessary plots of corrected standard deviations against geometric means. It is apparent that we are in some trouble on this assumption. There is considerably greater scatter about any possible regression line; a linear relation does not exist; and although the correlations obtained when least-squares regression lines are fitted are relatively high, the lines do not seem to adequately represent the data. In addition, the *Y*

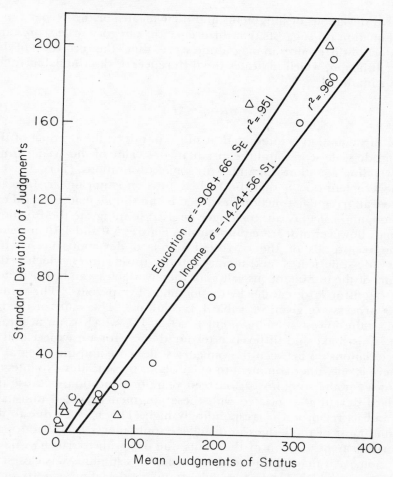

Figure 4.8. Standard deviation of magnitude judgments of status as function of mean judgments; income (circles) and education (triangles).

intercepts, which were positive in the previous test, are now negative, and this is not suggested by either our theory or the plots themselves.

All this suggests that equation (11) is not likely to describe accurately the relation between the scales, and this is in fact the case. The plots, not presented here, showed considerable systematic deviations from straight lines, particularly in the lower regions, and the deviations were such as to be worsened, rather than improved, by the q/k values we could calculate from the regression lines of Figure 4.8. We were forced, then, to take another approach to the problem.

Equation (11) was derived by integrating a differential equation one part of which was an expression describing the relation between the standard deviations of judgments and their means, or the Weber function. Equation (8) suggests that differences in category-scale scores are a product of differences in magnitude scores times the reciprocal of the Weber function, which indicates the difference, or discriminability, between stimuli:

$$dK = dR/(q + kR) .\qquad(8)$$

When this equation is integrated, it sums, in effect, the product of the magnitude scale scores and the instantaneous value of the Weber function, yielding equations (9) and, with some substitutions, (11).

The problem now is that the Weber function is not linear. Instead, we have an irregular function described by no simple mathematical expression, and calculus can no longer be used to integrate the function. We may, however, integrate numerically. Figures 4.9 and 4.10 are plots of the reciprocals of the corrected standard deviations versus the magnitude-scale scores; and the area under those curves, which is the product of the instantaneous values of these variables, can be calculated in a straightforward manner by the method of trapezoids.[6] The results of this process are given in Table 4.3, column 8. The value of the integral at the lowest stimulus point is set at 1.0, which is an arbitrary value. This makes no difference to our theory, for we expect only a linear relationship between the category scale score and the integral.

There is one other comment to make about these values. No integral is shown for the stimulus of fourteen years of education, because the standard deviation associated with these judgments seemed unusually low, and its reciprocal correspondingly high. This may be due to the fact that most of the judges were college sophomores, who had a particularly clear perception of the status due one with fourteen years of education; or it may be due to the fact that this stimulus was closest to the standard, which necessarily had a standard deviation of zero, or to

6. For a detailed discussion of this method see Eisler 1963*b*. The general idea can be sketched briefly, as follows: Equation (8) indicates that the category-scale score changes as a function of the magnitude-scale score multiplied by the reciprocal of the variability of the magnitude estimates at a given point. When Weber's law holds this variability is given by $\sigma_R = q + kR$, but when Weber's law does not hold we still have data on the variability at certain points on the continuum. Figure 4.9, for example, plots the reciprocals of the standard deviations as a function of the mean judgments. The concept of integration involves summing the value of an expression for every instantaneous value of the independent variable within a given range. In Figure 4.9 we know only a few values, but if we make the simplifying assumption that a linear relation between standard deviations and mean judgments exists between adjacent points, we can still estimate the value of the integral at each point for which we have data. This we do by assuming a value of the integral for the first (lowest) data point, and by adding to this the area under the curve between this and each succeeding data point. This area, of course, is that of the trapezoid described by the two data points and their projections on the X-axis, or the product of the difference in mean judgments and the mean variability between the two points in question.

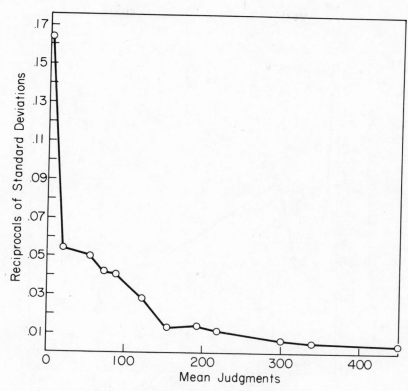

Figure 4.9. Reciprocals of standard deviations of judgments of status as function of mean judgments, status "income" data.

some other cause. We have no way of knowing, but it seemed best to eliminate the doubtful point. The integral calculated, then, is the area beneath the *dotted* line in Figure 4.10.

Our theory predicts that there will be a linear relation between the category scale scores and values of the Fechner integral at each point. Figures 4.11 and 4.12 demonstrate the extent to which this is the case. As can readily be seen, the fit of the points to the straight lines is very good, the correlations are very high, and there appears to be only random scatter around the regression lines.

Recalculating the Relation for "Unimportance" of Political Offices

In an earlier report of this research (Shinn 1969*b*), the regression line in Figure 4.4 was calculated by fitting at least-squares lines through all the data points shown, with the result that a smaller q/k was used for the unimportance data. This had no great effect, but it did result in the appearance of a slight curvature in Figure 4.7. S. S. Stevens, in a per-

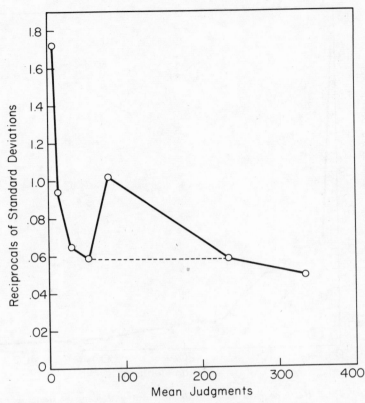

Figure 4.10. Reciprocal of standard deviations of judgments of status as function of mean judgments, status "education" data.

sonal communication, pointed this out and argued that the data did *not*, therefore, demonstrate that the relation between the scales was logarithmic. In an attempt to answer this criticism, I calculated the Fechner integrals for the data in question, using the methods just described. If the data given in Figure 4.4 had accurately described the Weber function, the relation between the category-scale scores and the Fechner integrals should have been linear, as we have just seen. In fact, however, the relation was not linear in the lower range; the bottom three points showed considerable deviation from the straight line. It was at this point that I decided to let the six points in the middle range determine the Weber function to be used, and the result was Figure 4.4 as it is shown. The observed standard deviations from the bottom three points were "adjusted" so that they fell on the line, and these adjusted values were then used in calculating the Fechner integrals. The calcula-

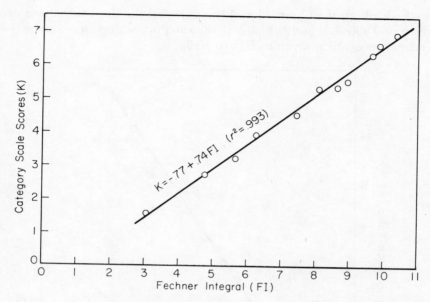

Figure 4.11. Category-scale scores for status as function of Fechner integral of magnitude-scale scores, status "income" data.

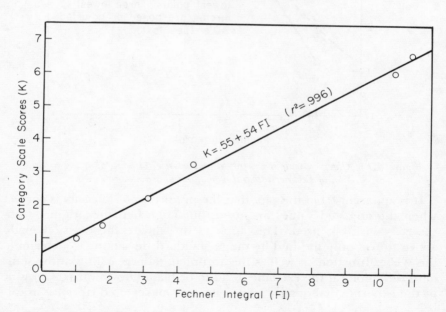

Figure 4.12. Category-scale scores for status as function of Fechner integral of magnitude-scale scores, status "education" data.

tions with both the observed and the adjusted standard deviations are given in Table 4.4, and the plot of the category-scale scores versus the Fechner integrals is given in Figure 4.13.[7]

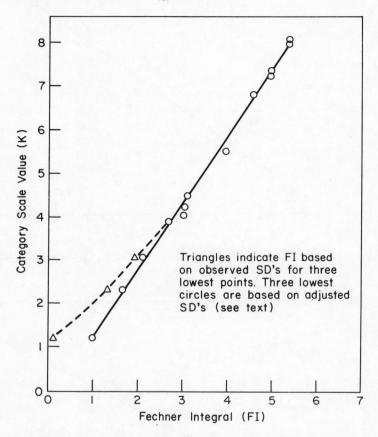

Figure 4.13. Category-scale scores for "unimportance" of political offices as function of Fechner integral of magnitude-scale scores.

It is apparent from the plot that the prediction of linearity is correct when the adjusted values are used, but not when the originally observed values are used. This appears to validate the decision made above to use only the middle-range standard deviations to determine the Weber function, as well as the argument (above, n. 5) that the standard deviations at the extremes tend to be biased downward as a result of the experimental design used. This bias makes no difference in cal-

7. In these calculations, the standard deviations were not "corrected," as they were in Table 4.3, by multiplying them by the ratio of the geometric to the arithmetic mean. The results without using this correction are so similar to those achieved when it is used that the extra effort does not seem to be justified.

culating the Fechner integrals at the high end of the scale, for here the standard deviations are high, their reciprocals correspondingly small, and the calculations are very insensitive to small errors. At the low end of the scale, however, the effect is critical.

This recalculation also demonstrates, as we would expect, that the procedure of Fechnerian integration, when the Weber function is in fact linear, yields results equivalent to the logarithmic relation predicted by equation (11).

Table 4.4. Summary of Data on "Unimportance" of Political Offices Used to Test the Model Relating Category and Magnitude-Scale Scores

Stimulus (1)	Magnitude Geo. Means (2)	Category Arith. Means (3)	SD (4)	1/SD (5)	Fechner Integral (6)
President	7.31	1.21	5.76 (12.50)	.1740 (.0800)	.11 (1.0)
Supreme Court justice	16.62	2.33	11.17 (15.7)	.0895 (.0638)	1.33 (1.67)
U.S. senator	23.85	3.09	12.89 (18.3)	.0777 (.0547)	1.94 (2.10)
U.S. representative	36.35	3.93	23.16	.0430	2.69
Federal judge	44.46	4.09	25.76	.0389	3.02
Mayor, N.Y.C.	44.61	4.27	25.51	.0398	3.03
Governor	46.71	4.52	28.24	.0354	3.11
State senator	73.54	5.56	36.80	.0272	3.95
County judge	97.70	6.83	45.13	.0222	4.55
County sheriff	115.85	7.28	48.85	.0205	4.94
Mayor, small city	116.29	7.38	49.49	.0202	4.95
Alderman, small city	135.67	8.09	45.77	.0219	5.36
Justice of peace	135.68	8.02	47.81	.0210	5.36

NOTE: Figures in parentheses indicate SD's adjusted to fall on the regression line in Figure 4.4, and calculations based on these SD's.

Interpretation of Category Scales

The findings described above suggest a revised interpretation of category scales. When Weber's law in its linear generalization holds, integration of the expression for a change in the category scale leads to a logarithmic relation (eq. [11]) between the category and magnitude scales, and this relation led us to see the results of category scaling as a logarithmic interval scale, one in which adjacent points were separated by equal, although unknown, ratios.

But when Weber's law does not hold, integration leads to an irregular relation between the two scale types. The category scale remains a scale based on the equating of similarities, (or differences, or discriminabilities), but since discriminability is no longer a simple function of magnitude scale values, there is no simple relation between the category and magnitude scale scores. The category scale may still be thought of as the integral of the product of the magnitude scale and the reciprocal of the Weber function—that is, as a Fechner integral —but as we have seen, this integral does not lead to a simple relation between the two scales. Adjacent points on the category scale will not be separated by equal ratios when this condition exists, and the category scale under these conditions must be considered to yield only ordinal data about the stimulus magnitudes.

These findings seem to cast grave doubts on the adequacy of category scales as measurement devices, for there seems no easy way to interpret the scale scores in terms of magnitudes on an equivalent interval- or ratio-level scale. Category-scale scores must be interpreted in terms of similarities rather than magnitudes, and while it would be possible to calculate similarities with magnitudes known, it would not be possible to reverse the process unless other information were available. If one had magnitude judgments for a set of stimuli, one could easily calculate equivalent category-scale scores, using equation (11) if Weber's law held, or the numerical integration process described above if it did not hold. This is so because the constants α and β in equation (11) are arbitrary in the sense that values on the category (K) scale are determined only within a linear transformation, so that we could consider equivalent all sets of K-scale scores derived by assuming any values at all for α and β. The same is true for the relation between the category-scale scores and the Fechner integrals.

But this would not be true if the process were reversed. If in equation (11) we solve for $R + (q/k)$, we have

$$R + (q/k) = e^{K-\beta/\alpha}$$

Since R scores are determined only within a ratio transformation, we may define the unit by setting α equal to any constant. But we may not assume a value for β, since a change in this value would determine a new set of scores which would not agree with the previous set within a ratio transformation, and this agreement is a necessary requirement for a ratio-level scale. In fact, since the constant appears in an exponent, a change in it would result in new scores which would not agree with previous scores even within a linear transformation; this is why we use the term *logarithmic interval scale* to describe the results of the category-scaling technique.

The discussion so far has proceeded on the assumption that Weber's law holds, but it will be readily seen that if Weber's law does not hold, the situation is made more rather than less complex, and the same basic problem remains.

On a hierarchy of scales, then, we must see the category scale as at best a logarithmic interval scale—superior to an ordinal scale, which can easily be derived from it; inferior to a ratio scale, from which it could be derived; and on an equivalent level with an interval scale, in the sense that neither could be derived from the other (Stevens 1959a).

There is only one sure solution to the problem. If it is felt necessary to use category-scaling techniques, because of their simplicity, in a research problem, it will be necessary to establish the relation between the category scale and a corresponding ratio-level scale, for the stimuli in question, either in a pretest or with a subsample of the population of interest. Such a test involves scaling the stimuli by both methods and then regressing the category-scale scores on the magnitude scores, which thus determines the constants in equation (11) if Weber's law holds, or an equivalent set of scale scores if it does not. With this information the category scale can then be used to collect data in further research, and the results easily converted to equivalent measurements on a ratio level.

The General Psychophysical Differential Equation and Similarity Scaling

In more recent work Eisler (1963c, 1965a; Mashhour 1964) has derived a more general statement of the dependence of interscale relations on the respective Weber functions involved. He shows (1963c, pp. 266-67) that the following equation for the general relation between two scale types can be derived:

$$\frac{dy}{dx} = \frac{\sigma_y\,(y)}{\sigma_x\,(x)} \, , \tag{12}$$

where the right-hand term in the equation refers to the ratio of the Weber functions of the two scale types. This equation he terms a General Psychophysical Differential Equation (GPDE). For the category scale the Weber function is typically a constant; therefore, if we assume that the Weber function for a magnitude scale is given by

$$\sigma_R = q + kR \, ,$$

and let y and x represent the category scale K and the magnitude scale R, respectively, then substitution of the Weber functions just given into equation (12) and integration of the resulting equation will again yield equation (11):

$$K = \alpha \log [R + (q/k)] + \beta \, .$$

The GPDE could be thought of as simply a more general way to state the theory relating magnitude and category scales, which it is. But it also suggests that relations between other types of scales are also dependent on their respective Weber functions. In the same paper (1963c), Eisler goes on to show that equation (2),

$$S_{ij} = \frac{2R_i}{R_i + R_j} \quad (R_i < R_j),$$

given earlier for the relation between similarity scales and magnitude scales, can be derived from the GPDE, starting from the known fact that the Weber function is a parabola for pairs of stimuli when either similarities or ratios of magnitudes are estimated (Eisler 1960). Since magnitudes derived from a set of ratio estimates ordinarily agree within a ratio transformation with magnitudes estimated directly, equation (2) should hold in cases where the Weber function is either Weber's law or the linear generalization of Weber's law with the correction q/k used.

If we think of the parameter q/k as a correction to error introduced by the method used for constructing a magnitude scale, as argued above (n. 4), we might assume that in most cases the true Weber function would be Weber's law. Under that assumption, equation (2) could be used to convert similarity estimates to equivalent magnitude-scale scores.

County Judge
Federal Judge

Dissimilar: ____:____:____:____:____:____:____: Similar

Figure 4.14.

This possibility offers another way around the problem of category scales, for the format used in similarity scaling can be quite simple, and very much like a category scale. Thus we may be able to combine the simplicity of category-scaling procedures with the accuracy of magnitude-scaling procedures. For instance, data on the relative importance of various political offices could be developed by presenting subjects with pairs of offices in the format shown in Figure 4.14. and asking them to "rate the similarity of these offices with respect to their importance to society." The results of this procedure could be converted, by use of equation (2), to the equivalent magnitude-scale values. Evidence of the utility of this approach is rather limited (Eisler and

Table 4.5. *Summary of Relations among Different Scale Forms, under Differing Conditions of Weber Function for Magnitude Scales*

	Weber Function	Similarity* Scales (S)	Category Scales (K)	Thurstonian Scales (T)
Magnitude scales (R) / Magnitude estimation	Weber's law ($q/k = 0$) or linear generalization: $R + (q/k)$	$S_{ij} = \dfrac{2R_i}{R_i + R_j}$	$K = \alpha \log R + \beta$	$T = \alpha \log R + \beta$ (Case VI)
	Constant: metathetic continua	$S_{ij} = \dfrac{2}{1 + e^{(R_j - R_i)/\alpha}}$	$K = \alpha R + \beta$	$T = \alpha R + \beta$ (Case V)
	Irregular	$S_{ij} = \dfrac{2}{1 + e^{(FI_j - FI_i)/\alpha}}$	$K = \alpha FI + \beta$	$T = \alpha FI + \beta$ (Case ?)
Ratio estimation	Parabola (Eisler 1963c, p. 269)		$K = \alpha \log R + \beta$	$T = \alpha \log R + \beta$ (Case VI)
Similarity* scales (S)	Parabola (Eisler 1963c, p. 269)		$S_{ij} = \dfrac{2}{1 + e^{(K_j - K_i)/\alpha}}$	$S_{iJ} = \dfrac{2}{1 + e^{(T_j - T_i)/\alpha}}$
Category scales (K)	Constant (Eisler 1963c, p. 267)			$T = \alpha K + \beta$

NOTE: Throughout the table, α and β are arbitrary constants dependent on choice of units and origin.

*The relation between category and similarity scales is assumed constant for all conditions of the Weber function for magnitude scales, since under our theory the category scale is interpreted directly in terms of similarities or discriminabilities. It is also assumed that magnitude estimation under Weber's law and ratio estimation when the Weber function is a parabola yield equivalent results. From these assumptions the other relations involving the similarity scale can be derived, but only that involving the magnitude scale constructed by ratio estimation, with a parabolic Weber function, has been checked empirically.

Ekman 1959; Eisler 1960; Ekman, Goude, and Waern 1961), and none of it appears to have come from experiments using stimuli of interest to social scientists. It seems like a promising avenue, however, and one which should be investigated more fully.

Different Weber Functions

It is obvious from the discussion thus far that the Weber function on any continuum will have a great deal to do with the form of the relations between scale forms. We have dealt mainly with the case in which Weber's law or its linear generalization holds, and to a lesser extent with situations in which the Weber function is irregular. There will be some situations in which a magnitude scale is used, however, in which the Weber function will be constant; that is, the variability of estimates will not increase with the magnitude. This class of continua has been termed "metathetic" in contrast with the class in which Weber's law holds, which can be termed "prothetic" (Stevens 1957; Eisler 1963*a*). The class of metathetic continua is probably rather small, but for a continuum of this class the similarity relation will not be equation (2), but rather the relation given in Table 4.5, and the relation between the category and the magnitude scale will be linear. For this class of continua, then, the category scale could be regarded as producing true interval-level measurement.

Unfortunately, there appear to be few continua in this class, and probably fewer still of interest to social scientists, although there is some evidence (Kuennapas and Sillén 1965) that the dimension of political liberalism and conservatism is such a continuum. In view of the limited number of continua which appear to fall into this class, it appears prudent to verify the form of the Weber function before relying on the assumption that category scales and magnitude scales are linearly related.

Relations Involving Indirect (Thurstonian) Scales

It will be sufficient here to simply summarize the relations to be expected between the various scale types we have discussed and the scales constructed according to Thurstone's "law of comparative judgment" or "law of categorical judgment," with which are associated, respectively, the methods of paired comparisons and of successive intervals. An excellent description of the basic Thurstonian models is contained in Torgerson (1958, chaps. 8-10); and empirical work relating these scales to category and magnitude scales is described by Kuennapas and Sillén (1965), Ekman and Kuennapas (1962, 1963*a*, 1963*b*), and Kuennapas and Wikstroem (1963). By far the best treatment of the theory underlying the interscale relations is given by Eisler (1965*b*).

Basically, we find that when Weber's law or its linear generalization holds for the magnitude scale, scales constructed according to Thurstone's Case V stand in a logarithmic relation to a magnitude scale, and in a linear relation to a category scale. When the Weber function for the category scale is constant, all three scale types are linearly related. To understand why this is so, it is necessary to understand that the information developed empirically by Thurstonian methods is ordinal in nature, and that it is raised to a higher level by way of a set of arbitrary assumptions which may not be tested by the data themselves. In Case V—the usual case—the assumptions are (1) that perceptions of stimuli are normally distributed on the psychological continuum; (2) that their standard deviations are constant, which is to say that the Weber function is assumed to be constant; and (3) that the ordinal data may be interpreted as reflecting differences in the scale positions of the stimuli.

If these assumptions hold, it can be shown that the scale scores developed according to the model will agree with "true" scores within a linear transformation, and it is thus commonly argued that Case V produces an interval scale. As we have seen, however, the Weber function in estimating magnitudes is typically not constant at all, and there is also good evidence (Stevens and Guirao 1962) that perceptions of magnitudes are not normally, but rather are lognormally, distributed. If these conditions hold, but we apply the assumptions of Case V, we should not be surprised to get a scale which is a logarithmic function of a magnitude scale, since a logarithmic transformation of the magnitude-estimation data would be sufficient to make them normally distributed with constant standard deviations, as Case V assumes they are in the first place. Thus it seems clear that the observed logarithmic relation between Case V scales and magnitude scales results from applying an inappropriate set of assumptions to the data.

With metathetic continua, however, for which the Weber function for magnitude estimation is constant, the Case V assumptions are likely to be reasonably correct, and hence for these continua we get the observed linear relation between the scale forms.

It is possible, of course, to apply another set of assumptions to the ordinal data developed by Thurstone's methods. One possible set would be (1) lognormal distributions; (2) Weber's law, that is, standard deviations proportional to magnitudes; and (3) interpretation of the observed ordinal data in terms of ratios between stimuli rather than differences (Eisler's Case VI). If these assumptions are applied the data will produce a logarithmic interval scale. Unfortunately, it is not possible to get from this sort of scale to either a ratio or an interval scale without outside information, and therefore this scale has rather limited utility. As a practical matter, then, we find few situations in which either of the Thurstonian methods would produce satisfactory results, and since the experimental work involved in gathering the data is typically much greater than that for other methods, their use is not recommended.[8]

Summary and Conclusions

Table 4.5 provides a summary of the expected relations between the various scaling forms discussed in this chapter. The relations that have not been discussed specifically follow logically from the key relations whose theoretical and empirical foundations have been considered (see Table 4.5, n.*). It would not be difficult to design an experiment to check the form of each of the relations given.

From the practical standpoint of social science research, I would draw several conclusions from this information. First, it is obvious that some scaling methods are better than others for most research. The simple category scale, for instance, has been shown to be definitely nonlinear relative to perceived magnitude, and I would recommend that its use be severely curtailed; in its stead I prefer the routine use of magnitude- or ratio-estimation methods, since they provide data which easily meet the interval-level assumptions underlying many statistics and provide additional ratio-level information which may be useful in some contexts. As we move from linear to nonlinear hypotheses in much social theory, this additional capability will assume greater importance.

This is not to say that the category scale should never be used. In some cases accuracy of measurement is not very important, and here the nonlinearity in the scale will not be particularly troubling —especially when the range of the scale is narrow, for over short ranges the maximum divergence between a magnitude scale and the best category scale for the same stimuli will be small. Also, of course, for some continua which are "metathetic" in character category scales will provide undistorted measurement. Finally, it can always be argued that the category scale gives us accurate measurement in terms of the similarity or discriminability of the stimuli used, and where these quantities are of interest, there is nothing wrong with using category scales as the measure. But it seems likely that most social theorists will wish to deal with the perceptual magnitudes of variables in their theories, rather than with discriminabilities or the like, although the latter will certainly be of interest to those studying the process of perception itself.

I should like to qualify my blanket endorsement of magnitude scaling by noting again that there may be a good bit of potential in similar-

8. For a possible exception to this generalization, in situations involving existing data—such as roll-call votes—which might be interpreted as reflecting some sort of regularized conflict, see Shinn 1971*b*.

ity scaling, since when Weber's law holds the results of this method appear to be related to perceptual magnitudes in a simple manner. The possibility that this relationship exists for most continua of interest to social scientists should be carefully explored.

The Thurstonian methods have never been widely used, largely because of the labor involved in collecting data by the methods of paired comparisons or successive intervals. Thus few researchers will be upset to learn that these methods, too, should be avoided because of distorted results. Where the Case V results may be regarded as a true interval scale—that is, in situations in which the Weber function is linear—it has been shown that a category scale may also be used, and it will generally be much less difficult to administer and process. Case VI, because it produces data which must be regarded as a logarithmic interval scale, must be considered largely a technical curiosity.

My most general recommendation, however, is that a much greater level of interest in scaling and other aspects of measurement on the part of all social scientists should be encouraged. Scaling theory is indeed complex, but researchers who wish to use it should learn enough about how different scales work to avoid the more glaring mistakes in conducting their research. For measurement *is* important, and we shall not be able to achieve the advances in social theory which we might otherwise expect until social science researchers have the practical command of measurement techniques that is automatically expected in the other sciences.

References

Bonjean, Charles M., R. J. Hill, and S. Dale McLemore
  1967. *Sociological Measurement: An Inventory of Scales and Indices.* San Francisco: Chandler.
Eisler, Hannes
  1960. "Similarity in the Continuum of Heaviness with Some Methodological and Theoretical Considerations." *Scandinavian Journal of Psychology* 1:69-81.
  1962a. "On the Problem of Category Scales in Psychophysics." Ibid. 3:81-87.
  1962b. "Empirical Test of a Model Relating Magnitude and Category Scales." Ibid. 3:88-96.
  1963a. "How Prothetic is the Continuum of Smell?." Ibid. 4:29-32.
  1963b. "Magnitude Scales, Category Scales, and Fechnerian Integration." *Psychological Review* 70:243-53.
  1963c. "A General Differential Equation in Psychophysics: Derivation and Empirical Test." *Scandinavian Journal of Psychology* 4:265-72.
  1965a. "On Psychophysics in General and the General Psychophysical Differential Equation in Particular." Ibid. 6:85-102.
  1965b. "The Connection between Magnitude and Discrimination Scales and Direct and Indirect Scaling Methods." *Psychometrika* 30:271-89.
Eisler, Hannes, and Goesta Ekman
  1959. "A Mechanism of Subjective Similarity." *Acta Psychologica* 16:1-10.
Ekman, Goesta
  1958. "Two Generalized Ratio Scaling Methods." *Journal of Psychology* 45:287-95.
  1961. "A Simple Method for Fitting Psychophysical Power Functions." *Journal of Psychology* 51:343-50.
Ekman, Goesta, and Teodor Kuennapas
  1962. "Measurement of Aesthetic Value by Direct and Indirect Methods." *Scandinavian Journal of Psychology* 3:33-39.
  1963a. "A Further Study of Direct and Indirect Scaling Methods." Ibid. 4:77-80.
  1963b. "Scales of Conservatism." *Perceptual and Motor Skills* 16:329-34.
Ekman, Goesta, and Lennart Sjoberg
  1965. "Scaling." *Annual Review of Psychology* 16:451-74.
Ekman, Goesta, Gunnar Goude, and Yvonne Waern
  1961. "Subjective Similarity in Two Perceptual Continua." *Journal of Experimental Psychology* 61:222-27.
Fechner, Gustav T.
  1966. *Elements of Psychophysics.* Leipzig: Breitkopf & Hartel, 1860; New York: Holt, Rinehart & Winston. (Translated by H. E. Adler.)
Galanter, Eugene, and Samuel Messick
  1961. "The Relation between Category and Magnitude Scales of Loudness." *Psychological Review* 68:363-72.
Guilford, Joy Paul
  1954. *Psychometric Methods.* New York: McGraw-Hill.
Guttman, Louis
  1944. "A Basis for Scaling Qualitative Data." *American Sociological Review* 9:139-50.
  1947. "The Cornell Technique for Scale and Intensity Analysis." *Educational and Psychological Measurement* 7:247-80.

Hamblin, Robert L.
    1971a. "Mathematical Experimentation and Sociological Theory." *Sociometry* 50, no. 4:423-52.
    1971b. "Ratio Measurement for the Social Sciences." *Social Forces* 50, no. 2:191-206.
Jones, Bryan, and Richard Shorter
    1972. "The Ratio Measurement of Social Status: Some Cross Cultural Comparisons." *Social Forces* 50, no. 4:499-511.
Junge, Kenneth
    1960. "The Category Scale Equation." *Scandinavian Journal of Psychology* 1:112-14.
Kuennapas, Teodor, and Monica Sillén
    1965. "Measurement of Political Preferences: A Further Study of Direct and Indirect Scaling Methods." *Scandinavian Journal of Psychology* 6:162-72.
Kuennapas, Teodor, and Inger Wikstroem
    1963. "Measurement of Occupational Preferences: A Comparison of Scaling Methods." *Perceptual and Motor Skills* 17:611-24.
Likert, Rensis
    1932. "A Technique for the Measurement of Attitudes." *Archives of Psychology* 140:1-55.
Mashhour, Madjid
    1964. "On Eisler's General Psychophysical Differential Equation and His Fechnerian Integration." *Scandinavian Journal of Psychology* 5:225-33.
Osgood, Charles E., George J. Suci, and Percy H. Tannenbaum
    1957. *The Measurement of Meaning.* Urbana: University of Illinois Press.
Pfanzagl, J.
    1968. *Theory of Measurement.* New York: Wiley.
Rainwater, Lee
    1971. "Interim Report on Explorations of Social Status, Living Standards, and Family Life Styles." Mimeographed. Cambridge, Mass.: Joint Center for Urban Studies of M.I.T. and Harvard.
Robinson, John P., Jerrold G. Rusk, and Kendra B. Head
    1968. *Measures of Political Attitudes.* Ann Arbor: Institute for Social Research, University of Michigan.
Robinson, John P., Robert Athanasiou, and Kendra B. Head
    1969. *Measures of Occupational Attitudes and Occupational Characteristics.* Ann Arbor: Institute for Social Research, University of Michigan.
Sellin, J. Thorsten, and Marvin E. Wolfgang
    1964. *The Measurement of Delinquency.* New York: Wiley.
Shinn, Allen M., Jr.
    1969a. "An Application of Psychophysical Scaling Techniques to the Measurement of National Power." *Journal of Politics* 31, no. 4:932-51.
    1969b. *The Application of Psychophysical Scaling Techniques to Measurement of Political Variables.* Chapel Hill: Institute for Research in Social Science, University of North Carolina.
    1971a. "Measuring the Utility of Housing: Demonstrating a Methodological Approach." *Social Science Quarterly* 52:88-102.
    1971b. "On Measuring Power: Psychophysical Approaches among Nations and on the Supreme Court." Mimeographed. Austin: Department of Government, University of Texas.
Stevens, S. Smith
    1946. "On the Theory of Scales of Measurement." *Science* 103:677-80.
    1957. "On the Psychophysical Law." *Psychology Revue* 64:153-81.
    1959a. "Measurement, Psychophysics, and Utility," Chapter 2 in *Measurement:*

Definitions and Theories, edited by Charles West Churchman and Philburn Ratoosh. New York: Wiley.

1959*b*. "Sic Transit Gloria Veritatis?" *Contemporary Psychology* 4:388-89.

1960. "Ratio Scales, Partition Scales, and Confusion Scales." Chapter 6 in *Psychological Scaling: Theory and Applications*, edited by Harold Gulliksen and Samuel Messick. New York: Wiley.

1961. "To Honor Fechner and Repeal His Law." *Science* 133:80-86.

1966. "A Metric for the Social Consensus." Ibid. 151:530-41.

1968. "Ratio Scales of Opinion." In *Handbook of Measurement and Assessment in Behavioral Sciences*, edited by D. K. Whitla. Reading, Mass.: Addison-Wesley.

Stevens, S. Smith, and Eugene Galanter

1957. "Ratio Scales and Category Scales for a Dozen Perceptual Continua." *Journal of Psychology* 54:377-411.

Stevens, S. Smith, and Miguelina Guirao

1962. "Loudness, Reciprocality, and Partition Scales." *Journal of the Acoustical Society of America* 34:1466-71.

Summers, Gene F., ed.

1970. *Attitude Measurement*. Chicago: Rand McNally.

Thurstone, Louis Leon

1927. "A Law of Comparative Judgement." *Psychological Review* 34:273-86.

1928. "Attitudes Can Be Measured." *American Journal of Sociology* 33:529-44.

Thurstone, Louis Leon, and E. J. Chave

1929. *The Measurement of Attitude*. Chicago: University of Chicago Press.

Torgerson, Warren S.

1958. *Theory and Methods of Scaling*. New York: Wiley.

1960. "Quantitative Judgement Scales." Chapter 3 in *Psychological Scaling: Theory and Applications*, edited by Harold Gulliksen and Samuel Messick. New York: Wiley.

Zinnes, Joseph L.

1969. "Scaling." *Annual Review of Psychology* 20:447-78.

Chapter 5

MEMORY AND THE ASSESSMENT OF BEHAVIOR

Roy G. D'Andrade

Roy G. D'Andrade is currently Professor of Anthropology, University of California, San Diego. He received his Ph.D. from the Department of Social Relations, Harvard University in 1962. Professor D'Andrade's research has been primarily in cognitive anthropology, and in the applications of mathematical and statistical models to social and cultural data.

In the social sciences people have been used as measuring instruments for the investigation of many aspects of behavior. To find out if the subjects in an experiment are *acting aggressively*, for example, an investigator will typically use other people as measuring instruments. On the basis of their understanding of what constitutes acting aggressively, the observers will judge whether various segments of the subjects' behavior are *aggressive* or not. Attempting to specify what *aggressive* means by defining the term with reference to more specific acts, such as *hitting* or *insulting*, still fails to make the decision process explicit, since the rules for coding behavior remain dependent on a set of undefined terms. Unless the measurement process is based solely on physical properties, at some point such verbal coding rules always fall back on undefined terms.

The advantages of methods using human judgment as a means of measurement are generally thought to outweigh the disadvantages. A few social scientists require that all their measurements be mechanically recorded in units of mass, time, and distance, but if the behavior to be recorded is even· slightly complex, it becomes enormously difficult to attempt such a mechanization of the measuring process. Primarily, this difficulty involves the lack of one-to-one correspondences between the properties of physical signals and the distinctions perceived by human observers. For example, in the area of speech at least three quite different acoustic signals are heard as initial *d*, depending on the following vowel (Liberman et al. 1967).

These many-to-one and one-to-many types of correspondence, which make mechanical decoding of complex human behavior inefficient and costly, occur between many levels besides the physical medium and the perceptual response. For example, there are many ways to indicate *agreement* besides the sentence "I agree." There are alternatives in vocabulary and syntax, and in the use of a medium such as speech rather than gesture or writing. A mechanical device which could determine as well as a human judge when a respondent agreed with a statement, whatever the means of agreement used, would be a most amazing and complex piece of machinery. At present, it is much easier to use humans than to try to build behaviorscopes from wire and glass.

The Validity and Reliability of Human Behaviorscopes

The low cost of using human judges to assess attributes of human behavior is offset by a number of disadvantages. Traditionally, these disadvantages have been discussed as problems of *reliability* and *validity*. Reliability is usually thought of as the degree to which measuring instruments of the same type give the same results. A large literature has developed concerning the causes, effects, and remedies for deficiencies in reliability. In general, present-day social science shows a high degree of sensitivity to problems of reliability.

In contrast to problems of reliability, problems of validity are not at present well formulated. In a classic article, Campbell and Fiske (1959) presented one of the first methodological assessments of validity. They argue that validity, like reliability, involves agreement between measures. Validity, however, involves agreement between maximally different, or independent, measurement procedures; whereas reliability involves agreement between maximally similar measures. Thus two different methods producing very divergent results cannot both be measures of the same thing, although both might be valid measures of different things. From examples in Campbell and Fiske's article, it appears that very few of the social sciences' methods show this type of validity in measuring any aspect of human behavior.

Obviously, high reliability alone does not insure validity. It is easy to show that under certain conditions highly reliable judgments can be quite invalid. The Muller-Lyer optical illusion, for instance, provides a simple example of conditions which elicit reliable but invalid judgments about the lengths of two lines. The clinical illusion, in which clinicians reliably interpret projective tests with invalid predictions, is a similar phenomenon, but it is cognitive rather than perceptual (Chapman 1967).

This chapter attempts to demonstrate that one of the methods used in the social sciences is invalid because it is subject to a special effect analogous to that of an illusion; an effect in which there is a reliable and systematic distortion of judgments under certain conditions. The general procedure in which this method is often used, and in which the distortion biases the results the most drastically, can be described as follows: First, one or more human observers are asked to judge one or more subjects on a number of traits of behavior; the judgments are expressed in ratings or rankings (scores) based on the observers' long-term (i.e., more than ten minutes') memory of the subjects' behavior. Second, a single score is computed for each subject for each trait, usually by taking the mean of all the scores given to each subject for each trait. Third, to find out how the traits are related to each other, some measure of association, such as the product-moment correlation, is computed from the subjects' scores for all pairs of traits. Finally, the measures of association are analyzed to determine how the traits are organized with respect to each other. A number of kinds of analysis may be used, ranging from simple clustering by inspection to factor analysis or multidimensional scaling. The results of such analyses indicate which traits tend to go together, and the similarity structure of the trait measurements is taken as a representation of the structure or organization of the subjects' behavior.

The motive for using this procedure is usually to simplify the description of human behavior by grouping similar traits into multibehavior units, such as clusters or dimensions. Since there appears to be a wide variety of human behaviors, each of which can be described in a large number of ways, some procedure is needed for constructing economical descriptions of a person's or a group's behavior. The reason for using ratings or rankings based on long-term memory in this procedure appears to be that such judgments are easy to obtain. One can consider the memory of each observer to be a storehouse, where the impressions left by hundreds of thousands of the subject's past acts may be inexpensively and quickly recovered.

Unfortunately, it appears that an observer's memory cannot be considered trustworthy for many kinds of judgments. The evidence to be presented below indicates that in such judgments there is a systematic distortion, in that traits the observer considers similar will be recalled as applying to the same person, even when this is not the case. As a result of this effect, the correlations found between traits prove to be due more to the observer's conception of "what is like what" than to covariation in the behavior of the subjects.

In an earlier paper on this topic it was argued that procedures which try to classify behavior from data consisting of global judgments by human observers reveal which behavior terms are semantically similar, not which behaviors of the subjects go together (D'Andrade 1965). The evidence used to support this contention was a demonstration that in at least two cases judgments of the semantic similarity of trait terms gave approximately the same results as the analysis or correlations based on the ratings of subjects' behavior made by informed observers. This evidence was equivocal, however, since it can be argued that the semantic similarity of trait terms corresponds to the way these traits actually go together, perhaps because the actual relations between traits become semantically coded into the trait terms. Given this *isomorphism* hypothesis, the fact that the same type of similarity structure can be obtained both from judgments of semantic similarity and from observer ratings would be expectable, and it certainly would not invalidate psychological theories which assume that people can be accurately described in terms of multibehavior units of some kind.

Multitrait-Multimethod Matrix Correspondence Technique

In order to decide between the *isomorphism* hypothesis and the *systematic distortion* hypothesis, a comparison between ratings based on long-term memory and the actual behavior of the subjects is needed. If the observer's memory-based ratings showed a very different pattern of correlations from that found for the data based on the actual behavior of the subjects (but a pattern similar to judgments of semantic similarity), it would be reasonable to reject the isomorphism hypothesis and to consider the systematic-distortion hypothesis supported. This strategy is similar to Campbell and Fiske's multitrait-multimethod matrix technique, except that entire patterns of correlation coefficients, instead of specific correlation coefficients, are to be compared. Pattern comparison is needed here because it is not the validity of specific traits or categories which is in question, but the validity of the correlations found between traits.

Ideally, for recording the actual behavior of the subjects, a mechanical device should be constructed to count frequencies of different kinds of behavior. Unfortunately, for all the reasons discussed above, a mechanical measuring instrument is not practical at present for any judgment more complex than *is making noise* versus *is not making noise*. The closest approximation to a mechanical device appears to be a trained observer using a simple coding scheme to record a subject's behavior as it occurs. The immediacy of the observer's assessment and the simplicity of the coding decisions should, it is hoped, protect against systematic distortion of the type thought to take place in long-term memory.

The most frequently used coding scheme for recording ongoing behavior is the Bales *Interaction Process* category system. The Bales categories are relatively simple in terms of coding rules and are also usable for ratings or rankings based on long-term memory. A schematic classification of the Bales system is presented in Figure 5.1.

A: Positive Reactions

1. Shows solidarity, raises others' status, jokes, gives help, reward
2. Shows tension release, shows satisfaction, laughs
3. Agrees, shows passive acceptance, understands, concurs, complies

B: Problem Solving Attempts

4. Gives suggestion, direction, implying autonomy for other
5. Gives opinion, evaluation, analysis, expresses feeling, wish
6. Gives orientation, information, repeats, clarifies, confirms

C: Questions

7. Asks for orientation, information, repetition, confirmation
8. Asks for opinion, evaluation, analysis, expression of feeling
9. Asks for suggestion, direction, possible ways of action

D: Negative Reactions

10. Disagrees, shows passive rejection, formality, withhold help
11. Shows tension increase, asks for help, withdraws "Out of Field"
12. Shows antagonism, deflates others' status, defends or asserts self

Figure 5.1. Bales interaction-process analysis categories (taken from Parsons and Bales 1955, p. 267).

The Borgatta, Cottrell, and Mann Study

Because of the general applicability to different methods of measurement of the Bales category system, a search was made to find published studies using the Bales categories in which both immediate recording of ongoing behavior and judgments based on memory had been carried out. Two such studies were found in which the data were reported completely enough to permit the necessary multitrait-multimethod matrix comparisons. The first study was conducted by Borgatta, Cottrell, and Mann (1958); the second was conducted by Richard Mann and reported in his Ph.D. dissertation (1959).

As part of the Borgatta, Cottrell, and Mann study a number of small groups were observed directly, with immediate recording of ongoing behavior according to the Bales category system. After twenty hours of small-group contact the individuals in each group also ranked each other on a variety of personality traits, including a set of behavior descriptions which correspond approximately to the Bales category system.

The subjects in the study were forty-seven graduate students enrolled in a class on interpersonal relations. They were divided into five small groups, each meeting for a two-hour discussion period every week throughout the semester. The groups had little or no external supervision. The primary focus of discussion was the analysis of processes that go with "democratic leadership."

The questionnaire ranking data were collected by the course instructor after the ninth week, ostensibly as part of a "student evaluation procedure." Rankings were made on a total of forty traits, with each person ranking all members of his group. Since the groups were of slightly different sizes, rank scores for each group were equalized. The traits most closely approximating the Bales categories were:

1b. Shows solidarity and friendliness (Bales no. 1)
2b. Is responsive to laughter (Bales no. 2)
4b. Makes the most suggestions (Bales no. 4)
10b. Disagrees most (Bales no. 10)
11b. Tends to be nervous (Bales no. 11)
12b. Tends to be antagonistic (Bales no. 12)

Presumably the investigators felt that their rephrasings of the category labels made it easier for the subjects to rate each other.

The immediate recording of ongoing interaction was carried out by a trained observer using the Bales category system. Each of the five groups was observed during the ninth and tenth weekly sessions. Interaction scores were adjusted to the individuals' rate of initiated acts per 100 minutes. Generally the groups show slightly different and stable interaction profiles.

To relate trait rankings to the results of the immediate recording of ongoing behavior, product-moment correlations were computed between all variables. These correlation coefficients indicate the degree to which individuals who have high scores on one variable also have high scores on the other variable. From the complete matrix of correlations it is possible to compare the pattern of correlations found between Bales category scores for rates of behavior based on immediate recording and the pattern of correlations found between Bales category scores for ranking based on long-term memory. Borgatta and his associates did not obtain measures of semantic similarity, however; so—to make possible a comparison of the pattern of semantic similarity occurring between the Bales categories and the patterns of correlations found for the other types of data—a test of semantic similarity had to be constructed and administered.

Because the wording of the trait descriptions used by Borgatta, Cottrell, and Mann is slightly different from that used in the original Bales category system, a modified set of behavior descriptions was constructed for the test of semantic similarity which is somewhat closer to Bales's wording. The phrases used were:

1s. Shows solidarity (Bales no. 1)
2s. Jokes, laughs (Bales no. 2)
4s. Suggests, gives direction (Bales no. 4)
10s. Disagrees (Bales no. 10)
11s. Shows tension, nervous (Bales no. 11)
12s. Shows antagonism (Bales no. 12)

The test was administered in questionnaire form to ten graduate students, none of whom were previously acquainted with the Bales category system. The format used for this questionnaire is presented in Figure 5.2.

Table 5.1 presents the correlation matrices from Borgatta, Cottrell, and Mann for the relevant Bales categories for rates of behavior based on immediate recording, for rankings based on long-term memory, and for the mean ratings of semantic similarity (ranging potentially from -3.0 for "very dissimilar" to $+3.0$ for "very similar").

For comparing matrices, the agreement in rank order for corresponding coefficients was used as a measure of overall pattern similarity. Degree of agreement in rank order is given by the Spearman rank-order correlation coefficients, which indicate how well the degree of similarity found between a given pair of Bales categories for one method of measurement predicts the degree of similarity to be found between the same pair of categories for a second method of measurement. Thus the coefficients inside a matrix indicate how much alike the Bales categories are for a particular method of measurement, while the rank-order coefficients between matrices indicate the degree to which different methods of measurement yield similar patterns of association between Bales categories.

The results presented in Table 5.1 may be summarized as follows:

1. Correlation coefficients for behavior rates based on immediate recording tend to be smaller in absolute size than the correlation coefficients for rank judgments based on long-term memory.
2. The correlation matrix for behavior rates is not strongly similar to the correlation matrix for rank judgments ($r_s = .34$).
3. The matrix of semantic-similarity ratings is fairly similar to the correlation matrix for rank judgments ($r_s = .60$), but not similar to the correlation matrix for behavior rates ($r_s = .03$).

Generally, information revealing which Bales categories are most

Judgment of Behavioral Descriptions

The purpose of this questionnaire is to obtain your judgment about the degree of *similarity* between a series of descriptions of human behavior. Base your judgments of similarity on the meanings of the terms and the degree to which the descriptions typically refer to the same kinds of behavior.

Each question on the test consists of a pair of behavior descriptions to be judged on a seven point scale ranging from *'very similar'* to *'very dissimilar.'*

In the example below, please rate the descriptive terms *'cooperative'* and *'helpful'* according to your estimate of their degree of similarity.

cooperative : : helpful

very similar	generally similar	slightly similar	unrelated not similar not dissimilar	slightly dissimilar	generally dissimilar	very dissim- ilar
+3	+2	+1	0	−1	−2	−3

Place an X in the slot which corresponds most closely to your judgment of how similar the descriptive term 'cooperative' is to the term 'helpful'.

Now go on to the rest of the test. Please answer all the questions.

shows solidarity : : suggests, gives direction

very similar	generally similar	slightly similar	unrelated not similar not dissimilar	slightly dissimilar	generally dissimilar	very dissim- ilar
+3	+2	+1	0	−1	−2	−3

Figure 5.2.

alike when behavior rates based on immediate recordings are used will not predict very well which Bales categories are most alike when rank judgments based on long-term memory are used. The pattern of association for the rank judgments for the Bales categories resembles the pattern of semantic similarity for these categories more than it resembles the pattern of association found for the observed rates of these behaviors.

These results appear to support the hypothesis that people tend to recall traits considered similar as characteristic of the same individuals. The evidence from the behavior rates based on immediate recording does not support the isomorphism hypothesis, since the categories considered similar in meaning are not the categories showing strongly correlated behavior rates.

What seems to happen in this type of small-group situation is that, while group members agree to a certain extent in their assessments, a

Table 5.1. *Comparison of Correlation Matrices for Behavior Rates Based on Immediate Recordings, Rank Judgments based on Long-term Memory, and Semantic Similarity Ratings, All Using Bales Interaction Process Analysis Categories*

Correlations for

Behavior Rates

	1a	2a	4a	10a	11a	12a
solidarity	1a		.35	.35	.06	.09	.17
jokes	2a			.22	.08	−.11	−.13
suggests	4a				.17	.04	−.06
disagrees	10a					.08	.13
tension	11a						.05
antagonism	12a						

Rank Judgments

	1b	2b	4b	10b	11b	12b
solidarity	1b		.32	.24	−.33	−.22	−.50
jokes	2b			.34	−.04	.08	−.04
suggests	4b				.35	.00	.17
disagrees	10b					.35	.75
tension	11b						.28
antagonism	12b						

Semantic Similarity Ratings

	1s	2s	4s	10s	11s	12s
solidarity	1s		.0	.2	−.7	−1.4	−1.5
jokes	2s			.1	−.9	.3	−1.0
suggests	4s				−1.1	−1.4	−1.1
disagrees	10s					.3	.7
tension	11s						1.0
antagonism	12s						

$r_s = .03$

$r_s = .34$

$r_s = .60$

NOTE: r_s coefficients are Spearman's rank order correlation measure.

number of these assessments are based, not on fact, but on a combination of other assessments. For example, according to the behavior rate correlations, individuals who *show solidarity* are slightly more likely than not to also *show antagonism* ($r = .17$). But since people conceive of solidarity as very dissimilar to antagonism (semantic-similarity rating of -1.5), they will remember an individual who shows a good deal of *solidarity* in his behavior as *not* showing *antagonism* (rank judgment based on long-term memory $r = -.50$).

Further information about the relation between the behavior rates and the rank judgments can be obtained from an inspection of the correlations between these two sets of scores. These correlations, presented in Table 5.2, are based on the scores assigned to individual subjects; a high correlation coefficient between a particular behavior-rate category and a particular rank-judgment category means that, if an individual's score on one measure is given, a fairly good prediction can be made of that individual's score on the other measure. In Campbell and Fiske's terminology, Table 5.2 presents a *hetromethod* correlation matrix, and the correlations between categories with the same label are validity coefficients.

Table 5.2. Correlations between Behavior-Rate Category Scores and Rank-Judgment Category Scores

Behavior rate category		Rank-judgment Category					
		1b	2b	4b	10b	11b	12b
Solidarity	1a	.23	.48	.36	.31	.03	.22
Jokes	2a	.00	.17	.14	.17	.03	.17
Suggestion	4a	.08	.17	.38	.09	.06	.00
Disagrees	10a	-.03	.05	.11	.30	.11	.22
Tension	11a	.07	.00	.29	.16	.29	.00
Antagonism	12a	.17	.43	.20	.08	.06	.14

NOTE: Correlations $\geq \pm.24$ significant at $p \leq .05$ for $n = 47$.

While the underlined validity coefficients average slightly higher than the hetromethod-hetrotrait coefficients, the sizes of these coefficients are not impressive.

The Richard Mann Study

The complex pattern of correlations found in Table 5.2 raises a possibility which might explain the lack of correspondence between the behavior-rate correlations and the rank-judgment correlations. This is the possibility that the Bales categories may mean something different to the subjects, who make the rank judgments, than to the observer, who does the coding of ongoing behavior. A related possibility is that behavior-rate scores may be overly influenced by the general activity level of the individual; for example, a person who says very little, but whose statements often contain suggestions, may receive a lower rate score on *suggests* than an individual who performs a much wider variety of behaviors but is extremely active. In contrast, the ranking judgments may more nearly reflect the proportions of a person's behavior which fall in the various categories.

Controlling for these possibilities requires a study in which the category scores for the immediate recording of behavior are given in terms of proportions of the individual's total output of behavior, and in which the observer not only does the immediate recording of behavior but also makes memory-based judgments about what proportion of each person's behavior falls into the various categories.

A study using both these procedures was carried out by Richard Mann (1959). The study has an extra feature, in that the small-group sessions took place under two different experimental conditions, with all subjects taking part in both types. Mann's research is an excellent example of comprehensive and careful data reportage. It includes test and performance scores for every subject on all variables, complete intercorrelation matrices, and examples of the test forms and instructions.

The major purpose of Mann's study was to test the relationship between personality and small-group performance. For purposes of this chapter, it is the group-performance measures which are of interest. These include the use of a modified Bales category system for the immediate recording of ongoing interaction. The same categories were also used for memory-based ratings, made after the small-group sessions by both the small-group participants and the observer.

For this study 100 male undergraduates, all of whom had recently pledged fraternities, were enlisted as subjects. After taking the questionnaire tests each subject was assigned to two different five-man groups in which none of the participants were well known to each other. No two subjects were put into the same two groups. One of the groups in which each subject participated worked on a relatively specific task (the "mined-road" problem) for fifty minutes, with the promise of a substantial reward if it came up with the best solution.

The other group for each subject worked for fifty minutes on a more emotional and diffuse problem concerning "the way houses should handle pledge training." First, the subjects attempted to formulate a compromise group policy, after which they ranked the five fraternities represented by the group members in terms of their closeness to this ideal policy. Experimental conditions were balanced for order, with half the subjects beginning with the "task" condition, and half with the "social-emotional" condition.

Group sessions were held in a social science laboratory and were observed through a one-way mirror. After each fifty-minute session a postmeeting questionnaire was given to the subjects, who sat at separate tables; the observer also rated each group member.

The interaction during the fifty-minute session was scored by means of a modified version of the Bales category system. Each act was scored in only one category. The modified system is presented below:

Modified Categories (Bales-Mann)	Bales Categories
(1) Agreement and solidarity	*Shows solidarity* (no. 1) except for omission of all joking behavior plus *shows agreement* (no. 3)
(2) Laughing and joking	*Shows tension release* (no. 2) plus all joking behavior
(3) Suggestions	*Gives suggestions* (no. 4)
(4) Opinions and orientations	*Gives opinions* (no. 5) and *gives orientation* (no. 6)
(5) Questions	*Asks for orientations* (no. 7) *Asks for opinions* (no. 8) *Asks for suggestions* (no. 9)
(6) Disagreement and antagonism	*Shows disagreement* (no. 10) *Shows antagonism* (no. 12)
(7) Tension	*Shows tension* (no. 11)

By grouping the Bales categories into fewer classes Mann hoped to make a simpler and more reliable coding scheme and to achieve a more normal distribution of categories. The observer, who had previously worked with Bales, achieved reliabilities of approximately .90 on the majority of the categories.

The scores for the immediate-recording data were transformed into percentages by dividing the subject's act frequencies for each of the Bales-Mann categories by the subject's total number of acts.

The questionnaire administered to the subjects after each session contained sixteen rating measures. Each of the five subjects rated the other four on these measures, using a ten-point rating scale with no ties

permitted. The questions for the ratings on the Bales-Mann categories
are:

1. (Agreement) Regardless of how much he talked altogether, how would
   you rate each member of this group (excluding yourself) on how much
   he tended to agree with what others had said?
2. (Laughing and Joking) Regardless of how much he talked altogether,
   how would you rate each member of this group (excluding yourself) on
   how much he tended to laugh and joke around?
3. (Suggestions) Regardless of how much he talked altogether, how would
   you rate each member of this group (excluding yourself) on how much
   he tended to give suggestions about what the group should do next or
   what decisions should be made?
4. (Opinions and Orientations) Regardless of how much he talked altogether, how would you rate each member of this group (excluding
   yourself) on how much he tended to give his opinion or state the facts
   about things?
5. (Questions) Regardless of how much he talked altogether, how would you
   rate each member of this group (excluding yourself) on how much he
   tended to ask questions of other people?
6. (Disagreement) Regardless of how much he talked altogether, how would
   you rate each member of this group (excluding yourself) on how much
   he tended to disagree with what others said?
7. (Tension) Regardless of how much he talked altogether, how would you
   rate each member of this group (excluding yourself) on how much he
   tended to be nervous, tense, or ill at ease?

The score for each individual on each measure was computed by simply summing the ratings given by the other four members.

The observer's ratings were based directly on his estimates of each
person's act proportions for the six Bales-Mann categories *agreement
and solidarity* (no. 1), *laughing and joking* (no. 2), *suggestions* (no. 3),
questions (no. 5), *disagreement and antagonism* (no. 6), and *tension* (no. 7).
No reason is given for the observer's not using Bales-Mann category 4,
opinions and *orientations*. The observer also made ratings on a number
of other measures, such as *leadership* and *likability*.

A comparison of the Bales-Mann immediate-recording category definitions and the wording of the questionnaire ratings shows that the
category descriptions were simplified for the questionnaire. Where two
of the Bales categories were combined, the questionnaire usually used
only the higher frequency category as the basis for the questionnaire
rating. Thus *agrees* (Bales no. 3) has an average percentage rate of
about 9.5, while *shows solidarity* (Bales no. 1) has a percentage rate of
only 2.3. In the questionnaire, Mann uses the phrase "tended to agree"
as the crucial frame of reference for the Bales-Mann category 1 of
agreement-solidarity.

Comparing the correlations computed from the immediate-recording percentages and the questionnaire ratings with the semantic-similarity ratings for the Bales-Mann categories required that some choices be made in the wording of the category definitions for a semantic-similarity test. As in the Borgatta, Cottrell, and Mann study, an attempt was made to stay as close as possible to the wording of the immediate-recording categories, but at the same time to follow the technique, used in the questionnaire, of excluding the less frequent Bales category in which combinations of the Bales categories were involved. The phrasing of the Bales-Mann categories for the semantic-similarity test is:

Bales-Mann 1	Agrees with others, complies
Bales-Mann 2	Laughs and jokes
Bales-Mann 3	Gives suggestions
Bales-Mann 4	Gives opinions and states facts
Bales-Mann 5	Asks questions
Bales-Mann 6	Disagrees with others, indicates contrary opinion
Bales-Mann 7	Shows tension and nervousness, withdraws

Originally, a questionnaire similar to that used in the Borgatta study to measure semantic similarity was constructed. However, perhaps because of the increase in the number of categories, and the somewhat smaller but more complex range of meaning contained in the Bales-Mann categories, the rating test proved relatively unreliable. The results showed a systematic but weak correspondence to correlations of the subjects' and observer's questionnaire ratings.

A more reliable and sensitive rating test was constructed by using the method of complete triads. The instructions are given in Figure 5.3. As can be seen, every triad occurs three times. This makes a longer test than one simply using a scale rating for each pair of terms.

Twenty-eight university undergraduates were tested. The correlation between two randomly split groups of the respondents yielded an r of .94, computed by using mean scores for the number of times each pair of terms was found to be "similar in meaning."

The correlation matrices for immediately recorded behavior and postsession subject and observer ratings, for each of the two experimental group conditions, are presented in Table 5.3. Table 5.4 presents the mean semantic-similarity rankings, and Figure 5.4 the Spearman rank-order correlation coefficients for the comparison of the different matrices.

The results presented in Tables 5.3 and 5.4 and Figure 5.4 reinforce the findings reported from the Borgatta, Cottrell, and Mann study and give additional information concerning the way in which changes in

This is a test concerning the meaning of words. On each page there will be a word or phrase printed at the top of the page, and then a number of pairs of words or phrases. For example:

Young Man

--------	------
2. youth	3. boy
--------	------
3. boy	4. guy
--------	------
2. youth	4. guy
--------	------

Circle the word or phrase on each line which is *most similar in meaning* to the word or phrase printed at the top of the page.

Sometimes it will be difficult to choose, but please DO NOT SKIP any of the pairs. Base your judgments on the ordinary, conventional meanings of the words. Work as quickly as you can.

(Ignore the numbers beside each word or phrase. These numbers are for convenience in coding the results.) Now go on to the rest of the test.

Figure 5.3.

situation affect the different methods. The results may be summarized as follows:

1. As in the Borgatta, Cottrell, and Mann study, the correlations for the immediately recorded behavior percentages are generally smaller than the correlations for the ratings (both the subjects' ratings and the observer's ratings).

2. Even more strikingly than in the Borgatta study, the correlation matrices for the immediately recorded behavior percentages are *not* similar to subject-rating correlation matrices ($r_s = .07$ and $-.03$).

3. Most critically, the correlation matrices for the observer's ratings are *not* strongly similar to the correlation matrices for the immediately recorded behavior ($r_s = .20$ and $.27$).

4. There is a fairly strong degree of similarity between the correlation matrices for the subjects' ratings and the correlation matrices for the observer's ratings ($r_s = .52$ and $.76$).

5. The semantic-similarity rankings of the Bales-Mann categories correspond fairly strongly to the correlations for the subjects' ratings ($r_s = .75$ and $.67$).

6. The semantic-similarity rankings of the Bales-Mann categories correspond strongly to the correlations for the observer's ratings ($r_s = .61$ and $.91$).

7. The semantic-similarity rankings of the Bales-Mann categories do not correspond strongly to the correlations for immediately recorded behavior percentages ($r_s = .20$ and $.14$).

8. The correlation matrices for the observer and subject ratings are very similar across experimental conditions ($r_s = .92$ for subject ratings, and $.90$ for observer ratings). The immediately recorded behavior percentages, on the other hand, do not show a high degree of cross-situation stability ($r_s = .42$).

Table 5.3. Correlations for Immediate Recordings, Subject Ratings, and Observer Ratings Using Bales-Mann Categories under Two Experimental Group Conditions

		Task Conditions						Social-Emotional Conditions					
		Correlations for behavior percentages from immediate recordings						*Correlations for behavior percentages from immediate recordings*					
		2	3	4	5	6	7	2	3	4	5	6	7
Agree	1	.14	−.26	−.25	.17	−.32	−.13	.01	.02	−.44	.01	−.30	−.11
Joke	2		−.27	−.34	−.20	.06	.00		−.37	−.30	−.25	−.18	.02
Suggest	3			−.18	−.23	−.11	−.28			−.33	.37	.25	−.07
Orient	4				−.27	−.16	−.22				−.33	−.33	−.32
Question	5					−.20·	.24					.22	−.06
Disagree	6						.06						.14
Tension	7												

		Correlations for subject ratings						*Correlations for subject ratings*					
		2	3	4	5	6	7	2	3	4	5	6	7
Agree	1	.16	−.35	−.41	−.18	−.61	.32	.20	.18	−.15	.14	−.55	.04
Joke	2		.31	.34	.28	.16	−.19		.32	.37	.23	.23	−.16
Suggest	3			.83	.53	.49	−.35			.58	.61	.25	−.24
Orient	4				.47	.50	−.46				.39	.43	−.34
Question	5					.45	−.01					.32	−.11
Disagree	6						−.03						.12
Tension	7												

		Correlations for observer ratings						*Correlations for observer ratings*					
		2	3	(4)	5	6	7	2	3	(4)	5	6	7
Agree	1	.28	.05		.40	−.34	−.32	.40	.33		.41	−.42	−.48
Joke	2		.34		.16	.05	−.15		.40		.41	−.17	−.33
Suggest	3				.39	.54	−.25				.63	.35	−.24
(Orient)	4												
Question	5					.09	−.26					.07	−.28
Disagree	6						.12						.30
Tension	7												

SOURCE: Mann 1959, Appendix H, Tables 2-J and 3-J.

The pattern of results shows a consistent network of congruence between the semantic-similarity rankings and the correlation matrices for ratings made on the basis of long-term memory, regardless of whether the ratings were made by subjects or by the observer, or under group task conditions or group social-emotional conditions. In contrast, the correlation matrices for the immediately recorded behavior percent-

Table 5.4. Mean Semantic-Similarity Rankings (Based on
Triads Test)

		1	2	3	4	5	6	7
Agree	1		8.4	5.4	4.9	4.8	0.3	5.0
Joke	2	8.4		4.8	3.6	4.7	2.0	3.2
Suggest	3	5.4	4.8		9.1	7.8	6.0	1.9
Orient	4	4.9	3.6	9.1		6.6	8.2	2.3
Question	5	4.8	4.7	7.8	6.6		6.6	4.0
Disagree	6	0.3	2.0	6.0	8.2	6.6		5.1
Tension	7	5.0	3.2	1.9	2.3	4.0	5.1	

NOTE: The greater the mean figure, the higher the similarity ranking.

ages are *not* strongly similar to any kinds of ratings made on the basis of long-term memory, and they show considerable change across group conditions.

The hetromethod correlation matrices for immediately recorded behavior percentages, subject ratings, and observer ratings are presented in Table 5.5.

The correlations in Table 5.5 show only a slightly more consistent pattern than the hetromethod matrix from the Borgatta, Cottrell, and Mann study (Fig. 5.4). Generally, the categories for the immediately recorded behavior percentages have their highest correlations with the properly corresponding categories for subject and observer ratings (underlined coefficients). These *validity* coefficients for the immediately recorded behavior percentages and the observer ratings are slightly higher than the validity coefficients for the immediately recorded behavior percentages with the subject ratings. However, the median validity correlation coefficient, which is between .33 and .36, is still unacceptably small. These data indicate that there has been considerable slippage in the recall of events.

General Formulation

The argument presented in this chapter is not just that there is memory drift when people make ratings or rankings of other people's behavior, but that this 'drift' is systematic, nonrandom, biased in the direction of the rater's conception of "what is like what." More abstractly stated, it is hypothesized here that, given a series of attributes (such as behavior traits) which can apply to a class of objects (such as other people), there will be systematic shift in the individual's recall of which attributes are possessed by which objects, such that the more strongly the individuals conceive of the attributes as belonging together, the more likely it will be that the individual recalls both attributes as belonging to the same objects. With this type of memory error, any at-

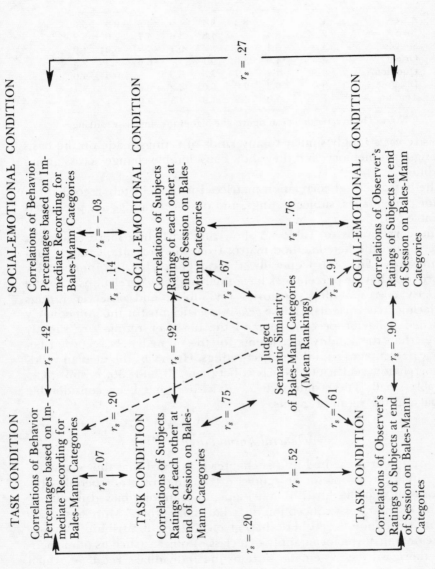

Figure 5.4. *Comparison of correlation matrices for behavior percentages based on immediate recording, postsession subject ratings, postsession observer ratings, each under two group-experimental conditions, with semantic-similarity rankings, all using Bales-Mann category system.*

tempt to discover how human behavior is organized into multibehavior units—such as dimensions or clusters—which is based on data consisting of long-term memory judgments will result in conclusions which primarily reflect the cognitive structure of the raters.

Rediscovery

After completing a first draft of this chapter, I discovered a reference in an older textbook on psychometric methods (Guilford 1936) to a study done in 1931 which clearly states the major hypotheses presented here, supported by differences in correlations found between observer ratings based on long-term memory and the correlations found between immediately recorded behavior frequencies (Newcomb 1931). The subjects were thirty problem boys sent to a summer camp for five weeks. The boys were under the constant observation of a psychiatrist and six or more trained counselors. A daily record was kept of specific incidents involving twenty-six categories of behavior for each boy by his own counselor. Some 8,500 incidents involving these categories were also recorded by the experimenter. At the close of the camp period ratings were obtained from each of the seven observers on the frequency of these twenty-six categories of behavior for every boy.

A mean correlation of .41 was found for the relation between daily record scores and the memory based ratings, indicating a weak degree of correspondence between methods. The correlations between behavior categories, however, showed a considerable degree of distortion when the results from the two different methods were compared. Intercorrelation of the categories for nine general traits yielded a mean correlation figure for the memory-based ratings of .49, but a figure of only .14 when computed from the daily records. Concerning these results Newcomb states: "The conclusion may therefore be drawn that the halo effect, inevitable in the ratings, *worked in such a way as to cause the rater to rate similarly logically related behaviors* . . . . The close relation between the intra-trait behaviors which is evident in the ratings may, therefore, be presumed to spring from logical presuppositions in the minds of the raters, rather than from actual behaviors" (Newcomb 1931, p. 288; italics added).

Similarity

A critical problem in the formulations presented above concerns the lack of specificity in some of the terms, and especially the vagueness of the term "similarity" when used with reference to an individual's conceptions. In this chapter measures of conceptual similarity have been phrased primarily in terms of semantic similarity. Thus the instructions for the questionnaire and the ranking task stressed that the similarity

Table 5.5. Hetro Method Correlations for Bales-Mann Categories under Two Experimental Group Conditions

Subject rating	Task Condition								Social-Emotional Condition						
Immediately recorded %	1	2	3	4	5	6	7	1	2	3	4	5	6	7
1	+.41	+.29	−.44	−.21	+.31	−.30	+.30	+.36	+.27	−.14	+.10	−.08	−.53	−.24
2	+.07	+.37	−.17	+.16	−.10	+.10	−.13	.00	+.25	−.10	+.09	+.04	−.00	−.44
3	+.01	−.23	+.20	+.42	−.14	+.03	−.39	+.19	−.23	+.20	+.12	+.30	−.16	−.45
4	+.06	−.17	+.20	+.54	−.16	−.01	−.37	−.02	−.26	+.05	+.23	+.07	+.06	−.49
5	+.04	−.20	+.03	+.10	+.10	+.03	−.21	+.11	−.18	+.04	+.08	+.36	−.09	−.28
6	−.30	−.26	+.07	+.29	−.06	+.32	−.15	−.31	−.31	+.04	+.10	+.15	+.53	−.07
7	+.19	+.16	−.22	−.07	+.59	+.13	+.55	−.16	+.15	−.13	+.06	−.10	−.02	+.14

Observer rating	Task Condition								Social-Emotional Condition						
Immediately recorded %	1	2	3	4	5	6	7	1	2	3	4	5	6	7
1	+.34	−.01	−.05	(.08)	+.14	−.49	−.29	+.30	+.09	−.05	+.08	+.01	−.41	−.46
2	−.00	+.24	−.06	(.09)	+.09	−.10	−.29	+.25	+.33	−.06	+.08	+.12	−.10	−.30
3	−.19	−.30	+.29	(.30)	−.14	+.02	−.37	+.12	−.21	+.33	+.18	+.30	+.12	−.47

Table 5.5—Continued

	Task Condition							Social-Emotional Condition						
Subject rating \ Immediately recorded %	1	2	3	4	5	6	7	1	2	3	4	5	6	7
5	+.14	−.32	+.05	(.19)	+.18	−.29	−.31	+.20	−.02	+.18	−.07	+.48	−.01	−.36
6	−.13	−.19	−.02	(.24)	−.10	+.51	−.06	−.18	−.27	+.20	−.20	.18	+.65	+.07
7	−.20	.00	−.38	(.00)	+.06	+.22	.59	−.21	+.04	+.12	−.17	−.05	+.35	+.55

	Task Condition							Social-Emotional Condition						
Observer rating \ Subject rating	1	2	3	4	5	6	7	1	2	3	4	5	6	7
1	+.26	+.18	+.19	(+.17)	+.30	−.16	−.09	+.24	+.16	+.26	(+.28)	+.21	−.16	−.22
2	+.11	+.52	+.25	(+.32)	+.12	+.02	−.32	+.18	+.33	+.28	(+.24)	+.15	−.09	−.25
3	−.40	+.28	+.64	(+.68)	+.28	+.39	−.42	−.13	+.34	+.61	(+.48)	+.33	+.23	−.35
5	−.12	+.26	+.46	(+.42)	+.34	+.16	−.16	+.02	+.15	+.48	(+.32)	+.39	+.05	−.34
6	−.37	+.10	+.41	(+.38)	+.10	+.41	−.16	−.47	+.04	+.06	(+.15)	+.01	+.51	−.02
7	+.08	−.23	−.22	(−.27)	−.13	−.01	.25	−.29	−.13	−.22	(−.19)	−.21	+.17	+.20

SOURCE: Mann 1959, Appendix G.

NOTE: 1 = agrees; 2 = jokes; 3 = suggests; 4 = orients; 5 = questions; 6 = disagrees; 7 = tension.

judgments should be based on the degree to which the events named by the terms were actually alike, rather than the degree to which the terms elicited the same associations.

In my earlier paper on trait psychology and componential analysis the theoretical discussion emphasized *denotative similarity*; that is, the degree to which different terms shared the same *distinctive features*, or *criterial attributes* (D'Andrade 1965).

Shweder (1972), in a study which demonstrates that the structural organization of variables obtained by Bales (1969) in his work with small groups can also be obtained by having respondents sort the relevant variables on the basis of "similarity," has pointed out that any assumption that the respondents are actually using overlap in distinctive features as the primary basis for making similarity judgments is unwarranted. Shweder argues that the basis on which the respondents make similarity judgments of this type is the degree to which attributes contiguously go together in making up a symbolic *behavioral type*, which he treats as a learned cultural construct.

Work by other investigators also indicates that a number of different kinds of relationships may be involved in judgments of similarity. Flavell and Flavell (1959) and Flavell and Stedman (1961) have presented evidence that judgments about similarity in meaning are affected by the *logico-grammatical relationships* occurring between terms. In the Flavell and Stedman study children and adults judged which of two pairs of terms were more similar in meaning (e.g., *big-large* versus *throw-ball*). Across a large number of such judgments, a relatively stable and consistent rank order in similarity was found for the various categories of logico-grammatical relationships by approximately age ten. Highest in the rank order of similarity were *synonymous* pairs (big-large, steal-rob), then *similar-dimension* pairs (small-tiny, smile-laugh), then *superset-subset* pairs (bird-sparrow, tree-oak), followed closely by *whole-part* pairs (bird-wing, shoe-heel), *object-attribute* pairs (lemon-sour, mouse-small) and *common-action-of* pairs (dog-bark, lion-roar).

Further down the scale were *coordinate* pairs (cow-horse, pipe-cigar), *common-action-upon* pairs (sweep-floor, chew-gum), *common-use* pairs (dog-bone, farmer-tractor), and *part-part* pairs (pedal-handlebars, wallfloor). Last were *contrast-on-a-dimension* pairs (hard-easy, strong-weak).

Results such as the Flavell and Stedman rank ordering could not be due to judgments based solely on overlap in distinctive features. Many other kinds of criteria appear to be involved in similarity judgments. In any case, it is somewhat ironic that the problem of not knowing what is happening when people are used as measuring instruments, raised at the beginning of this chapter and given as the reason why certain procedures in the social sciences produce invalid results, returns to plague a later formulation about exactly how these invalid results come about.

Wider Implications and Alternative Schemas

If the argument presented here concerning the lack of validity of procedures for discovering how behavior is organized when these procedures are based on correlations of long-term memory judgments is correct, a large number of studies in the social sciences are brought into question. Correlational studies relying on memory-based checklists, ratings, or interviews are obviously placed in the "dubious" category (Burton 1970). Most of these correlational studies have attempted to show that certain general traits or dimensions of behavior make possible an economic description of personality, or child rearing, or interpersonal behavior. But if the correlations on which these studies rest are primarily an artifact of the rater's or the questionnaire taker's cognitive structure, and not a reflection of the real world, there is little or no evidence that human behavior can be described by large multibehavior units. What remains is a world in which human behavior is to be described in terms of specific behaviors occurring in specific situations, as Mischell and others have argued (Mischell 1968).

A world made up of numerous ungroupable behaviors might seem disadvantageous for attempts to describe human behavior. Without multibehavior unit constructs, such as extroversion, assertiveness, intelligence, and so forth, it might seem that the goal of accounting for a large portion of an individual's behavior with a relatively small number of descriptive terms is not feasible. There is an alternative to the multibehavior unit schemata, however, one based on the analysis of the distribution of frequencies with which specific behaviors are performed.

Frequency distributions for category systems applicable to human behavior display very common forms or shapes, and these shapes make possible brief descriptions which account for large portions of behaviors. The shape of a frequency distribution for the nominal or unordered classes typical of most behavior-category systems is usually drawn as a rank-frequency graph. On this graph the categories are arranged in rank order of frequency along the horizontal axis, with the most frequent category next to the origin and with the actual frequencies (or proportions of the sum total of all categories) scaled along the vertical axis. Obviously, for any set of frequencies, a line through the frequency plots for each rank will decrease monotonically (i.e., each point will be lower than the point to its left). Figure 5.5 presents an example of a rank-frequency graph, with four possible kinds of rank-frequency relations plotted by the curves *A, B, C,* and *D.*

One of the most general findings in the social sciences is that rank-frequency plots for a variety of classifications of behavior have shapes

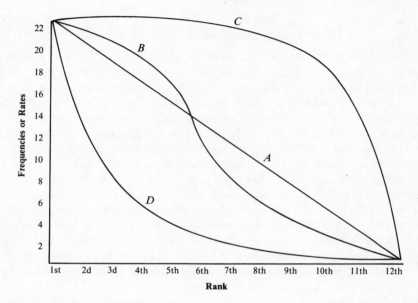

Figure 5.5.   Rank-frequency graph.

like curve *D*, which shows a rapid drop from the first- to the second-ranked category, and successively smaller drops as rank decreases. In a number of cases these concave-shaped frequency relations, when graphed on log-log coordinates, display straight lines. Such curves are often called Zipf curves. For the argument here, however, the curve does not have to be a true Zipf curve, but it must have a pronounced concave shape.

Figures 5.6 and 5.7 present rank-frequency plots for the proportional-frequency data from the two experimental group conditions of Mann's 1959 study. Both plots show pronounced concave forms, with the social-emotional condition displaying an even steeper initial drop than the task condition. There are other interesting differences between the two group conditions; *suggests* and *disagrees* are lower in rank order for the social-emotional condition than for the task condition, while *jokes* is higher.

The steep initial drops from the high-ranking categories show that most of the behavior of these small groups occurs in just a few categories. In the task condition group the two categories of *opinions* and *suggestions* account for 65 percent of all the behavior. In the social-emotional condition group the two categories of *opinions* and *agreement* account for about 70 percent of all the behavior.

A concave shape of a rank-frequency curve indicates that a good prediction of what the group or individual is doing can be gained simply by guessing that the group or individual is performing a behavior

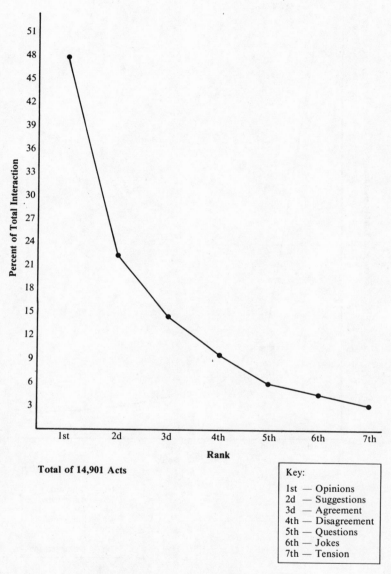

Figure 5.6. *Bales-Mann categories for task-oriented group*.

belonging to a high-rank category. Or, to put it another way, the con-cave curve indicates that the group or individual mainly performs its most frequent behaviors. It should be stressed that, if the rank-frequency plot does not have a concave form, one cannot obtain a good prediction by assuming that an individual is performing his most fre-quent behaviors. If the shape of the curve is convex, for example, like

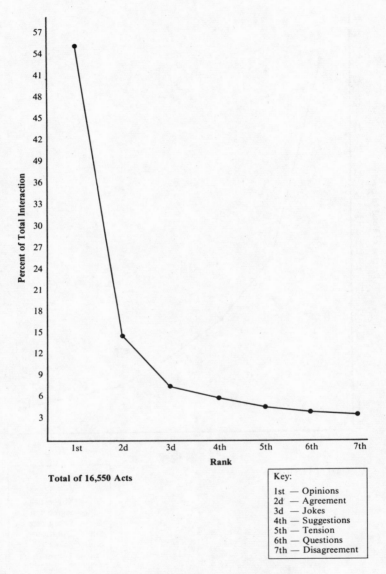

Figure 5.7. Bales-Mann categories for social-emotional group.

curve *C* in Figure 5.5, there is little improvement in prediction in saying that the individual is performing his most frequent behavior rather
than his next-to-most frequent behavior.

The concave form of rank-frequency relations implies that it is not
necessary to group behaviors into clusters, or traits, or dimensions to be
able to give an economical description of an individual's behaviors. In-

stead, by using a number of different category systems and plotting the rank-frequency relations for each one, a good description of a person's behavior can be given by "skimming off" the top-ranking categories from each classification system and then describing that person as highly likely to be performing these few behaviors. Thus, if one categorizes a person's gestures, his paralinguistic repertoire, the durations of his speech and silence, his choice of conversational topics, his selection of behavior settings, and so forth, and simply picks the highest frequency category for each of these classifications, a remarkably predictive description can be obtained.

The usefulness of describing individuals or groups in terms of their high-frequency behaviors depends on the degree of concavity of the rank-frequency relation. But why does the rank-frequency relation almost always show a concave shape for behavior-category systems? There seem to be various possible causes. Zipf curves, for example, can be generated by a random-walk process (Miller and Newman 1958); and other random processes, such as binomial series, typically show concave curves when plotted in rank-frequency charts. Thus the concavity of the rank-frequency relation may simply be a result of the nonorganized features of behavior determined by our descriptive methods.

The critical difference between this behavior-specific approach to description and the multibehavior unit approach is that the former does *not* assume that, because an individual performs one specific aggressive act (such as insulting others) with high frequency, he will perform other aggressive acts (like *hitting* or *using threat stares*) with high frequency. No generality in behavior is assumed, as in the multibehavior unit approach.

The failure of the multibehavior unit approach to yield good predictions of individual or group behavior is still a moot point in some areas of the social sciences. The pattern of evidence seems clear, however: the conception of humans in terms of dimensions, general traits, and so forth, has not been found to have reasonable validity (Hunt 1965; Vernon 1965; Mischell 1968). With respect to culture and personality studies this means that the descriptions of specific high-frequency behaviors said to be typical of a culture are probably useful in accounting for a considerable number of behaviors in that culture; whereas the more abstract descriptions of cultures as *Appollonian*, or *gentle*, probably lack validity, in that cultures thus described most likely provide many particular examples of high-frequency, non-Appollonian—or nongentle—behaviors.

References

Bales, R. F.
1969. *Personality and Interpersonal Behavior*. New York: Holt, Rinehart & Winston.

Borgatta, E. F., L. S. Cottrell, and J. H. Mann
1958. "The Spectrum of Individual Interaction Characteristics: An Inter-Dimensional Analysis." *Psychological Reports* 4:279-319.

Burton, Roger V.
1970. "Validity of Retrospective Reports Assessed by the Multitrait-Multimethod Analysis." *Developmental Psychology Monograph* 3, no. 3, pt. 2:1-15.

Campbell, D., and D. Fiske
1959. "Convergent and Discriminant Validation by the Multitrait-Multimethod Matrix." *Psychological Bulletin* 56:81-105.

Chapman, Loren J.
1967. "Illusory Correlation in Observational Report." *Journal of Verbal Learning and Verbal Behavior* 6:151-55.

D'Andrade, R. G.
1965. "Trait Psychology and Componential Analysis. *American Anthropologist* 67, no. 5, pt. 2:215-28.

Flavell, J. F., and E. H. Flavell
1959. "One Determinant of Judged Semantic and Associative Connection between Words. *Journal of Experimental Psychology* 58:159-65.

Flavell, J. F., and D. J. Stedman
1961. "A Developmental Study of Judgments of Semantic Similarity." *Journal of Genetic Psychology* 98:279-93.

Guilford, J. P.
1936. *Psychometric Methods*. New York: McGraw-Hill.

Hunt, J. McV.
1965. "Traditional Personality Theory in the Light of Recent Evidence. *American Scientist* 53:80-96.

Liberman, A. M., F. S. Cooper, D. P. Shankweller, and M. Studdert-Kennedy
1967. "Percepting the Speech Code." *Psychological Review* 74, no. 6:431-61.

Mann, R. D.
1959. "The Relation between Personality Characteristics and Individual Performance in Small Groups." Ph.D. dissertation, University of Michigan.

Miller, G. A.
1956. "The Magical Number Seven, Plus or Minus Two: Some Limits on Our Capacity for Processing Information." *Psychological Review* 63:81-97.

Miller, G. A., and E. G. Newman
1958. "Tests of a Statistical Explanation of the Rank-Frequency Relation for Words in Written English." *American Journal of Psychology* 71:209-18.

Mischell, W.
1968. *Personality and Assessment*. New York: Wiley.

Newcomb, T.
1931. "An Experiment Designed to Test the Validity of a Rating Technique." *Journal of Educational Psychology* 22:279-89.

Parsons, T., and F. Bales
1955. *Family, Socialization and Interaction Process*. Glencoe, Illinois: Free Press.

Shweder, Richard
1972. "Semantic Structures and Personality Assessment." Ph.D. Dissertation, Harvard University.

Chapter 6

MEASUREMENT ERROR IN SOCIOMETRY

PAUL W. HOLLAND
SAMUEL LEINHARDT

Paul W. Holland received his Ph.D. in Statistics from Stanford University in 1966. Currently, he is senior research associate at the National Bureau of Economic Research, Computer Research Center, Cambridge, Massachusetts, and lecturer in statistics at Harvard University. Professor Leinhardt received his Ph.D. in Sociology from the University of Chicago in 1968, and is presently Associate Professor of Sociology at Carnegie-Mellon University. Together, Dr. Holland and Professor Leinhardt have published several recent articles that deal with models and measurement in sociology.

It has been suggested that "the potential of sociometry for studying total social structures has been neglected" (Boyle 1969, p. 99). We take this to mean that the complexity of sociometric data has led to an emphasis on the analysis of local structure in groups, while total structure has been underanalyzed. Customarily, sociometric networks are assumed to possess face validity, and thus, to represent the actual organization of interpersonal relations within groups.[1] This assumption and the observed complexity of sociometric data suggest two intertwined research strategies. The first calls for ignoring part of the data to sim-

This chapter is a condensation of "The Structural Implications of Measurement Error in Sociometry," by P. Holland and S. Leinhardt, the *Journal of Mathematical Sociology*, January (1973), Vol. 3, No. 1, pp. 85-112; Gordon and Breach Science Publishers. Research support for Paul Holland was provided through National Science Foundation grants GP-8774 and GS-2044X to the Department of Statistics, Harvard University. Samuel Leinhardt held a Social Science Research Council Postdoctoral Fellowship when the research reported in this chapter was initiated.

1. Morton (1959, p. 11) expresses this common assumption in this manner: "The value of the sociogram lies in its face validity and in its possibility of providing a compelling and easily understandable picture of the data."

plify the network—for example, the common practices of ignoring asymmetric choices (see Coleman 1963; Hunter 1953),[2] and of concentrating on outlying individuals (see Moreno 1934). The second leads to the development of increasingly more complicated models—as indicated by the series: Cartwright and Harary (1956); Davis (1967); Davis and Leinhardt (1972); Holland and Leinhardt (1970, 1971); Leinhardt (1972); and Davis, Holland, and Leinhardt (1971).

It is a traditional statistical conception that all data are composed of a true structure plus noise. From this perspective the customary assumption of face validity for sociometric data amounts to assuming that any noise introduced by the sociometric procedure itself may be safely ignored. It is our purpose here to demonstrate that this assumption carries with it a high degree of risk.

While it is important to develop models of the true structure underlying sociometric data, we believe that not enough effort has been made to understand the inherent fallibility of these data. In this chapter we illustrate how most extant sociograms distort the networks of relationships they are presumed to represent. Such distortion cannot be removed or rendered less obscuring by throwing away data or by applying more complex structural models. We submit that although techniques of sociometric analysis have become increasingly more sophisticated they have failed to yield unequivocal results because of their inability to distinguish structural complexity from measurement error.

In the first section we shall discuss the meaning of measurement error in sociometric data and show how it is generated in a variety of common sociometric procedures. To provide a better understanding of the process of distortion we introduce the notion of compatibility, essentially a question whether the observed structure of sociometric data contains or is contained in the underlying, or true, structure of the group. In the next section we examine the likelihood that fixed-choice sociometric tests, tests in which a set number of responses is requested from every group member, yield sociograms of low compatibility. Free-choice tests, tests in which each group member is permitted to decide on the number of choices he or she wishes to make, are then considered briefly. The importance of sociometric data for the study of small-scale social systems leads us to suggest two approaches that may help to make these data more useful. The first is to develop robust data-analysis techniques that measure statistical tendencies and are not

2. Davis and Leinhardt (1972) collected a data bank of 917 sociograms of groups containing seven or more members by combing the literature and polling investigators privately. Fifty-eight of these sociograms contain only mutual positive choices. Since these were "raw" data the tendency to use only symmetric choices in empirical studies would be underestimated by the frequency of mutual choice sociograms in this data bank.

dependent upon the reconstruction of actual networks of interpersonal sentiment. The second is to develop techniques for gathering sociometric data that minimize the effects of measurement error (cf. Hallinan 1972). We have made some contribution to these two approaches elsewhere (Holland and Leinhardt 1970, 1972; Leinhardt 1972; Holland and Leinhardt 1973), which we briefly describe; and we conclude the chapter with a summary and some suggestions for future research using sociometric data.

The problem of measurement error in sociometric data is an example of a general problem likely to be encountered when data on networks of relations are gathered. By far the most common data on networks encountered in sociology are data on networks of positive interpersonal-sentiment relations. We therefore restrict our comments to this type of data with the understanding that most are equally applicable to data on networks of nonsentiment relations such as interaction, literature citations, dominance, kinship, acquaintance, association, recognition, and so forth.

Measurement Error In Sociometric Data

We assume that all groups possess an underlying pattern of generalized affect that is not directly observable but that generates the responses of group members in sociometric tests. We call this underlying pattern the *true structure* of the group and distinguish it from the *observed structure*, or *sociogram*. Conceptualizing sociometric measurement in this way puts it into the standard statistical model for all measurement—namely, that an observation (the sociogram) is a combination of a signal (the true structure) and noise (measurement error).

The mathematical nature of the observed structure, or sociogram, is generally understood to be a directed graph with a directed edge proceeding from node x to node y if and only if person x chooses person y in the sociometric test. Because the true structure is a hypothetical construct analogous to the "true score" of psychological test theory and is unobservable, there is no single, best, or obvious mathematical representation for it. We shall assume that it is a directed graph with a directed edge from node x to node y if and only if person x possesses any degree of positive sentiment for person y regardless of whether or not this sentiment is recorded by the sociometric test. We ignore the case of negative sentiment or disliking, though the argument is similar. Other mathematical representations for the true structure are available. The directed graph model can be generalized to a valued graph in which each edge is given a "weight" to indicate the strength and/or valence of the implied sentiment (see, e.g., Cartwright and Harary 1970). A different type of model would be one in which each group member possesses a set of rankings of the other members along various relevant continua (to be distinguished from the sociometric procedure, which requests ranks but treats the different rankings as equivalent in valence). Indeed, these or other mathematical models of the true structure may turn out to be more fruitful theoretical tools than the one we have adopted for this chapter, but for the points we wish to make here the "zero/one" model is sufficient. (In Holland and Leinhardt 1971, we describe an algebraic representation that is equivalent to the directed-graph notion.)

In sociometry, measurement error occurs when, regardless of the cause, the response made by a subject in a sociometric test fails to agree with the underlying true structure. Measurement error in zero/one sociograms occurs for two reasons: (1) no choice is recorded in the sociogram for a sentiment relation that exists in the true structure, or (2) a choice is recorded in the sociogram for which there is no corresponding sentiment relation in the true structure. In essence then, measurement error in sociometric data is a misclassification problem in which the relation between a pair of nodes is erroneously recorded. While the existence of this problem has been observed before (e.g., "Sociometric data are known to be a little sloppy" [Boyle 1969, p.109]) it is its implications for theoretical inference that are important and that have not been fully appreciated.

All procedures designed to gather information on empirical phenomena are to some extent prone to measurement error. At the very least, all require care in administration if their validity as measurements is not to be discounted. In sociometry, as elsewhere, measurement error can inadvertantly be introduced by "sloppy" technique. The mistaken transcription of choices, inadequate description of the task, unwillingness on the part of subjects to cooperate, accidental interference with the procedure, and so forth, can severely affect both the reliability and the validity of the test. Although not entirely removable, these contaminants are minimized straightforwardly. A more subtle generator and major source of measurement error resides in the formalities of common sociometric procedures. If the procedure employed constrains the number of choices obtained from each subject, and if any component of the true structure cannot be exactly rendered within the context of these constraints, the structure observed in the data can only be a distorted representation of the underlying, or true, structure of the group's interpersonal relations.

The amount of distortion introduced by the formalities of the procedure depends on the nature of the group's true structure and the type of procedure employed. How critical this distortion is will depend on the structural variables of concern to the investigator. Many reasonable structures cannot be exactly rendered by the most common sociometric procedures. On the other hand, certain characteristics of structure are more robust than others and can be consistently measured irrespective of the procedure used in gathering the sociometric data. In general, the greater the dependence of a structural characteristic on the exact rendition of structure and the greater the interest in fine structure, the more critical will be the choice of the procedure. We shall consider each of these factors in turn. We limit our concern in the remainder of this section to the last factor, the effect of the form of the sociometric procedure.

Several varieties of sociometric tests predominate in the literature. For later reference we summarize them here. The most common is the *fixed-choice* procedure. Here, every group member is required to make the same number of choices from among the other group members on some criterion such as "friendship." In this case the number of choices a group member makes is fixed by the investigator before the test is carried out.

A second commonly used sociometric test is the *free-choice* procedure. This is exactly the same as the fixed-choice test except that there are no overt restrictions on the number of choices each group member can make.

A third technique is to obtain from each group member a complete ranking of all the other members on some criterion such as friendship. Related to this is the method of paired comparisons, which requires each group member to compare every *pair* of other members and to indicate which group member in each of the pairs is preferred to the other.

Some intermediate varieties of sociometric procedures combine features of two or more of those described above. One, the partial ranking procedure, is like a fixed-choice test except that the choices are ordered—first choice, second choice, and so forth, up to some imposed limit. Another involves applying the fixed-choice procedure repetitively during one administration, with different choice criteria used with each replication. The results of such replications can be viewed as separate fixed-choice tests or combined into one grand test that is something like a weighted free-choice test with no redundant choices for individuals allowed (see, e.g., Leinhardt 1972). Examples of these and other techniques can be found in the literature, but for reasons of administrative simplicity and tradition the fixed-choice test, typically with a three-choice limit, is the most common; the free-choice is next in popularity.[3] In all these techniques negative choices, or "rejections,"

---

3. In Davis and Leinhardt's collection of 917 sociograms, 427 are probably fixed-choice sociograms and 386 are probably free-choice sociograms. The mean choices made per member average 2.6 ($\sigma = 1.4$) for fixed-choice and 6.4 ($\sigma = 4.8$) for free-choice. Several relatively recent research reports have utilized fixed-choice sociograms with two- or three-choice limits (Murray 1965; Coleman, Katz, and Menzel 1966; Caplow and Finsterbusch 1967).

can be and occasionally are requested. This is an extraneous and complicating factor, and we ignore it here.

The popularity of the fixed-choice procedure provides an initial empirical observation of the extent of measurement error in extant sociometric data. The standard deviation of the row sums of a fixed-choice sociomatrix should be zero. Since all group members are required to make the same number of choices, there should, by definition, be no variability between the total numbers of choices made by different individuals. However, of 384 sociomatrices (taken from the data collected by Davis and Leinhardt) reported by investigators to have been generated by fixed-choice procedures, the row standard deviation exceeded one for 138 sociograms and was equal to zero for only 65. Apparently, in more than 35 percent of these sociograms something had interfered with execution of the formal test design.

In the light of our definition of measurement error, let us now consider the effect on the resulting observation of interpersonal structure of a fixed-choice test in which each group member complies with the formal request to name "three best friends." Each person is required to make three choices. Obviously, if the group members name different numbers of friends, the use of this procedure must produce a sociogram that distorts the underlying pattern of affect. Furthermore, if differential affect is an important aspect of a theoretical model of the true structure, the data will make its exact confirmation impossible. Last, if the investigator's objective is to draw conclusions about the particular group tested or about individual group members, many conclusions are likely to be entirely erroneous.

The fixed-choice procedure provides a simple vehicle for illustrating the role played by measurement error in sociometry, and since this procedure has enjoyed widespread use, its inherent difficulties should be made explicit. Consequently, the next section is devoted to examining the fixed-choice case in detail.

When the distortion-laden character of the fixed-choice procedure is pointed out, it is natural to suggest that the free-choice procedure might be preferable. While the free-choice procedure does result in a much wider class of sociograms (and thereby removes an obvious source of measurement error), more subtle problems may remain. We shall discuss these other possibilities in the following section.

Effects of the Fixed-Choice Procedure

In this section we shall refer to "compatibility" between a sociogram and the true structure. In a fixed-choice test in which each person makes l choices, compatitility of the true structure and the sociogram means that the l directed edges (arrows) emanating from each node of the sociogram satisfy the following three conditions:

i. If *exactly* l arrows emanate from a given node in the true structure, these same l arrows, only, emanate from the corresponding node in the sociogram.

ii. If *more than* l arrows emanate from a given node in the true structure, the l arrows emanating from the corresponding node in the sociogram are a subset of them.

iii. If *fewer than* l arrows emanate from a given node in the true structure, they are a subset of the l arrows emanating from the corresponding node in the sociogram.

An example may help to clarify the meaning of compatibility. Consider a three-choice test in which each subject is asked to choose three friends from among the group members. Each subject is in one of three situations:

1. *Exactly three* other members are liked and are chosen, as the test requires.

2. *More than three* other members are liked, and therefore only a subset of three of them is chosen, which satisfies the constraints of the test.

3. *Fewer than three* other members are liked and are chosen, but so, too, are persons besides these, in accord with the requirement of three choices.

In cases 2 and 3, the subject's choices are not determined uniquely by the true structure. If the subject has four "friends," we assume that three are chosen from this set of four in response to the sociometric test. If the subject has only two friends, we assume that they are chosen with certainty and that one additional person outside this circle is chosen to fill the quota of three. A number of processes could be posited to generate the actual choices made in cases 2 and 3, but it is not directly relevant for us to do so here. The simplest model is to assume that in case 2 all subsets of three within this larger circle of friends are equally likely, and that in case 3 the persons needed to fill the quota of three are chosen at random from outside the smaller circle of friends. Regardless of the mechanism that generates these choices, we shall say that whenever the l-choice sociogram agrees with the true structure as indicated in the above prescription it is *compatible with the true structure*. To tie the true and observed structures together (i.e., give a reason for doing sociometry at all), we assume in this discussion that the true structure and the observed sociogram are compatible. It should be noted that our definition of compatibility can be extended to the free-choice case with no essential modification.

Our strategy in this section is to explicate a variety of examples in which we first posit a specific underlying true structure and then examine the distorting effects of measurement error induced by a fixed-choice test. The three-person group, because of its structural simplicity, is a useful starting point. It should be viewed as an easily appreciated ideal type rather than as a realistic example. This discussion is followed by an investigation of measurement error in larger, more realistic groups of six and twenty members.

If a three-person group is given a sociometric test requiring each member to choose one other person, only two types of sociograms can result. These are illustrated in Figure 6.1. In Figure 6.1*a* person A chooses *B*, as does person *C*, and person *B* reciprocates *C*'s choice. The *B-C* edge of Figure 6.1*a* is a mutual pair; the *A-B* edge is an asymmetric pair; and the *A-C* edge is a mutual nonchoice, or null pair. In Figure 6.1*b*, *A* chooses *B* who chooses *C* who chooses *A*. All these edges are unreciprocated choices, or asymmetric pairs. Although Figures 6.1*a* and 6.1*b* illustrate the only possible types of one-choice sociograms for three people, six versions of Figure 6.1*a* and two versions of Figure 6.1*b* can be obtained by rearranging the labels of the individuals.

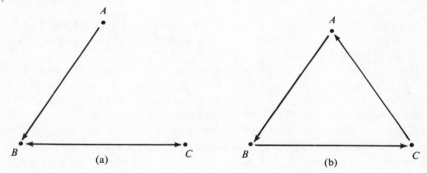

Figure 6.1.　One-choice sociograms for three-person groups.

In Figure 6.2 all possible nonisomorphic classes of triads (digraphs with three nodes) are graphed. These sixteen configurations are identified by a code standing for the number of mutual, asymmetric, and mutually null edges they contain, respectively, and in some instances they are further differentiated by the letters *U, D, C*, or *T*, which code the orientation of asymmetric pairs (see Holland and Leinhardt 1970).[4] Under this system the sociogram in Figure 6.1*a* would be identified with the triad 111*D*, and the sociogram in Figure 6.1*b* would be a triad of type 030*C*.

4. The letters *U* and *D* orient the asymmetric pairs "up" out of the mutual choice or nonchoice or "down" into it, respectively, as in 021*U* and 021*D*; the letters *C* and *T* are associated with some cyclic and transitive triads.

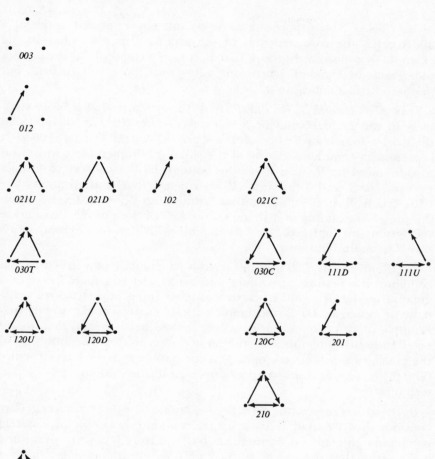

Figure 6.2.   Nonisomorphic triad types (following Holland and Leinhardt 1970).

Two cliques. Suppose a 102 triad represents the true structure of a three-person group: *A* and *B* are mutual friends, while *C* is not a member of their clique. This is a trivial example of a "balanced" graph (Harary, Norman, and Cartwright 1965). Only one of the possible three-person, one-choice sociograms in Figure 6.1 (the 111*D* triad, Fig. 6.1*a*) is compatible with this true structure. A 030*C* triad such as Figure 1*b* is not compatible with this underlying structure because *A* and *B* must choose each other in the sociogram. In this case the true structure cannot be reproduced identically by the sociogram.

One Clique. Now suppose that the completely connected graph of a 300 triad is the true structure of the group. This is another simple example of a balanced group, that is, a single clique. In this case *both* sociograms in Figure 6.1 are compatible with the true structure, but neither one is identical to it.

Transitive Hierarchy. The 030T triad is a structure that is more common in the animal-behavior literature (Landau 1951a, 1951b, 1953) than in sociometry (cf., however, French 1956 and Friedell 1967). It represents a complete ranking of the three group members, with A on top, followed by B, with C on the bottom. In the context of human groups, Davis and Leinhardt (1972) suggest that configurations like 030T triads illustrate the idea that "admiration flows up levels." As in the previous example of a single clique, *both* of the possible one-choice sociograms in Figure 6.1 are compatible with this hierarchical structure, but again both distort it.

Two Ranked Cliques. The 120D triad is an example of a structure that combines the features of cliques and ranks and is a special case of a general model (the ranked-clusters model) for group structure originally proposed by Davis and Leinhardt (1972). It is similar to our first example of two cliques, but C is now ranked below A and B, who are equal in status as members of the same clique. In this case, only one of the possible one-choice sociograms is compatible with the true structure (Fig. 6.1a), and, as in previous examples, it distorts the underlying pattern of affect.

Disconnected Components. As a final example of a three-person group, consider the 102 triad. This structure is another example of a system combining cliques and hierarchies, but it differs from the preceding example in that the clique formed by C is noncomparable with the hierarchically ranked system formed by A and B. Such a structure is an example of the transitive graph (t-graph) explored in Holland and Leinhardt (1971). This particular structure contradicts the hypothesis of Davis and Leinhardt's (1972) model that null pairs only pass between groups of equal status. Empirically, the structure is commonly found among groups of schoolchildren, who tend to segregate their choice preferences by making choices only among members of their own sex. In this case only the 111D triad of Figure 6.1 (fig. 6.1a) is compatible with the underlying structure, but it also distorts it.

These five examples were chosen because they are simple illustrations of various models that have been proposed for the structure of interpersonal relations. They obviously do not exhaust the possibilities of true structures for three-person groups. In every case examined, limiting each individual's choices to one led to misrepresentation of the true structure. *This distortion is serious enough to make it impossible to distinguish, in the data, among two unranked cliques, two ranked cliques, a three-level hierarchy, a single clique, or a system of two disconnected components.*

The examples of measurement error in a one-choice sociogram of a three-person group have extensions to larger groups. If, in an *n*-person group, each person is asked to name his "best friend" (i.e., make exactly one choice) the form of the resulting sociogram is still quite limited, as a little reflection reveals (see, e.g., Harary, Norman, and Cartwright 1965, p. 324). In particular, the only general features the one-choice sociogram, or "functional digraph" (a digraph with exactly one directed line emanating from each node; see Harary 1967) may possess are "cycles" (directed paths beginning and ending at the same node) of varying lengths with or without one or more "tails" (asymmetric pairs oriented toward one node of a cycle) of varying lengths and complexity. Such sociograms may contain only half of the sixteen nonisomorphic types of triads. Only triads of varieties 003, 012, 021*U*, 102, 021*C*, 030*C*, and 11*D* (top half of Fig. 6.2) may appear, since the other nine require at least one member to make two choices (see Hallinan 1972). Some versions of the possible configurations in which no node has an out-degree (the number of directed lines emanating from a node) in excess of one appear in Figure 6.3. Figure 6.3*a* is a mutual pair (a cycle of length 2), 6.3*b* is a cycle of length 2 with two tails, 6.3*c* is a cycle of length 4, and 6.3*d* is a cycle of length 5 with a complex tail. Any one-choice sociogram must be made up of a system of configurations like those exemplified in Figure 6.3. Because these are the only types of configurations that can result from a one-choice sociometric test, interpreting them in substantive terms (i.e., cliques, admiration flows, and so forth) must be done with caution. Authors who have cited one-choice sociograms as data include Cunningham (1951), Caldwell (1959), Criswell (1939), Faunce and Beegle (1945), Venable (1954), and Grossman and Wrighter (1948).

The one-choice sociometric test is an extreme example, but one that clearly illustrates the type and extent of the constraints the fixed-choice procedure imposes on the resulting sociogram. It is also simple enough that the effects of measurement error on the true structure are relatively easy to see. In the general *l*-choice test, the effects of measurement error are not as easy to visualize, but it is apparent that the true structure can still be seriously distorted. To argue this point further, we shall now investigate some larger structures and illustrate the effects of two- and three-choice tests, situations in which all sixteen triads are possible.

Figure 6.4 is a six-person group that is a transitive graph, or *t*-graph (a graph containing none of the triads listed on the right side of Fig. 6.2), and another example of the ranked-clusters model of Davis

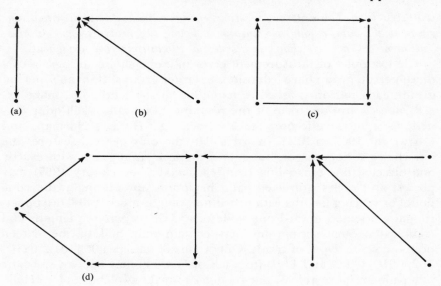

Figure 6.3.   Several possible one-choice sociograms.

and Leinhardt (1972). We follow the general interpretation of small-scale social structure presented by Holland and Leinhardt (1971) and Davis and Leinhardt (1972). There are three levels of status: *A* is at the top; *B, C, D,* and *E* are equivalent in status (receive the same number of choices) and rank below *A*, while *F* is on the bottom; and *B* and *C* form a clique, as do *D* and *E*.

Suppose Figure 6.4 represents the true structure of a six-person group that is given a two-choice sociometric test. What sort of sociogram would result? Persons *B, C, D,* and *E* all have positive affect with two other people; so if the resulting sociogram is to be compatible with Figure 6.4 they must all make those two choices (e.g., *B* must choose *C* and *A*, and so forth. But *F* would like to choose everybody and can only choose two, while *A* does not reciprocate affect with anyone and hence is forced to make choices where none exist. There are 100 sociograms which are compatible with Figure 6.4 and the two-choice sociometric test. Person *A* can make ten different *pairs* of choices, as can *F*. For the purposes of this discussion we shall reduce the number of compatible sociograms by fixing *A*'s choices and varying only *F*'s. Because *A* is forced to make two choices, we assume that he chooses people closest to him in status—for example, *B* and *E*. These arbitrary restrictions on *A* are not essential to our argument, and while they are consistent with some sociological theory (e.g., Homans [1950] expects individuals to choose up to those nearest, i.e., to go through channels), we only employ them to cut down the number of compatible graphs to a manage-

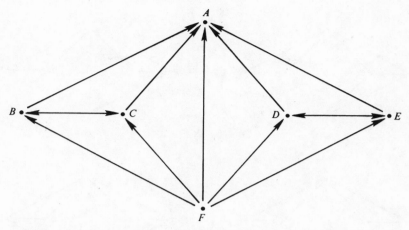

Figure 6.4.   *Example of six-person group whose underlying structure is a system of ranked clusters.*

able size. The ten remaining compatible sociograms are found by varying *F*'s choices. Of these only six are essentially different (nonisomorphic). These six appear in Figure 6.5.

Sociograms can always be drawn to emphasize particular structural features. In Figure 6.5 we have emphasized the similarities between these six possible sociometric observations and the true structure in Figure 6.4. As in the three-person groups, limiting choices has distorted the underlying true structure, but each version does this in a different way. The differences between the graphs in Figure 6.5 are subtle (e.g., each has four mutual pairs, four asymmetric pairs and seven null pairs); consequently, it is interesting to see how they compare according to some quantitative sociometric measures. We shall compare four measures: sociometric status; δ, an index of structure for the ranked-clusters model proposed by Davis and Leinhardt (1971); τ, a standardized measure of transitive organization (Holland and Leinhardt 1970, 1971); and τ*, a more sensitive indicator of transitivity (Leinhardt 1972). These measures are defined below.

Sociometric Status

Choice status (or the number of choices received) is a traditional measure used to describe the results of sociometric tests. Table 6.1 gives the choice statuses for individuals *A* through *F* for the graphs depicted in Figure 6.4 and Figures 6.5*a*-6.5*f*. Obviously, there is a considerable agreement between choice statuses in these six structures. Person *A* is nearly always the "star" receiving more choices than anyone else, and *F* is always an "isolate" never receiving any choices. Persons *B, C, D,* and *E* share various intermediate ranks. Measurement error has made *B*

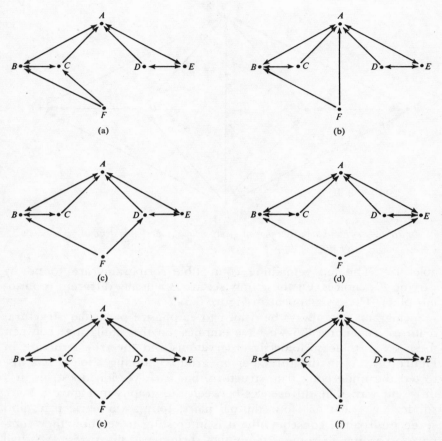

Figure 6.5.   Six possible sociograms generated in response to a two-choice
sociometric test when underlying structure is that of Figure 6.4.

Table 6.1. Choice Status by Individual for
Graphs of Figures 6.4 and 6.5

| Individual | Figure | | | | | | |
	6.4	6.5a	6.5b	6.5c	6.5d	6.5e	6.5f
A	5	4	5	4	4	4	5
B	2	4	3	3	3	2	2
C	2	2	1	1	1	2	2
D	2	1	1	2	1	2	1
E	2	2	2	2	3	2	2
F	0	0	0	0	0	0	0

and *E* appear slightly higher in status than *C* and *D*. This is due to our
arbitrary assumption that *A* chooses them. While measurement error

has interfered with the choice-status distribution in this example, it certainly has not distorted it beyond recognition. This is not an artifact of this particular example, but a general consequence of our assumption that the sociogram is compatible with the true structure.

The number of choices received is a very gross measure of the pattern or structure of the choices that appear in a sociogram. Since only *A* and *F* were clearly distinguishable, it is understandable that sociometric status finds its principal use in discussions of extreme positions in the social structure such as those of stars and isolates. It is clearly less useful when it is necessary to discriminate among individuals who are not characterizable as extremes in distributions. To examine these graphs more deeply we consider several measures which are capable of analyzing fine structure.

Measures of Structure Based on Triad Censuses

Several measures of structure based on combinations of the sixteen nonisomorphic triads have been advanced by Davis and Leinhardt (1972), Holland and Leinhardt (1970, 1971), and Leinhardt (1972). These measures are designed to assess the deviation from randomness of an observed sociogram in the direction of general models of group structure. Each of these models contains as special cases such diverse structures as clusterable graphs (graphs containing only symmetric pairs and which can be arranged so that all positive pairs connect individuals in a clique and all negative pairs connect cliques) and transitive tournaments (complete asymmetric digraphs containing no cycles). The *t*-graph model of Holland and Leinhardt (1971) is the most general; the Davis and Leinhardt (1972) model is a special case of a *t*-graph. The measures for these models take into account the character of every triad in the group and therefore delve far deeper into the structure of the sociogram than does sociometric status. Since neither the structural models upon which the measures are based nor the notion of randomness they employ are widely used in sociometry, we shall briefly review them here. We present first the ranked clusters model of Davis and Leinhardt (1972) and then note the changes introduced by the more general *t*-graph model of Holland and Leinhardt (1971).

The essential feature of Davis and Leinhardt's ranked-clusters structural model is that unreciprocated choices or asymmetric pairs are taken as evidence of ranking or hierarchy, while mutual choices are interpreted in terms of cliquing. The resulting model has two features: (i) a single system of hierarchically arranged levels, and (ii) within each level a cluster of one or more cliques. Individuals on the lower levels make unreciprocated choices to those on higher levels. Within a level, individuals in the same clique make only mutual choices to each other, while individuals in different cliques do not choose each other. The number of levels and the number of cliques in any level are not specified. Balance (Cartwright and Harary 1956) occurs when there is only one level and at most two cliques on that level. Clustering (Davis 1967) occurs when there is only one level but more than two cliques (to distinguish it from balance). A transitive tournament occurs when there are as many levels as there are group members and only one clique on each level (i.e., each member defines a level and clique). Davis and Leinhardt (1972) show that a sociogram can be arranged into an example of their general model if and only if eight nonisomorphic types of triads are absent (the seven triads on the right of Figure 6.2 plus the 012 triad). They propose a statistical test of the fit of their model based on the actual number of these nonpermissible triads that appear in the given sociogram.

To give their measure a statistical basis, they employ the following notion of a "random sociogram." They assume that the numbers of mutual pairs, m, asymmetric pairs, a, and null pairs, n, are given and that all sociograms with these given values of m, a, and n are equally likely. This differs from the more traditional random model employed in sociometry. The traditional assumption in the fixed-choice case is that each person distributes his l choices at random to the other $N - 1$ group members. These two methods of constructing random sociograms are not equivalent. For reasons we shall not detail here, we believe that the Davis-Leinhardt random model is more appropriate for the analysis of triadic structure than the traditional one (see Holland and Leinhardt 1970).

In proposing a t-graph model Holland and Leinhardt have asserted that the essential structural principle of positive interpersonal sentiment is transitivity. There are few operational differences between the ranked-clusters model and the general t-graph model. Within t-graphs, mutual pairs define equivalence classes and asymmetric pairs determine ordering relations. Seven of the triads cannot occur in a t-graph (those on the right of Figure 6.2), and of these, none can occur in a system of ranked clusters. One essential difference, mentioned earlier, is that t-graphs can contain disconnected components, a difference characterized by the permissibility of one particular triad, 012, in the t-graph model and by its nonpermissibility in the ranked-clusters model.

Holland and Leinhardt provide a standardized statistical measure for their model; that is, approximate significance levels for the measure can be obtained by reference to a table of the percentage points of the normal distribution. Let T be the number of intransitive triads, and μ and σ their expected value and standard deviation, respectively, if the graph is random. The standardized measure of deviation from randomness toward a t-graph, τ, given by Holland and Leinhardt (1970), is

$$\tau = \frac{T - \mu}{\sigma}$$

The measure τ is a minimum when the graph is transitive and has mean zero and variance one under the assumption that the graph is random. An alternative measure of transitivity is provided by Leinhardt (1972). This measure, τ^*, is analogous to τ except that it counts each intransitive triple rather than each intransitive triad (an intransitive triad may be intransitive from as many as three points of view and as few as one). Since the variance of the triad types was not known when their paper appeared, Davis and Leinhardt suggested the measure $\delta = (T_{DL} - \mu_{DL}) / \mu_{DL}$ (where T_{DL} is the observed frequency of the eight triads critical to the ranked-clusters model, and μ_{DL} is their expectation in a random graph) to determine whether an empirical sociogram tends to be a system of ranked clusters.

Table 6.2 presents the results of applying these measures (plus δ_{STZD}, a standardized version of δ) to the true structure in Figure 6.4 and the six sociograms in Figure 6.5. The true structure has a value of -100.00 for δ, which indicates that there are 100 percent fewer nonpermissible triads than the number expected in this example of a ranked clustering. The standardized measures for the true structure are all significantly negative, ranging from -3.83 for τ^* to -5.87 for δ_{STZD}. When we compare the measures for Figures 6.5a-6.5f, however, we obtain a wide distribution of values. These range from a factor of 3.2 to 1,250 times less than the value for the true structure in the case of τ^*. In other words, while all the values are negative and indicate tendencies in the direction of the various models, the differences among them indicate that in terms of their triads Figure 6.4 and Figures 6.5a-6.5f are quite different.

Table 6.2: Four Triadic Measures of Structure for
Graphs in Figures 6.4 and 6.5

Figure	Triadic Measure			
	δ	δ_{STZD}	τ	τ^*
6.4	-100.00	-5.87	-4.74	-3.83
6.5a	$-\ 7.77$	-0.58	-1.46	-1.63
6.5b	$-\ 30.83$	-2.33	-1.46	-1.63
6.5c	$-\ 7.77$	-0.59	-0.20	-0.77
6.5d	$-\ 0.08$	-0.01	-0.20	-0.77
6.5e	$-\ 15.47$	-1.17	-0.20	-0.78
6.5f	$-\ 23.14$	-1.75	-0.83	-1.20

It is clear that the structural measures vary in their sensitivity to the distortion occurring in the graphs of Figure 6.5. In terms of the ranked-clusters model, Figure 6.5*b* has 31 percent fewer nonpermissible triads than the number expected, while 6.5*d* has only 0.1 percent fewer. The calculation of an analogous measure for the intransitive triads would yield a similar spread. While the standardized measure τ^* varies less, in none of the graphs in Figure 6.5 is a statistically significant tendency (i.e., a value less than -1.96, the one-sided 5 percent point of the standard normal distribution) toward transitivity detected. Note that the enormous spread of values in δ has been achieved by varying the choices of only one member of the group, F, the assumedly lowest-status group member.

It may be argued that a six-person group is much too small to do these measures justice. There are only twenty triads in a group of this size, and, as we have seen, a change of one choice (e.g., 6.5*a* to 6.5*b*) can have an unduly large effect on the values of these measures. Indeed, the standardized measures have highly discontinuous sampling distributions for small-group sizes, a characteristic that invalidates the assumption of normality for the standardized measures. This problem is not present in large groups. Another reason for examining the effects of measurement error in larger groups rests in their greater frequency in empirical data. In the data bank of sociograms collected by Davis and Leinhardt, the mean group size was 24.06 ($\sigma = 14.4$). Thus, to address the issue of size and gain a greater understanding of the degree to which measurement error is present in extant data, we look at some examples of synthetic groups involving twenty persons.

For this analysis we used three different *t*-graphs as the true structure: a transitive tournament, a balanced graph with two ten-person cliques, and a two-level Davis-Leinhardt model with one five-person clique in the top level and one fifteen-person clique in the bottom level. These three structures were then distorted so as to agree with the requirements of a three-choice sociometric test. This was accomplished "at random" in the following way: If, in the true structure, exactly three arrows emanated from a group member, these were taken as the choices made in the sociogram. If more than three arrows emanated from the group member, we chose three of these at random and made them the choices in the sociogram. Finally, if fewer than three arrows emanated from the group member these became part of the required three choices, and the remaining choices were selected at random. Sociomatrices for three underlying structures and the distorted simulated observations of these structures appear in Figure 6.6.

Let us briefly examine the matrices in Figure 6.6. The structures are presented in the common sociomatrix notation, with the number "1" in the i, j position of the matrix if person i chooses person j, and with the

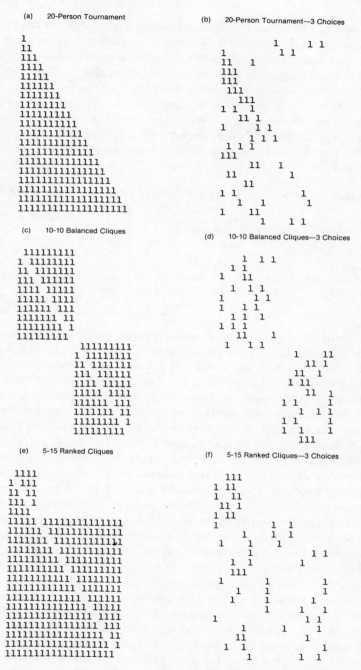

Figure 6.6. Three true structures and distorted sociomatrices generated by simulated three-choice sociometric procedure.

cell left blank otherwise. Immediately below each idealized true structure is a sociomatrix produced by using the "random" procedure previously described. Note that in the three-choice simulations we have
retained the arrangement of rows and columns that, in the sociomatrices of the true structures, render the nature of the network quickly
apparent. Were these examples of empirical observations rather than
computer simulations, such conveniences would be purely fortuitous
and extremely unlikely. If these were "real" data the rows and columns
would be permuted randomly, and visual recognition of structure
made impossible.

Table 6.3. Measures of Triadic Structure for groups in Figure 6.6

	True structures				Simulated observations			
	δ	δ_{STZD}	τ	τ^*	δ	δ_{STZD}	τ	τ^*
Tournament	−100.	−19.49	−19.49	−19.49	−3.05	−1.31	+0.08	−0.13
5-15 ranked clusters	−100.	−43.08	−43.08	−38.01	+2.11	+0.09	−1.18	−1.51
10-10 balanced clusters	−100.	−29.45	−29.45	−29.45	+2.82	+1.19	−3.69	−2.63

The results of analyzing these twenty-person groups agree quite well
with our findings for the six-person group. Table 6.3 presents the re-
sults of calculating δ, δ_{STZD}, τ, and τ^* for the true structures and the
three-choice simulated observations. The Davis-Leinhardt measure-
ment, δ, is −100 for every true structure, which indicates that each of
these three matrices represents a structure that fits this model and,
therefore, has 100 percent fewer critical triads than would be expected
on the basis of chance. The standardized measures, δ_{STZD}, τ, and τ^*, are
all significantly negative for the true structures, which indicates that
each deviates strongly from randomness toward the ranked-clusters
and *t*-graph models. The distorted versions of these true structures
present us with a completely different picture. The measure δ varies
from −3.05 for the tournament to 2.83 for the balanced cliques. Its
standardized version, δ_{STZD}, is negative only once—for the tournament.
The measure τ fares slightly better; it is negative twice and is significant
for the balanced cliques. The measure τ^* appears to fare the best; it is
negative in all cases and is significant for the balanced cliques.

Results such as these indicate that the kind of structure measured by
the triad indices is extremely sensitive to measurement error. Although
one measure, τ^*, was able to detect tendencies in the direction of the
t-graph model in every instance, it must be emphasized that only three
simulations were generated for the purposes of this discussion. It is
altogether possible that a different set of simulated observations generated from the same three true structures might yield completely differ-

ent results. Furthermore, although the range of differences in the measures is not as vast as that in the six-person groups, it is still great enough to imply that attempts to reconstruct the true structures from the "sociometric" observations would be extremely hazardous.

The results for choice status are variable, too. The correlations between the rank orders of individuals according to choice status before and after distortion are .53 for the transitive tournament, .88 for the ranked clusters, and .71 for the balanced cliques. Note that for the two ten-person cliques no choices in the distorted version can cut across the cliques. This, of course, is due to the fact that each person makes nine choices within his or her clique in the true structure and, since we have forced compatibility, chooses three from among the nine. This suggests that a gross structural feature like sex-cleavage in children's groups will not be affected by fixed-choice errors if there are more children of both sexes than allowed choices and if complete connectivity (all nodes linked to every other node by a directed line) within the cliques is not a requirement of the clique-detection technique.

Measurement Error in the Free-Choice Case

The tendency of the fixed-choice sociometric procedure to distort the underlying group structure was demonstrated in the previous section. We believe, however, that it is a serious mistake to view the problem of measurement error solely as an unfortunate property of the fixed-choice procedure. In the fixed-choice case the *mechanism* causing measurement error is easy to identify and document, but the problem of the relationship between the true structure and the results of the sociometric test exists no matter what form of test is employed (and no matter what structural model is used). Measurement error in some form occurs in all sociometric data; the problem is to assess its effects in each particular investigation. In this section we shall briefly discuss why the free-choice procedure may not be the ready panacea it appears to be. The situation in the free-choice case is more subtle than the situation in the fixed-choice case, and we know of no data that directly bear on the issues (however, see Holland and Leinhardt 1972). Consequently, this section rarely rises above the level of conjecture.

To begin with, we ask, What is the task of a subject in a free-choice test? The task of a three-choice test is easily discerned—the subject is to create a list of three names in accordance with some criterion. But in the free-choice test the subject has to decide how long the list will be, in addition to who will go on it. The blithe assumption that the respondent will continue to add names until all those considered "friends" are mentioned does not take other aspects of the test situation into consideration. In particular, it is not inconceivable that the instructions or behavior of the test administrator may contain an implicit "response norm" to the effect that most subjects will list only some specific small number of names regardless of their positions in the group or of the true numbers of their friends. For example, Bjerstedt (1956) found that in free-choice tests subjects often gave only three or four names, and he used this fact to justify using the fixed-choice test as an adequate substitute. This may, in fact, be evidence of the existence of a "response norm" such as the above. Another aspect of this response norm is the possibility that individuals are reluctant in a sociometric test to choose all the others or none of the others, even if their positions in the true structure suggest that this would be appropriate. Note that the t-graph model implies that vast variation in the distribution of choices made can result when hierarchical systems exist. A response norm would directly affect the ability of a free-choice test to reveal a true structure like that of Figure 6.4. Neither the top nor bottom individuals could respond in a nondistorted fashion. It is not at all clear how to eliminate the effects of such a response norm if it exists. Merely telling the group members to "make as many or as few choices as you want" will not necessarily make the response norm vanish, especially if the subjects have become accustomed to sociometric tests. One possible technique which may be of help is discussed in Holland and Leinhardt (1973).

A second line of evidence for measurement error in sociometry concerns negative choices, or rejections. Gronlund (1959) found that the literature on rejections is small, and various authors (e.g., White 1961) have indicated that negative choices procedurally distinct from positive choices are difficult to elicit from subjects. This might indicate that some parts of the true structure (or perhaps some of its implications) are unpleasant, evoke anxiety, or are difficult for subjects to make explicit. Exactly this type of mechanism would prevent the true structure from being identical to the sociogram. Obviously, it can operate in either a fixed- or a free-choice test.

Finally, a third mechanism that produces distortion might be termed "structural confusion." The true structure underlying a group may have different components such as admiration, friendship, and common side interests. Indeed, a single term such as friendship could have effectively different role connotations to group members who occupy different positions in the structure. This type of structure would really need a "multigraph" to describe it—for example, several different directed graphs on the same nodes considered collectively. Confusion of these distinct graphs would occur when, to a particular sociometric instruction like "name your best friends," responses recorded on only one graph are based on different components of the true structure. Thus, persons on the bottom of the structure might respond to the "admiration" component of the affective network and choose those at the very top. Persons on the top of the structure might respond to the "common side interests" component and choose those on nearby lower levels. Given the notion of measurement error and what we now know about it (at least in the fixed-choice case), we are not surprised to find in the literature the suggestion that it makes little difference how the sociometric question is phrased. Certainly the suggestion does not directly refute the notion of "structural confusion" as a possible fact of sociometric life.

Summary and Discussion

We began this chapter by raising the question whether sociometrics could serve as a data source for sophisticated analyses of social structure. Since sociometric data have been available for almost thirty-five years it seems peculiar to us that only those insights into group structure found by Moreno—that is, the skewness of the distribution of choices received, and the prevalence of mutuality—have come forth. We held that the fault lies in the data-collection procedure. Our argument revolved around the concept of measurement error, an inherent quality of any empirical data-collecting technique. We defined sociometric measurement error conceptually as the difference between the underlying, true structure of a group and the sociogram produced by the responses of the group members to a particular sociometric test. A number of examples of increasing complexity illustrating the distortion introduced by sociometric tests were developed, and we attempted to explain why we feel that the free-choice procedure is not the panacea one may have naïvely assumed.

Throughout the chapter the gist of our argument has been that commonly available sociometric data are unlikely to be adequate for the task of accurately re-creating the underlying network of interpersonal relations in small groups. We do not believe, however, that the vast and diverse body of extant sociometric data is useless, nor that it is of little relevance to theoretical issues concerning the structures of small-scale social systems. Its utility, it seems to us, rests primarily in its role as a source of data in which the statistical tendencies of structural properties can be assayed. Elsewhere (Leinhardt 1972; Holland and Leinhardt 1972), we have carried out analyses of large aggregations of common sociometric data and have shown that these data strongly and consistently support the t-graph model of the structure of positive interpersonal sentiment in small groups. Only through studies such as these is it likely that we shall be able to tease some general meaning from existing sociometric data given the very small structural signal they contain and the extensive noise of sociometric measurement error in which this signal is embedded.

References

Boyle, R. P.
1969. "Algebraic Systems for Normal and Hierarchial Sociograms." *Sociometry* 32 (March):99-119.

Bjerstedt, A.
1956. *Interpretations of Sociometric Choice Status.* Lund: CWK Gleerup; Copenhagen: Ejnar Munksgaard.

Caldwell, E.
1959. *Creating Better School Climate in the Classroom through Sociometric Techniques.* San Francisco: Fearon.

Caplow, T., and K. Finsterbusch
1967. "France and Other Countries: A Study of Interaction." Paper presented at the 62nd Annual Meeting of the American Sociological Association, 28 August, San Francisco, California.

Cartwright, D., and F. Harary
1956. "Structural Balance: A generalization of Heider's Theory." *Psychological Review* 63:277-93.
1970. "Ambivalence and Indifference in Generalizations of Structural Balance." *Behavioral Science* 15 (November):497-513.

Coleman, J. S.
1963. *Adolescent Society.* Glencoe, Ill.: Free Press.

Coleman, J. S., E. Katz, and H. Menzel
1966. *Medical Innovation: A Diffusion Study.* New York: Bobbs-Merrill.

Criswell, H. J.
1939. "A Sociometric Study of Race Cleavage in the Classroom." *Archives of Psychology*, no. 235.

Cunningham, R.
1951. "Understanding Group Behavior of Boys and Girls." Mimeographed. New York: Teachers College.

Davis, J. A.
1967. "Clustering and Structural Balance in Graphs." *Human Relations* 20, no. 2:181-87.

Davis, J. A., and S. Leinhardt
1972. "The Structure of Positive Interpersonal Relations in Small Groups." In J. Berger, M. Zelditch, Jr., and B. Anderson, eds., *Sociological Theories in Progress* Volume II. Boston: Houghton Mifflin.

Davis, J. A., P. Holland, and S. Leinhardt
1971. "Comments on Professor Mazur's Hypothesis about Interpersonal Sentiments." *American Sociological Review* 36:309-11.

Faunce, D., and J. A. Beegle
1945. "Cleavages in a Relatively Homogeneous Group of Rural Youth." *Sociometry* 8:207-16.

French, J. R. P.
1956. "A Formal Theory of Social Power." *Psychological Review* 63 (May): 181-95.

Friedell, M.
1967. "Organizations as Semilattices." *American Sociological Review* 32 (February):46-54.

Gronlund, N. W.
  1959. *Sociometry in the Classroom*. New York: Harper & Bros.
Grossman, B., and J. Wrighter
  1948. "The Relationship between Selection-Rejection and Intelligence." *Sociometry* 11:346-55.
Hallinan, M.
  1972. "Comment on Holland and Leinhardt." *American Journal of Sociology* 72 (May):1201-5.
Harary, F.
  1967. *A Seminar on Graph Theory*. New York: Holt, Rinehart & Winston.
Harary, F., R. Z. Norman, and D. Cartwright
  1965. *Structural Models*. New York: Wiley.
Holland, Paul, and Samuel Leinhardt
  1970. "A Method for Detecting Structure in Sociometric Data." *American Journal of Sociology* 76 (November):492-513.
  1971. "Transitivity in Structural Models of Small Groups." *Comparative Group Studies* 2 (May):107-24.
  1972. "Some Evidence on the Transitivity of Positive Interpersonal Sentiment." *American Journal of Sociology* 72 (May):1205-9.
  1973. "The Structural Implications of Measurement Error in Sociometry." *Journal of Mathematical Sociology* 3 (January):85-112.
Homans, G. C.
  1950. *The Human Group*. New York: Harcourt, Brace & World.
Hunter, F.
  1953. *Community Power Structure*. Chapel Hill: University of North Carolina Press.
Landau, H. G.
  1951-53. "On Dominance Relations and the Structure of Animal Societies." I, "Effect of Inherent Characteristics"; II, "Some Effects of Possible Social Factors"; III, "The Condition for a Score Structure." *Bulletin of Mathematical Biophysics* 13 (March):1-19; 13 (September):245-62; 15 (June):143-48.
Leinhardt, S.
  1972. "Developmental Change in the Sentiment Structure of Children's Groups." *American Sociological Review* 37 (April):202-12.
Moreno, J. L.
  1934. *Who Shall Survive?* Washington, D. C.: Nervous and Mental Disease Publishing Co. (second edition, 1953, New York, Beacon).
Morton, A. S.
  1959. *Similarity as a Determinant of Friendship: A Multi-dimensional Study*. Princeton, N. J.: Educational Testing Service.
Murray, T. R.
  1965. *Sociological Differences in the Classroom*. New York: David McKay.
Venable, T. C.
  1954. "The Relationship of Selected Factors to the Social Structure of a Stable Group." *Sociometry* 17:355-57.
White, H. C.
  1961. "Management Conflict and Sociometric Structure." *American Journal of Sociology* 67 (September):185-99.

II

MULTIPLE INDICATOR APPROACHES

Chapter 7

AN EMPIRICAL AND ALGEBRAIC ANALYSIS OF ALTERNATIVE TECHNIQUES FOR MEASURING UNOBSERVED VARIABLES

ALVIN L. JACOBSON
N. M. LALU

Alvin L. Jacobson received his Ph.D. in Sociology from Cornell University, in 1969. In 1968 he assumed his present position in the Department of Sociology at the University of North Carolina, Chapel Hill. Recent papers by Jacobson reflect his continuing interest in comparative studies of intranational conflict. N. M. Lalu is Assistant Professor of Sociology, University of Missouri, St. Louis. He received his Ph.D. in that same field in 1972 from the University of North Carolina, Chapel Hill. Professor Lalu's research interests include methodology and population problems.

The most striking and significant development in social science methodology in the last five years concerns the study of measurement models, or, more specifically, the causal analysis of unobserved variables. In view of the rapid growth in the number of such studies as well as the technical advances reflected in many of these works, the analysis of measurement problems now appears to stand at the forefront of the methodologists' concerns. Sociology, in particular, has become fertile ground for the cross-marriage of psychometric and econometric theories of measurement; and if the initial enthusiasm greeting these

We should like to thank Hubert M. Blalock, Jr., Arthur S. Goldberger, J. William McPherson, and Charles Werts for their helpful comments on earlier drafts of this chapter. This is a revised version of a paper presented at the 1972 Annual Meeting of the Southern Sociological Society, New Orleans.

developments is an indication, it is reasonable to suppose that studies of this kind will continue to proliferate.

All this, of course, portends well for a field like sociology, which in the past has been beset with measurement "problems." We are beginning to approach the time when heretofore untested assumptions in social science research may be tested explicitly. Even at this nascent stage, however, it is instructive to pause momentarily and ask the simple but nevertheless necessary question—What impact is the current study of measurement models having (or likely to have) on actual social science research? Additionally, we may raise the corollary question of the relationship between current interests in measurement theory and more conventional measurement practices as they are reflected in existing empirical studies. It is our conviction that it is neither too early nor inappropriate to raise these questions; indeed, if we are to realize the potential contributions this work holds, we should keep these questions at the center of our attention.

This chapter is directed toward some of these more pragmatic ends. Specifically, our principal concern is with comparing the estimates of a known structural parameter obtained from three different measurement strategies (i.e., single indicators, indexes, and multiple indicators). The comparison is made under each of four variable conditions common to all measurement operations: (1) varying the magnitude of the structural parameter to be estimated, (2) varying the strength of the epistemic correlations linking measurable indicators to unmeasured variables, (3) varying the magnitude of the correlation between error terms of measured indicators, and (4) varying the number of measured indicators used in the model. The first section of this chapter gives a brief review of some of the central characteristics, advantages, and disadvantages of the single-indicator, index, and multiple-indicator methods as exemplified in current sociological literature. This discussion is followed by an empirical comparison of the means and variances of each of three estimation procedures for a common measurement model.

Types of Measurement Procedures

Central to the process of empiricism is the issue of measurement, or the assignment of numbers to observable objects and events. Except in the case of the extreme positivist, this assignment procedure invariably involves an explicit or implicit set of rules for relating data to a corresponding theory (Coombs 1964). In practice, such rules have generally remained implicit, and analysts have usually allowed familiar conventions to influence their choices of types of procedures to follow. Two of the more common strategies chosen in this manner are the single-indicator and index techniques. A third procedure, originally advanced by Curtis and Jackson (1962) and forwarded by Siegel and Hodge (1968), Costner (1969), and Blalock (1969), represents still a different method of relating measurable indicators to underlying variables. In the following review and analysis, we have limited our attention to measurement models in which it is assumed that the unobserved variable "causes" the measured "effect" indicators (see Blalock 1969; Land 1970; and Heise 1972 for a discussion of techniques appropriate to models for which the unobserved variable is assumed to be an intervening factor).

Single Indicators
By far the most simplistic, and in a sense the most vulnerable, of the three techniques to be examined is the single-indicator method. Where only a single indicator of an underlying and unmeasured variable is identified, the analyst must essentially assume (1) that it is a "good" indicator of the unobserved variable (i.e., it accounts for most of the variation in the true variable); and (2) that there is no "specification error" (Heise 1969), or what Costner (1969) refers to as "differential bias." In other words, given two theoretical variables,[1] both of which are measured by single indicators, these two indicators are assumed to be associated *only* through the posited relationship linking the two theoretical variables. If the latter condition cannot be reasonably assumed—and in most practical situations it cannot—estimates of the structural parameter will be biased even when the first assumption holds.

The use of single indicators to measure underlying variables appears limited, especially in most sociological work. The reasons for this are no doubt varied, but in part they derive from one or more of the following: (1) problems of missing data, which are especially troublesome when only one measure of a given variable is used; (2) the abstract quality of most theoretical variables, which does not permit a useful "summarization" when a single indicator is employed; and (3) a general belief in the idea that the more indicators used, the "better" the resultant measure.[2]

Nevertheless, in some areas of study, such as demography, single indicators can be and have been used with some frequency. If, for example, one wishes to measure variables like "population size," "age-sex composition," or "birth and death rates," census data contain fairly reliable individual measures on each of these variables. Even such variables as "educational level," "economic status," "religious identification," and "social mobility" have been adequately measured with single indicators. All other things being equal, parsimony indicates a more

1. In this and the following discussion, "theoretical" variable is used synonymously with "unobserved," "unmeasured," or "underlying" variable.
2. This assumption is discussed and tested in a later section of the chapter.

widespread use of this measurement procedure; but current practice does not follow, nor has past practice necessarily followed, this simple rule of thumb.

Indexes

The second and perhaps the most common technique of measurement involves the *combined* use of several individual indicators to build a summary score, or index. With respect to our specific interest in "effect" indicators only, two general theoretical models which have given rise to the use of indexes may be identified. The first is represented in the work of Lazarsfeld and Rosenberg (1955). They suggest that an index serves as a useful summary measure for identifying a locus of points composing the attribute space of a given conceptual variable; and that, since the attribute space of most variables of sociological interest is *multidimensional*, the use of a single indicator is inadequate in describing the location of any one observation in that space. Coming more directly out of the psychometric tradition, Heise and Bohrnstedt (1970), on the other hand, speak of composite scores of a *single* underlying trait. Hence, a single variable (trait, dimension) is considered to have a number of specific and measured indicators. The difference between the two models seems to be one of the degree of abstractness of the measurement process; Lazarsfeld and Rosenberg's conceptualization of indexes is more general than Heise and Bohrnstedt's.

The general statistical model used in constructing indexes is extremely variable. Measures may vary in (1) the number of items included in an index, (2) the weights assigned to particular items, and (3) the manner in which the items are combined. In practice, the techniques described for aggregating scores across a number of indicators range from a simple additive and unweighted procedure to the kind of estimation techniques considered by Hauser and Goldberger (1971). Moreover, the number and variety of applications of indexes appearing in social science studies are almost limitless. Bonjean, Hill, and McLemore (1967) reported finding 3,609 references to 2,060 different scales purporting to measure 78 different variables (e.g., occupational status, religious orthodoxy, and social distance).

The widespread popularity of approaching measurement tasks by means of index construction appears understandable. Effectively, this measurement strategy reduces the likelihood of occurrence of the chief disadvantages noted earlier for the single-indicator model—namely, the problem of measuring multidimensional conceptual variables, and the problem of missing data. Further, this technique tends to cancel the effects of a nonrandom error term which may be associated with a single measure. What is not as readily obvious is that the use of several indicators in building composite scores increases the possible sources of specification error contained in one's model. In other words, where the error terms between any two measured indicators are themselves related through unspecified but common variables, estimates of the structural parameter will be biased. Moreover, once values have been aggregated on a number of different indicators, it is impossible to calculate estimates for the magnitude of this source of error.

A second difficulty encountered in the use of indexes is the frequent absence of a well-formulated theory to be used in the interpretation of the constructed variable. Some of the instances wherein factor analysis or item analysis has been employed for purposes of building scales or identifying underlying traits highlight the kinds of extreme abuses to which a posteriori theoretical inference is prone. When we implicitly invoke the simple adage "The more indicators, the better," it is well to ask the question—Better for what? Do we mean "better" in that the composite score is statistically valid (see Heise and Bohrnstedt 1970, eq. [2]), and/or "better" in that all of a number of underlying dimensions are represented? The lack of distinction between the two arises in part because of the failure to distinguish between the two types of models indicated above, and this is particularly a problem in the measurement of macro-level variables; here, the quality and quantity of data available to the researcher are generally such that one often combines many indicators in the belief that many "poor" indicators are "better" than one or two—or, even better than one "good" one. Part of the analysis and results presented below is designed to test this underlying belief.

Multiple Indicators

The third and final measurement procedure considered in the following analysis is one advanced by Costner (1969) and Blalock (1969).[3] The underlying logic of this technique is similar to that of the index technique in that it makes use of multiple indicators, but dissimilar in that the *separate identity* of each of the measured indicators is maintained. The measured indicators are used in solving for specified "unknowns" in a series of simultaneous equations. The greater the proportion of "known" quantities to "unknowns" (i.e., the more indicators used in measuring any one variable), the greater is one's ability to reject alternative auxiliary theories linking the measured variables with unmeasured ones.

Costner (1969) suggests three desiderata to be gained from this approach: (1) that it is possible to arrive at an estimate for each of the specified unknown coefficients; (2) that it is possible to test for some

3. Earlier references to this line of inquiry appear in the works of Lazarsfeld (1959), Curtis and Jackson (1962), and Siegel and Hodge (1968).

types of differential bias, if present; and (3) that it is possible to test the implications of the causal model outlined in the main theory. It should be emphasized that when indexes are used, neither the first nor the second desideratum is possible to fulfill. In a simple two-variable model in which indicators of each variable have been combined into a single measured variable (i.e., index), we are left in the hopeless situation of having three unknowns and one known quantity (i.e., $r_{x_1 y_1}$); in this circumstance, it is impossible to calculate unique estimates of the unknown coefficients, and we cannot test for differential bias. In fact, and as observed in our previous discussion, any existing differential bias is obscured when we aggregate separate indicators.

Not unlike the previous two procedures reviewed, the Costner (1969) technique raises peculiar problems in its own right. First, more so than the single indicator or index strategy, the multiple-indicator method requires for its analysis an explicit statement of the "cause and effect" relationships between the measured and unmeasured variables.[4] As Blalock (1971) has noted, decisions of this type are especially troublesome when an indicator is simply regarded as "an aspect of," "a part of," or "correlated with" the underlying variable. Second, it is possible to satisfy Costner's second consistency criterion (i.e., that all nine estimates of the three indicator model be approximately equal) with a number of alternative auxiliary theories. As the number of measured indicators and unmeasured variables increases, it is extremely difficult, if not impossible, to consider all logical combinations of relationships. A third problem noted by Hauser and Goldberger (1971) concerns the choice of an estimation method; if the model is overidentified, there is some question of how one ought to proceed in the selection (or construction) of a single estimate from among a number of possible estimates. A fourth and final problem has recently been raised by Althauser and Heberlein (1970). They have shown that Costner's (1969) consistency criterion is too easy to satisfy when the correlations between pairs of selected indicators falls below .30. To the extent to which the multiple-indicator method gains wider attention and application in social science research, some of these difficulties noted above will no doubt be provided workable solutions.

Analysis

The basic measurement model upon which the present analysis was conducted is shown in Figure 7.1. Following notational conventions already established in similar studies, X and Y here symbolize the two underlying or unobserved variables. The respective indicators of X and

---

4. See Blalock (1969), Land (1970), and Heise (1972) for examples of how "the indicators causes construct" model differs from the "construct causes indicators" situation.

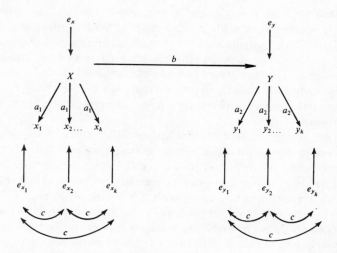

Figure 7.1. Basic measurement model.

Y are denoted by $x_1, x_2, \cdots, x_j$ and $y_1, y_2, \cdots, y_k$, and their corresponding error terms by $e_{x_1}, e_{x_2}, \ldots, e_{x_j}$ and $e_{y_1}, e_{y_2}, \ldots, e_{y_k}$. In addition, the error terms of X and Y (i.e., e_x and e_u, respectively), indicate exogenous sources of variance of the two underlying variables. The small alphabetic characters a, b, and c refer to (1) the epistemic correlations, (i.e., r_{Xx_y} or r_{Yy_k}), (2) the structural parameter (i.e., ρ_{xy}), and (3) the correlation between error terms (i.e., $re_{x_1}e_{x_k}$ and $re_{y_1}e_{y_k}$), respectively. To simplify the analysis we have assumed that all the a's are equal for all the conditions we have chosen to examine. In effect, this assumption means that we are willing to treat all our indicators as equally "good" or equally "bad" measures.[5]

Using the exact mean and variance formulas given in the Appendix, we calculated the means and variances of each of the three estimation procedures for all combinations of the desired test conditions.[6] These conditions were empirically set as follows: (1) a (epistemic correlations)

5. A preliminary analysis of data which did not make such an assumption showed that large differences were obtained between the single-indicator and index strategies (the only two techniques tested) when the set of epistemic correlations varied. It was not uncommon to find that one "good" indicator for each of the two underlying variables provided a closer approximation to the underlying parameter, than several "poor" ones combined together. It has been correctly pointed out to us that when we assume all the a's are equal we have an underidentified system of equations. In other words, we have two distinct correlations and three parameters to be estimated. Since for our purposes, we have confined our attention to estimating the parameter relating the two unmeasured variables, this limitation was non-problematical in the present study.

6. Scores for the index technique were obtained by a simple unweighted sum of the indicators for X and Y. The reader is encouraged to see Hauser and Goldberger (1971) for a discussion of an alternative way of combining indicators.

= .80 ("high"), .50 ("moderate"), and .30 ("low"); (2) b (structural parameter) = .90 ("very high"), .80 ("high"), .50 ("moderate"), and .30 ("weak"); and (3) c (correlated error) = .60 ("high"), .30 ("moderate"), and .00 ("none"). In addition, the number of indicators used in the calculation of the index estimates was systematically varied from two to four.[7] The range of values used in testing each of the above conditions was established so as to approximate a broad but realistic set of empirical constraints.

Before we discuss the major findings of the study, two preliminary points need to be emphasized. First, it is important to note that the measurement model depicted in Figure 7.1 represents only *one* type of model arising in social science research. In the language of factor analysis, we are essentially dealing with a "confirmatory factory analysis model" (Hauser and Goldberger 1971). *No* assumption is being made that this is the only such model, nor are we assuming that the results of this analysis are generalizable to other types of models (for a discussion of some of these differences, see Chapter 9 in this volume, by Werts, Linn, and Jöreskog). Second, though the values for the variances were calculated directly from the formulas given in the Appendix, this was not true for the variances of the Costner estimates. Since Costner's estimation equation for d (here, b) is a ratio of the products of two correlations (see eq. 17 in Appendix), the computational formula for this estimate is exceedingly complex. To obtain an estimate of the variance for this estimation procedure, we therefore calculated the variance of the sampling distribution on the basis of 100 samples, each of size 500.[8] These samples were selected at random from the computer, and the data were then generated according to the appropriate parameter values.[9]

With the possible exception of the latter estimate, there is a sense in which the numerical analysis presented below is redundant with the algebraic treatment given in the Appendix. We have included both forms of analyses here for the convenience of readers who might find one mode preferable to the other. At least in one respect, however, the following numerical results provide an additional opportunity for assessing measurement strategies which cannot be gained by a simple inspection of the algebraic equations—namely, that we have included in

7. By definition, estimates from the single- and multiple-indicator methods will be unaffected by changes in the number of indicators available for study. The only effect of a change in the number of indicators on the multiple-indicator technique is an increase in the number of pairs of estimates of b^2 (see eq. [42] in Costner 1969).

8. The subroutine used in the construction of this data set was GAUSS, a part of the IBM Scientific Subroutine Package. The sample size equaled 500.

9. As noted below, whenever any one of the sample statistics yielded a value for b^2 greater than 1.0 or less than 0.0, these were reassigned values of 1.0 and 0.0, respectively.

our analysis mean estimates of b based on a simple random sample of 500 observations. Hence, for each set of conditions we have (1) calculated the exact population means and variances of b, except in the case of the variance for b using the Costner technique, where the variance has been determined from the sampling distribution of 100 samples; and (2) calculated estimates of b from a single sample. Together, these two sets of statistics tell us, first, how the three estimation procedures compare in an absolute sense, and second, how far from these values we are likely to be when the analysis is realistically limited to a single set of observations.

Varying the Strength of the Structural Parameter

The first condition on which we wished to compare each of the measurement techniques was variation in the strength of b, or ρ_{yx}. Table 7.1 summarizes the results of this test while controlling for (1) the strength of the epistemic correlations, (2) the number of indicators used in the index and multiple-indicator procedures (i.e., three), and (3) the strength of the correlation between error terms. For this as well as all subsequent tests the exact mean and variance values are reported in columns 1 and 3. The biases of the estimates (or $\rho_{yx} - r_{yx}$) are given in column 2, and the mean square errors (MSE, which is a measure of dispersion about the true value and may be expressed as the variance of the estimate plus the square of the bias of the estimate) are presented in column 4. Column 5 contains estimates of ρ_{yx} based on the data obtained from the single sample of 500 cases.

It may be seen from Table 7.1 that, regardless of which value ρ_{yx} assumes (i.e., .90, .80, .50, or .30), the MSE for the multiple-indicator method is always lower than the corresponding values for the single-indicator or the index method. The one exception occurs when $b = .30$, $a = .30$, and $c = .00$. In this case the large MSE value, .117, is due totally to the variance of the mean, since the mean itself is an unbiased estimate of the population parameter (the variance of the multiple-indicator method is discussed in greater detail below).

If we look more specifically at the trend in the bias and variance as we vary the correlation between X and Y, two general conclusions may be made: (1) the value of the bias for each of the three estimation procedures decreases as ρ_{yx} decreases, except for the multiple-indicator method when $c = 0$; and (2) the variance of each of the estimates increases as ρ_{yx} decreases. Although these results are, of course, generalizable from an inspection of the estimation formulas given in the Appendix, they do serve to emphasize the point that the variability of each of the three measurement strategies is more troublesome when ρ_{yx} is assumed to be less than or equal to .50.

Two final comments concerning the effects of varying the correlation

Table 7.1. Comparisons of Means, Bias, Variance, Mean Square Error (MSE) and Sample Means for b under Varying Test Conditions for Three Estimation Techniques

Test Conditions* and Estimation Technique	Population and Sample Statistics				
	Mean (1)	Bias (2)	Variance (3)	MSE (4)	Sample Mean (5)
$a = .8, b = .9, c = .0$					
Single	.576	.324	.00089	.10587	.577
Index	.758	.142	.00036	.02056	.760
Multiple	.900	.000	.00115	.00115	.898
$a = .8, b = .8, c = .0$					
Single	.512	.288	.00109	.08403	.512
Index	.674	.126	.00060	.01655	.663
Multiple	.800	.000	.00078	.00078	.780
$a = .8, b = .5, c = .0$					
Single	.320	.180	.00161	.03401	.340
Index	.421	.079	.00135	.00759	.446
Multiple	.500	.000	.00242	.00242	.534
$a = .8, b = .3, c = .0$					
Single	.192	.108	.00186	.01352	.242
Index	.253	.047	.00175	.00400	.320
Multiple	.300	.000	.00315	.00315	.377
$a = .8, b = .9, c = .3$					
Single	.576	.324	.00089	.10587	.580
Index	.692	.208	.00054	.04368	.705
Multiple	.770	.130	.00082	.01771	.791
$a = .8, b = .8, c = .3$					
Single	.512	.288	.00109	.08403	.547
Index	.615	.185	.00077	.03485	.652
Multiple	.684	.116	.00103	.01438	.718
$a = .8, b = .5, c = .3$					
Single	.320	.180	.00161	.03401	.335
Index	.385	.115	.00145	.01477	.402
Multiple	.428	.072	.00195	.00716	.441
$a = .8, b = .3, c = .3$					
Single	.192	.108	.00186	.01352	.183
Index	.231	.069	.00179	.00659	.216
Multiple	.257	.043	.00373	.00561	.236
$a = .8, b = .9, c = .6$					
Single	.576	.324	.00089	.10587	.600
Index	.637	.263	.00071	.06979	.669
Multiple	.673	.227	.00075	.05232	.711
$a = .8, b = .8, c = .6$					
Single	.512	.288	.00109	.08403	.554
Index	.566	.234	.00092	.05550	.610
Multiple	.598	.202	.00096	.04171	.646
$a = .8, b = .5, c = .6$					
Single	.320	.180	.00161	.03401	.333
Index	.354	.146	.00153	.02285	.368
Multiple	.374	.126	.00164	.01755	.388

Table 7.1–Continued

Test Conditions* and Estimation Technique	Population and Sample Statistics				
	Mean (1)	Bias (2)	Variance (3)	MSE (4)	Sample Mean (5)
$a = .8, b = .3, c = .6$					
Single	.192	.108	.00186	.01352	.218
Index	.212	.088	.00182	.00950	.240
Multiple	.224	.076	.00227	.00801	.232
$a = .5, b = .9, c = .0$					
Single	.225	.675	.00180	.45743	.237
Index	.450	.450	.00127	.20377	.485
Multiple	.900	.000	.00911	.00911	1.116
$a = .5, b = .8, c = .0$					
Single	.200	.600	.00184	.36184	.181
Index	.400	.400	.00141	.16141	.362
Multiple	.800	.000	.01498	.01498	.750
$a = .5, b = .5, c = .0$					
Single	.125	.375	.00194	.14256	.134
Index	.250	.250	.00176	.06426	.265
Multiple	.500	.000	.01562	.01562	.502
$a = .5, b = .3, c = .0$					
Single	.075	.225	.00198	.05260	.054
Index	.150	.150	.00191	.02441	.110
Multiple	.300	.000	.02099	.02099	.318
$a = .5, b = .9, c = .3$					
Single	.225	.675	.00180	.45743	.168
Index	.346	.554	.00155	.30830	.265
Multiple	.474	.426	.00433	.18607	.374
$a = .5, b = .8, c = .3$					
Single	.200	.600	.00184	.36184	.217
Index	.308	.492	.00164	.24401	.336
Multiple	.421	.379	.00520	.14880	.463
$a = .5, b = .5, c = .3$					
Single	.125	.375	.00194	.14256	.156
Index	.192	.308	.00185	.09653	.236
Multiple	.263	.237	.00610	.06219	.306
$a = .5, b = .3, c = .3$					
Single	.075	.225	.00198	.05260	.090
Index	.115	.185	.00195	.03603	.136
Multiple	.158	.142	.00650	.02669	.163
$a = .5, b = .9, c = .6$					
Single	.225	.675	.00180	.45743	.148
Index	.281	.619	.00170	.38455	.188
Multiple	.321	.579	.00301	.33776	.208
$a = .5, b = .8, c = .6$					
Single	.200	.600	.00184	.36184	.205
Index	.250	.550	.00176	.30426	.256
Multiple	.286	.514	.00249	.26698	.289

Table 7.1–Continued

Test Conditions* and Estimation Technique	Population and Sample Statistics				
	Mean (1)	Bias (2)	Variance (3)	MSE (4)	Sample Mean (5)
$a = .5, b = .5, c = .6$					
Single	.125	.375	.00194	.14256	.144
Index	.156	.344	.00190	.12007	.178
Multiple	.179	.321	.00375	.10706	.195
$a = .5, b = .3, c = .6$					
Single	.075	.225	.00198	.05260	.068
Index	.094	.206	.00196	.04450	.084
Multiple	.107	.193	.00304	.04024	.093
$a = .3, b = .9, c = .0$					
Single	.081	.819	.00197	.67273	.096
Index	.206	.694	.00183	.48356	.238
Multiple	.900	.000	.08902	.08902	1.106
$a = .3, b = .8, c = .0$					
Single	.072	.728	.00198	.53196	.078
Index	.183	.617	.00187	.38249	.196
Multiple	.800	.000	.11603	.11603	.743
$a = .3, b = .5, c = .0$					
Single	.045	.455	.00199	.20902	.042
Index	.114	.386	.00195	.15063	.113
Multiple	.500	.000	.12947	.12947	2.413
$a = .3, b = .3, c = .0$					
Single	.027	.273	.00200	.07653	.047
Index	.069	.231	.00198	.05551	.119
Multiple	.300	.000	.11703	.11703	.618
$a = .3, b = .9, c = .3$					
Single	.081	.819	.00197	.67273	.061
Index	.141	.759	.00192	.57832	.108
Multiple	.223	.677	.01197	.47011	.117
$a = .3, b = .8, c = .3$					
Single	.072	.728	.00198	.53196	.061
Index	.125	.675	.00194	.45737	.101
Multiple	.198	.602	.00955	.37153	.163
$a = .3, b = .5, c = .3$					
Single	.045	.455	.00199	.20902	.014
Index	.078	.422	.00198	.17988	.023
Multiple	.124	.376	.00672	.14812	.103
$a = .3, b = .3, c = .3$					
Single	.027	.273	.00200	.07653	.053
Index	.047	.253	.00199	.06604	.095
Multiple	.074	.226	.00565	.05656	.177
$a = .3, b = .9, c = .6$					
Single	.081	.819	.00197	.67273	.054
Index	.107	.793	.00195	.63088	.072
Multiple	.127	.773	.00401	.60099	.064

Table 7.1–Continued

Test Conditions* and Estimation Technique	Population and Sample Statistics				
	Mean (1)	Bias (2)	Variance (3)	MSE (4)	Sample Mean (5)
$a = .3, b = .8, c = .6$					
Single	.072	.728	.00198	.53196	.054
Index	.095	.705	.00196	.49889	.070
Multiple	.113	.687	.00396	.47564	.073
$a = .3, b = .5, c = .6$					
Single	.045	.455	.00199	.20902	.000
Index	.059	.441	.00199	.19610	.000
Multiple	.071	.429	.00392	.18818	.047
$a = .3, b = .3, c = .6$					
Single	.027	.273	.00200	.07653	.038
Index	.036	.264	.00199	.07188	.051
Multiple	.042	.258	.00252	.06885	.044

*a = epistemic correlation; b = structural parameter; c = correlation of error terms.

between X and Y relate to (1) the relative performances of the single-indicator and index techniques, and (2) the results of the sample statistics. With respect to the first point it is evident that for comparable conditions the bias, variance, and MSE are greater when ρ_{yx} is estimated on the basis of single indicators of X and Y than when it is calculated from a composite index of X and Y. Second, the associated estimates of the sample statistics for the three measurement procedures do not appear to bear any systematic relationship with ρ_{yx}. Under most of the tested conditions, the sample values are within one and one-half standard deviations of the expected mean score.

Varying the Strength of the Epistemic Correlations

In most measurement situations one is faced with the task of selecting measurable indicators of a given variable from a larger pool of all possible indicators. The criteria governing this selection process may involve (1) theoretical, (2) empirical, and/or (3) pragmatic factors. Here, we are basically concerned with examining the differential effects on each of the three measurement strategies as the empirical criterion varies; that is to say, when the strength of the epistemic correlation between a given indicator and its corresponding conceptual variable is systematically altered (for a more complete discussion of the criteria and procedures governing this selection process, see the following chapter, by Sullivan).

While it is generally true that the strength of this association is an unknown quantity, it seems reasonable to state that *general assessments* regarding its relative magnitude are possible.[10] Using the Costner (1969) technique and solving for these unknowns through a set of simultaneous equations, or using the kind of factor analytic procedure described by Heise and Bohrnstedt (1970), does provide a more substantial basis for calculating the values of these unknowns. Even if this information is not known, in some circumstances it may be reasonable to assume that a researcher can generally and accurately evaluate his indicator(s) as either being "strongly," "moderately," or "weakly" correlated with the respective theoretical variable, and it is this situation we have attempted to recreate in our analysis. As mentioned above, we have assumed that for any given estimate *each* of the three indicators of a given variable has the *same* degree of association with the theoretical variable.

Again, the main results of this test when a is successfully set equal to .80, .50, and .30 are shown in Table 7.1. As might be anticipated from the algebraic discussion, these results show that if we hold b and c constant, the amount of bias of any one of the techniques increases as a decreases. The only exception to this finding occurs for the multiple-indicator method when $c = 0$. In this case it is easily shown that equation (17) in the Appendix yields an unbiased estimate of ρ_{yx}. Under the more realistic assumption that for most applications c will not be equal to zero, it is important to observe that the bias for the Costner method is considerable as a decreases. For $a = .30$ and $c = .60$, for instance, the results in Table 7.1 show that the biases for all three methods are approximately equivalent, regardless of which value b assumes. With respect to bias alone, however, the Costner technique enjoys a slight advantage over the index technique, and the latter method consistently has a smaller bias than the single-indicator strategy.

Nevertheless, one of the more prosaic, yet noteworthy, observations is that *none* of the three measurement strategies does an especially good job of estimating the structural parameter when all the indicators of each of the two theoretical variables are only "moderate" (i.e., .50) or "poor" (i.e., .30) measures of the underlying variable. There is nothing particularly encouraging in asserting that one technique is different —and "better"—than another, if both are "equally bad"; essentially this is the case we are faced with in Table 7.1 as the epistemic correlations assume values equal to .50 and .30. If we add to this the conditions of correlated error terms and weak structural parameters, the situation seems to be one of overwhelming despair. To remain somewhat sanguine about such a prospect, however, we might argue that it is unrealistic to assume the worst of all possible conditions. (One possible but partial "solution" for such a situation, should it arise, is suggested below under the topic "Varying the Number of Indicators Used.")

10. See Costner and Schoenberg (1973) and Chapter 8 in this volume, by Sullivan, for fuller discussions of the criteria and techniques for evaluating multiple indicators.

An equally serious and associated feature of reduced epistemic correlations concerns the variability of the estimates. From a practical and especially predictive standpoint, the amount of bias of a particular estimation technique may be of less concern than its variability. All we really know when faced with an unbiased estimate is that over the long run we expect the mean of the sampling distribution to approximate the population parameter; but this is of small comfort to the researcher who is only dealing with the results of a single sample.

It is evident from Table 7.1 that the variances of all three estimation procedures increase as a decreases. What is especially striking about this trend is that the variance for the Costner technique seems to be disproportionately affected by changes in the epistemic correlations. To illustrate this pattern, let us assume $b = .90$ and $c = 0$. Then when $a = .80$, the variance for the Costner estimate is .00115, which is only slightly larger than the corresponding variances for the single-indicator (.00089) and index (.00036) estimates. When $a = .50$, the variance increases by a factor of about eight, to .00911; and when $a = .30$ the variance further increases about tenfold (to .08902). The corresponding increases for the single-indicator and index methods are considerably less.

A general understanding of this finding may be gained by recalling Costner's (1969) estimation equation (20) b^2 (see eq. 17 in the Appendix). Estimates of b^2 are obtained by calculating the ratio of the products of $r_{x_1 y_1}$ and $r_{x_2 y_2}$, and $r_{x_1 x_2}$ and $r_{y_1 y_2}$. As a decreases in magnitude, each of these correlations will be extremely small, and hence subject to greater sampling variability.[11] By then taking the product of these correlations, it is entirely possible that either the numerator or the denominator may tend to zero, whereas the other component may not. Indeed, our results, based on 100 random samples of $N = 500$, indicated that values for b^2 were commonly larger than 1.0 and less than 0.0. For these cases we somewhat arbitrarily let $\hat{b} = 1.00$ and 0.00, respectively. The obvious rationale for this decision was that, were such values actually derived in a real analysis, the analyst would have to either discard the results altogether or reassign them extreme but meaningful values. The general effect of assigning 1's and 0's was conservative estimation of the reported variances in Table 7.1.

For reasons similar to those just mentioned, it is likewise understandable why the variance for the single-indicator strategy decreases as a increases. Since for this procedure we are not concerned with products or ratios of correlations, for similar size N's the sampling variability of $r_{x_1 y_1}$ will become smaller as the epistemic correlations increase. Unlike

11. For large samples drawn from a normal population with true correlations close to zero, estimates of the standard error of the correlation coefficient are approximately $(1 - r^2)/(n - 1)^{1/2}$ (Ezekiel and Fox 1966; p. 295). Hence, sampling variations of correlation coefficients which are nearly zero are subject to greater sampling variations.

the multiple-indicator technique, this method avoids the compounding effects of error terms, but on the other hand, it has the general effect of yielding a more biased estimate of the underlying parameter.

It is worthwhile to reflect momentarily on the meaning of our findings in the light of Costner's (1969) original paper. In that discussion his second consistency criterion (eq. [42]) stated that, in the absence of differential bias, estimates of b^2 "should be identical, except for random measurement error." What our own results and the discussion above strongly suggest, however, is that even when we can safely rule out differential bias, random error may be especially troublesome. Given the somewhat dubious quality of a large number of sociological measures, we may go further and say that random error will generally be a problem—with or without specification error.

Related to the concept of variability of the estimates is the variation due to sample size. Although the data are not shown here, we made a preliminary test for this relationship by drawing five replicate samples, each of size 100, 500, 1,000, and 4,000. Setting $\rho_{yx} = .50$ and $a = .50$, we tabulated the means and standard deviations for the three measurement techniques. In general, for $c = .00$ and $c = .60$, the results were similar to those shown in Table 7.1. The Costner technique was the least biased of the three methods, but it also tended to have the highest standard deviation. An increase in sample size had the predicted effect of reducing sampling variability; yet the returns were negligible for sample sizes greater than 500. Nevertheless, the data suggested that for $N = 100$, the variance is substantially greater (usually four times as great) than for larger samples. Because these results were based on only five samples each, considerable caution should be exercised in their interpretation. Besides the need for expanding the number of samples used in the examination of this problem, additional data are required for the study of small-sample ($N < 100$) properties.

A final comment pertaining to the effects of varying the strength of the epistemic correlations relates to the results of the single-sample statistics. With a few minor and nonsystematic exceptions, the sample means are within or very close to plus or minus one standard deviation of the exact mean values. Evidence of the relatively large variance associated with the multiple-indicator method is provided when $c = 0$. For this case, and when $a = .50$ and $b = .90$, the sample data yielded a value of $\hat{b} = 1.116$; when $a = .30$ and $b = .50$, the sample estimate was equal to 2.413. We obtained these estimates by simply averaging the nine pairs of estimates obtained from Costner's (1969) equation (20).[12] Despite the fact that in this context values of $\hat{b}$ greater than one or less

12. Since we were *not* testing for differential bias, only the left-hand side of Costner's equation (20) was used in calculating these mean values. These data were therefore based on nine estimates of d^2, not eighteen.

than zero had little empirical meaning, we included these estimates to illustrate the kinds of figures which might be obtained.

Varying the Strength of the Correlation between Error Terms

The third general condition on which we wished to compare each of our measurement strategies was variation in the strength of the correlation between error terms of indicators of the same variable. From a practical standpoint, it is difficult to assume realistically that error terms of indicators of the same variable will not be correlated—at least to some degree—with one another. On the other hand, it *is* more reasonable to assume only weak correlations between error terms of indicators of *different* variables.[13] We have thus defined three progressive situations of correlated error between indicators of the same variable: (1) where the error terms are independent of one another, except for sampling variability, (2) where all the error terms for the same variable are related moderately (i.e., $c = .30$), and (3) where the error terms for the same variable are highly correlated with one another (i.e., $c = .60$).

In Table 7.1, again, the main results of this test are presented while controlling for (1) the strength of the structural parameter, (2) the strength of the epistemic correlation, and (3) the number of indicators used. Somewhat expectedly, the data show that the bias, the variance, and hence the MSE of the single-indicator strategy are not affected by changes in the assigned values of c. Obviously this has to be the case, since the effect of positively correlated error terms is the inflation of the relationship between the two variables whose error terms are associated—not between one of those variables and a third variable.[14] Hence, while $r_{x_1 x_2}$, $r_{x_1 x_3}$, and $r_{x_2 x_3}$ should increase, it does not follow, for example, that $r_{x_1 y_2}$ or $r_{x_2 y_1}$, should similarly increase.

In contrast to the bias of the single-indicator procedure, and under the assumption of positively correlated error terms and epistemic correlations,[15] the biases of the index and multiple-indicator techniques increase as c increases. With respect to the effects of c on the variance, however, the two techniques behave differently. Generally speaking, the variance tends to decrease as c increases for the multiple-indicator estimates, while for the index estimates the variance increases. To un-

13. Blalock (1971) has rightfully pointed out that this assumption depends on "how we have measured" our variables. If the aggregating principle is one of "geographical proximity," this assumption will generally be invalidated.

14. Since in these tests the correlation between *all* error terms, as well as between *all* epistemic correlations, was assumed to be positive, the effect was an *increase* in the correlation between pairs of variables with correlated error. Under the *opposite* condition of *negatively* correlated error terms and positive epistemic correlations, the effect would be *attenuation*, not inflation, of the correlation coefficient.

15. See n. 14 above.

derstand why this pattern holds, it is helpful to refer to formulas (16) and (17) in the Appendix.

From equation (17), which shows the computational form of $\hat{b}$, it may be seen that as c increases positively, the denominator term will increase and $\hat{b}$ will be reduced. If, on the other hand, c is negative, the general effect will be a reduction of the denominator and an increase in the value of $\hat{b}$. Since in this analysis we are only dealing with positive values of c (see n. 14), $\hat{b}$ will always appear to be attenuated. Correspondingly, the decrease in the variance as c increases is due to the fact that $r_{x_1 x_2}$ and $r_{y_1 y_2}$ increase, and thus are less influenced by sampling variability (see n. 11). In effect, as we saw earlier, this reduced variability in the terms composing the denominator yields a less variable estimate of the underlying parameter.

For the index method a somewhat different explanation is required. Here, we are simply adding indicators of X together, and similarly for Y, and then correlating the composite scores for each. In obtaining a value for $r_{(x_1 + x_2 + x_3)(y_1 + y_2 + y_3)}$ we simply follow the customary procedure of dividing the covariance of X' and Y' by the square root of the variance in X' times the square root of the variance in Y'. When there is no correlated error among the indicators of X and Y, the total variance in X' and Y' is simply equal to the sum of the variance in x_1, x_2, and x_3 plus the sum of the covariance terms (in a like manner, we can decompose the total variance for Y'). By adding the assumption of correlated error terms and maintaining the assumption that all these terms are positive, we essentially increase the total variance in X' by increasing the values of the covariance terms. As a result, the denominator portion of our equation for computing r will be greater, and r itself will be lower and, thus, will reflect a greater bias. Likewise, as r decreases, the effects of sampling variability will increase (i.e., there will be greater variance of the estimate).

Because with the index method we divide the covariance (or numerator) by the square root of the denominator, the biasing effects tend to be smaller than those for the multiple-indicator approach. It is precisely this differential effect of correlated error terms on all three procedures which accounts for the convergence of estimates as c increases. It may be seen from Table 1 that when $c = .60$ the three estimates are approximately equivalent (regardless of what values a or b assume). Owing to this near equivalence, the multiple-indicator method seems to be the preferable strategy to adopt when there is sufficient reason to believe correlated error is substantial. As Costner (1969) and Costner and Schoenberg (1973) have shown, an overidentified system of equations allows one to make consistency checks for evaluating this type of specification error. Given these values, the analyst may then "correct" for the bias of the estimate.

Varying the Number of Indicators Used

The final condition on which we sought to compare our three measurement strategies was the number of indicators actually employed in the measurement process. Earlier we noted that there is, in effect, an unspoken rule in sociology—the more indicators one uses to measure a given variable, the "better" the resultant measure. This belief is frequently expressed in the form "having more confidence," or "faith," in the measurement instrument. In practice, however, we often use too *few* indicators to measure relatively abstract variables (e.g., prejudice, industrialization).

Basically, two underlying arguments appear to be used in the defense of selecting numerous indicators of a given variable. The first and perhaps the most common rationale given in sociology is the one, reviewed earlier, from Lazarsfeld and Rosenberg's (1955) work. We assume that the theoretical variable we are attempting to measure is multidimensional and then try to select a large number of indicators which will "tap" all the dimensions. This, in fact, is what is meant when a measure is claimed to be "representative"; it measures all the relevant aspects of a more generalized variable. When, as Lazarsfeld and Rosenberg recommended, this procedure is carried out in a deductive fashion, it seems to be a reasonable one to follow; yet, in reality, the procedure often works very inductively. It is more often than not *vaguely* assumed that there are a number of frequently unspecified components of a general variable, and it is *hopefully* anticipated that a large array of indicators will indeed measure these components.

In contrast to this theoretical or conceptual argument, a more statistically oriented justification is commonly cited for the use of additional indicators—most frequently by psychometricians such as Kerlinger (1966, p. 422). The emphasis is placed on maximizing the explained variance in the unmeasured variable by using efficient estimation techniques, as described by Hauser and Goldberger (1971). This is done by continuing to add items to one's measurement instrument to increase the accuracy of the measure. One positive effect of following this strategy is that, as the number of items of a measure increases, and as the proportion of variance explained increases, the problems of correlated error terms decrease and the stability of various coefficients (either factor weights or beta weights) increases.[16] The obvious dif-

---

16. The variance of b_{ij} is proportional to $(1 - R^2_{1.2 \ldots jk})/(1 - R^2_{j.2 \ldots k})$, where the first variable is the dependent variable and $2 \ldots k$ are the independent variables. If $R^2_{1.2 \ldots k}$ is near unity, the sampling variance of b_{ij} will be small. A similar argument holds for the variance of factor "loadings" or weights. See Stone (1945) for a more technical discussion of this issue.

ficulty, however, is making theoretical "sense" out of an underlying variable which has a wide assortment of measures; but from a purely predictive standpoint this may not be a particularly troublesome problem.[17]

For purposes of our test we have essentially assumed (1) a unidimensional variable and (2) a noncorrelated error between indicators of the same variable. Our analysis applies best, therefore, to the delineation of a relatively nonabstract variable without multiple dimensions and, subsequently, to the attempt to secure data on a number of similar indicators for that quantity. Or, to look at it in a slightly different manner, we are interested in obtaining multiple measures on one particular aspect of a more general variable.

Table 7.2 summarizes the results obtained with the use of two, three, and four indicators. Since estimates of the mean and variance for the single- and multiple-indicator models are unaffected by an increase in the number of indicators,[18] these results are applicable only to an analysis of the index technique. Finally, it will be noted that because of project limitations we have confined our comparison to the situation in which $a = .80$ and $.50$ and $c = 0$ for all values of a and b. The estimation equations for calculating the mean and variance are identical with those given in equations (5) and (16) of the Appendix.

The main finding of this test is revealed by a simple inspection of the MSE column. In every instance the MSE is reduced as we add more indicators to our measure. This pattern holds as well for the bias of the estimate as for the variance. Theoretically, of course, we would expect that the payoffs of adding indicators would reach an optimum number (i.e., where decrements in the bias and variance are negligible), but that the number would undoubtedly be greater where the epistemic correlations are small. Practically speaking then, the procedure of using additional indicators may be especially helpful when we have reason to believe that all or most of our selected indicators are only poorly related to a variable of theoretical interest (and for these results, when the error terms are mutually uncorrelated). This, of course, assumes that any additional variables will not seriously introduce other sources of measurement error into the model.

Conclusions

In the prologue to the 1970 edition of *Sociological Methodology* (Borgatta and Bohrnstedt 1970) the editors commented that "measurement in

---

17. That is, if we are mainly interested in prediction as distinct from explanation, the precise meaning of the theoretical construct may be less significant.

18. See n. 7 above.

Table 7.2. Comparison of Population Means, Biases, Variances, and Mean Square Error (MSE) for the Index Method While Varying the Number of Indicators and Specified Test Conditions

Test Conditions* and No. of Indicators	Population Statistics			
	Mean	Bias	Variance	MSE
$a = .8, b = .9, c = .0$				
2	.702	.198	.00051	.03954
3	.758	.142	.00036	.02056
4	.789	.111	.00028	.01260
$a = .8, b = .8, c = .0$				
2	.624	.176	.00074	.03158
3	.674	.126	.00060	.01655
4	.701	.099	.00052	.01024
$a = .8, b = .5, c = .0$				
2	.390	.110	.00144	.01348
3	.421	.079	.00135	.00759
4	.438	.062	.00131	.00511
$a = .8, b = .3, c = .0$				
2	.234	.066	.00179	.00612
3	.253	.047	.00175	.00400
4	.263	.037	.00173	.00310
$a = .5, b = .9, c = .0$				
2	.360	.540	.00152	.29312
3	.450	.450	.00127	.20377
4	.514	.386	.00108	.14986
$a = .5, b = .8, c = .0$				
2	.320	.480	.00161	.23201
3	.400	.400	.00141	.16141
4	.457	.343	.00125	.11880
$a = .5, b = .5, c = .0$				
2	.200	.300	.00184	.09184
3	.250	.250	.00176	.06426
4	.286	.214	.00169	.04761
$a = .5, b = .3, c = .0$				
2	.120	.180	.00194	.03434
3	.150	.150	.00191	.02441
4	.171	.129	.00188	.01841

*a = epistemic correlation; b = structural parameter; c = correlation of error terms.

sociology probably has been as poor as in any other discipline, if not poorer. The effects of errors in measurement have received attention in some disciplines, especially educational psychology, but have largely been ignored in sociology. It is hoped that the next decade will see progress in this very crucial area." It is already apparent from recent literature that progress *is* being made and that these advances are especially welcomed in a field long troubled with measurement "problems."

Certainly, it is clear from these studies as well as from our own that considerably more work must be accomplished before we arrive at definitive solution—or better yet, programmatic paradigms—for these problems. Nevertheless, there is a basis for optimism—if for no other reason than that today we are more aware and alert to sources of measurement error, as well as to provisional techniques for dealing with these difficulties.

Underlying this effort, however, rests a potentially counterproductive tendency. A number of the studies upon which this analysis has drawn seem to have unwittingly mistaken a lack of mathematical formalization for a lack of rigor. The real danger in this misassociation lies in the fact that "elegance" and "precision" alone are insufficient for persuading researchers to employ the study of measurement models in their own work. If we are to avoid the division between "methodologists" and "empiricists" alluded to by Hill (1969), we need to continuously seek out more "conventional" techniques for communicating these methodological developments to their intended audience.

It is our belief that the use of numerical illustrations, generated with the assistance of computer simulation methods, provides a mode of analysis which adequately serves both an "analytical" and a "communicative" function. Particularly in the study of sampling properties, solutions gained through the investigation of simulated data often supply the only meaningful and systematic means of tackling such problems. Moreover, this type of analysis has the virtue of combining a familiar and readily comprehensible output with the ability to isolate the effects of desired conditions on a known structure.

Although we have attempted throughout this chapter to indicate the limitations of this study and the areas requiring further exploration, it may be useful to summarize briefly some of the more salient questions remaining. First, it bears repeating that this study has purposefully restricted its attention to what Hauser and Goldberger (1971) refer to as a "confirmatory factor analytic" measurement model. Subsequent investigations of this type could profitably examine the measurement qualities of other basic models (e.g., causal and mixed indicators, oblique and orthogonal relations between unmeasured variables). Second, it seems imperative that we relax the restrictive assumptions we have imposed on our data—that the epistemic correlations and correlated error terms are all equal. A third and related point concerns the effects on our estimates if we misspecify the occurrence of errors between indicators of different variables. And fourth, we need to look more intensely at the small-sample properties of measurement strategies. Clearly these questions do not exhaust the range of research opportunities available on this subject, but we hope they will stimulate others to pursue a similar line of inquiry.

Appendix: An Algebraic Analysis

Assuming that all variables reported in Figure 7.1 are in standard form (i.e., mean zero and variance unity), we may express the model in the form of the following equations:

$$Y = bX + e_y\sqrt{1 - b^2} \, , \tag{1}$$

$$x_i = a_1 X + e_{x_i}\sqrt{1 - a_1^2} \, , \tag{2}$$

$$y_i = a_2 Y + e_{y_j}\sqrt{1 - a_2^2} \tag{3}$$

$$(i, j = 1, 2, \cdots, k) \, .$$

It may be noted that a_1, a_2, and b can only assume values between -1.0 and 1.0; otherwise the quantities under the radical sign in equations (1)-(3) may be negative. Further, it should be clear that, if X and the error terms in (1), (2) and (3) are in standard form, Y, x_i, and y_j will also be in standard form.

Single Indicators

In this case one indicator of each of the unmeasured variables is selected to represent that variable. To estimate b, the correlation between X and Y, we use as our estimate $r_{x_i y_j}$. From (1), (2) and (3) it can be seen that

$$r_{x_i y_j} = a_1 a_2 b \, . \tag{4}$$

In deriving (4) we have assumed that the error terms (i.e., e_{x_i}, e_{y_j}) are uncorrelated with one another and with other variables. Equation (4) shows that $r_{x_i y_j}$ will be an accurate estimate of b as *both* a_1 and a_2 approach unity (in absolute value).

In the event that $r_{e_{x_i} e_{y_j}}$ is *not* zero, $r_{x_i y_j}$ will be attenuated or increased depending on the sign of the correlation, $r_{e_{x_i} e_{y_j}}$. This situation is not examined here, since we have restricted our attention to correlated error terms between indicators of the *same* unmeasured variable.

The variance of (4) is given by the standard formula

$$\text{Var}\,(r_{x_i y_j}) = \frac{(1 - \rho_{x_i y_j})^2}{N - 1} \, . \tag{5}$$

It may easily be seen from this expression that as $\rho_{x_i y_j}$ increases (without respect to sign), the variance will decrease. Likewise, other things being equal, the variance will decrease as N increases.

Index Method

Imagine from Figure 7.1 that we form an index of X and of Y, say, X' and Y', from the measured indicators of each. A general additive model for forming such an index is as follows:

$$X' = W_1 x_1 + W_2 x_2 + \cdots + W_k x_k$$

and

$$Y' = V_1 y_1 + V_2 y_2 + \cdots + V_k y_k ,$$

where the W's and V's represent assigned weights associated with the measured indicators of X and Y, respectively.

Taking $r_{x'y'}$ as our estimate of b, we shall examine the error of this procedure under the desired test conditions. From (2) and (3) we obtain

$$r_{x_i x_j} = a_1{}^2 + (1 - a_1{}^2) r_{e_{x_i} e_{x_j}} \tag{6}$$

and

$$r_{y_i y_j} = a_2{}^2 + (1 - a_2{}^2) r_{e_{y_i} e_{y_j}} . \tag{7}$$

Let

$$c_1 = r_{e_{x_i} e_{x_j}} \quad \text{and} \quad c_2 = r_{e_{y_i} e_{y_j}} ; \tag{8}$$

the variance of X' is then given by

$$\text{Var}(X') = \sum_{i=1}^{k} W_i^2 + \sum_{i \neq j} W_i W_j r_{x_i x_j} . \tag{9}$$

Using (6) and (8), we may rewrite (9) as

$$\text{Var}(X') = \sum_{i=1}^{k} W_i^2 + \sum_{i \neq j} W_i W_j [a_1{}^2 + (1 - a_1{}^2) c_1] . \tag{10}$$

Similarly, the variance of Y' may be written

$$\text{Var}(Y') = \sum_{i=1}^{k} V_i^2 + \sum_{i \neq j} V_i V_j [a_2{}^2 + (1 - a_2{}^2) c_2] . \tag{11}$$

The covariance of $(X'Y')$ is then defined as

$$E(X'Y') = \sum_{i,j}^{k} E(W_i V_j x_i y_j) ,$$

which is equal to

$$E(X'Y') = \sum_{i,j}^{k} W_i V_j E(x_i y_j) .$$ (12)

Substituting (4) in (12) we get

$$E(X'Y') = \sum_{i,j}^{k} W_i V_j a_1 a_2 b .$$ (13)

From (10), (11), and (12) we may now express $r_{x'y'}$ as the covariance of $X'Y'$ divided by the square root of the variance of X' times the variance of Y', or

$$r_{x'y'} = \frac{\sum_{i,j}^{k} W_i V_j a_1 a_2 b}{[\text{Var}\,(X') \cdot \text{Var}\,(Y')]^{-\frac{1}{2}}} .$$ (14)

In the numerical analysis given in the text we have assumed (i) that the weights assigned to each of the indicators of X and Y are all equal to one, (ii) that the epistemic correlations are equal (i.e., $a_1 = a_2 = a$), and (iii) that the correlated error terms are likewise all equal (i.e., $c_1 = c_2 = c$). Under these assumptions, and using a simple additive model involving equal weights for aggregating the indicators (see Hauser and Goldberger [1971] and Costner and Schoenberg [1973] for a discussion of analyses which do not make such assumptions), we may reexpress (14) as

$$r_{x'y'} = \frac{k^2 a^2 b}{k + k(k-1)[a^2 + (1-a^2)c]} .$$ (15)

Dividing both numerator and denominator by $k^2 a^2$ and simplifying the results, we get:

$$r_{x'y'} = \frac{b}{1 + \left(\dfrac{1-a^2}{a^2}\right)\left(c + \dfrac{1-c}{k}\right)}$$ (16)

From (16) it is easy to see (i) that as c tends to zero, and for a relatively large number of indicators, k, the denominator will approximate 1 and hence the estimator $r_{x'y'}$ will approach b; and (ii) that as a tends to unity, $r_{x'y'}$ will also approach b. Since the variance of (16) is given by (5), the same conclusions hold for the variance of the index method as for the single indicator case.

Multiple Indicators

The algebraic expression for b given by Costner (1969) in his equation (20) is

$$\hat{b} = \left[\frac{(r_{x_1 y_1})(r_{x_2 y_2})}{(r_{x_1 x_2})(r_{y_1 y_2})} \right]^{\frac{1}{2}} \tag{17}$$

For the constraints we have assumed (i.e., $r_{x_1 y_1} = r_{x_2 y_2}$ and $r_{x_1 x_2} = r_{y_1 y_2}$), it should be noted that the ratios in (17) are redundant with one another. In the more general case, however, this will not be so. From (4), and under the assumption that the epistemic correlations are all equal to a, we may rewrite (17) as

$$\hat{b} = \frac{a^2 b}{a^2 + (1 - a^2)c}. \tag{18}$$

Case 1: Uncorrelated error ($c = 0$). Equation (18) will give an unbiased estimate of b.

Case 2: Correlated error ($c \neq 0$). The estimate of b obtained from (18) will be biased. As noted above, the effects of the bias will depend on both the magnitude and direction of c.

As suggested in the text, the complexity of the computational formula for the variance of (17) would make its algebraic presentation less than meaningful. We have therefore relied on simulated data results to provide the appropriate estimates for this statistic, shown in Table 7.1.

References

Althauser, Robert P., and Thomas A. Heberlein
  1970. "Validity and the Multitrait-Multimethod Matrix." In Edgar F. Borgatta and George W. Bohrnstedt, eds., *Sociological Methodology, 1970*. San Francisco: Jossey-Bass.
Blalock, Hubert M., Jr.
  1969. "Multiple Indicators and the Causal Approach to Measurement Error." *American Journal of Sociology* 75 (September):264-72.
  1971. "Aggregation and Measurement Error." *Social Forces* 50 (December):151-65.
Bonjean, Charles M., Richard J. Hill, and S. Dale McLemore
  1967. *Sociological Measurement*. San Francisco: Chandler.
Borgatta, Edgar F., and George W. Bohrnstedt, eds.
  1970. *Sociological Methodology, 1970*. San Francisco: Jossey-Bass.
Costner, Herbert L.
  1969. "Theory, Deduction, and Rules of Correspondence." *American Journal of Sociology* 75 (September):245-63.
Costner, Herbert L., and Ronald Schoenberg
  1973. "Diagnosing Indicator Ills in Multiple Indicator Models." In Arthur S. Goldberger and Otis Dudley Duncan, eds., *Structural Equation Models in the Social Sciences*. New York: Seminar Press.
Coombs, Clyde
  1964. *A Theory of Data*. New York: Wiley.
Curtis, Richard F., and Elton F. Jackson
  1962. "Multiple Indicators in Survey Research." *American Journal of Sociology* 68 (September):195-204.
Ezekiel, Mordecai, and Karl A. Fox
  1966. *Methods of Correlation and Regression Analysis*. New York: Wiley.
Hauser, Robert M., and Arthur S. Goldberger
  1971. "The Treatment of Unobservable Variables in Path Analysis." In Herbert L. Costner, ed., *Sociological Methodology, 1971*. San Francisco: Jossey-Bass.
Heise, David R
  1969. "Problems in Path Analysis and Causal Inference." In Edgar F. Borgatta, ed., *Sociological Methodology, 1969*. San Francisco: Jossey-Bass.
  1972. "Employing Nominal Variables, Induced Variables, and Block Variables in Path Analyses." *Sociological Methods and Research* 1 (November):147-74.
Heise, David R., and George W. Bohrnstedt.
  1970. "Validity, Invalidity, and Reliability." In Borgatta and Bohrnstedt, eds., *Sociological Methodology, 1970*. San Francisco: Jossey-Bass.
Hill, Richard J.
  1969. "On the Relevance of Methodology." Reprinted in Norman K. Denzin, ed., *Sociological Methods*. Chicago: Aldine.
Kerlinger, Fred N.
  1966. *Foundations of Behavioral Research*. New York: Holt, Rinehart & Winston.
Land, Kenneth C.
  1970. "Path Coefficients for Unmeasured Variables." *Social Forces* 48 (June):506-11.

Lazarsfeld, Paul F.
   1959. "Problems in Methodology." In Robert K. Merton, Leonard Broom, and Leonard S. Cottrell, Jr. eds., *Sociology Today*. New York: Basic Books.
Lazarsfeld, Paul F., and Morris Rosenberg, eds.
   1955. Introduction to *The Language of Social Research*. New York: Free Press.
Siegel, Paul M., and Robert W. Hodge
   1968. "A Causal Approach to the Study of Measurement Error." In Hubert M. Blalock and Ann B. Blalock, eds., *Methodology in Social Research*. New York: McGraw-Hill.
Stone, Richard
   1945. "The Analysis of Market Demand." *Journal of the Royal Statistical Society* 108, nos. 3, 4:286-382.

Chapter 8

MULTIPLE INDICATORS:
SOME CRITERIA OF SELECTION

JOHN L. SULLIVAN

John L. Sullivan is Associate Professor of Political Science, Indiana University, and received his Ph.D. from the University of North Carolina, 1970. He has recently contributed articles both to political science journals and to various edited volumes, primarily in the areas of public opinion, political ideology, causal modeling, and multidimensional scaling analysis.

Jacobson and Lalu have compared three measurement strategies, the single-indicator approach, the index approach, and the multiple-indicator approach. Their major findings are (1) that the multiple-indicator approach generally yielded the best parameter estimates; (2) that this advantage was diminished as the strength of the parameter decreased, the strength of the epistemic correlation decreased, and the magnitude of the correlation between the error terms increased; and (3) that none of the three approaches yielded good estimates when the indicators were only weakly associated with the underlying unmeasured construct.

The present chapter deals with a situation in which the multiple-indicator approach is advantageous. The models to be tested involve variables which are almost certainly highly related; hence, the epistemic correlations and structural parameters are very strong. Further, the indicators are selected under conditions suggesting a strong relationship with the unmeasured construct. Therefore, the multiple-indicator approach appears best in the current instance. Under this assumption, this chapter deals more specifically with criteria for the selection of

I wish to thank Hubert ___ Jr., for his insightful and useful suggestions.

indicators, given several from which to choose. In particular, some aspects of measurement error—auxiliary theory, redundancy, and repetitiveness—are examined as they apply to the situation of aggregate data analysis, and to an approach based upon multiple-partial correlation coefficients.

Measurement Error

The problem of measurement error is a recurrent one in social science research, since with extremely indirect measurements, that is, empirical indicators of underlying theoretical constructs, measurement error of some sort is certain to exist. The consequences of this error differ, however, depending upon whether it is random or nonrandom. If it is entirely random, least-squares estimates will be attenuated, and relatively unbiased estimates can be obtained by means of instrumental and exogenous variables (Blalock 1968). If, however, the measurement error is nonrandom, such procedures break down.

Costner (1969) has proposed a criterion to determine whether measurement error is random or nonrandom, provided one has multiple indicators of each theoretical construct and can express the correlations among indicators in terms of path coefficients. Also, for indicators assumed to be effects rather than causes of the theoretical constructs, Costner has shown that an additional criterion, providing an unbiased estimate of the parameters among the unmeasured constructs, must be met. Such a model, with two indicators per variable, two unmeasured constructs, and only random measurement error, is shown in Figure 8.1. Writing the correlations in terms of path coefficients, we get

$$r_{x_1 x_2} = ab \,, \tag{1}$$

$$r_{x_1 y_1} = acd \,, \tag{2}$$

$$r_{x_1 y_2} = ace \,, \tag{3}$$

$$r_{x_2 y_1} = bcd \,, \tag{4}$$

$$r_{x_2 y_2} = bce \,, \tag{5}$$

$$r_{y_1 y_2} = de \,. \tag{6}$$

Therefore, $\tag{7}$

$$(r_{x_1 y_1})(r_{x_2 y_2}) = (r_{x_1 y_2})(r_{x_2 y_1}) = abc^2 de \,.$$

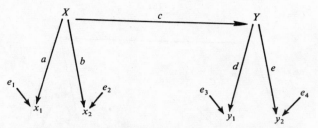

Figure 8.1. Costner's two-variable four-indicator model with random error

If there is nonrandom measurement error across variables, as in Figure 8.2, consistency criterion (7) will not hold. For example:

Equations (1)-(3),

$$r_{x_2 y_1} = bcd + fg,$$

$$(4a)$$

Equations (5)-(6)

but

$$(r_{x_1 y_1})(r_{x_2 y_2}) \neq (r_{x_1 y_2})(r_{x_2 y_1})$$

$$(7a)$$

because

$$(acd)(bce) \neq (ace)(bcd + fg).$$

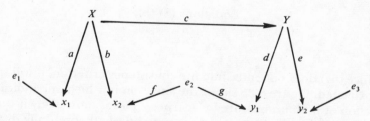

Figure 8.2. Costner's two-variable four-indicator model with detectable nonrandom error.

So if the left- and right-hand sides of (7) are equivalent, the model of Figure 8.2 cannot hold. We can check this empirically, since we derive the six correlations from our data.

Costner has noted that even with "effect indicator" models there are two situations of *nonrandom* error in which this particular consistency criterion will still be approximately satisfied. They are illustrated in Figure 8.3. Figure 8.3a shows the situation in which there is *within-set*

(a)

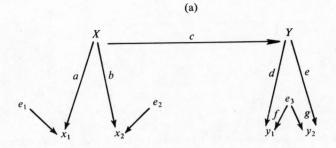

(b)

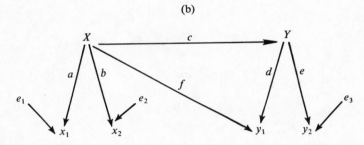

*Figure 8.3.   Costner's two-variable four-indicator model with nonrandom error
that is not detectable*

nonrandom error, likely in questionnaire data if y_1 and y_2 happen to be
contiguous questions:

Equations (1)-(5),

$$r_{y_1 y_2} = de + fg. \tag{6a}$$

But since (6a) does not enter into the consistency criterion, it will still be
approximated. Figure 8.3b shows the situation in which one indicator is
a function of both unmeasured constructs. This is most likely if the two
constructs are highly related and are not entirely theoretically distinct:

Equation (1),

$$r_{x_1 y_1} = acd + af, \tag{2a}$$

Equation (3),

$$r_{x_2 y_1} = bcd + bf, \tag{4b}$$

Equations (5)-(6),

Therefore, $$(r_{x_1 y_1})(r_{x_2 y_2}) = (r_{x_1 y_2})(r_{x_2 y_1})$$ (7)

because $$(acd + af)(bce) = (ace)(bcd + bf) \, .$$

This first consistency criterion is therefore not a sufficient condition for the absence of nonrandom measurement error, unless one can safely rule out nonrandom error between indicators of the same concept, *and* the presence of an indicator which is a product of more than one theoretical construct.[1] If the criterion is met and these complications are ruled out, a relatively unbiased estimate can be obtained, as noted, by means of exogenous variables. Many times this is not possible, and in such cases attenuation can be corrected as follows:

Equations (1)-(6).

Therefore, there are six equations and five unknowns; but since

$$(r_{x_1 y_1})(r_{x_2 y_2}) = (r_{x_1 y_2})(r_{x_2 y_1}) \, ,$$ (7)

we can write $r_{x_1 y_1}$ as a function of the other three correlations, and we have five equations and five unknowns:

$$r_{x_1 x_2} = ab \, ,$$ (1)

$$r_{x_1 y_2} = ace \, ,$$ (3)

$$r_{x_2 y_1} = bcd \, ,$$ (4)

$$r_{x_2 y_2} = bce \, ,$$ (5)

$$r_{y_1 y_2} = de \, .$$ (6)

We can now solve for the unknowns (path coefficients):

$$(r_{x_1 y_2})(r_{x_2 y_1}) = (ace)(bcd) \, ,$$
$$(r_{x_1 y_2})(r_{x_2 y_1}) = abc^2 de \, ,$$ (8)
$$\frac{(r_{x_1 y_2})(r_{x_2 y_1})}{abde} = c^2 \, ,$$

1. Provided, of course, that we have an "effect indicator" model. If we do not, there are additional situations which will satisfy the first consistency criterion even in the presence of nonrandom error (see Blalock 1971*b*).

$$\frac{(r_{x_1 y_2})(r_{x_2 y_1})}{(r_{x_1 x_2})(r_{y_1 y_2})} = c^2 \ ,$$

$$\pm \sqrt{\frac{(r_{x_1 y_2})(r_{x_2 y_1})}{(r_{x_1 x_2})(r_{y_1 y_2})}} = c \ ,$$

and, from (7),

$$\pm \sqrt{\frac{(r_{x_1 y_1})(r_{x_2 y_2})}{(r_{x_1 x_2})(r_{y_1 y_2})}} = c \ .$$

So we can solve for c, the epistemic path coefficient (and correlation coefficient in this case) in terms of the known correlations among indicators. The two estimates of c provide a second consistency criterion; these estimates should be virtually identical, given approximate satisfaction of the first consistency criterion.[2] We can go on to solve, with two estimates each, the other path coefficients, a, b, d, and e, which link each indicator with the abstract construct (see Costner 1969).

This approach can be generalized to more than two indicators per construct (see Fig. 8.4.) In such instances, there are nine tests of the consistency criterion:

$$(r_{x_1 y_1})(r_{x_2 y_2}) = (r_{x_1 y_2})(r_{x_2 y_1}) \ , \tag{7}$$

$$(r_{x_3 y_1})(r_{x_2 y_2}) = (r_{x_3 y_2})(r_{x_2 y_1}) \ , \tag{9}$$

$$(r_{x_1 y_1})(r_{x_3 y_2}) = (r_{x_1 y_2})(r_{x_3 y_1}) \ , \tag{10}$$

$$(r_{x_1 y_3})(r_{x_2 y_2}) = (r_{x_1 y_2})(r_{x_2 y_3}) \ , \tag{11}$$

$$(r_{x_3 y_3})(r_{x_2 y_2}) = (r_{x_3 y_2})(r_{x_2 y_3}) \ , \tag{12}$$

$$(r_{x_1 y_3})(r_{x_3 y_2}) = (r_{x_1 y_2})(r_{x_3 y_3}) \ , \tag{13}$$

$$(r_{x_1 y_1})(r_{x_2 y_3}) = (r_{x_1 y_3})(r_{x_2 y_1}) \ , \tag{14}$$

2. Hauser and Goldberger (1971) point out that an efficient estimate of c can be obtained by taking the weighted average of these two estimates, taking into consideration the relative sizes of their standard errors.

$$(r_{x_3 y_1})(r_{x_2 y_3}) = (r_{x_3 y_3})(r_{x_2 y_1}) \,, \tag{15}$$

$$(r_{x_1 y_1})(r_{x_3 y_3}) = (r_{x_1 y_3})(r_{x_3 y_1}) \,. \tag{16}$$

For the model of Figure 8.4, (9), (10), (15) and (16) are not met, while (7), (11), (12), (13), and (14) are approximately met. Since the only correlation common to the four not met is $r_{x_3 y_1}$, the researcher can conclude that there is some source of nonrandom error between x_3 and y_1, eliminate those two, and proceed with the analysis. If all nine were met, there would then be nine estimates of c, all of which should be approximately equal. The point is simply that nonrandom error can often be eliminated if we have more than two indicators of at least some constructs.

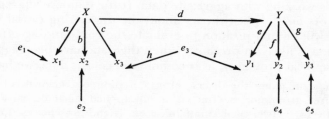

Figure 8.4.   *Costner's two-variable six-indicator model with detectable nonrandom error.*

This approach can also be generalized to the k-variable case. The consistency criterion remains the same, even if two variables are separated by a series of intervening variables, as long as their correlation can properly be expressed as equivalent to at least one set of path coefficients (Sullivan 1970).

It can be concluded from the discussion thus far that, in making decisions about indicators, the researcher should carefully examine the possibility of nonrandom measurement error between indicators of the same construct, and for indicators that might be products of more than one construct in the system, before he checks the consistency criterion.

Other Considerations

Obviously, the researcher cannot simply collect multiple indicators and try out various combinations until the criterion is approximated. There are other, equally important considerations, one of which is parsimony. If the hypothesized model is a complex one, and each indicator is used in testing the correctness of the model, the number of tests quickly becomes unmanageable. One approach to the problem is that of using multiple-partials in testing the predictions of the model. This allows all "blocks" of indicators to operate simultaneously while the advantages of multiple indicators, including multiple tests of each prediction, are retained (Sullivan 1971).

A second consideration is that the basic model must be specified clearly and must make sense theoretically. That is, the causal relationship between each unmeasured construct and its indicators must be both specifically posited and theoretically plausible. Otherwise, these consistency criteria, although they may be met, do not indicate the absence of nonrandom error. The criteria hold only when the correlations may be written in terms of path coefficients, and this imposes certain restrictions on the form of the model. For example, Blalock (1971a) has pointed out that the causal relationships between true and measured values are often poorly understood, especially when the researcher is working with aggregate data. If the data are aggregated on the basis of some explicit theory about the underlying causal relationships, we will be in a position to evaluate the confounding effects that aggregation is likely to produce. When the data have been aggregated by geographical proximity, as is common in census data, we have

> confounded together the diverse effects of common regional cultures and subcultures, group norms, effects of locally applied sanctions, early socialization patterns, networks of communication, friendship choices, family patterns, and selective in- and out-migration. The criterion for grouping will thus almost surely be related to most of the remaining variables in the system, but because of its complexity it will be extremely difficult to theorize very precisely about such relationships. [Blalock 1971a, p. 159]

In many situations, then, the geographical units being analyzed will differ significantly on most of the variables included in the system, and also on many variables not explicitly included but which comprise the error terms. It will thus be difficult to rely on the consistency criteria.

In such cases, how is one to proceed? One possible approach is first to recognize that the causal relationships among indicators cannot be sorted out, theoretically or empirically, and then to explore the relationships among the abstract constructs. If we conceptualize each construct as a block, and each indicator as one variable in that block, and then hypothesize that some of the variables in one block have a direct causal effect on some of the variables in the other (but not vice versa), we have a block-recursive situation. Often we will not be in a position to state which variables in block 1 affect which variables in block 2, although we may be relatively certain that there are direct asymmetric relationships. The multiple-partial approach is useful in handling these situations because it allows the hypothesized model to be tested in spite of the fact that the specific causal interrelationships cannot be sorted out. Additionally, as noted above, it allows multiple tests of each prediction.

Block-recursive Systems and Multiple-partials

The multiple-partial strategy is, briefly, as follows: Since we are not certain exactly how the within-block indicators are related to one another, we allow them to operate on the dependent variable simultaneously and attribute the resultant multiple correlation to the block as a whole. Whenever the model implies a relationship between two blocks controlling for a third, we allow all variables in the control blocks to operate before examining the relationship between the residuals. Since a multiple-partial cannot handle more than one dependent variable at a time, we take each indicator of the dependent variable block, one at a time. This gives us the multiple tests of each prediction, which may reveal whether the blocks affect the various components of the dependent block in the same way. If they do not, additional insights are obtained (Sullivan 1971).

If this approach is used, certain guidelines should be followed. First, there should be equal numbers of indicators per construct. Although it is perfectly correct, in terms of Costner's criterion, to work with unequal numbers of indicators, certain problems arise when the model is tested by means of multiple-partial coefficients. Gordon (1968) distinguishes between differential repetitiveness and unequal redundancy. The former refers to unequal numbers of indicators across constructs. If a regression analysis is run on a dependent variable which is related to two independent variables, but there are more indicators of one independent variable than of the second, "it could even happen that the regression coefficients of the construct having the *weaker* relationship with the dependent variable would attain statistical significance when the remainder did not, simply as a result of its being less repetitively represented" (Gordon 1968, p. 598). This is because the total effect of an independent variable on the dependent variable tends to be divided among its indicators. The larger the number of indicators, therefore, the smaller effect each one has on the dependent variable; hence, the more likely it is that *none* of them will have significant regression coefficients. In the case of an independent variable with a weaker total effect but fewer indicators, each indicator may reach significance because the effects are concentrated rather than diluted.

This problem is likely to be reversed in the present case, since we are relying on multiple-partials, which allow all indicators of the independent variables to operate at the same time. We are not attempting to eliminate indicators that do not reach significance in a regression equation, but rather to allow each indicator to add whatever explained variance it can. The more repetitive set, therefore, is likely to come out ahead, since the common variance between a dependent variable and an independent variable can only increase or stay the same if we *add* indicators of the independent variable to the equation.

Another consideration is what Gordon calls *unequal redundancy*. By redundancy he means a high correlation among the indicators of a variable. In general, the less the redundancy, the larger the regression coefficients for each indicator. Therefore, even with equal repetitiveness (same number of indicators per construct), if the within-set correlations are higher for the indicators of one independent variable than for those of another, the regression coefficients for the indicators in the set with lower within-set correlations are more likely to achieve significance. This effect is magnified if the between-set correlations are high. It is therefore important that the intra-set correlations be as similar as possible. With the multiple-partial approach, if there is unequal redundancy, the set with the smallest internal intercorrelations will account for the most total variance in the dependent variable; there will be less overlap in that set's indicators' separate relationships with the dependent variable. If the indicators of two sets are, individually, equally related to the dependent variable, but the indicators of set X are less highly related to each other than are those of set Y, set X will explain more total variance in the dependent variable; there will be less redundancy in their relationships with the dependent variable. This leads to the guideline that the intra-set correlations must be as similar as possible.

A corollary of the guideline above is that the intra-set correlations should be not only similar across sets, but relatively high as well. If the indicators indeed "indicate" the same thing, they ought to be highly related to one another. Further, if all indicators in a set accurately measure the underlying construct, and are therefore highly correlated to one another, they ought to be approximately equally related to the indicators in the other sets. That is, each indicator of construct A ought to be approximately equally related to the indicators of construct B.

The final and perhaps the most important guideline is that there should be a theoretical relationship between indicator and construct. Given a number of indicators from which to choose, one should of course select those with the closest and most direct relationships to the abstract concept. Which indicators these are is not always clear; a suggested general strategy in such instances is as follows: If the indicators are of similar quality, select those that best meet the criteria mentioned above (and summarized immediately below). Then factor analyze all the indicators of the same construct and compare the factor loadings of the selected indicators with those rejected. If their loadings are similar in magnitude to those which did not meet various of the other criteria, one can assume that the selected indicators are representative of the total set considered and can generalize the results to the theoretical concept rather than interpret the findings merely in terms of the particular indicators selected. This strategy will be illustrated below.

In summary, then, the guidelines in testing complex models with multiple indicators and multiple-partials are (1) that there should be a theoretical relationship between indicator and construct, (2) that there should be equal numbers of indicators per construct, (3) that there should exist relatively high and equal within-set correlations among indicators, and (4) that there should be similar between-set correlation patterns. Additionally, it is useful to check Costner's first consistency criterion under the assumption that all indicators of the model are, in fact, effect indicators, unless it is certain that this is not the case; and then to relax that restriction and test the model by the multiple-partial approach. Some illustrative data are analyzed below.

Specific Models

The original theoretical model is presented in Figure 8.5.[3] The evidence and theory which led to the causal assumptions are discussed elsewhere (Sullivan 1970). The indicators noted in Table 8.1 were employed in the original analysis of this model, and the results were generally confirmatory, although there are certain problems with these data. First, there are unequal numbers of indicators per construct, the effects of which have just been noted. Second, the within-set correlations vary considerably, and several are of low magnitude. Third, the indicators do not meet Costner's consistency criterion.[4] More specifically, there is nonrandom measurement error among the indicators of discrimination, party competition, and choice (Sullivan 1970, chap. 4). Even though the data seem to confirm the model, confidence in·the results cannot be high. As a result, additional indicators were collected, with the above criteria in mind. They are listed in Table 8.2.

There are more indicators per construct than can reasonably be dealt with, except in the construct of choice. Therefore, within-set correlation matrices were computed for each set, and some indicators were eliminated because they did not correlate significantly with the other within-set indicators. After this elimination, two criteria were applied simultaneously: the consistency criterion, and the size of the within-set correlations. The two "best" indicators per construct are listed first in Table 8.2; their correlations are presented in Table 8.3. The within-set correlations are high and range from .82 to .94 (with one exception noted below); the between-set correlations are similar; and, as noted in Table 8.4, the consistency test is closely approximated.

3. The unit of analysis is the American states. The indicators of each concept are noted below.

4. This *may* be due to the inappropriateness of simple "cause-effect" models in the case of aggregated data.

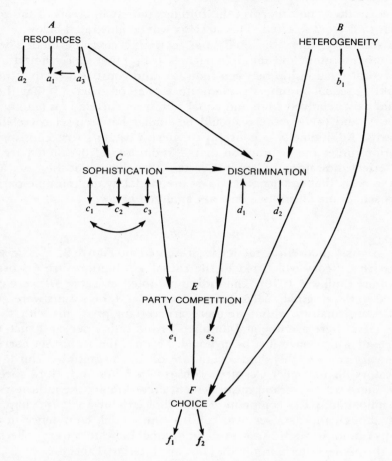

Figure 8.5.   Original model (error terms not represented).

The one exception to the rule that the within-set correlations be high is the ultimate dependent variable, the amount of choice offered in the election. These two indicators, the amount of choice offered in the Senate election of 1966 and the average amount of choice offered in the House elections in each state that same year, are only correlated .55. This could mean that there is no unitary concept of choice that can be applied to state political systems (i.e., separate forces are operating to determine the amount of choice offered in different types of elections), or it could mean that, since in all but two states there was only one senatorial election, there is considerable error variance because of sampling errors. Since there were several House elections in most states, there was less sampling error within the states.

Table 8.1. Original Set of Indicators

Indicator	Definition	Indicator	Definition
a_1	% home ownership	e_1	% for presidential candidate carrying the state, 1966
a_2	Median income		
a_3	% white collar	e_2	Mean difference, winner's % − loser's %, by congressional district, 1966
b_1*	Index		
c_1	% college educated	f_1‡	Difference score, Senate race, 1966
c_2	Median education	f_2‡	Mean difference score by congressional district, 1966
c_3	% functionally illiterate		
d_1	% Negro		
d_2†	Home-ownership ratio		

SOURCES: f_1, f_2 from data collected by *Congressional Quarterly* for N.B.C. News-Election Unit; all other indicators taken from *Congressional District Data Book, 1963*.

NOTE: Sample size is thirty-two states.

*Summation of the standard deviation, by congressional district, of seven socioeconomic variables.

†Difference between the ratio of home ownership to renter-occupied dwellings for whites vs. nonwhites.

‡Issue position, on a liberalism-conservatism scale of attitudes toward public policy, of candidate 1 minus the issue position of candidate 2 when both candidates are running for the same office; they represent the amount of choice the electorate had between the two candidates. See Sullivan and O'Connor 1972.

Whichever explanation is correct, this deviation from the general pattern of within-set correlations does not result in the kind of problems discussed by Gordon. The problem of unequal redundancy applies only to the independent variables. The less redundant should have a greater joint effect on the dependent variable, but the concept of choice and its indicators are never considered to be anything but dependent variables. At no time do they enter the same regression equation; at no time is their influence on another variable compared with the influence of other variables.

As noted above, the within-set correlations for the independent variables range from .82 to .94. Although not a considerable range, it does mean that the effects of the sophistication and party competition indicators will be more redundant than the indicators of resources and heterogeneity.

Table 8.2. Additional Indicators

Construct and Indicator	Definition
A. Resources	
a_1	% white collar
a_2	Median income
a_3	% families under $3,000
a_4	Per capita revenue
a_5	% home ownership
a_6	% families under $6,000
a_7	% families over $10,000
a_8	100−% engaged in farming, fishing, forestry
a_9	Industrialization factor score
a_{10}	Natural-resources factor score
B. Heterogeneity	
b_1*	Socioeconomic diversity index (within-state)
b_2*	Socioeconomic diversity index (within congressional district)
b_3	Original index
C. Sophistication	
c_1	Cultural-enrichment factor rank
c_2	Median education
c_3	% college educated
c_4	% functionally illiterate
c_5	% urban
c_6	Per pupil expenditures
c_7	Welfare-Education factor score
c_8	Number of newspapers/number of families
D. Discrimination	
d_1	Discrimination ratio, professionals' income
d_2	Discrimination ratio, craftsmen's income
d_3	% Negro
d_4	Home-ownership ratio
E. Party competition	
e_1	Dawson and Robinson Competitiveness Index
e_2	Ranney Competitiveness Index
e_3	% for presidential candidate carrying state, 1966
e_4	Mean difference, winner's % − loser's %, by congressional district, 1966
e_5	Hofferbert Competitiveness Index
F. Choice	
f_1 and f_2	See definition, Table 8.1

SOURCES: a_3, a_4, c_6, c_8, *Statistical Abstracts, 1963*; a_8, *U.S. Census, 1960*, pp. 1-281; a_9, c_1, Hofferbert 1968; a_{10}, c_7, Sharkansky and Hofferbert 1969; b_1, b_2, Sullivan 1973; d_1, d_2, Dye 1969; e_2, Ranney 1965, p. 65; e_5, Hofferbert 1964; all other variables, *Congressional District Data Book, 1963*, unless otherwise noted in Table 8.1.

*Proportion of social, economic, and religious characteristics upon which two randomly selected individuals·from each state would differ, restricting selection of individuals to the entire state and to congressional districts, respectively.

Table 8.3. Correlations, Second Set of Indicators

Variable	Correlation										
	2	3	4	5	6	7	8	9	10	11	12
1. %white collar	**.83**	.70	.64	.74	.70	−.42	−.57	.56	.67	.33	.26
2. Median income		.86	.74	.73	.74	−.57	−.75	.73	.81	.32	.46
3. State diversity			**.82**	.47	.61	−.43	−.58	.66	.71	.30	.22
4. District diversity				.52	.58	−.37	−.46	.60	.64	.34	.28
5. Cultural factor					**.93**	−.77	−.79	.70	.79	.54	.67
6. Median education						−.78	−.84	.66	.76	.55	.63
7. Discr. ratio, professionals							**.87**	−.67	−.74	−.56	−.74
8. Discr. ratio, craftsmen								−.76	−.83	−.56	−.69
9. Dawson and Robinson									**.94**	.49	.59
10. Ranney										.55	.62
11. Choice, Senate											**.55**
12. Choice, House											
13. % under $3,000*	**−.78**	−.87	−.74	−.80	−.75	+.65	+.82	−.75	−.83	−.41	−.52

NOTE: All correlations in boldface are within-set correlations.

*Later replaces number 2, median income. Therefore, the first correlation listed, −.78, is with the first variable, % white collar.

Table 8.4. Distribution, Consistency Criterion Results

Test No.*	Diff. from 0	Test No.*	Diff. from 0
5	.0686	15	.0207
6	.0446	7	.0168
2	.0366	11	.0106
4	.0355	9	.0092
1	.0324	3	.0089
10	.0306	13	.0063
12	.0283	8	.0036
14	.0280		

*See Appendix.

As for the first consistency criterion, the results of these tests are presented in Table 8.4. It is difficult to evaluate them in the absence of a test of significance, although, in comparative terms, they appear to be good. The first set of indicators, noted in Table 8.1, resulted in four-teen of twenty-four difference scores higher than the largest difference score obtained with this second set. The highest of the fourteen larger scores was .4168, and eleven of them were higher than .1000. This second set better approximates Costner's criterion for random meas-urement error.

In Table 8.4, four of the five highest difference scores involve the indicators of resources, and all of the seven highest scores involve the indicators of either resources or sophistication. This strongly suggests that any nonrandom measurement error in this set is due to these indicators. The source of the nonrandom error can be determined, as noted earlier, by using additional indicators; and the consistency criterion is better met when percentage of families with incomes under $3,000 is substituted for median income as an indicator of resources. Table 8.5 presents the results, which are to be compared with those of Table 8.4. It should be noted that the addition of any other indicator from the twenty listed in Table 8.2 increases the probability of nonrandom measurement error.

Table 8.5. Consistency Criterion Results, Percentage of Families under $3,000 Replacing Median Income

Test No.	Diff. from 0	Test No.	Diff. from 0
2*	.0670	4*	.0177
6	.0446	7	.0168
1*	.0388	11	.0106
10	.0306	9	.0092
12	.0283	13	.0063
14	.0280	8	.0036
3*	.0261	5*	.0001
15	.0207		

*New values due to change in indicators.

The most dramatic change is in test number 5, between the indicators of resources and those of choice. This test, which was the most deviant from zero with median income as the indicator of resources, is now the closest to zero. Now, the most obvious source of nonrandom measurement error is the indicators of sophistication. Five of the six highest values in Table 8.5 represent tests including some of these indicators.

Other indicators of sophistication were tried, but in every case the consistency tests were less well satisfied. That in itself is not sufficient to exclude them, but the differences were generally much larger and the theoretical connections between indicators such as per pupil educational expenditures, percentage of adults functionally illiterate, and so on, and the sophistication construct are no clearer or more straightforward than those for the indicators cultural factor and median education.

The model of Figure 8.1 can now be retested using the second set of indicators, with percentage under $3,000 replacing median income. The results of the tests of the predictions of this model are presented in Table 8.6. Whereas these tests are generally satisfied if the first set of indicators is used, only one of the six is satisfied with this second set. It must be concluded that the results obtained with the second set of measures are more likely to be valid, and so the model must be rejected.

The multiple tests of each prediction except the sixth are consistent. The indicators of resources seem to have independent impacts on the average choice by congressional district, but not on the choice offered in the senatorial elections. This could reflect either a true difference or a sampling error, as noted earlier.

A Revised Model

Clearly, model 1 (Fig. 8.1) is not supported by these data. The results of Table 8.6 can be used in reformulating the relationships among these variables. In particular, there are strong correlations between resources and heterogeneity, and between sophistication and heterogeneity. One possibility is a direct relationship between resources and heterogeneity, resulting in a spurious relationship between sophistication and heterogeneity. Certainly, the presence and development of

Table 8.6. Test of Model 1, Second Set of Indicators

Fit Between Model and Data

1. $r_{AB} = 0$
    (1) $a_1 b_1 = +.70*$
    (2) $a_1 b_2 = +.64*$
    (3) $a_2 b_1 = -.87*$
    (4) $a_2 b_2 = -.74*$
2. $r_{BC} = 0$
    (1) $b_1 c_1 = +.47*$
    (2) $b_1 c_2 = +.61*$
    (3) $b_2 c_1 = +.52*$
    (4) $b_2 c_2 = +.58*$
3. $r_{BE \cdot D} = 0$
    (1) $e_1(b_1 b_2) \cdot (d_1 d_2) = +.47*$
    (2) $e_2(b_1 b_2) \cdot (d_1 d_2) = +.54*$
4. $r_{CF \cdot DE} = 0$
    (1) $f_1(c_1 c_2) \cdot (d_1 d_2 e_1 e_2) = +.09\dagger$
    (2) $f_2(c_1 c_2) \cdot (d_1 d_2 e_1 e_2) = +.17\dagger$
5. $r_{AE \cdot CD} = 0$
    (1) $e_1(a_1 a_2) \cdot (c_1 c_2 d_1 d_2) = +.39*$
    (2) $e_2(a_1 a_2) \cdot (c_1 c_2 d_1 d_2) = +.45*$
6. $r_{AF \cdot CD} = 0$
    (1) $f_1(a_1 a_2) \cdot (c_1 c_2 d_1 d_2) = +.13\dagger$
    (2) $f_2(a_1 a_2) \cdot (c_1 c_2 d_1 d_2) = +.40*$

NOTE: $N = 32$
*Significant, .05 level.
†Not significant, .05 level.

resources should affect heterogeneity by producing more varied social and economic strata, especially as a result of industrialization and its accompanying urbanization. If this is the case, the multiple-partials between sophistication and heterogeneity, controlling for resources, should drop to zero; but in fact they are .39 with b_1 and .14 with b_2 as dependent variables. This seemingly rules out a direct relationship between resources and heterogeneity coupled with a spurious relationship between sophistication and heterogeneity.

Another possibility, then, is an indirect relationship between resources and heterogeneity, via sophistication. This seems doubtful on theoretical grounds, but if it is the case, the multiple-partials between resources and heterogeneity, controlling for sophistication, should drop to zero; instead, they are .59 for b_1 and .81 for b_2. A more plausible alternative, then, is a direct relationship for both resources and sophistication with heterogeneity.

A second useful result shown in Table 8.6 is that the multiple-partials between heterogeneity and party competition, controlling for discrimination, do not drop to zero. Perhaps, then, there is a direct relationship between the two (see Sullivan 1973 for a theoretical exposition based on Madisonian theory regarding the relationships among heterogeneity, discrimination, and party competition). It is possible, however, that the residual relationship, once discrimination is controlled, is spurious via sophistication, since the model now assumes a direct relationship between sophistication and heterogeneity. If so, the multiple-partials between heterogeneity and party competition, controlling for sophistication and discrimination, should be zero. They are .53 for e_1 and .58 for e_2, and therefore a direct relationship seems more plausible.

A third pertinent result shown in Table 8.6 is the fact that the multiple-partials between resources and party competition did not drop to zero once sophistication and discrimination were controlled. In this reevaluation of the model, however, it has become evident that a direct relationship between resources and heterogeneity, on the one hand, and a direct relationship between heterogeneity and party competition, on the other hand, add another control variable to this test, because the residual relationship may be due to this intervening link rather than to any direct relationship between resources and party competition. Indeed, when heterogeneity is added as a control, the multiple-partials are .18 for e_1 and .00 for e_2. This is consistent with the assumption of only intervening links between resources and party competition.

The last consideration shown in Table 8.6 is the relationship between resources and choice, controlling for sophistication and discrimination. The results are inconsistent, which indicates a direct role for resources in determining the amount of average choice by congressional districts, but none for choice in Senate races. We now add another control, heterogeneity, because of the possibility of an intervening residual relationship. The results stay the same: .16 for f_1 and .41 for f_2.

The results suggest a revised model, illustrated in Figure 8.6. The correspondence between its predictions and assumptions, on the one hand, and the data, on the other, is presented in Tables 8.7 and 8.8. Generally, the data seem to fit this model, which is considerably different from the original model. The only inconsistent result seen in Table 8.7 is that just noted—the relationship between resources and choice.

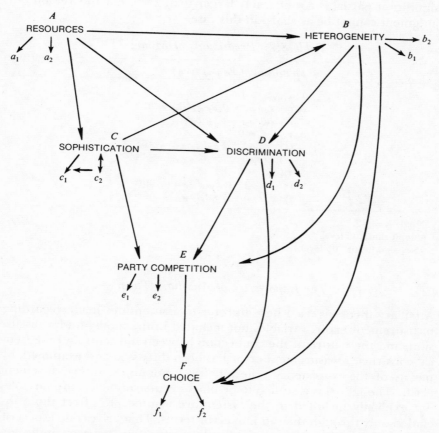

Figure 8.6.   Revised model (hypothesized relationships between indicators and constructs, and among indicators, are necessary only for consistency criterion and may be dropped when testing model by means of multiple-partials).

The results shown in Table 8.8 indicate that the same is true of the relationship between heterogeneity and choice (see assumption 7). Since the evidence is so consistent, it may be concluded that social and economic characteristics affect choice in statewide elections through political variables such as discrimination and party competition, but that they have independent effects on choice at the district level.

One other inconsistent result is evident in Table 8.8, at least at the .05 level. Discrimination has a larger residual relationship with choice at the district level than at the statewide level, which results in one significant and one nonsignificant multiple-partial. This is consistent with the effects of resources and heterogeneity on choice; yet the non-significant partial is considerably larger than zero. For this reason our judgment cannot be as sharp in this case.

Table 8.7. Predictions of Model 2

Fit Between Model and Data

1. $r_{AE \cdot BCD} = 0$
   (1) $e_1(a_1a_2) \cdot (b_1b_2c_1c_2d_1d_2) = .18\dagger$
   (2) $e_2(a_1a_2) \cdot (b_1b_2c_1c_2d_1d_2) = .00\dagger$
2. $r_{AF \cdot BDE} = 0$
   (1) $f_1(a_1a_2) \cdot (b_1b_2d_1d_2e_1e_2) = .16\dagger$
   (2) $f_2(a_1a_2) \cdot (b_1b_2d_1d_2e_1e_2) = .41*$
3. $r_{CF \cdot BDE} = 0$
   (1) $f_1(c_1c_2) \cdot (b_1b_2d_1d_2e_1e_2) = .09\dagger$
   (2) $f_2(c_1c_2) \cdot (b_1b_2d_1d_2e_1e_2) = .06\dagger$

NOTE: $N = 32$.
*Significant, .05 level.
†Not significant, .05 level.

The Importance of Auxiliary Theory

Auxiliary theory is used here to refer to assumptions made regarding measurement error, variables not included in the model under discussion, and the nature of the connection between indicator and theoretical construct. Measurement error has been discussed and examined, by means of the consistency criterion for randomness of measurement error. The model is assumed to be block-recursive; hence any variables not explicitly included in the system are assumed to affect those included only through the random error terms. That leaves one aspect of the auxiliary theory unexamined—the connection between indicator and theoretical construct. It is perhaps the most important, and certainly the most difficult, criterion to be applied to the selection of indicators.

Table 8.8. Assumptions of Model 2

Fit Between Model and Data

1. $r_{AB \cdot C} \neq 0$
   (1) $b_1(a_1a_2) \cdot (c_1c_2) = +.59*$
   (2) $b_2(a_1a_2) \cdot (c_1c_2) = +.81*$
2. $r_{AC} \neq 0$
   (1) $a_1c_1 = -.80*$
   (2) $a_1c_2 = -.75*$
   (3) $a_2c_1 = +.74*$
   (4) $a_2c_2 = +.70*$
3. $r_{AD \cdot BC} \neq 0$
   (1) $d_1(a_1a_2) \cdot (b_1b_2c_1c_2) = +.47*$
   (2) $d_2(a_1a_2) \cdot (b_1b_2c_1c_2) = +.51*$
4. $r_{BC} \neq 0$
   (1) $b_1c_1 = +.47*$
   (2) $b_1c_2 = +.61*$
   (3) $b_2c_1 = +.52*$
   (4) $b_2c_2 = +.58*$
5. $r_{BD} \neq 0$
   (1) $b_1d_1 = -.43*$
   (2) $b_1d_2 = -.58*$
   (3) $b_2d_1 = -.37*$
   (4) $b_2d_2 = -.46*$
6. $r_{BE \cdot D} \neq 0$
   (1) $e_1(b_1b_2) \cdot (d_1d_2) = +.47*$
   (2) $e_2(b_1b_2) \cdot (d_1d_2) = +.54*$

7. $r_{BF \cdot DE} \neq 0$
   (1) $f_1(b_1b_2) \cdot (d_1d_2e_1e_2) = +.09\dagger$
   (2) $f_2(b_1b_2) \cdot (d_1d_2e_1e_2) = +.41*$
8. $r_{CD} \neq 0$
   (1) $c_1d_1 = -.78*$
   (2) $c_1d_2 = -.84*$
   (3) $c_2d_1 = -.77*$
   (4) $c_2d_2 = -.79*$
9. $r_{CE \cdot BD} \neq 0$
   (1) $e_1(c_1c_2) \cdot (b_1b_2d_1d_2) = +.44*$
   (2) $e_2(c_1c_2) \cdot (b_1b_2d_1d_2) = +.45*$
10. $r_{DE} \neq 0$
    (1) $d_1e_1 = -.67*$
    (2) $d_1e_2 = -.74*$
    (3) $d_2e_1 = -.76*$
    (4) $d_2e_2 = -.83*$
11. $r_{DF \cdot E} \neq 0$
    (1) $f_1(d_1d_2) \cdot (e_1e_2) = +.26\dagger$
    (2) $f_2(d_1d_2) \cdot (e_1e_2) = +.55*$
12. $r_{EF} \neq 0$
    (1) $e_1f_1 = +.49*$
    (2) $e_1f_2 = +.59*$
    (3) $e_2f_1 = +.55*$
    (4) $e_2f_2 = +.62*$

NOTE: $N = 32$.
*Significant, .05 level.
†Not significant, .05 level.

The gap between theory and research has been noted often, but left unresolved. It cannot be resolved here, nor can an attempted resolution be undertaken. Rather, several points can be illustrated as they pertain to the complexity of the linkage between concept and measurement that is inherent in all research but is even more obvious and difficult with aggregate data.

The first point is that indicators can usually be conceptualized as either determinants of or consequences of the theoretical concept. The models in Figures 8.1 and 8.2 illustrate such hypothesized causal relationships between the indicators and concepts used in this analysis.[5] Indeed, for Costner's consistency criterion to be used, it is important that most if not all indicators be consequents of the unmeasured variable so that the correlations can be expressed in terms of path coefficients.

5. Again, caution is urged, since this may be inappropriate with aggregate data.

A related point is that the causal connection between indicators and their theoretical abstractions is more direct at some times than at others, and the major reason appears to be conceptual ambiguity at the theoretical level or lack of appropriate data at the empirical level. To illustrate, consider the concepts of model 2 (Fig. 8.2). Resources are defined as the "raw materials" available to a state, including primarily, but not exclusively, economic potential and/or development (see Sullivan 1970 for definition and discussion of all concepts included). Two consequences of a high level of economic resources are a small percentage of families with incomes below $3,000 and an increase in the percentage of white-collar employees needed to manage and develop these resources. Indeed, all the indicators noted under resources in Table 8.2 can be conceptualized as results of the presence and development of economic resources. Because of the vagueness of the concept, however, it is difficult to judge any indicators, a priori, as better than the others.

The second confounding factor, a lack of empirical indicators, is illustrated by the concept sophistication. Although somewhat vague in and of itself, its primary meaning, originally, was the central tendency of the degree of political awareness, knowledge, and interest of the citizenry of the state. But national survey data, which provide measures of these components of political sophistication, do not include respondents from all states and often do not provide enough subjects in more than a few states for it to be possible to avoid large sampling errors. Therefore, the concept had to be conceptualized (redefined) as a direct function of general sophistication, and measured primarily in terms of educational level.[6]

The other concepts are measured in a more direct fashion. For example, heterogeneity is defined as the degree of variation among the electorate of each state in social, economic, and religious characteristics. It implies cross-cutting cleavages and a series of minority groups rather than one clear-cut majority group. It is measured by an index of diversity, whose value for each state represents the percentage of social, economic, and religious characteristics not shared by two average residents of that state (see Sullivan 1973). The second indicator reflects the degree of unshared characteristics by congressional district rather than by state. In both cases, they measure directly what is implied in the abstract discussion of the theoretical construct. Discrimination, defined as unequal treatment of equals and measured as the income differences between whites and nonwhites at the same occupational levels, is also quite directly measured, as are the concepts party competition and choice.

6. It is with concepts such as this that we are often unable to determine whether we have cause or effect indicators, or both. Hence the inappropriateness of relying exclusively on Costner's criteria.

An important question thus arises. What happens when we know there is a rather large gap between some of our concepts and their indicators? On the face of it, it appears that we must sacrifice generality and stick close to the indicators themselves in our analysis and interpretation. To illustrate, consider one of the concepts in this situation, resources. As noted above, using the theory of path coefficients, we can solve for the value of the path coefficients between indicators and constructs (*a, b, d, e* in Fig. 8.1). Therefore, we can, seemingly, empirically link our abstract system of concepts with our empirical estimates of those concepts. Two computed estimates of the path coefficient between white-collar percentage (a_1) and resources are .853 and .849; those of the percentage of families with incomes under $3,000 are .914 and .918.[7] Therefore, the nature of the abstract notion resources seems to be determined by the kind of indicators used. It shares more than 70 percent common variance with "percentage white collar," and more than 80 percent common variance with "percentage under $3,000." Regardless of how we initially define resources, the resulting model, including the abstract concepts, is apparently determined by the nature of the indicators selected.

The researcher may, nevertheless, continue to adhere to the original formulation, if he is willing to run the risk of overgeneralizing his results. For example, if the concept resources is primarily unidimensional and is directly related to the indicators listed in Table 8.2, the major consideration is in fact the nature of the measurement error among various sets of indicators. Model specification and parameter estimation should yield similar results regardless of the particular set of indicators used, unless there are major differences in the nature of their measurement error. In the present case, the results may differ because all other indicators of resources appear to involve nonrandom error with other sets of indicators. Because of this, it is crucial that we use the selected indicators; but if we can assume that the original notion of resources encompasses (as consequents) all indicators considered, the indicators are primarily (but not exclusively, as assumed in factor analysis) spuriously related and do not directly affect any of the remaining theoretical constructs in the system. The primary impact, then,

---

7. The estimates are obtained by solving the paths between resources and sophistication, as in Figure 8.1. The equations are

$$a_1{}^2 = r_{a_1 a_2} \left(r_{a_1 c_2} / r_{a_2 c_2} \right) = r_{a_1 a_2} \left(r_{a_1 c_1} / r_{a_2 c_1} \right),$$

$$a_2{}^2 = r_{a_1 a_2} \left(r_{a_2 c_2} / r_{a_1 c_2} \right) = r_{a_1 a_2} \left(r_{a_2 c_1} / r_{a_1 c_1} \right).$$

Therefore, the path coefficient is the square root of these terms. Further, the path coefficients are the same as correlation coefficients in this case (see Costner 1969). Here, a_1 = percentage white collar, a_2 = percentage under $3,000, c_1 = cultural factor, and c_2 = median education.

is through the originally specified but unmeasured concept resources, and we can interpret our results in more abstract terms, thus overcoming the apparent redefinition caused by the use of particular indicators.

In the present instance, the two most tenuous connections are between resources and sophistication and their indicators. Both sets of indicators (listed in Table 8.2) were factor analyzed (verimax orthogonal rotation), for determining the number of factors best describing each set, as well as for comparing the loadings of the indicators used in the analysis with those (with nonrandom measurement error) discarded before model specification was carried out. In both cases, two orthogonal factors were extracted (an eigenvalue cutoff of 1.0 was used). For the construct resources, the first factor is almost perfectly correlated with median income, which could not be used because of the consistency criterion.[8] However, the two indicators used load .97 and .85 on the first factor, and of the indicators in Table 8.2 (under construct resources), only percentage of home ownership and natural-resources factor score fail to load highly on the first factor.

For the construct sophistication, the two indicators used load more highly on the first factor than any discarded indicators.[9] Further, only the indicators percentage urban and number of newspapers/number of families fail to load highly on the first factor. In fact, percentage urban is perfectly correlated with the second factor, which indicates a split in the sophistication indicators between education and urbanization indicators.

In both cases, almost all the indicators load highly on the first factor extracted, and the indicators used in this analysis loaded *very* highly on it. This does not in any sense solve our theoretical problems, but it does mean that the indicators which best satisfied the consistency criterion are typical (good) representatives of the total set considered, and that the results can be generalized (with a certain amount of risk) in terms of the abstract theoretical constructs, which include portions of the indicators which did not satisfy the consistency criterion.[10]

The suggestion here, then, is to select indicators on the basis of theory. Given equal theoretical usefulness, select those that best satisfy the criteria for within- and between-set correlations, and for random-

8. The highest loadings are: median income, .99; percentage under $6,000, −.99; percentage under $3,000, −.97; percentage white collar, .85; percentage over $10,000, .73; and per capita revenue, .67.

9. The highest loadings are: median education, .92; cultural factor, .92; percentage with less than five years' education, −.87; welfare-education factor, .71; per pupil expenditures, .64.

10. A common practice is factor analyzing each set of indicators and then using the factor scores to represent each construct. However, the advantages of multiple indicators are lost and the nonrandom measurement error is confounded when that is done. A better procedure seems to be to use the indicators separately, but to check their loadings to make sure they are not weakly related to the "commonality" present among all indicators of the same construct.

ness of measurement error. These indicators should be best for model specification, if the assumptions of Costner's criteria are met. One can then determine how free one is to generalize, on the basis of a factor analysis of same-concept indicators. The major advantage of this procedure over factor analysis is that the problem of randomness of measurement error cannot be handled if one uses factor scores directly; in the latter instance, in order to specify a model, the researcher must assume that the "commonality" of all his indicators contains only random measurement error, but he cannot check this assumption.

Concluding Remarks

Several criteria for the selection and analysis of indicators with aggregate data have been discussed, among them the theoretical relationship between indicator and construct, the number of indicators per construct, high and equal within-set correlations, similar between-set correlations, and the consistency criterion for the randomness of measurement error. It would be useful to rank order these in terms of importance, but that is probably impossible. All of them are of considerable importance. For example, if the construct and its indicators are only weakly related, any generalizations at the theoretical level are so risky as to be useless. On the other hand, even if this problem is handled satisfactorily, the existence of nonrandom error means incorrect model specification, and the nature of the specification errors will usually be completely unknown. Suffice it to say that each criterion ought to be explicitly taken into account, and any conflicts between or among them should be handled on an individual basis, depending on the nature of the problem at hand. Certainly, whenever data are being collected, a priori consideration of these criteria will allow the researcher more flexibility once and analysis phase begins.

Appendix
Results of Consistency Criterion Test with Second Set of Indicators

Pairs of Concepts Tested	Test Results
1. Resources with heterogeneity	$(.74)(.70) - (.86)(.64) = -.0324$
2. Resources with sophistication	$(.73)(.70) - (.74)^2 = -.0366$
3. Resources with discrimination	$(-.75)(-.42) - (-.57)^2 = -.0089$
4. Resources with party competition	$(.81)(.56) - (.73)(.67) = -.0355$
5. Resources with choice	$(.46)(.33) - (.32)(.26) = .0686$

6. Heterogeneity with
   sophistication $(.47)(.58) - (.61)(.52) = -.0446$
7. Heterogeneity with
   discrimination $(-.58)(-.37) - (-.43)(-.46) = .0168$
8. Heterogeneity with party
   competition $(.71)(.60) - (.66)(.64) = .0036$
9. Heterogeneity with choice $(.22)(.34) - (.30)(.28) = .0092$
10. Sophistication with
    discrimination $(-.84)(-.77) - (-.78)(-.79) = .0306$
11. Sophistication with party
    competition $(.76)(.70) - (.66)(.79) = .0106$
12. Sophistication with choice $(.63)(.54) - (.55)(.67) = -.0283$
13. Discrimination with party
    competition $(-.74)(-.76) - (-.67)(-.83) = .0063$
14. Discrimination with choice $(-.74)(-.56) - (-.56)(-.69) = .0280$
15. Party competition with
    choice $(.59)(.55) - (.49)(.62) = .0207$

References

Blalock, Hubert M.
    1968. "Simultaneous-Equation Estimation Techniques." Manuscript. Seattle: Department of Sociology, University of Washington.
    1969. "Multiple Indicators and the Causal Approach to Measurement Error." *American Journal of Sociology* 75 (September):264-72.
    1971a. "Aggregation and Measurement Error." *Social Forces* 50 (December): 151-65.
    1971b. "Causal Models Involving Unmeasured Variables in Stimulus Response Situations." In Hubèrt M. Blalock, ed., *Causal Models in the Social Sciences*. Chicago: Aldine.
Costner, Herbert L.
    1969. "Theory, Deduction, and Rules of Correspondence." *American Journal of Sociology* 75 (September):245-63.
Dye, Thomas R.
    1969. "Inequality and Civil Rights Policy in the States." *Journal of Politics* 31:1080-97.
Gordon, Robert A.
    1968. "Issues in Multiple Regression." *American Journal of Sociology* 68 (September):195-204.
Hauser, Robert M., and Arthur S. Goldberger
    1971. "The Treatment of Unobservable Variables in Path Analysis." In Herbert L. Costner, ed., *Sociological Methodology, 1971*. San Francisco: Jossey-Bass.
Hofferbert, Richard I.
    1964. "Classification of American State Party Systems." *Journal of Politics* 26:550-67.
    1968. "Socioeconomic Dimensions of the American States: 1890-1960." *Midwest Journal of Political Science* 12:410-13.
Ranney, Austin
    1965. "Parties in State Politics." In Herbert Jacob and Kenneth N. Vines, eds., *Politics in the American States*. Boston: Little, Brown.
Sharkansky, Ira, and Richard I. Hofferbert
    1969. "Dimensions of State Politics, Economics, and Public Policy." *American Political Science Review* 63 (September):876.
Sullivan, John L.
    1970. "Linkage Models of the Political System." Ph.D. dissertation, University of North Carolina.
    1971. "Multiple Indicators and Complex Causal Models." In Hubert M. Blalock, ed., *Causal Models in the Social Sciences*. Chicago: Aldine.
    1973. "Political Correlates of Social, Economic, and Religious Diversity in the American States." *Journal of Politics* 35 (February):70-84.
Sullivan, John L., and Robert E. O'Connor
    1972. "Electoral Choice and Popular Control of Public Policy." *American Political Science Review* 66 (December):1256-68.

Chapter 9

QUANTIFYING UNMEASURED VARIABLES

C. E. WERTS
R. L. LINN
K. G. JÖRESKOG

Charles E. Werts received his Ph.D. from the University of Minnesota in 1960. He is currently Research Psychologist at the Educational Testing Service, Princeton, N.J. His main interests lie in educational research. Robert L. Linn received his Ph.D. in Psychology from the University of Illinois, where he now holds a position of Associate Professor of Educational Psychology. His major interests are test theory and educational research on which subjects he has published several articles recently. Professor Linn also serves at present as Editor of the Journal of Educational Measurement. *K. G. Jöreskog received his Ph.D. in 1963 from the University of Uppsala, where he is presently Professor of Statistics. His main research interests lie in applications of multivariate analysis in the behavior sciences, particularly factor analysis, covariance structures, and structural equation models; in these areas he has published several articles recently.*

Social scientists frequently make inferences about the "effects" of hypothetical constructs which are not directly measured; for example, only the symptoms, antecedents, or consequences of those constructs may be measurable. In recent years various statistical procedures designed to help quantify the relationships among observed variables and constructs have been introduced in an attempt to increase the rigor and validity of such inferences. The purpose of this chapter is to introduce the concepts and to consider the numerous assumptions involved in these procedures.

The research reported herein was performed pursuant to Grant no. OEG-2-700033(509) with the United States Department of Health, Education, and Welfare, and the Office of Education.

270

Validity

A basic concept in the discussion of indirectly measured variables is that of *validity*. Although the term "validity" has been used in a number of different senses, we shall use it to refer to the relationship between an observed variable, X, and the unmeasured construct, Y. We shall discuss models in which it is assumed that the relationship is linear, that is,

$$X = bY + I + e, \tag{1}$$

where b is the slope of the regression of X on Y, I is the intercept of this regression line, and e is a residual taken to be independent of Y. Econometricians (see Goldberger 1970) typically specify $b = 1$ and $I = 0$, and e is labeled a *disturbance* instead of the psychometric term *errors of measurement*. Despite the crucial importance of this linear relationship, data analysts seldom substantively justify this assumption. For example, ability and achievement-test scores are generally assumed to have a linear relationship with their underlying *true* scores, however persuasively Carver (1969) has argued that there is a curvilinear relationship between knowledge (the construct) and test scores in classroom learning—that is, that more knowledge is required to increase the test score one point at the high end of the scale. Psychologists commonly use the term *validity coefficient* to refer to the correlation (R_{XY}) between the observed variable and the construct (true score), assuming the residuals of X on Y to be independent of Y (Guilford 1954, chap. 14).

It is useful to distinguish between the terms *reliability* and *validity*. A traditional test theorist will typically consider the correlation between *equivalent*, *parallel*, or *alternate* forms (X_1 and X_2) of a test to be the *reliability coefficient*. As illustrated in Figure 9.1a, the model here is $X_1 = b_1Y + I_1 + e_1$ and $X_2 = b_2Y + I_2 + e_2$, where e_1 and e_2 are assumed independent of each other and of Y; which implies that $R_{e_1 e_2} = R_{e_1 Y} = R_{e_2 Y} = 0$. Test forms are said to be equivalent when the variances of e_1 and e_2 are equal ($V_{e_1} = V_{e_2}$) and $b_1 = b_2$. It follows that the correlation between the observed measures will equal the square of the correlation of either measure with the construct, that is, $(R_{X,Y})^2 = (R_{X,Y})^2 = R_{X_1 X_2} =$ reliability coefficient. If Y, the variable being measured by the parallel forms, is itself a symptom of Z, another construct, new assumptions must be made, for example, $Y = bZ + \mu$, where μ is independent of Z, e_1, and e_2, as shown in Figure 9.1b. In this case the correlations between equivalent observed measures and Z are $R_{X,Z} = R_{X_2 Z} = R_{YZ}R_{X_1 Y} = R_{YZ}R_{X,Y} = R_{YZ}(R_{X,X_2})^{1/2}$. In this model the X_i on Z residuals have the form $X_i - b_i bZ = b_i\mu + e_i$, and the covariance between the X_1 and X_2 on Z residuals will equal $b_1 b_2 V_\mu$. Therefore, these

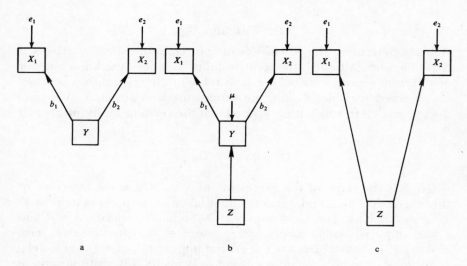

Figure 9.1.   Reliability and validity models

residuals are in general correlated, and $(R_{X_1 X_2})^{1/2} \neq R_{X_1 Z}$ or $R_{X_2 Z}$, which means that $R_{X_1 Z}$ and $R_{X_2 Z}$ cannot be estimated. However, $(R_{X_1 X_2})^{1/2}$ is the upper limit for these correlations; that is, reliability sets an upper bound on validity.

For illustrative purposes, consider the problem of measuring achievement in mathematics for ninth grade students in city A. Two (or more) equivalent forms of widely used mathematics tests, standardized on national samples, can be readily obtained and administered. These forms have almost identical item formats, the items differing mainly with respect to the numbers inserted in the problems. Because these tests cater to a wide variety of schools, the items necessarily cover material common to most curricula at this level. Insofar as the curriculum in city A has special emphases, not generally taught elsewhere, the nationally standardized tests will be partly irrelevant (invalid) to city A. The equivalent forms correspond to X_1 and X_2 in Figure 9.1b, the variable Y represents achievement on generally taught problems, and Z is the achievement of students in city A. If the discrepancy between Y and Z is very great, as inferred from curricular differences, city A can build equivalent forms more precisely covering their coursework, which may then correspond to the model in Figure 9.1c. It is always necessary for the researcher to examine test materials in order to see how well the construct being measured by that test corresponds to the construct relevant to the research project. In many cases he may decide to use two measures of a construct with very different types of item formats in order to obtain a model like Figure 9.1c, since the very similarity of item formats may give the scores some covariation not representative of association due to the underlying construct to be measured (as in Fig. 9.1*b*).

Instead of validity coefficients, factor analysts (see Harman 1967) refer to *factor loadings*. A factor loading is the regression weight of an observed score on a factor (namely, construct). The models in Figures 9.1*a* and 9.1*c* correspond to a *single-factor* model, and the standardized factor loading, like the corresponding reliability and validity coefficients, is equal to the correlation of the observed score with the factor. If there is more than one factor, but these factors are uncorrelated, as in an *orthogonal solution*, the standardized factor loading is still equal to the correlation. With correlated factors, as in an *oblique solution*, the standardized factor loadings are standardized partial regression weights, called *path coefficients* by path analysts (Duncan 1966; Wright 1934).

The regression weight in equation (1) basically states the relationship between the unit of measurement of the observed variable and that of the construct. A weight equal to unity corresponds to the assumption that the observed measure and the construct have the same unit of measurement. Psychological test theorists and econometricians usually make this assumption, whereas path analysts (Blalock 1969; Costner 1969) and factor analysts commonly assign the factor a variance of unity ($V_Y = 1$). As shall be noted later, this assumption creates no difficulty until the problem involves multiple measures of a construct and/or growth along the same dimension over time (Werts, Jöreskog, and Linn 1972).

Multiple Measures of a Single Construct

Although econometricians are rarely concerned with multiple measures of a construct, test theorists and path and factor analysts have written extensively on this topic. Much of modern test theory (Lord and Novick 1968) is based on the assumption that there are at least two *essentially tau equivalent* measures of the underlying *true score* (i.e., construct). *Essentially tau equivalent* measures (e.g., X_1 and X_2) are those in which the observed on true regression weights are unity ($b_1 = b_2 = 1$) and the errors of measurement are independent of each other and of the true score. In contrast to the *equivalence* assumptions discussed previously, the essentially tau equivalent assumption means that the tests may have different reliabilities (i.e., differing error variances). Since $X_1 = Y + I_1 + e_1$ and $X_2 = Y + I_2 + e_2$, the covariance $C_{X_1 X_2} = V_Y$: the covariance between the observed scores is equal to the variance of the true scores. The true variance divided by the observed variance ($V_Y \div V_{X_i}$) yields the test's reliability.

The essentially tau equivalent assumption also means that the observed measures of the construct are assumed to have the same unit of measurement. It is quite common for different symptoms or indicators of an underlying construct to have different units—for example, income and occupation—since, typically, indicators of social-class status are measured in different units. When the indicators have different units, the unit of the construct is arbitrary and is usually fixed by the assignment of a variance of unity, although it is also possible to identify the unit of one of the measures with that of the construct by specifying the corresponding regression weight to be unity. Jöreskog (1971) calls the various measures of the construct *congeneric* measures ($b_1 \neq b_2 \neq b_i$), whereas factor analysts would say that a single-factor structure has been assumed. Both assume that the errors or residuals are independent of each other and of the construct.

Identification

The concept of *identification* is crucial to any comparison of methods. Mathematicians and econometricians (Fisher 1966) have long been interested in developing procedures for dealing with identification problems. Whereas psychometricians and path analysts usually attempted to build identified models, the majority of factor analysts have dealt with highly underidentified models. Although in principle sociologists were exposed to the identification issue in relation to latent structure analysis (Lazarsfeld 1950), the recent papers on this subject by path analysts (e.g., Boudon 1965; Blalock 1966) have probably had a wider impact. The term *identifiable* will be used here in the sense defined by Fisher (1966, p. 25): "We shall speak of that equation as identifiable (or identified) if there exists some combination of prior and posterior information which will enable us to distinguish its parameters from those of any other equation in the same form."

To illustrate the identification problem, let us consider a single-factor model from the perspective of path analysis (Costner 1969). Suppose we are given four observed measures (X_1, X_2, X_3, X_4) of the factor Y. The single-factor model specifies that $X_i = b_i Y + I_i + e_i$, where all e_i are independent of each other and of Y. The model is depicted in Figure 9.2, in which path-analysis notation is used; that is, when variables are independent, no arrows connect them. To obtain the *expected* covariances C_{ij} between two observed measures X_i and X_j, we multiply the corresponding pair of equations to obtain

$$C_{ij} = b_i b_j V_Y \, , \tag{2}$$

$$V_{X_i} = b_i^2 V_Y + V_{e_i} \, . \tag{3}$$

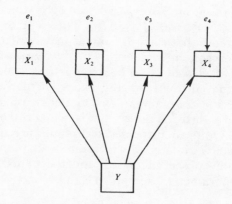

Figure 9.2.   A single-factor model.

The term *expected* refers to the value of a parameter to be expected in a model without *sampling* or *model specification* errors. *Specification errors* refer to the incorrect choice of a statistical model (Theil 1957). In the four-variable case, it is convenient to arrange the expected variances and covariances given by equations (2) and (3) into an expected *variance-covariance matrix* Σ:

$$\Sigma = \begin{bmatrix} V_1 & C_{12} & C_{13} & C_{14} \\ C_{12} & V_2 & C_{23} & C_{24} \\ C_{13} & C_{23} & V_3 & C_{34} \\ C_{14} & C_{24} & C_{34} & V_4 \end{bmatrix}$$

To see if this model is identified, the path analyst (e.g., Costner 1969) typically standardizes all variables $(V_{X_1} = V_{X_2} = V_{X_3} = V_{X_4} = V_Y = 1)$ and then derives the equations for each expected correlation, R_{ij}, in terms of b_i^*, the path coefficients of the model:

$$R_{12} = b_1^* b_2^*,$$

$$R_{13} = b_1^* b_3^*,$$

$$R_{14} = b_1^* b_4^*,$$

$$R_{23} = b_2^* b_3^*,$$

$$R_{24} = b_2^* b_4^*,$$

$$R_{34} = b_3^* b_4^*,$$

By means of any three measures, X_i, X_j, and X_k, it is possible to solve for the unknown: $(b_i^*)^2 = (R_{ij}R_{ik}) \div R_{jk}$. Thus all parameters, b_i^* are identified, in the sense that each parameter may be stated as a function of potentially observable information. The *actually observed* sample variances and covariances could also be arranged in a matrix S. The observed matrix S may differ from the expected matrix $\sum$ because of sampling and specification errors. The model is usually judged to be incorrect if $\sum$ and S differ greatly—that is, when the observed data do not *fit* the model. Quite sophisticated techniques are now available for obtaining parameter estimates which minimize in some sense the difference between the observed matrix and the expected matrix computed from the parameter estimates (Hauser and Goldberger 1971; Jöreskog 1970).

The equations relating the expected correlations R_{ij} to the model parameters b_i^* are called *path equations* by path analysts. Given that the parameters are identified by these equations, a model is called *just identified* when the number of observable quantities R_{ij} equals the number of unknown parameters b_i^* in the path equations, and *overidentified* when the observables exceed the parameters. When the number of unknown parameters exceeds the number of observables, the model is *underidentified* even though a subset of the parameters may be identified.

Jöreskog labels overidentified models as *confirmatory*. In confirmatory factor studies the experimenter has already obtained a certain amount of knowledge about the variables measured and therefore is in a position to formulate a model to be tested for fit to data. Most factor analysts deal with highly underidentified models, with which *exploratory* factor procedures are used to suggest the appropriate number of factors and a preliminary interpretation of the data. In contrast, econometricians, path analysts, and classical test theorists usually deal with identified models which reflect substantive theoretical considerations. It is logically possible for the model suggested by exploratory procedures to be identified, but factor analysts have typically not examined this question because their main interest is in fit, not in identifiability.

Multifactor Models

Let us consider a simple two-factor (Y_1 and Y_2) model (Fig. 9.3) in which there is only one observed measure (X_1 and X_2) of each factor: $X_1 = b_1 Y_1 + I_1 + e_1$ and $X_2 = b_2 Y_2 + I_2 + e_2$, where e_1 and e_2 are independent of each other and of Y_1 and Y_2. When all variables are standardized there is one observed correlation, R_{12}, and three unknown correlations, $R_{X_1 Y_1} = b_1^*, R_{Y_1 Y_2}$, and $R_{X_2 Y_2} = b_2^*$, among variables (i.e., the model is underidentified), and $R_{12} =$

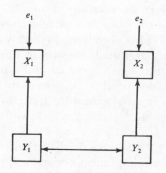

Figure 9.3.   A simple two-factor model.

$R_{X_1 Y_1}$ $R_{Y_1 Y_2}$ $R_{X_2 Y_2}$. Psychometricians call the correlation between the factors $(R_{Y_1 Y_2})$ the *unattenuated correlation*. For the tests, the publisher usually provides test reliabilities (labeled R_{11} and R_{22}), which in this model equal the squares of the correlations with the appropriate factors: $R_{11} = (R_{X_1 Y_1})^2$ and $R_{22} = (R_{X_2 Y_2})^2$. Given these reliabilities, we may estimate (denoted by "^") the correlation between factors as

$$\hat{R}_{Y_1 Y_2} = R_{12} \div \sqrt{R_{11} R_{22}}.$$

This procedure is called *correcting for attenuation*. Estimates of reliability are sometimes obtained from *internal consistency* procedures (Stanley 1971) which are based on the variance-covariance matrix among the test items.

Exact Functional Relationship among Factors

Statisticians (e.g., Kendall and Stuart 1961) and econometricians (Johnston 1963, chap. 6) have been interested in the variation of the Figure 9.3 model in which $b_1 = b_2 = 1$ and the factors have an *exact functional relationship*: $Y_2 = I + BY_1$ and $R_{Y_1 Y_2} = 1$. It might, for example, be hypothesized that in a class of equally intelligent and motivated students, the amount they will learn in a math course, Y_2, will be exactly proportional to their relevant mathematics skills, Y_1, at the beginning of the course because those who know more are better able to understand the teacher. If variable means are neglected, it is clear that, since there are three unknown parameters (V_{Y_1}, V_{Y_2}, B) and only one observed correlation (R_{12}), this model is underidentified. Isaac (1970) reviews the estimating formulas for the case in which the error variances V_{e_1} and/or V_{e_2} or their ratio $V_{e_1} \div V_{e_2}$ are known.

Stochastic Components

Johnston (1963, p. 148) notes that the model with an exact functional relationship among its factors "hardly seems appropriate for econometric work, since if it were true, all points would be exactly on a straight line. A stochastic component of behavior would seem an essential in economics." This comment probably applies to all the social sciences in which it is generally necessary in linear structural models to assume that all the other *unmeasured* variables influencing a variable of interest are independent of the measured influences (Blalock 1967). It seems most unlikely, for example, that there are not other, one hopes random, disturbing factors which will influence mathematics achievement.

With the addition of a stochastic disturbance term, μ, representing these other variables, the equation between the factors becomes $Y_2 = I + \beta Y_1 + \mu$, where μ is independent of Y_1 and $b_{1.} = b_2 = 1$. The analysis of this stochastic model is discussed by Johnston (1963, chap. 6). One approach assumes that the error variances V_{e_1} and V_{e_2} are known, which is equivalent to the psychometrician's approach, since, if the error variances are known, the reliabilities can be computed: $R_{ii} = (V_{X_i} - V_{e_i})/V_{X_i}$, where $V_{Y_i} = V_{X_i} - V_{e_i}$. Because $R_{Y_1 Y_2}$ is identified by the formula for attenuation, it follows that β and therefore V_μ are also identified, that is, $\beta = R_{Y_1 Y_2}(V_{Y_2} \div V_{Y_1})^{1/2}$ and $V_\mu = V_{Y_2} - \beta^2 V_{Y_1}$. The difficulty with this approach lies in the problem of obtaining reasonable estimates of the error variances. Even when reliabilities are given, as in many published tests, these figures may be erroneous to an unknown degree for the particular subpopulation being tested.

Another approach is the use of *instrumental* variables, in this case a variable Z which is independent of both error e_1 and error e_2. The regression weight β may be estimated as $\hat{\beta} = \text{cov}(Y_2 Z) \div \text{cov}(Y_1 Z)$. It may be shown that the reliability coefficient for X_1 is $R_{11} = R_{X_1 Z} R_{X_1 X_2} \div R_{X_2 Z}$, which from the previous section can be seen as the solution for the squared factor loading in the single-factor model in which X_1, X_2, and Z are *congeneric* measures where

$$(\hat{R}_{X_2 Y_1})^2 = R_{X_1 X_2} R_{X_2 Z} \div R_{X_1 Z}$$

and

$$(\hat{R}_{Y_1 Z})^2 = R_{X_1 Z} R_{X_2 Z} \div R_{X_1 X_2}.$$

Further analysis would show that V_{e_2} and V_μ are not identified. The basic problem in using instrumental variables is that we are seldom in a position to check whether this variable is in fact independent of errors; yet the estimates are likely to be highly dependent on which such variable is selected (Blalock, Wells, and Carter 1970). The same problem plagues the use of the congeneric model, since it is seldom obvious exactly which observed measures really are indicators of the same underlying trait assuming independent errors. It is interesting to note that in these models an instrumental variable substitutes for a congeneric measure; what we really need is a third measure which is independent of the errors in the other two variables. For illustrative purposes, consider the problem of measuring differential student math achievement, given the scores from two different nationally distributed objective exams—one perhaps using a problem format and another a multiple-choice format—whose validities for the curriculum of interest are unknown. A third congeneric measure might well be the course grades given by the teacher. The logic here is that these should all be tapping the achievement dimension, but to differing degrees, and there is no a priori reason to believe that errors of measurement among these measures are correlated, since very different formats are involved. Sometimes, however, achievement tests are given in batteries, so that English-achievement scores, say, might be available. It is unlikely that the English scores are correlated with errors of measurement on the two objective math tests, and they could therefore serve as an instrumental variable. We might, however, be more concerned about the English-subtest scores' independence of grades (which might reflect oral facility). If all four measures are available, they should fit a single-factor model. A poor fit with the observed data will probably lead to the rejection of the independent-residuals assumption, in which case a model with one set of nonindependent errors may be tested for fit.

Model with Multiple Indicators

Economists (Goldberger 1970) and sociologists (Blalock 1969; Costner 1969) rarely have the data with which to estimate reliability from independent sources, whereas psychometricians and factor analysts (at least implicitly) frequently do. A traditional technique of this type used by psychometricians is the split-half procedure (Guilford 1954, p. 377). The items on a test are split in half (odd items might be assigned to one of the halves, and even items to the other), and the correlation between the halves is used to estimate the reliability of the whole test. It is assumed that the halves are *equivalent* measures. Various formulas are used to adjust for the fact that the halves are not as long as the whole test and therefore are not as reliable (Guilford 1954, chap. 14). These reliability estimates may then be used to estimate the unattenuated correlation between two tests, that is, the correlation between the two true factors underlying the observed measures.

The logic of the split-half approach is worth further study. The change to a double subscript is made for each observed measure: X_i becomes X_{ij}, where j refers to the jth construct (Y_j), and i to the ith indicator of the jth construct. Then, in the split-half procedure, the equations are

$$X_{11} = b_{11} Y_1 + I_{11} + e_{11},$$

$$X_{21} = b_{21} Y_1 + I_{21} + e_{21},$$

$$X_{12} = b_{12} Y_2 + I_{12} + e_{12},$$

and

$$X_{22} = b_{22} Y_2 + I_{22} + e_{22} .$$

Using path analytic procedure, we find that

$$R_{X_{11} X_{21}} = b^*_{11} b^*_{21} ,$$

$$R_{X_{11} X_{12}} = b^*_{11} R_{Y_1 Y_2} b^*_{12} ,$$

$$R_{X_{11} X_{22}} = b^*_{11} R_{Y_1 Y_2} b^*_{22} ,$$

$$R_{X_{21} X_{12}} = b^*_{21} R_{Y_1 Y_2} b^*_{12} ,$$

$$R_{X_{21} X_{22}} = b^*_{21} R_{Y_1 Y_2} b^*_{22} ,$$

and

$$R_{X_{12} X_{22}} = b^*_{12} b^*_{22}$$

The solution of these equations indicates that all the reliabilities, b^*_{ij}, and the unattenuated correlation, $R_{Y_1 Y_2}$, are identified without further assumptions. This model is *overidentified*, since there is one more equation than unknown parameters—that is, there is *one degree of overidentification* equivalent to *one degree of freedom* in Jöreskog's (1970) general model for the analysis of covariance structures (which may be used for estimation purposes). Because the model is identified, we may check to see whether it is reasonable to believe that $b^*_{11} = b^*_{21}$, $b^*_{12} = b^*_{22}$, $V_{e_{11}} = V_{e_{21}}$, and $V_{e_{12}} = V_{e_{22}}$, as asserted in the assumption that split halves are equivalent (Werts and Linn 1972). Even without the equivalence assumption the model may be tested for fit to the data. As Guilford (1954, p. 377) notes, the difficulty with the odd-even method is that the observed correlation between the splits will generally be too high because of "extra-test determiners contributing positively to the observed correlation." For example, testing conditions and amount of time devoted to each half will be nearly constant for the halves. In contrast, the alternate-forms method, with at least a day between administrations, introduces a change of conditions which "is more like those changes between administration of two different tests or between test administration and measurement of some criterion in validation" (Guilford 1954, p. 377). If these other determiners are independent of the true score, we may assert that the corresponding errors in our model are not in fact independent (e.g., $R_{e_{11}e_{21}} \neq 0$), which it is possible to interpret as a lack of model fit to the observed data. Psychometricians have various other procedures for estimating whole-test reliability from item data (Stanley 1971), the logic of which is much like that discussed here except that each item now becomes an observed measure. To the degree that the item data do not fit a single-factor model, these estimates become difficult to interpret (Werts and Linn, 1970*a*). Nonetheless, in practice this fit is seldom checked.

The Multitrait-multimethod Approach

The multitrait-multimethod matrix technique (Campbell and Fiske 1959) has been of considerable interest to psychologists because it provides information on the *convergent* (confirmation by independent measurement procedures) and *discriminant* (separation of one trait from another) *validity* of theoretical constructs (i.e., traits). The problem of measuring mathematics achievement, as opposed to that of measuring achievement in English, may be used to illustrate these concepts. To measure math achievement we might use three measures, including one "subjective" measure—course grades—and two "objective" measures consisting of a multiple-choice and a mathematics-reasoning test (perhaps constructed by the publisher of the course material). Despite the differences in format, each measure, in principle, is simply another demonstration of the student's grasp of the subject matter and should therefore tend to give fairly consistent results. Insofar as the results are indeed consistent, convergent validity is demonstrated. The logic underlying convergent validity is much like that of the congeneric model previously discussed. The emphasis on different methods of measurement represents an attempt to insure that the correlations among variables as much as possible represent commonality with the underlying trait rather than consistencies due to similarities of testing methods. Thus, the use of different methods tends to support the assumption of independent errors required by the congeneric model.

Now suppose that English achievement is also obtained from the three measures used for obtaining math achievement—course grades and a multiple-choice and a reasoning test. Discriminant validity is demonstrated if it can be shown that the trait (i.e., factor) underlying the math measures is distinctly different from the trait underlying the English measures. According to Campbell and Fiske, convergent validity is demonstrated by at least moderate correlations between different methods' measures of the same trait, and discriminant validity is shown by a higher correlation between independent efforts (i.e., method) to measure the same trait than between measures designed to detect different traits using the same method. From our perspective, discriminant validity consists in demonstrating that the true correlation between two traits is meaningfully less than unity. Werts and Linn (1970*b*) have criticized the Campbell-Fiske approach from this perspective. The analytical procedures devised by Campbell and Fiske (1959) are not of interest here, because no attempt was made to specify the nature of the relationship between the observed measures and the trait or methods factors. It should be clear from our previous statements that an observed variance-covariance matrix is interpretable only from the perspective of a hypothesized model. Campbell and Fiske's argument that, to improve convergent validity, the researcher should obtain measures of a trait which differ as much as possible in measurement technique is very pertinent. These authors would especially criticize the typical psychometric approach, which attempts to devise alternate forms with almost identical formats, as lacking in convergent validity.

Of the various analytical methods proposed for multitrait multimethod data (Boruch et al. 1970), only Jöreskog's confirmatory factor analytic approach will be considered here. Assume that each observed measure is a function of only one trait factor, Y_j, and one method factor, M_k, in a linear model which assumes no trait by method interaction, that is,

$$X_{jk} = a_{jk}Y_j + b_{jk}M_k + I_{jk} + e_{jk} ,$$

where

X_{jk} = measure reflecting combination of trait j and method k ,

a_{jk} = regression weight of X_{jk} on trait Y_j ,

and

b_{jk} = regression weight of X_{jk} on method M_k .

Assume also that all residuals are independent of each other and of all factors. It may be shown that at least three traits and three methods must be used in order for this model to be identified, given that all factors may be *oblique*, that is, correlated. To understand the connection with models discussed earlier, consider two different-method measures of the same trait, X_{11} and X_{12} (illustrated in Fig. 9.4). It can be seen that there are several sources of the observed correlation $R_{X_{11}X_{12}}$:

$$R_{X_{11}X_{12}} = a^*_{11}a^*_{12} + a^*_{11}R_{Y_1M_2}b^*_{12} + a^*_{12}R_{Y_1M_1}b^*_{11} + b^*_{11}R_{M_1M_2}b^*_{12}.$$

If the methods factors are independent of the trait factor, the model, in principle, is like a congeneric model with correlated residuals. Such a model has been proposed by Guttman (1953) in relation to obtaining reliability estimates from nonindependent item data. If the methods factors are independent, we have the congeneric model basic to true-score theory. Thus we see that the traditional approaches to test theory discussed earlier may be considered the special case of the multitrait-multimethod approach in which methods factors are assumed to be independent of each other and of the trait factors. The notion of reliability as the ratio of true variance to observed variance is only mean-

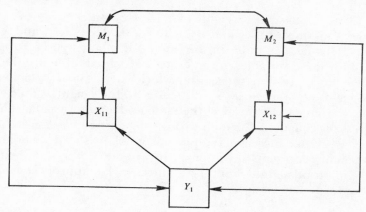

Figure 9.4.   A two-method, one-trait model.

ingful in the case where errors are independent in this way; no such neat partitioning of variance is possible in the general multitrait-multimethod approach.

Functional Relationships Among Factors

Whereas econometricians and path analysts invariably postulate functional relationships among the factors, psychologists and factor analysts seldom do so. Both the multitrait-multimethod approach and the true-score theory focus only on errors of measurement. In part, this situation arises because psychologists are usually taught to avoid making causal inferences from correlations. Sometimes *antecedent* (i.e., causally prior) variables are statistically *controlled*, to insure that a particular correlation is not *spurious*; however, systematic procedures for analyzing sources of a correlation (e.g., path analysis) are viewed with suspicion.

The function of causal hypotheses can be illustrated by an example taken from Werts and Linn (1970*b*). Suppose there is a linear causal relationship between variables: $Y_2 = BY_1 + \mu$, where Y_2 is measured directly, and Y_1 indirectly, by two indicators, $X_1 = b_1Y_1 + e_1$ and $X_2 = b_2Y_1 + e_2$. This is a single-factor model, and $B*$ may be estimated as

$$\hat{B}* = \sqrt{R_{X_1 Y_2} R_{X_2 Y_2}} \div R_{X_1 X_2} \; .$$

For example, if $R_{X_1 Y_2} = .20$, $R_{X_2 Y_2} = .40$, and $R_{X_1 X_2} = .80$, then $\hat{B}* \cong$ .32. Most educational psychologists, in their search for school effects, would not even consider the possibility that several measured variables might be indicators of the same underlying construct (i.e., Y_1) and would proceed, using the regression equation

$$Y_2 = b_1 X_1 + b_2 X_2 + I_3 + e_3 \; ,$$

which yields standardized weights of $b_1^* \cong -.33$ and $b_2^* \cong +.67$. If, for example, X_1 is the proportion of faculty with doctorates, and X_2 the number of books per pupil in the library, it might well be supposed that both of these variables are indicators of school affluence (i.e., Y_1). Certainly the regression procedure, which is typical of school-effects studies, yields no hint of how Y_1 influences Y_2; the weights b_1^* and b_2^* are opposite in sign, yet both reflect the same underlying variable. The use of regression equations for the purpose of finding *influences* by seeing whether a variable increases the percentage of predictable variance in the outcome represents an attempt to avoid theory. It is better to specify the postulated theoretical structure, so that appropriate analytical procedures may be designed.

Change Studies

Specifying functional relationships is also important in the study of the determinants of change. Panel studies are typically designed for this purpose. Test theorists have long been concerned with the problem of estimating change in the presence of errors of measurement (Harris 1963). The *initial status* and *final status* variables have identical units of measurement. If the initial status is $X_1 = b_1 Y_1 + I_1 + e_1$ and the final status is $X_2 = b_2 Y_2 + I_2 + e_1$, the equal-units assumption is equivalent to $b_1 = b_2$. Various procedures (e.g., see Cronbach and Furby 1970) attempt to estimate the true change $Y_2 - Y_1$ from the observed scores and known reliability coefficients for the initial and final measures. From these data the *reliability of differences*—that is, the squared correlation of the observed difference $X_2 - X_1$ with the true difference $Y_2 - Y_1$—may be obtained. It was originally thought that, if the reliability of differences was low, our ability to estimate true change would be low; but Cronbach and Furby (1970) and Werts and Linn (1970a) have demonstrated the use of information about other variables in helping to estimate change. The logic of this approach is an extension of the rationale enunciated earlier with regard to instrumental variables: both causes and effects and other correlates of growth carry information which can be used for estimating model parameters and, therefore, for improving estimates of factor scores.

Several educational researchers (Bloom 1964; Thorndike 1966) have been concerned with the determinants of $Y_2 - Y_1$ and in essence have argued that, if the initial status Y_1 is uncorrelated with gain $Y_2 - Y_1$, the determinants of change during this time interval are different from those which produced the initial level of competence Y_1. No such conclusion is warranted (Werts, Jöreskog, and Linn 1972), since without including in the functional model various determinants of growth, it is impossible to make any statements about the *effect* of these determinants. As the path analysts have frequently shown, no correlation, even zero, is interpretable in a causal sense except within the framework of a causal model. It is quite possible, because of counterbalancing influences, for $Y_2 - Y_1$ to be uncorrelated with Y_1 and yet for initial status to influence gain either positively or negatively.

An important feature of growth studies is that the variance of the initial and final status factors Y_1 and Y_2 is identified by the scaling assumption $b_1 = b_2$. For convenience, test theorists usually assign the value $b_1 = b_2 = 1$; that is, the factors are assigned the same units as the observed measures, and the variance of the factors is then determined by the known reliabilities. In the typical achievement study the *true variance* increases over time ($V_{Y_2} > V_{Y_1}$). An illustration of the cause of the increase is that some students will pursue the study of mathematics, whereas others will avoid advanced courses. The usual approach in factor and path analysis of standardizing all factors (e.g., $V_{Y_1} = V_{Y_2}$) is clearly unsatisfactory for growth studies because it ignores changes in true variance. Even if there are no errors of measurement, standardization of variables is undesirable in growth studies. Psychometricians have usually dealt with models in which one measure of a construct was available, but when several measures with different units are obtained the variance of the construct becomes arbitrary. If the initial status factor is assigned a variance of unity ($V_{Y_1} = 1$), the assumption $b_1 = b_2$ will identify the variance of the final status factor (Werts and Linn 1970*b*), given that b_1^* and b_2^* are identified.

Using a model identical to the split-half reliability model discussed earlier (see "Multifactor Models"), Werts, Jöreskog, and Linn (1972) show that if we have two congeneric measures of Y_1, say, X_{11} and X_{21}, which are repeated at a later time (X_{12} and X_{22}, respectively), it is possible to test whether the assumption $b_{11} = b_{12}$ is compatible with $b_{21} = b_{22}$. In other words, the ratio $V_{Y_2} : V_{Y_1}$, identified by the assumption that $b_{11} = b_{12}$, may be different from the ratio of these variances given by the assumption that $b_{21} = b_{22}$, and this will show up as a significant increase in the model's lack of fit to the data when the added restriction $b_{21} = b_{22}$ is imposed on the model. This test indicates whether it is reasonable to believe that the measures have equal units over time.

Other Constructs in Statistical Procedures

In this section we propose to demonstrate that statistical procedures frequently imply constructs of which many researchers are not aware. For illustrative purposes consider a *quasi-experimental* (Campbell and Stanley 1963) study in which four different procedures for teaching fifth grade mathematics are randomly assigned to four available schools in a district. The mathematics achievement of each student is measured at the beginning and end of fifth grade by means of parallel forms of a test which provide good coverage of the material taught in the various schools (the test has *face* validity). Because it is a naturalistic study, it is found that the mean achievement scores at the beginning of the fifth grade differ. To avoid interpretive complications, assume perfect validity. Suppose the mean results for schools are as shown in Figure 9.5: the ordering of the schools remains constant over time, but the spread of means increases in proportion to the initial mean. One possible statistical procedure which the data seem to fit is the analysis of variance of repeated measures (Winer 1962, chap. 7), which basically

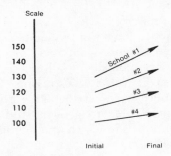

Figure 9.5.   Mean math scores.

consists in subtracting the initial means from the final means and testing to see if these differences are the same from school to school. Since these differences range from twenty units to five units for schools number 1 and number 4, respectively, it is clear that with this procedure one would conclude that there is a *treatment* (i.e., school) effect: school number 1 is the most effective, and number 4 the least. A second statistical procedure which the data fit is the analysis of covariance with initial status controlled (Winer 1962, chap. 11). Since the final means are perfectly correlated with the initial means, it may be shown that, given the standard assumptions of analysis of covariance (Werts and Linn 1971), this procedure will indicate no treatment effect. To understand these seemingly contradictory interpretations, we need to ponder the following hypothetical question: For any given school, what would the final mean be *if* no treatment had been applied? In a *true* experiment this would not be a question, because the design would provide for a group which did not receive the treatment but which, because of random assignment, had the same initial mean as that of a group receiving the treatment. In most naturalistic studies such information is usually not available, and its absence creates ambiguity. The analysis of variance assumes, in essence, that *if* no treatment has been given the final mean for each school is the same as the initial mean. In contrast, the analysis of covariance assumes that if no treatment has been given the final mean is completely *predictable* from the initial mean; in our illustration, for instance, the final means are perfectly correlated with the initial means. There is no law of nature that either case is necessarily so, which means that neither statistical procedure may be appropriate. Furthermore, our analysis has assumed the appropriateness of a linear additive model, which may not provide a reasonable simulation of the reality being investigated.

A slight variation in the problem above occurs when some measure is being obtained in a time series and at some point a new treatment is imposed. Such a case might be the measurement of math achievement of students followed from grade school into high school. Thistlethwaite and Campbell (1960) have argued that, if the past treatment trend continues on the pretreatment trend, no treatment effect may be inferred. In real life, however, students who go to superior high schools have probably gone to superior grade schools, and vice versa. If so, it is quite possible that the effective high school would do well if it could continue the learning progress its students were making before entry. A treatment effect might well be evidenced by a straight trend line from grade school through high school. Again, the unobserved construct is: What would the group mean be *if* there were no treatment? Without this information no statements about treatment effects are warranted, nor can anybody validly assert that a particular statistical analysis is appropriate.

Hypotheses About Changes in Means

The discussion to this point has been devoted to the analysis of the observed variance-covariance matrix. In some problems, however, hypotheses really concern structures (i.e., restrictions) on the means of variables. For example, if we give a class special assistance in vocabulary, we hope to observe an increase in the average vocabulary score of the group; hence, the correlation between initial and final vocabulary scores is not the relevant statistic to analyze. In such cases the neglect of means (common among path analysts) leads to uninterpretable results.

Educational researchers interested in growth have encountered the problem of means because of the way tests are constructed (see Carver 1970). The procedures used in test development typically strive to maximize the discrimination between individuals. Items answered correctly by almost everyone at the end of a course tend to be omitted, since these serve to show similarities among individuals; yet it may be precisely these items that show the general progress of the class during the course. From our perspective, the procedures of item analysis thus prevent measurement of true change in means over time. Consider the extreme case in which the students have no familiarity with the subject matter being taught, which means that an initial test of their knowledge in this subject would yield a zero score for the whole class. A parallel test given at the end of the course would show varying degrees of knowledge attained, that is, a positive mean and variance. The initial test scores would have a zero (meaningless) correlation with the final scores, and the final mean would represent the average level of course effectiveness. If there were some initial familiarity with the subject matter, the reliability of the initial test might be very low and yet be appropriate for measuring changes in student knowledge during the course. Obviously, path coefficients would be irrelevant to the issue.

Although not noted earlier, *equivalent* tests are also assumed to have the same underlying mean: observed differences in test means are presumed due to errors of measurement. Thus, underlying the various observed test means, there is assumed to be a common *unobserved* mean. This should be recognized as a problem in the analysis of variance (Winer 1962, chap. 4) in which, for example, rows represent the scores for an individual, columns correspond to the different tests, and the researcher wishes to test whether the column means differ from each other. If the means do not differ significantly, the best estimate of the *true mean* is the grand mean of the observed tests. Notice that if the grand mean is used as the best estimate of the common test mean, our estimates of variances and covariances will be affected, since these are measures of deviation from the grand mean. This mutual interdependence is recognized in Jöreskog's (1970) general model, which, within given restrictions on both the means and the variance-covariance matrix, allows for simultaneous estimation and hypothesis testing. We may, for example, wish to test the hypothesis that the true-score means over time increase linearly (or exponentially).

General Considerations

It is relatively easy to find a linear structural model which fits the data quite closely; factor analysts, for example, may keep adding factors till a good fit is obtained. With a modicum of thought it is also relatively easy to obtain a model consistent with our theory, when this model is *just* identified (i.e., there is a unique solution for each parameter), because the matrix estimated from the model Σ will in general equal the observed matrix S. Given overidentification, it is possible that the model may be rejected because of poor fit to the data. In such cases it is usually possible to find a less restrictive model which will fit the data better, but this model may not be substantively plausible. It is extremely difficult to demonstrate (a) that a model approximately simulates reality, (b) that it provides better simulation than another model, (c) that the constructs defined by the model have greater explanatory power than the observed variables from which they are derived, and (d) that these constructs are in any sense useful in promoting better research. In most cases it seems reasonable to suppose that several plausible models may be found, all of which are consistent with the observed data. It would then be necessary to deduce what data would need to be collected to discriminate among these models.

Some of the concepts discussed in previous sections suggest some cautions in interpreting observed variance-covariance matrices. Granting the validity of using correlations at all (see Tukey 1954, for a discussion of this question), it should be clear from the section on the multitrait-multimethod procedure that the probable existence of errors of measurement and multiple indicators of underlying variables will necessarily make any interpretation chancy. Furthermore, even if the unattenuated correlations among the relevant constructs are known, correlations are by no means self-interpreting in a causal sense (Blalock 1964). An observed correlation may thus be completely spurious, owing to the presence of a common antecedent variable (which must be controlled). Whereas most psychologists use the concept of spuriousness, the notion of controlling a variable in a chain of causes to see if this variable *explains* the observed association (Blalock 1964) is almost unknown at present. It should not be inferred, however, that a causal analysis of the correlations is appropriate to every problem (Bailey 1970).

In the light of the considerable flexibility present in Jöreskog's (1970) general model, it seems likely that in the near future some mathematician will be able to provide a general technique which will include all the techniques discussed in this chapter as special cases, differing only in specifications of or restrictions on the model parameters. Once the computational problem can be readily handled, we must face the issue of whether such a general technique should be applied to a particular problem. Most applications of factor analysis, path analysis, and test theory can probably be described as exploratory or speculative in the sense that a particular analytical technique is performed because the researcher is familiar with it rather than because he can demonstrate that it provides the best simulation of the process under study. We are thus in the unenviable position of discussing statistical techniques without knowing when they should be used.

References

Bailey, K. D.
  1970. "Evaluating Axiomatic theories." In E. F. Borgatta and G. W. Bohrn-stedt, eds. *Sociological Methodology, 1970*. San Francisco: Jossey-Bass.
Blalock, H. M., Jr.
  1964. *Causal Inferences in Nonexperimental Research*. Chapel Hill: University of North Carolina Press.
  1966. "The Identification Problem and Theory Building." *American Sociological Review* 31 (February):52-61.
  1967. "Causal Inferences, Closed Populations, and Measures of Association." *American Political Science Review* 61:130-36.
  1969. "Multiple Indicators and the Causal Approach to Measurement Error." *American Journal of Sociology* 75 (September):264-72.
Blalock, H. M., C. S. Wells, and L. F. Carter
  1970. "Statistical Estimation with Random Measurement Error." In E. F. Borgatta and G. W. Bohrnstedt, eds., *Sociological Methodology, 1970*. San Francisco: Jossey-Bass.
Bloom, B. S.
  1964. *Stability and Change in Human Characteristics*. New York: Wiley.
Boruch, R. F., J. D. Larkin, L. Wolins, and A. C. McKinney
  1970. "Alternative Methods of Analysis: Multitrait-Multimethod Data." *Educational and Psychological Measurement* 30(4):833-54.
Boudon, R.
  1965. "A Method of Linear Causal Analysis: Dependence Analysis." *American Sociological Review* 30(3):365-74.
Campbell, D. T., and D. W. Fiske
  1959. "Convergent and Discriminant Validation by the Multitrait-Multimethod Matrix." *Psychological Bulletin* 56(2):81-105.
Campbell, D. T., and J. S. Stanley
  1963. "Experimental and Quasi-experimental Designs for Research in Teaching." In N. L. Gage, ed., *Handbook of Research on Teaching*. Chicago: Rand McNally.
Carver, R. P.
  1969. "A Model for Using the Final Examination as a Measure of the Amount Learned in Classroom Learning." *Journal of Educational Measurement* 6 (Summer):59-68.
  1970. "Special Problems in Measuring Change with Psychometric Devices." In *Evaluation Research: Strategies and Methods*. Pittsburgh: American Institute of Research.
Costner, H. L.
  1969. "Theory, Deduction, and Rules of Correspondence." *American Journal of Sociology* 75 (September):245-63.
Cronbach, L. J., and L. Furby
  1970. "How Should We Measure 'Change'—or Should We?" *Psychological Bulletin* 74(1):68-80.
Duncan, O. D.
  1966. "Path Analysis: Sociological Examples." *American Journal of Sociology* 72(1):1-16.

Fisher, F. M.
1966. *The Identification Problem in Econometrics*. New York: McGraw-Hill.
Goldberger, A. S.
1970. "Econometrics and Psychometrics: A Survey of Communalities."
Psychometrika 36:83-107.
Guilford, J. P.
1954. *Psychometric Methods*. New York: McGraw-Hill.
Guttman, L.
1953. "Reliability Formulas That Do Not Assume Experimental Indepen-
dency." *Psychometrika* 18:225-39.
Harman, H. H.
1967. *Modern Factor Analysis*. Chicago: University of Chicago Press.
Harris, C. W.
1963. *Problems in Measuring Change*. Madison: University of Wisconsin Press.
Hauser, R. M., and A. S. Goldberger
1971. "The Treatment of Unobservable Variables in Path Analysis." In H. L.
Costner, ed., *Sociological Methodology, 1971*. San Francisco: Jossey-Bass.
Isaac, P. D.
1970. "Linear Regression, Structural Relations, and Measurement Error."
Psychological Bulletin 74(3):213-18.
Johnston, J.
1963. *Econometric Methods*. New York: McGraw-Hill.
Jöreskog, K. G.
1970. "A General Method for Analysis of Covariance Structures." *Biometrika*
57:239-51.
1971. "Statistical Analysis of Sets of Congeneric Tests." *Psychometrica*
36:109-34.
Kendall, M. G., and A. Stuart
1961. *The Advanced Theory of Statistics*, vol. 2, *Inference and Relationship*. London: Griffin.
Lazarsfeld, P. F.
1950. "The Logical and Mathematical Foundation of Latent Structure
Analysis." In S. Stauffer, L. Guttman, E. A. Suchman, P. F. Lazarsfeld, S. A.
Starr, and J. A. Clausen, *Studies on Social Psychology in World War II*, vol. 4,
Measurement and Prediction. Princeton, N.J.: Princeton University Press.
Lord, F. M., and M. R. Novick
1968. *Statistical Theories of Mental Test Scores*. New York: Addison-Wesley.
Stanley, J. C.
1971. "Reliability." In R. L. Thorndike, ed., *Educational Measurement*.
Washington, D.C.: American Council on Education.
Theil, H.
1957. "Specification Errors and the Estimation of Economic Relationships."
Review International Statistics Institute 25:41-51.
Thistlethwaite, D. L., and D. T. Campbell
1960. "Regression-Discontinuity Analysis: An Alternative to the Ex Post
Facto Experiment." *Journal of Educational Psychology* 51:309-17.
Thorndike, R. L.
1966. "Intellectual Status and Intellectual Growth." *Journal of Educational
Psychology* 57:121-27.

Tukey, J. W.
   1954. "Causation, Regression, and Path Analysis." In O. Kempthorne, T. A. Bancroft, J. W. Gowen, and J. L. Lush, eds., *Statistics and Mathematics in Biology*. Ames: Iowa State College Press.
Werts, C. E., K. G. Jöreskog, and R. L. Linn
   1972. "A Multitrait-Multimethod Model for Studying Growth." *Educational and Psychological Measurement* 32(3):655-78.
Werts, C. E., and R. L. Linn
   1970a. "Cautions in Applying Various Procedures for Determining the Reliability and Validity of Multiple-Item Scales." *American Sociological Review* 35(4):757-59.
   1970b. "Path Analysis: Psychological Examples." *Psychological Bulletin* 74(3):193-212.
   1971. "Problems with Inferring Treatment Effects from Repeated Measures." *Educational and Psychological Measurement* 31(4):857-66.
   1972. "Corrections for Attenuation." Ibid. 32(1):117-27.
Winer, B. J.
   1962. *Statistical Principles in Experimental Design*. New York: McGraw-Hill.
Wright, S.
   1934. "The Method of Path Coefficients." *Annals of Mathematical Statistics* 5:161-215.

Chapter 10

THE CAUSAL APPROACH TO MEASUREMENT ERROR IN PANEL ANALYSIS: SOME FURTHER CONTINGENCIES

MICHAEL T. HANNAN
RICHARD RUBINSON
JEAN TUTTLE WARREN

Michael Hannan, currently Assistant Professor of Sociology at Stanford University, received his Ph.D. from North Carolina in 1970. At present he is analyzing family response to the Seattle-Denver Income Maintenance Experiment and conducting a longitudinal investigation of the relationship between national educational expansion and economic and political structures. Richard Rubinson is Assistant Professor of Sociology at Johns Hopkins University. He received his Ph.D. from Stanford University, his dissertation is a comparative study of political processes causing the expansion of national educational systems. His primary interests are in political sociology, stratification, and comparative research methods. Jean Tuttle Warren received a Ph.D. from Stanford University in 1973 and is currently an Assistant Professor in the Department of Sociology at the University of North Carolina, Chapel Hill. Her research interests include substantive and methodological issues in the study of social change on both a societal and an organizational level.

The research reported herein was performed pursuant to a contract with the United States Department of Health, Education, and Welfare, Office of Education, and was partially supported by NSF Grant GS-32065. John Boli performed many of the computations for this research.

There is considerable stress in current methodological discussion in sociology and political science on shifting focus from cross-sectional to longitudinal designs. Sociological research has been almost exclusively cross-sectional, and our methodology is suited primarily to this case. Attempts to shift to longitudinal designs raise a number of new issues—in particular, the many discontinuities between *cross-sectional* thinking, where many instances of a process are observed simultaneously; and *time-series* thinking, where a single instance is observed at many points in time. While both types of analysis are well understood, the nonexperimental social scientist is typically faced with a design falling somewhere between the two. The typical case involves observations on many instances of a process at only a few points in time. Sociologists and political scientists have relied almost exclusively on the *panel method* to address this case.

However, we may have greatly exaggerated the "power" of the panel design. While changing to a simple longitudinal design allows one to use time orderings to rule out some causal effects, it does not unambiguously resolve many questions concerning either direction or time sequencing of causal effects (Duncan 1969, 1972, 1975). In fact, as Heise (1970) and Duncan have shown, causal inferences in such simple longitudinal models depend on rather restrictive assumptions. It has become clear that most of the analysis problems arising in even the simplest cases are not yet well understood.

While the panel design has been used primarily to resolve difficulties in causal analysis, there has been a recent emphasis in the causal-models approach to measurement error on using panel observations to eliminate complications suggested by the acknowledgment of measurement imperfection. Blalock (1970) has suggested that a panel design will generally help in reducing the excess of unknowns which arises when the true sample values of substantive variables are assumed to be unknown and measured with error. Costner (1969) had demonstrated earlier that with three indicators for each substantive variable in a recursive cross-sectional model the analyst can both test measurement models and (if appropriate) estimate causal parameters. Obtaining three indicators of each variable is often not possible, however, and Blalock (1970) has shown that a rough trade-off exists between the number of indicators in a cross-section and waves of observations in a panel under certain specified conditions. In some situations, the researcher who can obtain only one or two indicators of some variables can generate tests and estimates if he can obtain repeated measurements in a panel design.

Work on measurement error in panel models has focused on only the very simplest cases. Attention has been limited to *single-variable models* (where a single substantive variable is measured at several points in time). This poses a serious problem for the analyst faced with a multivariate panel model (where several variables are measured at several points in time) measured with error. In attempting analysis, the researcher must deal simultaneously with the inference problems of linear panel models and with those arising from the existence of measurement error. We have begun to face such dual problems in our substantive research. *This chapter focuses, then, on the additional complications which arise when multivariate panel models are measured with random and nonrandom errors.* In spirit and approach, it relies heavily on the papers cited above.

In any didactic discussion it is difficult to introduce more than one complication at a time. We are primarily interested in measurement error and are willing for the present to employ highly restrictive assumptions to rule out other complications. It is highly likely in panel models that regression disturbances (residuals) will be correlated over waves of observations because of stability in these causal variables excluded from the model (see Heise 1970). Since the presence of both correlated regression disturbances and measurement error generally result in underidentification,[1] we shall generally assume that the disturbances are uncorrelated inter se and with substantive variables in our models. We are forced to adopt this position largely because we have no a priori information about measurement quality. Evidence in each case is *internal* to the model. We construct models incorporating substantive arguments as likely sources of measurement error and test them with our data. We do not, however, attempt to arrive at the appropriate error model inductively. Rather, the thrust of this chapter, and of the literature it follows, is to emphasize the practical impossibility of solving measurement problems inductively.

We follow the literature cited above in employing the technical apparatus of path analysis for testing and estimation. All the coefficients we discuss are *standardized* by sample variances. This approach simplifies the problem of generating the large number of structural equations containing unmeasured (true values) variables arising in realistic models, but it has serious disadvantages for panel analysis. Wiley and Wiley (1970) have demonstrated that the assumption of stable standardized coefficients requires that both the true population variances and the measurement-error variances be stable over the waves of observations. This is particularly problematic in "development" models, and we discuss its implications in terms of specific models below.

The substantive research application is a cross-national study of the interrelations of national educational systems and economic, social, and

---

1. This is not universally true, of course. In some realistic cases, sociologists may have access to enough measurements and a priori restrictions on the model so that both types of complications may be dealt with. This has not been the case in our research, however.

political development (Meyer and Hannan 1971). In this chapter we focus on one highly simplified model relating expansion of educational systems to economic development. Using data reported by the United Nations (*U.N. Statistical Yearbooks*) we follow a panel of ninety-six nations[2] through three waves of observations, 1955, 1960, and 1965. The research project is still in an early phase and we are less concerned here with substantive findings than with witnessing the import of measurement complications.

We have confined our attention to lagged cross-effects rather than instantaneous effects. Since this decision may often be problematic, we shall discuss our reasoning. Duncan (1969) has shown that in general one cannot take both the direction of cross-effects and the timing of causal effects as problematic. Consider the model, taken from Duncan's paper, drawn in Figure 10.1. As long as the analyst is unwilling to make at least one a priori restriction, for example, to rule out either the lagged effects or the instantaneous effects, this model is underidentified since there are seven parameters and only six independent equations. Alternatively, one can proceed by ruling out effects (either lagged or instantaneous) in one direction. What is clear is that, in the very general model drawn in Figure 10.1, one cannot employ sample information alone to infer either lagged or instantaneous effects in one, the other, or both directions.

However, the substantive significance of the distinctions between lagged and instantaneous effects seems to vary with the process being studied and the development of the theory. In Duncan's examples, the observation points correspond to socially meaningful categories (grade in school, stage in life cycle, etc.), and the variables can conceivably increase or decrease in magnitude between waves of observations. In our research the time periods of observations are more or less arbitrary indicator points, since the variables are cumulative (monotonically increasing) for almost all units. Whether the effects are lagged or instantaneous is not an important substantive issue (at least given the present state of development of the theories involved), and ignorance of appropriate lags is less likely to produce faulty inferences when all variables are monotonic over time. We make an argument below (for didactic purposes) for lags of different lengths—that is, an argument that the causal processes under study in a model differ in the lag with which they have an impact on the variables under study. Here Duncan's argument is compelling. The point is that for the present we take the direction and magnitude of cross-effects as particularly important and

2. When we employ two indicators of each variable, the number of observations drops to forty-six, owing to missing data on GNP in the earliest time period. Obviously this makes the single-indicator and two-indicator models noncomparable. We have chosen this option to minimuze the "ceiling effect" in primary school enrollments.

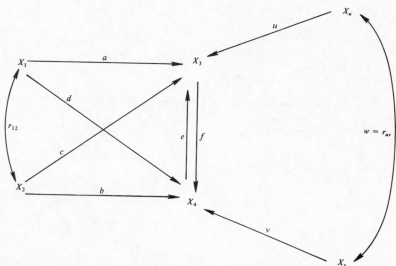

Figure 10.1. Redrawn from Duncan 1969, Figure 1.

do not systematically investigate the timing of causal effects. In particular, we impose the restriction that all causal effects be *lagged* effects.

A Three-wave, Two-variable, Two-indicator (3W-2V-2I) Model

We begin our analysis with a three-wave, two-variable model. Our data
enable us to select two indicators of economic development—per capita
gross national product and per capita consumption of electricity. Both
indicators have been logged to make their relationships to other variables linear. We also select two indicators of educational expansion:
the ratio of primary school students to the appropriate age-group population, and the ratio of secondary school students to the age-group
population.

This model, with uncorrelated residuals and purely random measurement error, is diagrammed in Figure 10.2. The curved arrow at the
left represents the summary of the history of the operation of the postulated causal processes. We further assume that all coefficients in the
model are stable over waves of observations. Throughout this chapter,
the underlying economic development variable will be represented by
X_i and the educational variable by Y_i, with the subscript standing for
the period of observation. The *indicators* of economic development will
be represented by X'_{ij} and the indicators of educational expansion by
Y'_{ij}, with the first subscript standing for the period of observation and
the second subscript for the specific indicator.

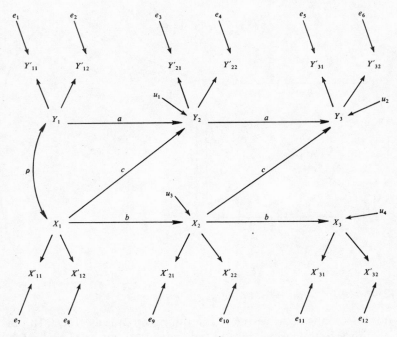

Figure 10.2.

The correlation matrix for this model is presented in Table 10.1. The matrix includes a pattern which, on initial inspection, is very perplexing. Examine the intercorrelations of the educational ratios. The primary ratio at the first time period is most highly correlated with the secondary ratio at the last time period, next-to-most highly correlated with the secondary ratio at the middle time period and least highly correlated with the cotemporal secondary ratio. The pattern for the primary ratio measured at the middle time period is similar in that the correlation with the secondary ratio of the last time period is the greatest. For the primary ratio measured at the last time period, the correlation is greatest at the same point in time and the correlation with secondary ratios decreases monotonically as one moves back in time.

We had originally intended to treat the two ratios of educational enrollment as related only through their common relationship to the un-

Table 10.1. Correlation Matrix of Educational Measures

	Secondary 1955	Secondary 1960	Secondary 1965
Primary 1955	.212	.303	.391
Primary 1960	.115	.149	.236
Primary 1965	.066	.089	.123

derlying variable educational expansion. We began with this hypothesis of "common factor variance" (or "congeneric tests") because, for scientific simplicity, this model represents the most parsimonious structure. Yet we find that indicators of variables measured at different points in time are more highly intercorrelated than are cotemporal measures of the variables. This result violates our conventional understanding of *validity* (see Campbell and Fiske 1959). And it is unlikely that such a simple causal structure could generate the observed correlation matrix. For instance, the educational portion of this model (Fig. 10.2) fails the consistency criterion for purely random measurement error developed by Costner (1969).

We were faced with the practical problem of how to proceed with such an unforeseen result. Two lines of investigation seemed open: (1) construct more complicated two-indicator models to generate the observed pattern of intercorrelation, and (2) decompose this model to allow the indicators to be directly causally related. We shall trace out the details and implications of each strategy.

To simplify the algebra we revise the model in Figure 10.2 to include only that portion relating to educational expansion. Since we assume that this variable is systematically affected by economic development, we allow the residuals to be correlated with the true (unobserved) values of the educational variables, where the correlations do not violate least-squares restrictions. Note that this model is now more restrictive than we should like, since we must postulate that U is uncorrelated with early values of educational expansion. This revised model is diagrammed in Figure 10.3. The new k terms will be used in the second of the models discussed below. For the moment k is fixed at unity.

Using the algorithm of path analysis, we write the fifteen equations (twelve of which are numbered) for the measurement model in Figure 10.3:

$$\rho_{Y'_{11} Y'_{12}} = cd , \tag{1}$$

$$\rho_{Y'_{11} Y'_{21}} = c^2 a , \tag{2}$$

$$\rho_{Y'_{11} Y'_{22}} = cda = \rho_{Y'_{12} Y'_{21}} , \tag{3}$$

$$\rho_{Y'_{11} Y'_{31}} = c^2 (ab + su) , \tag{4}$$

$$\rho_{Y'_{11} Y'_{32}} = cd(ab + su) = \rho_{Y'_{12} Y'_{31}} , \tag{5}$$

$$\rho_{Y'_{21} Y'_{22}} = cd , \tag{6}$$

$$\rho_{Y'_{21} Y'_{31}} = c^2 (b + srt + asu) , \tag{7}$$

$$\rho_{Y'_{21} Y'_{32}} = cd (b + srt + asu) = \rho_{Y'_{22} Y'_{31}} , \tag{8}$$

$$\rho_{Y'_{31} Y'_{32}} = cd , \tag{9}$$

$$\rho_{Y'_{12} Y'_{32}} = d^2 (ab + su) , \tag{10}$$

$$\rho_{Y'_{12} Y'_{22}} = d^2 a , \tag{11}$$

$$\rho_{Y'_{22} Y'_{32}} = d^2 (b + srt + asu) . \tag{12}$$

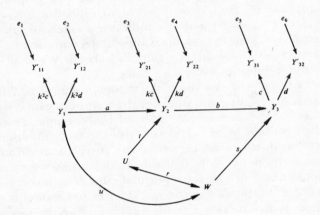

Figure 10.3.

Consider first the possibility, discussed above, that the primary and secondary ratios are two indicators of educational expansion, measured with random error, and related only through their relationship to unmeasured educational expansion. The ordering of magnitudes of the sample correlations between the primary ratio in 1955 (Y'_{11}) and the secondary ratios $(Y'_{12}, Y'_{22}, Y'_{32})$ gives rise to the following inequality:

$$r_{Y'_{11} Y'_{32}} > r_{Y'_{11} Y'_{22}} > r_{Y'_{11} Y'_{12}}$$

Substituting from the path equations (1), (3), and (5), we obtain corresponding values

$$cd(ab + su) > cda > cd,$$

or, with $cd > 0$,

$$ab + su > a > 1.$$

This result violates the basic model, since the two terms required to exceed unity are a zero-order correlation (a) and a sum of direct and indirect causal effects in standardized form ($ab + su$). Each term is bounded by plus and minus one. If they were not so bounded, we would be accounting for more than 100 percent of the variance in the dependent variables. This result argues against the common-factor model. Note, however, that this involves a statistical inference, since it is possible to obtain sample values exceeding unity when the population parameter is less than unity.

If we continue to accept the model diagrammed in Figure 10.3, we might proceed by allowing other complications in the model in order to generate the correlation matrix in Table 10.1. For example, we might allow the different indicators of educational expansion to be correlated at every wave because of common sources of measurement error (e.g., both pieces of information are processed by the same national bureaucracies); or, we might allow the same indicators to be correlated at different points in time because of stable sources of measurement-error variance (e.g., stability for units in the bureaucratic procedures for gathering and reporting educational statistics). Working through the resulting equations (where, for instance, e_1 and e_2, e_3 and e_4, and e_5 and e_6 are correlated, or e_1 and e_3, e_2 and e_4, etc.) quickly reveals that these added complications cannot reproduce the observed pattern of intercorrelations.

Allowing intertemporal correlation of the measurement-error terms of *different* indicators (i.e., allowing Y'_{11} and Y'_{32} and Y'_{22} to share common sources of error variance) will allow us to reproduce the correlation matrix. We reject this solution, however, for it merely represents a mechanical way to generate the matrix in the absence of substantive knowledge (i.e., it is a formalization of our ignorance).

We next develop a model which allows the random errors in variables to decrease proportionately with each wave of observation. This model is based on the assumption that with the secular trend toward national accounting the quality of the national statistics collected increases over time. Such an assumption seems reasonable for our educational statistics, since their collection and reporting is continually being supervised by the United Nations statistical office (UNESCO). To represent this secular trend in statistical quality, we allow the k term in our educational model (Fig. 10.3) to take on values different from unity and also require them to be between zero and one.[3] Other values will not produce decreasing random measurement error. (See Duncan 1972b for an analogous model.)

---

3. The k term must be less than one because the value of the total "epistemic correlation" (the decreasing component k times the stable random error component) *increases* over time to a maximum value of 1. In other words, the *residual paths* for the measured values (e.g., $[1 - (k^2 e)^2]^{1/2}$) *decrease* over time.

To evaluate this model, we consider the inequalities introduced above. Since k is no longer equal to unity, we have

$$k^2cd(ab + su) > k^3cda > k^4cd,$$

or (again assuming $cd > 0$)

$$ab + su > ka > k^2,$$

with $cd > 0$. We can no longer reject this model on logical grounds.

We can proceed to subject the model to an additional test using the seven overidentifying restrictions (the model has eight unknowns and fifteen equations). All seven restrictions can be written as quantities equal to zero, under the hypothesis that the model is correct (Blalock 1964). As noted previously, sampling error may produce deviations from zero even if the model is correctly specified and the analyst must make a statistical inference (where, unfortunately, the sampling distributions of the estimators are unknown). The overidentifying restrictions with the sample estimates are:

Prediction	*Estimate*
$\rho_{Y'_{11} Y'_{32}} - \rho_{Y'_{12} Y'_{31}} = 0$	.219
$\rho_{Y'_{11} Y'_{22}} - \rho_{Y'_{12} Y'_{21}} = 0$	.140
$\rho_{Y'_{21} Y'_{32}} - \rho_{Y'_{22} Y'_{31}} = 0$	.057
$\rho_{Y'_{11} Y'_{12}}\rho_{Y'_{31} Y'_{32}} - \rho_{Y'_{21} Y'_{22}} = 0$	.031
$\rho_{Y'_{11} Y'_{21}}\rho_{Y'_{12} Y'_{32}} - \rho_{Y'_{12} Y'_{32}}\rho_{Y'_{11} Y'_{32}} = 0$	.074
$\rho_{Y'_{11} Y'_{21}}\rho_{Y'_{22} Y'_{32}} - \rho_{Y'_{12} Y'_{32}}\rho_{Y'_{21} Y'_{31}} = 0$	.056
$\rho_{Y'_{12} Y'_{32}}\rho_{Y'_{21} Y'_{32}} - \rho_{Y'_{11} Y'_{31}}\rho_{Y'_{21} Y'_{31}} = 0$	.018

This fit does not seem particularly close. Nonetheless, we proceed to estimate the one obviously identified coefficient, k. Equations (1), (6), and (9) allow two ways of estimating k directly:

$$\hat{k} = \sqrt{\frac{\rho_{Y'_{11}}\rho_{Y'_{12}}}{\rho_{Y'_{21}}\rho_{Y'_{22}}}} = \sqrt{\frac{\rho_{Y'_{21}}\rho_{Y'_{22}}}{\rho_{Y'_{31}}\rho_{Y'_{32}}}}.$$

We follow Duncan (1972, 1975) and add these two expressions and insert sample estimates to arrive at an "ad hoc" estimate of k:[4]

$$\hat{k} = \sqrt{\frac{\sqrt{\rho_{Y'_{11}}\rho_{Y'_{12}}} + \sqrt{\rho_{Y'_{21}}\rho_{Y'_{22}}}}{\sqrt{\rho_{Y'_{21}}\rho_{Y'_{22}}} + \sqrt{\rho_{Y'_{31}}\rho_{Y'_{32}}}}}.$$

4. The issues involved in estimating overidentified path models are rather complex. Hauser and Goldberger (1971) have shown that for models like ours with *all* recursive

Inserting sample values of correlations gives an estimate of $k = 1.04$. This estimate for k is inconsistent with the hypothesis that the sources of measurement error are stable but decreasing with each new wave of observation. This failure is not surprising, given the poor fit of the entire model.

A Single-indicator Model

At this point (given our aims) we had only two choices. We could ignore one of the indicators of educational expansion and proceed with a single indicator, or we could entertain the hypothesis that the two "indicators" stand in some direct causal relationship. We should mention one variation of the latter alternative we did not pursue. The previous analysis suggests serious defects in the "common-factor" approach to the educational ratios. One alternative modification is to keep the common-factor model but to introduce additional direct causal links between the indicators (educational ratios). We did not pursue this approach, since the number of unknown quantities becomes too large.

Distinguishing Cross-Effects

In this section we pursue the single-indicator approach. Thus we revise the model of Figure 10.3 to create the three-wave, two-variable, single-indicator model drawn in Figure 10.4. This model contains only educational variables (primary and secondary ratios measured at three points in time). For purposes of algebraic simplicity, we continue to posit uncorrelated residuals and, for the present, assume uncorrelated random measurement errors. The latter assumption will be relaxed below. This model incorporates a conceptual shift. The enrollment ratios are now taken to be abstract causal *variables* measured with random error. We continue to denote the primary ratios by Y_{i1} and the secondary ratios by Y_{i2}. Measured values are primed.

This model allows for cross-effects in both directions. However, when we first began to examine the correlation matrix in Table 10.1, two of us were working on a version of the model in which the effect from secondary to primary ratios was assumed to be absent (i.e., $d = 0$). Call this case (i). We discovered that such a model is capable of generating the correlation matrix in question, given very high autocorrelation terms. In fact, the process can be represented in a simple and elegant

---

"arrows" allowed by the model specification to take on nonzero values, the best estimator is a maximum-likelihood procedure. Since for most of the models we use, some causal connections are assumed to be absent, this method is apparently not appropriate (given the present state of our knowledge). Thus we follow Duncan's heuristic method, although recognizing that the properties of the resulting estimators have not been studied. This procedure seems justified only so long as we are concerned mainly with the general properties of these models as distinct from precise estimates of causal parameters. At the point where attention focuses on estimation, we suggest following Hauser and Goldberger (1971) and Jöreskog (1970).

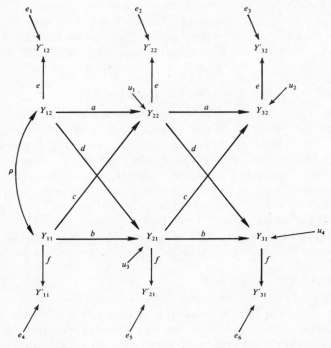

Figure 10.4.

form. To do this we alter our notation temporarily. Let P'_t and S'_t denote the primary and secondary ratios measured at time t, and P'_{t+1}, S'_{t+1} denote the measured values of the same variables at the next point in time, and so forth. This model is drawn at the top of Table 10.2, where we continue to assume purely random measurement error, stable coefficients, and uncorrelated residuals. Given this specification, the path equation for the population value of the zero-order cross-lag correlation takes on the form

$$\rho_{P_{t_1} S_{t+k}} = ef[\rho a^k + c \sum_{j=0}^{k-1} a^{k-j-1} c^j]$$

The behavior of these cross-lagged correlations is indeed time dependent as the difference-equation representation shows. With P_t fixed, the correlation $\rho_{P_{t_1} S_{t+k}}$ will increase as k increases up to a point and then begin to decrease. Both the length of the interval over which a maximum is attained and the behavior of the correlation around that interval (e.g., rapidity of decline in magnitude) depend on the values of the coefficients of the model. The important point for our purposes is that this model, together with reasonable regression estimates of the

Table 10.2. *Some Sample Results for Cross-lag Correlations*

$$\rho_{P_{t_1} S_{t+k}} = \rho a^k + c \sum_{j=0}^{k-1} c^{k-j-1} b^j$$

k	a = b = .9 ρ = .3 c = .1	a = b = .8 ρ = .3 c = .1	a = b = .7 ρ = .3 c = .1
1	.37	.34	.31
2	.42	.35	.29
3	.46	.34	.25
4	.49	.33	.21
5	.507	.30	.17
10	.49	.173	.004

	a = b = .9 ρ = .3 c = .2	a = b = .8 ρ = .3 c = .2	a = b = .7 ρ = .3 c = .2
1	.47	.44	.41
2	.60	.51	.43
3	.70	.54	.40
4	.78	.53	.34
5	.84	.51	.29
10	.86	.31	.08

coefficients, produces a correlation matrix very close to that reported in Table 10.1. The behavior of the cross-lag correlation over ten time periods for alternative hypothesized coefficients is reported in Table 10.2.

Consider an alternative specification of the model relating the two educational ratios in which only the direction of the cross-effect is changed (i.e., $d \neq 0$, $c = 0$); call this case (ii). Case (i) seems preferable on substantive grounds. Increases in primary enrollments create a demand for the expansion of secondary systems as larger cohorts pass through the primary schools. However, the possibility remains that educational systems expand down from the top. Secondary expansion creates a "pull" into primary school, owing to the changed opportunity structure. For this reason it is useful to subject both models to test.

First we consider the "dynamics" of our second model. This model generates a correlation matrix which is the transpose of the matrix produced by the first model. Thus the correlation matrix generated in this case is not at all close to that observed in our sample. This result lends considerable support to the model in which secondary ratios are taken as dependent on earlier primary ratios (case [i]).

Since this method of evaluating the competing causal models is somewhat novel in the social science literature (and involves a number of implicit assumptions and approximations), we were interested in also conducting a more standard path-analytic test of the models. To do this we write out the path equations for the two models as follows:

$$\text{Case } (i)(d = 0) \qquad\qquad \text{Case } (ii)(c = 0)$$

$$\rho_{Y'_{12} Y'_{22}} = e^2(a + \rho c) \qquad\qquad e^2 a$$

$$\rho_{Y'_{12} Y'_{32}} = e^2(a^2 + \rho ca + \rho bc) \qquad\qquad e^2 a^2$$

$$\rho_{Y'_{12} Y'_{11}} = e\rho f \qquad\qquad e\rho f$$

$$\rho_{Y'_{12} Y'_{21}} = e\rho b f \qquad\qquad ef(d + \rho b)$$

$$\rho_{Y'_{12} Y'_{31}} = e\rho b^2 f \qquad\qquad ef(\rho b^2 + db + ad)$$

$$\rho_{Y'_{11} Y'_{22}} = ef(c + \rho a) \qquad\qquad ef\rho a$$

$$\rho_{Y'_{11} Y'_{32}} = ef(\rho a^2 + ca + bc) \qquad\qquad ef\rho a^2$$

$$\rho_{Y'_{11} Y'_{21}} = f^2 b \qquad\qquad f^2(b + \rho d)$$

$$\rho_{Y'_{11} Y'_{31}} = f^2 b^2 \qquad\qquad f^2(b^2 + \rho db + \rho ad)$$

$$\rho_{Y'_{22} Y'_{32}} = e^2(a + a\rho bc + c^2 b) \qquad\qquad e^2 a$$

$$\rho_{Y'_{22} Y'_{21}} = ef(a\rho b + cb) \qquad\qquad ef(ad + a\rho b)$$

$$\rho_{Y'_{22} Y'_{31}} = ef(a\rho b^2 + cb^2) \qquad\qquad ef(d + adb + a\rho b^2)$$

$$\rho_{Y'_{21} Y'_{32}} = ef(c + acb + a^2 \rho b) \qquad\qquad ef(a^2 d + a^2 \rho b)$$

$$\rho_{Y'_{21} Y'_{31}} = f^2 b \qquad\qquad f^2(b + d^2 a + b\rho ad)$$

$$\rho_{Y'_{32} Y'_{31}} = ef(cb + acb^2 + a^2 \rho b^2) \qquad\qquad ef(ad + a^2 db + a^2 \rho b^2)$$

The two models do not share any prediction equations, which makes it difficult to choose between the two. Both cases fit better than the model tested earlier, as is shown in Table 10.3. If anything, case (ii) fits slightly better than case (i), according to the criteria of average departures from zero. Since as far as we know the sampling distributions of the series of prediction equations is not known, it is difficult to choose between the two cases purely on the basis of the small difference in fits. Proceeding to the estimation stage does not reduce the uncertainty. In each case only two coefficients are *obviously*[5] identified, the autoregression and "epistemic correlation" for the independent variable. There are five mathematically equivalent solutions for each of the autoregression terms. Using the Duncan procedure outlined above, we obtain $\hat{b} = .893$ for case (i) and $\hat{q} = 1.021$ for case (ii). Using these composite estimates, we can solve directly for $\hat{f}$ in case (i) and $\hat{e}$ in case (ii) in three equivalent ways. The combined estimates for the two quantities are 1.048 and .937, respectively.

Table 10.3. Deviations of Tetrad Differences from Zero

Case (i)	Case (ii)
.027	
.102	.084
.108	.001
.045	.016
.029	.052
.007	.086
.002	.065
.060	.087
.026	.014
	.012

Under the model specifications for the two cases, the four terms estimated are correlations as well as path coefficients. Each case violates this assumption, and neither model is satisfactory. The fact that none of the remaining parameters of either model are obviously identified greatly limits the usefulness of these models. Thus we do not continue this analysis in an effort to model the complications which might yield

5. The estimation equations for the coefficients we estimate are obvious from the path equations. It is possible both that more complicated estimates of these terms are available and that more complicated systems of equations yield solutions for the other terms. In the cases we investigated, this did not seem to be the case. Most often the systems of nonlinear equations were not amenable to direct algebraic solution. Where we were able to reduce the estimation equations to quadratic, cubic or quartic equations, we did not obtain real roots for all of the unknown terms. Since our search procedures were not entirely systematic, however, we cannot assert with confidence that no other estimates exist. In this and what follows we refer to "obvious" solutions when we refer to the estimation status of parameters.

more acceptable estimates; our ultimate objective is to relate these educational variables to other substantive variables (economic development in the present application). To do this we shall pursue a number of the issues which arise when single-indicator models are embedded in more complex models. The most obvious extension in this substantive research is to *three-variable*, three-wave panel models.

Since the path analysis is indeterminate in choosing between the two models, we shall take the argument based on dynamics (together with our substantive preference) as persuasive. Henceforth in the analysis we shall consider case (i) as the appropriate causal model.

The Problem of Identification

Before going on to more complex models, we shall comment briefly on the identification problem in this simple model with one-way cross-effects. It is rather surprising that even when we assume stability in all parameters (which implies constant true and error variances), purely random measurement error, and uncorrelated disturbances, only the autoregression of the "independent" variable and the coefficient associated with the measurement term for this variable are identified. *What is even more surprising is the finding that the addition of new waves of observations does nothing more than provide additional tests of the model and additional estimates of the coefficients already identified, even when the new waves do not add additional unknowns.* This is quite important. The bottom half of the model for case (ii) corresponds to the single-indicator case discussed in the literature cited at the outset. Our result conforms to what is already known—with single indicators measured with purely random error, uncorrelated disturbances, and three waves of observations, all parameters of interest are identified. However, the addition of a second substantive variable makes clear that the more general case is considerably more complicated. This is particularly puzzling, since the variable we add is exogenous (i.e., it is posited to be independent of the residuals in the regression equations for the educational ratios). We seem to have a case, then, where the addition of more information precludes the estimation of previously identified coefficients.

Inspection of the equations for case (ii) isolates the difficulty. Consider the expression for the population correlation of the primary ratios at the second and third observations, since the autoregression in this variable could be solved for before the addition of the exogenous variable:

$$\rho_{Y'_{22} Y'_{32}} = e^2 \left(a + a\rho bc + c^2 b \right) .$$

We see that the estimation complications arise because of the initial correlations represented by the curved double-headed arrows at the left-hand side of the model (denoted by ρ) and because of the over-time stability in all the substantive variables. When early values of the variables are correlated, owing to previous operation of the causal structure under study, and the variables are stable, the number of indirect paths connecting observations quickly becomes very large and expressions do not repeat themselves. This is the reason that the addition of waves of observations does not eliminate the estimation problem. This only gives rise to more complicated expressions relating early "independent" variables to later "dependent" ones.

This, plus the nonlinear manner in which the measurement error terms enter the equations, gives rise to systems of nonlinear equations in k unknowns (where k is fairly large, e.g., 4) which are unlikely, in our experience, to yield useful solutions. Even though the systems of equations may in principle have real roots, the actual work of solving the system (even using a computer) is enormous.

The technical problem is a failure of the *sufficient* conditions for identification. We have become accustomed to concerning ourselves only with the necessary conditions for identification. In the present context these may be stated in the form: the number of path coefficients to be estimated must not exceed the number of independent equations (Wright 1960). Clearly we have no difficulty satisfying this condition.

Our practical problem is accentuated, since we lack a readily applicable set of guidelines showing a priori for complicated cases (where a portion of the system is overidentified and another portion is underidentified) which, if any, coefficients are identified. In the usual representation of structural equations in an (unstandardized) econometric system, the application of both the necessary ("order") and sufficient ("rank") conditions to each equation is straightforward. Our difficulty has been in failing to be able to extend this approach to complicated path-analytic panel models. In principle, we should be able to follow Jöreskog's (1970) representation of the covariance structure and pinpoint identification problems from an inspection of the various variance-covariance matrices. To the present we have not been able, using this approach, to isolate the difficulties.

This brief discussion should make plain the fact that an investigation of the usefulness of single-indicator models measured with error must focus heavily on the conditions under which, in overidentified models, the parameters of interest are identified (or perhaps practically estimable). Unfortunately we have proceeded on a rather ad hoc basis, since we have not found any simple algorithms which allow one to make such a judgment prior to writing out the systems of equations and searching for estimates.

A Three-variable, Three-wave, Single-indicator Model
(3V, 3W, 1I)

We have already argued that primary enrollment ratios affect secondary ratios (and not the reverse), and it seems a natural extension to argue that economic development affects only primary ratios directly. To further simplify our analysis, we assume for the moment no cross-effect from either educational variable to development. The model drawn in Figure 10.5, incorporating our usual simplifying assumptions concerning disturbances and measurement error terms, represents the causal structure. Again we must require all our (standardized) coefficients to be stable or none will be identified.

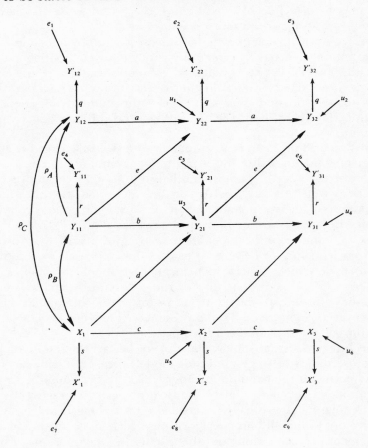

Figure 10.5.

This model has an excess of twenty-five equations over unknown coefficients. As before, each of the overidentifying restrictions (redundant equations) can be written as quantities (Spearman tetrad differences) equal to zero under the hypothesis of no specification error (i.e., the model is correct) and no sampling error. The fit of these twenty-five equations with our sample is extremely close. The largest deviation from the predicted value is .021, and the mean of the absolute values of the deviations is .0067. As the latter figure suggests, most of the predictions are almost exactly met.

The massive inadequacies of single-indicator models (even with strong simplifying assumptions such as those made above) become inescapable when we shift attention from testing to estimation. Just as with the cases analyzed earlier, only the autoregression coefficient for economic development, the most "independent" variable, and the path coefficient linking this variable with its indicator are apparently estimable. It is easy in this case to see that it is *only* the presence of measurement error which rules out the estimation of the remaining coefficients. In other words, if each of the path coefficients linking variables with indicators is a priori set equal to some value, all the remaining coefficients in the model can be solved for in a number of ways (i.e., they will not only be identified, they will be overidentified). If only partial information is available, perhaps the value of one of the "epistemic correlations," r, a portion of the remaining coefficients can be solved for (in this example, b, d and ρ_c).

As a further partial check on the model we estimate the available coefficients, with the result that $\hat{c} = 1.01$ and $\hat{s} = .987$. In this model c is a correlation and thus should not exceed unity. However, the discrepancy is smaller than was the case previously, and the estimated value of s is reasonable.

Duncan (1975) has shown that one need not stop here in a substantive analysis. In a number of the cases he examined, estimation of the model's remaining coefficients based on "provisional" estimates of some of the unknown quantities gave rise to either logical inconsistencies (e.g., correlations greater than unity, unreal solutions, etc.) or substantively uninterpretable results. Since we are more concerned at this point with the logic of the analysis problems, we do not pursue this strategy, but note its potential usefulness.

We have reached consistently negative conclusions about the usefulness of single-indicator models. Even under the most idealized conditions, such models do not allow us to estimate the parameters of the postulated causal structure. However, we should not totally dismiss the fact that single-indicator models are falsifiable and thus can contribute at least negative evidence to substantive problems. In addition, a focus on the dynamics of the difference equations conveys important information. Yet, any consideration of more realistic complications must inevitably lead to the study of multiple-indicator models. We make this shift in the next section.

A Two-variable, Three-wave, Two-indicator Model (2V, 3W, 2I)

In this section, we alter the model in Figure 10.2, with which we began the analysis, in an effort to eliminate the causal interconnections which produced the earlier anomalous results. Specifically, we choose as our indicators of educational expansion a combined ratio of primary and secondary students to the appropriate age-specific population and the ratio of students in tertiary schools to the total population. Economic development is measured by GNP/cap and KWH/cap. Unfortunately, the existing data is such that the inclusion of GNP/cap reduces our sample to the forty-six (presumably) most developed nation-states. This is particularly problematic when one uses, as we do, standardized coefficients. In such a case the changing variances will create unstable (standardized) population parameters even when the slopes are invariant across time periods.

A Model with Random Measurement Error

We shall continue to explore the consequences of measurement error in the context of a substantive model specifying asymmetric cross-effects from economic development to educational expansion over the time period of investigation. The revised model incorporating double indicators is diagrammed in Figure 10.6.

Before analyzing this model we must digress and consider an analysis problem raised by Blalock (1970) which seems to point to a problem with our model. To do this, we specialize the model drawn in Figure 10.6 in the following ways: Concentrate only on the educational "half" of this model, that is, treat the economic-development variable as unobserved, and thus part of the residual. Assume (contrary to the model drawn in Figure 10.6) that the residuals are uncorrelated with the included variables and are not stable over waves of observations (i.e., are intertemporally uncorrelated). Assume, further, that the measurement error terms are correlated both simultaneously for different indicators and intertemporally for the same indicators measured at different points in time. Finally, assume that the correlations of measurement error terms are stable over waves of observations. The restrictions give us the model discussed by Blalock (1970, Fig. 5), which is diagrammed in Figure 10.7. Note that this model requires the "epistemic correlations" to be stable but allows the autoregression terms to vary between waves of observations.

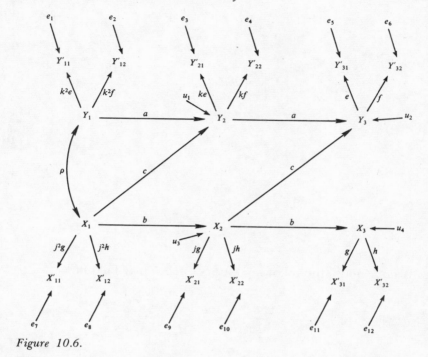

Figure 10.6.

This model gives rise to the following system of fifteen equations (redundancy is indicated by an asterisk):

$$r_{x_{11} x_{12}} = ab + a'b'f , \tag{1'}$$

$$*r_{x_{21} x_{22}} = ab + a'b'f , \tag{2'}$$

$$*r_{x_{31} x_{32}} = ab + a'b'f , \tag{3'}$$

$$r_{x_{11} x_{21}} = a^2 c' + (a')^2 g , \tag{4'}$$

$$r_{x_{21} x_{31}} = a^2 d' + (a')^2 g , \tag{5'}$$

$$r_{x_{11} x_{31}} = a^2 c'd' + (a')^2 g' , \tag{6'}$$

$$r_{x_{12} x_{22}} = b^2 c' + (b')^2 h , \tag{7'}$$

$$r_{x_{22} x_{32}} = b^2 d' + (b')^2 h , \tag{8'}$$

$$r_{x_{12}x_{32}} = b^2 c'd' + (b')^2 h' \,, \tag{9'}$$

$$r_{x_{11}x_{22}} = abc' \,, \tag{10'}$$

$$r_{x_{11}x_{32}} = abc'd' \,, \tag{11'}$$

$$*r_{x_{12}x_{21}} = abc' \,, \tag{12'}$$

$$*r_{x_{12}x_{31}} = abc'd' \,, \tag{13'}$$

$$r_{x_{21}x_{32}} = abd' \,, \tag{14'}$$

$$*r_{x_{22}x_{31}} = abd' \,. \tag{15'}$$

As Blalock notes, the following estimates obviously fall out:

$$c' = \frac{r_{x_{11}x_{32}}}{r_{x_{21}x_{32}}} = \frac{abc'd'}{abd'} \;; \quad d' = \frac{r_{x_{11}x_{32}}}{r_{x_{11}x_{22}}} = \frac{abc'd'}{abc'} \,.$$

However, one can obtain estimates of a and b by, for example, subtracting equation (4') from (5') and multiplying both sides by $(ab)^2$, as long as $c' \neq d'$. The above procedure depends on the assumption that

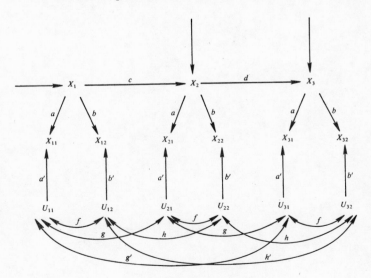

Figure 10.7. Redrawn from Blalock 1970, Figure 5.

$c' \neq d'$. If, in fact the two stability coefficients are nearly identical in the population, then even though their sample counterparts may be slightly different, there will be very large sampling errors for the estimates of the ratio a^2/b^2 and also for all the estimates dependent on this ratio. Therefore, for all practical purposes, the procedure will be useful only if the stability coefficients c' and d' are very different. [Blalock 1970, p. 109] While this statement is accurate as it refers to the estimation procedure Blalock employed, it is somewhat misleading if it is taken to apply more generally to the estimation of "stability" coefficients in this model.

To see this, let $c' = d'$, and rewrite the system of equations just considered:

$$r_{x_{11}x_{12}} = ab + a'b'f = r_{x_{21}x_{22}} = r_{x_{31}x_{32}} , \qquad (1''\text{-}3'')$$

$$r_{x_{11}x_{21}} = a^2 c' + (a')^2 g = r_{x_{21}x_{31}} , \qquad (4''\text{-}5'')$$

$$r_{x_{11}x_{31}} = a^2(c')^2 + (a')^2 g' , \qquad (6'')$$

$$r_{x_{12}x_{22}} = b^2 c' + (b')^2 h = r_{x_{22}x_{32}} , \qquad (7''\text{-}8'')$$

$$r_{x_{11}x_{22}} = abc' = r_{x_{12}x_{21}} = r_{x_{22}x_{31}} , \qquad (10''\text{-}13'')$$

$$r_{x_{11}x_{32}} = ab(c')^2 = r_{x_{12}x_{31}} . \qquad (14''\text{-}15'')$$

We see immediately that in this case we employ *different* equations to estimate all the coefficients. The estimation proceeds as follows:

$$\hat{c}' = \frac{r_{x_{11}x_{32}}}{r_{x_{11}x_{22}}} = \frac{ab(c')^2}{abc'} ;$$

$$\hat{\hat{ab}} = \frac{r_{x_{11}x_{22}} r_{x_{12}x_{21}}}{r_{x_{11}x_{32}}} = \frac{a^2 b^2 (c')^2}{ab(c')^2} .$$

Subtracting equation (6′) from (4′) and (9′) from (7′) and taking a ratio of these quantities gives

$$\frac{\hat{a}^2}{\hat{b}^2} = \frac{r_{x_{11}x_{21}} - r_{x_{11}x_{31}}}{r_{x_{12}x_{22}} - r_{x_{12}x_{32}}} = \frac{a^2 [c' - (c')^2]}{b^2 [c' - (c')^2]} .$$

Combining the above expressions yields

$$\hat{a}^4 = \frac{r_{x_{11}x_{22}} r_{x_{12}x_{21}}}{r_{x_{11}x_{32}}} \cdot \frac{r_{x_{11}x_{21}} - r_{x_{11}x_{31}}}{r_{x_{12}x_{22}} - r_{x_{12}x_{32}}} .$$

Given estimates of c and a, we can use equations (10'-13') to provide estimates of b, and of the disturbances.

It is obvious that this method faces a restriction similar to that discovered by Blalock. Our estimates of the ratio a^2/b^2 will have very large sample variance if c' is very close to $(c')^2$, that is, if c' is very close to unity in the population. Thus this method is useful only if the process is such that these correlations are considerably less than unity. However, in the multivariate applications, the "stability coefficients" will be "partial" coefficients and thus may exceed unity. This is a frequent occurrence in the models with which we have worked. The implication is that the estimation method is not restricted to the case of "unstable" systems, that is, those in which factors left out of the analysis are quite important in producing intertemporal variation in the variable under study. The method is applicable even when such variables are introduced explicitly into the analysis. The requirement is that the stability in the variable itself (as opposed to stability in other variables) not be so high as to produce almost no intertemporal variation. More concretely, if there are variables which produce systematic variation in the variable under study over time, the estimation method should not be expected to have exceedingly large sample variance.

The important point here is that the utility of any estimation method must be evaluated relative to the substantive model under study. A method which is optimal for unstable autoregression coefficients may not be optimal for the stable case. This conclusion is reinforced by the demonstration that our method of rewriting the system of equations so as to introduce the presumed complication does not contradict Blalock's analysis of the requirement of moderately low intratemporal correlations among at least two indicators in his discussion of the three-wave, three-indicator (single-variable model).

The point of this digression is to demonstrate that if our assumptions are justified we can expect to estimate the coefficients of the model drawn in Figure 10.6, even if the autoregression parameters are stable over waves of observations. With this assurance we can return to that model and proceed to examine the consequences of the complications thought to be most troublesome in this type of substantive application.

The first problem is familiar. With sixty-six equations and only eight unknowns, we face a bewildering variety of estimates for many of the coefficients. The autoregression in economic development, b, can be estimated at least fifty different ways. The problem is that the various estimates must surely differ in sampling variance. Some estimates are "direct" in the sense that they are given by ratios of two sample correlations. These "direct" estimates can then be used to solve rather more complicated systems of linear equations involving the quantity b. It is no simple matter just to identify all of the possible ways to estimate each coefficient in a model as simple as this (the complications arise through, for instance, the many possible paths connecting educational ratios between the last two time periods) or to establish which estimates are independent. The practical problem is that the various estimators differ considerably. One normally suspects that considerable divergence in the estimates suggests specification error in the model. As long as the sampling distributions of the estimators are unknown, however, such inferences do not have firm support. Consequently we have continued to report composite estimators which make use of some but not all of the information in the sample. We have made no attempt to incorporate all the logically possible independent estimates. Our estimates, then, are highly tentative, since, primarily, they make use of the most "direct" methods of estimation. As we shall see below, this approach if carried out in substantive analyses has some serious drawbacks.

Thus, assuming for the moment that $j = k = 1$, we proceed to estimation of the coefficients of the model in Figure 10.6:[6]

$$\hat{a} = 1.205,$$
$$\hat{b} = 1.003,$$
$$\hat{c} = -.210,$$
$$\hat{e} = 1.031,$$
$$\hat{f} = .368,$$
$$\hat{g} = .935,$$
$$\hat{h} = .978,$$
$$\hat{p} = .772.$$

The only obvious difficulty is that $\hat{e}$ exceeds unity (and, as a consequence, $\hat{f}$ is small in magnitude). However, $\hat{b}$ is so close to unity that, if we were limited to the estimation procedure presented as an alternative to the one suggested by Blalock, the estimates would be extremely responsive to sampling error. The fact that we have three waves and six indicators means that we have considerably more ways to estimate the model coefficients, although this may only serve to mask the consequences of the obviously high autoregression terms. We have not yet been able to assess the seriousness of such problems.

Models with Nonrandom Measurement Error

As before, we proceed to consider the implications of several types of nonrandom measurement error. As noted earlier, among the most realistic nonrandom errors in cross-nation research is organizational

6. All the coefficients but a and c are solved by the Duncan estimate of nine equivalent estimating expressions chosen unsystematically from the obvious possibilities. The estimation of a and c requires the solution of systems of two equations in two unknowns. There are a number of equivalent systems in the same two unknowns, and the method of combining the alternative solutions is not obvious. For the lack of a better method we took the arithmetic mean of five sets of solutions.

"memory." All the measures we employ are generated by national bureaucracies. These bureaucracies tend to err in the same sorts of ways consistently over time. We examine this type of complication by simplifying the argument to specify a five-year memory and allow for correlated measurement error for the same indicators over five-year intervals, but not longer—a restriction introduced to simplify the problem. We shall continue the analysis with the last substantive model considered, which is adapted for our present purposes and rediagrammed in Figure 10.8.

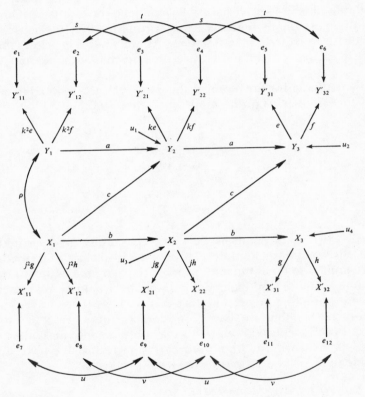

Figure 10.8.

Only twenty-six of the equations for this model are different from those in the previous model (Fig. 10.7). The addition of the "memory" terms eliminates numerous simple equation systems yielding estimates of b. As a result, assuming $j = k = 1$, the estimate of b becomes 1.06, perhaps enough greater than unity to cast doubt on this particular model. There is no apparent change in the estimation procedures for the remaining coefficients. More precisely, every valid estimate for any of the remaining terms in this model is also appropriate under the specification of the model with uncorrelated measurement error terms. Since the magnitudes of the correlations between measurement error terms are not obviously estimable, we can proceed no further without additional assumptions. The logic for proceeding with this model is not obvious, since it fits the logical bounds (on magnitudes of correlation coefficients) less well than the more restrictive model discussed earlier.

We could engage in a completely parallel analysis of the proposition that the bureaucracies tend to err in the same sorts of ways in a given time period in reporting *different* national account statistics. In such a case we would allow different indicators of the same variable, as well as indicators of different variables measured at the same point in time, to be correlated. Since we could not estimate the systematic error components in this case, we have shifted attention to other problems.

The final class of nonrandom measurement errors we consider in the context of this model is the systematically (proportionally) decreasing random error discussed in the first section. That is we relax the restriction that $j = k = 1$ in the model drawn in Figure 10.6.

By and large the estimation procedure is as above. One exception involves the proportionality terms for the decreasing error, j and k. In this case, we solve directly for these terms and then proceed as above using the estimates of j and k wherever such terms appear. Recall that our substantive understandings require $0 < j \leq 1$ and $0 < k \leq 1$. Our sample estimates are

$$\hat{j} = .991,$$
$$\hat{k} = 1.090.$$

The result for k is much like that obtained earlier for the single-indicator educational-ratio model. Clearly this particular hypothesis of nonrandom error is not appropriate for at least this portion of the model in Figure 10.7. Our examination of the data strongly suggests that failure here is due to a secular trend of decreasing cross-sectional variance in the primary-secondary ratio. This trend reflects a type of "ceiling effect" which is enormously problematic in standardized models. At any rate, given the unrealistic estimate of k, there is no point in proceeding to estimate terms depending on $\hat{k}$.

It is interesting to consider the consequences of proportionately decreasing error in the model's indicators of economic development. Allowing for this type of nonrandom error raises the estimates of path coefficients linking economic development with its indicators, $\hat{g}$ and $\hat{h}$, from .935 to .994 and from .978 to .989, respectively, and lowers the estimate for the autoregression, b, from 1.003 to .879. Both types of changes are quite encouraging for substantive analysis.

We had originally become interested in this type of nonrandom error because of an interest in eventually modeling substantive processes involving lags of *different* lengths. For example, we might argue that the lag in the causal effect of educational expansion on economic development is twice as long as the lag in the reverse effect. In cases like this we should expect that over any time period of observation the longer lagged effects will be more seriously affected by random measurement error. Unless the analyst takes the decrease in the time-dependent magnitude of random errors into account, he is likely to make incorrect inferences in comparing the magnitudes of the longer lagged and the shorter lagged effects.

An example of the type of model in which this would be problematic is drawn in Figure 10.9. Here the lag for the effect from educational expansion is two waves of observations (ten years), and the lag for the effect from economic development to educational expansion is one wave (five years).

The failure of our model for decreasing random error in the educational expansion of the model in Figure 10.7 rules out the possibility of estimating all the coefficients in this new model. Yet, we can see some of the consequences of this type of error using a hypothetical value of k. If we restrict $j = k = 1$, then $d = -.076$; but when we assume that $j = k = .991$, the estimate of d is increased to $-.220$, a considerable in-

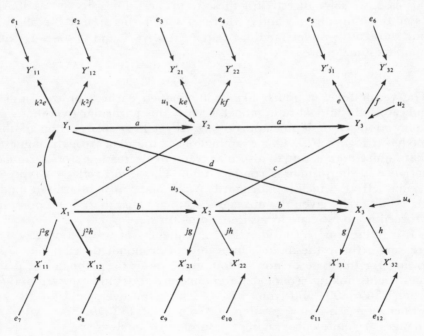

Figure 10.9.

crease. This exercise suggests that our original concerns were justified and that researchers modeling processes like that under study here ought to attend to such nonrandom error.

The model drawn in Figure 10.9 illustrates one further difficulty with ad hoc estimation methods for complicated path models. The addition of a long-lagged cross-effect has only a very slight effect on other estimates in the model, since the term appears in relatively few equations. This, given simple composite estimates, has the consequence of minimizing the difference between a model which has such an effect and one which does not. This factor will often make it very difficult to choose between two such models when both are confronted with the same sample data.

But the more serious problem lies with the "stepwise" method of estimation used by us, Duncan (1972, 1975), and Blalock (1970). In this procedure we first estimate (inserting sample estimates) those terms which appear simply as, say, ratios of population correlations. Those first-order estimates are then used to solve more complicated expressions to produce "derived" estimates for additional terms. In very complicated models like those considered in this chapter, the analyst may have to go through several steps. The difficulty is the following: We can solve directly for b in the model in Figure 10.9 without taking into account the presence of the other cross-effect, d; we then use this estimate of b to solve for d. However, it may be possible to solve more complicated systems of equations for b and d simultaneously. Obviously, the latter procedure is preferable, since it more faithfully represents the causal structure of the model by simultaneously taking into account the presence of both cross-effects. We should expect that estimates produced by such a procedure will ordinarily differ from those arrived at by the procedure we used. This estimation problem will loom importantly in the substantive research which motivated this analysis.

Concluding Remarks

We shall not attempt to recapitulate the series of technical results scattered throughout the chapter. The main point is that inferences in the multiwave, multivariable panel are much more complicated than has been generally realized. Results from single-variable models with measurement error are not easily generalized to more complicated cases. Moreover, the consequences of measurement error are not easily generalized but depend heavily on the specific features of the model in which it occurs. In this sense this chapter reinforces the developing consensus in social science methodology that simple formulations of the consequences of even random measurement error (e.g., attenuation) are not likely to be invariant across models. This new emphasis is beneficial, since social scientists appear to have begun to rely too heavily on stock reactions to the presence of measurement error.

We have noted difficulties of estimation at numerous points. This type of work is greatly hampered by the lack of a systematic theory of identification and of statistical inference for realistic panel models. The thrust of recent statements (Hauser and Goldberger 1971, Werts, Linn, and Jöreskog 1971) is to suggest that sociologists may not have to invent such a theory but may be able to borrow formulations from econometrics and biometrics. Unfortunately, the formulations applied to path models to this point are not easily generalizable to cases we have considered. It is clear that this sort of work must proceed before the causal approach to measurement error will be practically useful to sociologists employing panel models in substantive research.

References

Blalock, Hubert M.
  1964. *Causal Inferences in Nonexperimental Research*. Chapel Hill: University of North Carolina Press.
  1970. "Estimating Measurement Error Using Multiple Indicators and Several Points in Time." *American Sociological Review* 35 (February):101-11.
Campbell, Donald T., and Donald W. Fiske
  1959. "Convergent and Discriminant Validation by the Multitrait-Multimethod Matrix." *Psychological Bulletin* 56 (March):81-105.
Costner, Herbert L.
  1969. "Theory, Deduction, and Rules of Correspondence." *American Journal of Sociology* 75 (September):245-63.
Duncan, Otis Dudley
  1969. "Some Linear Models for Two-wave, Two-Variable Panel Analysis." *Psychological Bulletin* 72 (September):177-82.
  1972. "Unmeasured Variables in Linear Models for Panel Analysis: Some Didactic Examples." In H. Costner, ed., *Sociological Methodology*, 1972. San Francisco: Jossey-Bass.
  1975. "Some Linear Models for Two-wave, Two-Variable Panel Analysis, with One Way Causation and Measurement error." In H. M. Blalock et al., eds., *Quantitative Sociology*. New York: Academic Press (forthcoming).
Hauser, Robert M., and Arthur S. Goldberger
  1971. "Treatment of Unobservable Variables in Path Analysis." In Herbert L. Costner, ed., *Sociological Methodology, 1971*. San Francisco: Jossey-Bass.
Heise, David R.
  1970. "Causal Inference from Panel Data." In Edgar F. Borgatta and George W. Bohrnstedt, eds., *Sociological Methodology, 1970*. San Francisco: Jossey-Bass.
Jöreskog, K.
  1970. "A General Method for the Analysis of Covariance Structures." *Biometrika* 57(2):239-51.
Meyer, John, and Michael T. Hannan
  1971. "The Interrelationships of National Educational Systems with Political and Economic Institutions." Research proposal submitted to the National Science Foundation.
Nerlove, Marc
  1971. "Further Evidence on the Estimation of Dynamic Economic Relations from Time Series." *Econometrics* 39 (March):359-82.
Werts, Charles E., Robert L. Linn, and Karl G. Jöreskog
  1971. "Estimating the Parameters of Path Models Involving Unmeasured Variables." In Hubert M. Blalock, ed. *Causal Models in the Social Sciences*. Chicago: Aldine.
Wiley, David E., and James A. Wiley
  1970. "The Estimation of Measurement Error in Panel Data." *American Sociological Review* 35 (February):112-16.
Wright, Sewell
  1960. "Path Coefficients and Path Regressions: Alternative or Complementary Concepts." *Biometrics* 16 (June):189-202.

III

ORDINAL MEASUREMENT

Chapter 11

MEASURES OF ASSOCIATION FOR BIVARIATE ORDINAL HYPOTHESES

Thomas P. Wilson

Thomas P. Wilson received his graduate training in Sociology at Columbia University and is currently in the Department of Sociology at the University of California, Santa Barbara. His interests include a concern with the implications of measurement limitations in the social sciences on theory construction. Currently he is collaborating with Don H. Zimmerman in research into the nature of sociological description and context dependence in social interaction.

Although ordinal variables have a number of unsatisfactory characteristics (Wilson 1971), they are likely to remain a prominent feature of empirical social research for some time to come. Consequently, statistical techniques for ordinal variables are important heuristic methods for social science investigation, and a number of recent papers have been concerned with developing various rationales for measuring association between ordinal variables (Goodman and Kruskal 1954; Somers 1962, 1968; Davis 1963; Costner 1965; Leik and Gove 1969; Wilson 1969; Morris 1970). In this work, a question of increasing importance is that of choosing between the by now large number of available measures of ordinal association. The purpose of this chapter is to propose a framework for answering this question in terms of the type of research hypothesis under investigation.

This is a revision of a paper read at the American Sociological Association meetings, August, 1966. I wish to thank David Gold, Bruce C. Straits, and H. M. Blalock, Jr., for suggestions and critical comments.

327

The Problem

The concern here is with the problem of a researcher who has formulated a bivariate hypothesis—that is, a proposition asserting a relation between two variables—and must choose an appropriate measure of association. Such a hypothesis may be suggested by a theory, gleaned from the literature, or stimulated by the data themselves. But no matter what the source of his idea, it is assumed that the researcher is concerned with a specific hypothesis that a relation of some designated kind exists in his data.

Moreover, it is assumed that the data are measured at best at the ordinal level and that the researcher is unwilling to invoke the kinds of assumptions needed to justify an assignment of numbers to his scales for use in metric techniques such as product-moment correlation and regression. Further, it is supposed that the two variables in question have been measured with comparable refinement and that the cutting points and numbers of categories in the scales have been chosen with an eye to minimizing problems resulting from ties created by the mere crudeness of the categorizations.

Under these conditions, determinate choice of an appropriate measure of association depends upon two things: a logically precise formulation of the kind of relation under investigation, and a clearly formulated model for interpreting ordinal association. To meet these demands, three basic types of ordinal relation will be identified, and a simple model of interpretation will be proposed. The main result is that Goodman and Kruskal's γ, Somers's d_{yx}, and a new measure, e, are shown to be uniquely appropriate, respectively, for the three basic types of ordinal hypotheses.

Types of Bivariate Ordinal Hypotheses

A bivariate ordinal hypothesis asserts a relation between two ordinal variables. A relation can, of course, take many forms, but those most frequently considered in social science research are monotonic, that is, never decreasing or never increasing, as opposed to relations that increase and then decrease. Consequently, attention is confined here to monotonic relations.

An ordinal hypothesis is frequently stated in the form, "The higher the x, the higher the y." Often, however, it is not clear whether this assertion is meant to be taken literally or whether a weaker or stronger proposition is intended. In fact, at least three fundamentally different types of ordinal hypotheses can be identified, each using a different definition of "perfect association," and each requiring a different measure of association for appropriate study. Moreover, because the ordinal level of measurement permits the concept of directionality, each type of hypothesis has a positive and a negative form, depending on whether an increase or decrease in the dependent variable is asserted to be associated with an increase in the independent variable. The three types of hypotheses to be considered here concern the following types of ordinal relations:

Relations of no reversals
Positive: if x increases, y does not decrease
Negative: if x increases, y does not increase
Asymmetric relations
Positive: if x increases, y increases
Negative: if x increases, y decreases
Strict relations
Positive: if x increases, y increases, and if x does not vary, neither does y
Negative: if x increases, y decreases, and if x does not vary, neither does y

While no claim is advanced that these types are exhaustive, they appear to represent three salient possibilities for bivariate monotonic ordinal hypotheses.

A Model for Interpreting Ordinal Association

The next step is to construct a general procedure for measuring the extent to which a given set of data fits either the positive form or the negative form of a particular type of hypothesis. To begin with, since the variables in question are ordinal, the hypotheses must be interpreted as statements about pairs of cases rather than as statements about individuals. Thus, strictly speaking, a positive no-reversals hypothesis asserts that if one individual is higher than another on x, he will not be lower than the other on y. Now in any set of real data, there will generally be some pairs fitting the positive form of a particular type of hypothesis and some pairs fitting the negative form. Consequently, the preponderance of one kind of pair over the other can be used to assess the degree to which the entire set of data fits one form of the hypothesis or the other. Thus, a measure of fit can be constructed by taking the difference between the proportion of pairs fitting the positive form and the proportion fitting the negative form among all those pairs relevant to the type of hypothesis in question. In symbols,

$$\text{Degree of fit} = \frac{P - Q}{R}$$

where R is the number of pairs relevant to the type of hypothesis, P is the number of relevant pairs fitting the positive form, and Q is the number of relevant pairs fitting the negative form. This measure will be $+1$ when all the relevant pairs fit the positive form, it will be -1 when all the relevant pairs fit the negative form, and it will be zero when there are as many relevant pairs fitting the positive as the negative form.

The critical concept here, of course, is the notion of pairs relevant to a particular type of hypothesis. For the purpose of this measure, a pair is relevant to a particular type of hypothesis when it provides definite evidence supporting either the positive or the negative form of the hypothesis, but not both. More formally:

DEFINITION. *A pair is* relevant *to a particular type of hypothesis if and only if (a) it satisfies the antecedent conditions of the hypothesis, and (b) it is not consistent with both the positive and the negative forms of the hypothesis.*

Part (a) excludes those pairs about which the hypothesis makes no definite assertion (e.g., for no-reversals hypotheses, those tied on x), and part (b) exludes further those pairs that are consistent with both the positive and the negative forms and thus do not help distinguish between the two.

Measures for the Three Types of Hypotheses

To apply these concepts, some notation is required. A pair of individuals (i, j) is *concordant* when i is higher than j on both variables or lower than j on both variables. The pair is *discordant* when i is higher than j on one variable and lower than j on the other. If a pair is neither concordant nor discordant, it must be tied on x or y or both. A pair not tied on a given variable is *dispersed* on that variable. Let C be the number of concordant pairs, D the number of discordant pairs, T_x the number of pairs tied on x only, T_y the number tied on y only, and T_{xy} the number tied on both x and y.

Hypotheses of No Reversals

Stated precisely, a positive no-reversals ordinal hypothesis proposes that for all i and j,

if i is higher than j on x,
then i is at least as high as j on y.

An example of a perfect positive no-reversal relation is given in Table 11.1.

To find the pairs relevant to this type of hypothesis, note that it makes a definite assertion only about pairs that are dispersed on x, and this is so for both the positive and the negative forms. Thus, the pairs

Table 11.1. A Perfect No-Reversal Relation

y \ x	Very low	Low	Medium	High	Very high
Very high					100
High		100	100	100	100
Medium		100			
Low		100			
Very low	100				

NOTE: $\gamma = 1.000$; $d_{yx} = 0.750$, $d_{xy} = 0.819$; $e = 0.572$.

satisfying part (a) of the definition are those dispersed on x, the number of which is $C + D + T_y$. One of these pairs fits the positive form of the hypothesis if and only if it is either concordant or tied only on y, for in these cases, one individual is higher than the other on x and either higher or the same as, and thus not lower than, the other on y. Similarly, a pair fits the negative form if it is either discordant or tied only on y. Hence, by part (b) of the definition of relevant pairs, those that are tied only on y must be excluded, since they fit both the positive and the negative forms of a no-reversals hypothesis. Therefore, the number of relevant pairs is $C + D$, the number of these fitting the positive form is just C, and the number fitting the negative form is D. Hence the resulting measure of the extent to which the data fit a no-reversals hypothesis is

$$\gamma = \frac{C - D}{C + D},\tag{1}$$

which, of course, is Goodman and Kruskal's well-known measure.

Thus, the measure of association appropriate for investigating no-reversals hypotheses turns out to be the widely used γ. As will be seen below, moreover, γ is uniquely suited for this purpose, and it is not an appropriate measure for the remaining two types of hypotheses.

Asymmetric Hypotheses

The formal statement of a positive asymmetric ordinal hypothesis is that for all i and j,

if i is higher than j on x,
then i is higher than j on y.

The essential difference between no-reversal and asymmetric hypotheses is that a pair dispersed on x but tied on y fits both forms of a no-reversal hypothesis, but neither form of an asymmetric one. An example of a perfect asymmetric relation appears in Table 11.2.

Table 11.2. A Perfect Asymmetric Relation

y \ x	Low	Medium	High
Very high			100
High		100	
Medium		100	
Low		100	
Very low	100		

NOTE: $\gamma = 1.000$; $d_{yx} = 1.000$, $d_{xy} = 0.700$; $e = 0.700$.

It will be noted that, as with no-reversals hypotheses, a definite asser-
tion is made only for those pairs dispersed on x, of which there are $C + D + T_y$. In this case, however, only those pairs that are concordant fit
the positive form, while only those pairs that are discordant fit the
negative form. Hence the number of relevant pairs is simply $C + D + T_y$,
and the extent to which the data fit an asymmetric hypothesis is

$$d_{yx} = \frac{C - D}{C + D + T_y}, \tag{2}$$

which is Somers's asymmetric measure of association.

It should be noted that this type of hypothesis is logically asymmetri-
cal, since a perfect relation of y to x does not imply a perfect relation of
x to y. Thus, connected with an asymmetric hypothesis (that dispersion
on the independent variable is associated in a consistent way with dispersion on the dependent variable) is a *converse* hypothesis (that dispersion on the dependent variable is associated in a consistent way with
dispersion on the independent variable). An asymmetric hypothesis
does not logically imply its converse, however, and as can be seen in
Table 11.2, d_{yx} is $+1$; but d_{xy}, the appropriate measure for the converse, is 0.700.

Somers's d_{yx}, then, is the appropriate measure of association for investigating asymmetric hypotheses. Moreover, comparing Table 11.1
and Table 11.2, one can see that γ is not suitable for this purpose since
it is equal to 1 in Table 11.1 even though the relation is not a perfect
asymmetric one. And, d_{yx} is not appropriate for no-reversals hypotheses since it does not equal 1 in Table 11.1.

Strict Hypotheses

In formal terms, a positive strict ordinal hypothesis asserts that for all i
and j,

if i is higher than j on x,
then i is higher than j on y,
and if i and j are tied on x,
they are tied on y.

A strict hypothesis is equivalent to asserting simultaneously both an asymmetric hypothesis and its converse. Consequently, a strict hypothesis is always symmetric and amounts to asserting that x and y vary together. An example of a perfect strict ordinal relation is given in Table 11.3.

Table 11.3. A Perfect Strict Relation

y \ x	Very low	Low	Medium	High	Very high
Very high					100
High				100	
Medium			100		
Low		100			
Very low	100				

NOTE: $\gamma = 1.000$; $d_{yx} = 1.000$, $d_{xy} = 1.000$; $e = 1.000$.

It is clear that a strict ordinal hypothesis makes an assertion about every pair, the total number of which is $C + D + T_y + T_x + T_{xy}$. Of course, the pairs that satisfy the positive form are those that are either concordant or tied on both variables. Similarly, the pairs fitting the negative form are those that are discordant or else tied on both variables. Clearly, then, in terms of the definition, all pairs are relevant except those that are tied simultaneously on both variables, for the latter contribute no information distinguishing between the positive and negative forms. Hence, the extent to which the data fit a strict ordinal hypothesis is measured by

$$e = \frac{C - D}{C + D + T_y + T_x}. \tag{3}$$

This measure, which is called "e" here, may perhaps have appeared elsewhere in the widely scattered literature on ordinal association, but it is certainly not one of the better known or widely used ordinal statistics. Thus, while for no-reversal and asymmetric hypotheses the appropriate measures turn out to be already well known, for strict hypotheses an unfamiliar measure appears to be appropriate. Finally, it should be noted that neither γ nor d_{yx} is appropriate for investigating strict hypotheses, since both can assume the values $+1$ or -1 when not all the data fit a strict hypothesis, and e is similarly inappropriate for no-reversal and asymmetric hypotheses.[1]

Comparison of e *and Kendall's* τ_b

Because e is an unknown measure, it may be useful to compare some of its properties with another, more familiar statistic that might be used in the case of a strict hypothesis, namely, Kendall's τ_b, given by

$$\tau_b = \frac{C - D}{\sqrt{(C + D + T_x)(C + D + T_y)}}. \tag{4}$$

As is well known, τ_b, like e, takes the value $+1$ or -1 if and only if the data exhibit a perfect positive or a perfect negative strict ordinal relation, and, of course, both are zero when there is no association. Between these extremes, however, they generally differ, with e never greater than τ_b. This can be seen readily if the ratio of e to τ_b is examined, or, to avoid the square root stemming from the denominator of equation (4), the square of this ratio. To simplify the algebra, let $A = C + D$. Then

$$(e/\tau_b)^2 = \frac{(A + T_x)(A + T_y)}{(A + T_x + T_y)^2}. \tag{5}$$

A little algebra shows that equation (5) expands to equation (6), which is obviously less than one except when $T_x = T_y = 0$.

$$(e/\tau_b)^2 = \frac{(A + T_x)(A + T_y)}{(A + T_x)(A + T_y) + T_x{}^2 + T_y{}^2 + A(T_x + T_y) + T_x T_y}. \tag{6}$$

1. An interesting note is that the general model for "proportional-reduction-in-error" interpretations developed by Davis (1963) in connection with γ and applied by Somers (1968) to d_{yx} can be extended to e. The extension follows Somers exactly, with one addition: in case of a tie on the independent variable, a prediction is made according to the same procedure as employed when predicting without information concerning the independent variable, and error is determined by the same random device posited by Somers, with pairs tied on both variables excluded. It should be observed, however, in considering this interpretation for γ, d_{yx}, and e, that predictions from the independent to the dependent variable are made only for those pairs that are relevant in terms of the definition given above. Thus, no matter whether one prefers a proportional-reduction-in-error interpretation or the framework proposed here, the conclusion remains that γ, d_{yx}, and e are the appropriate measures for no-reversals, asymmetric, and strict hypotheses, respectively. The difficulties with proportional-reduction-in-error interpretations for ordinal variables (Wilson 1971) suggest, however, that the framework of interpretation proposed here is preferable.

Inspection of (5) shows that e and τ_b are identical if and only if there are no pairs tied on one variable but not on the other. This can be made more precise by examining the way the ratio (5) depends on the two quantities $T_x + T_y$ and $T_x - T_y$. Let $s = \frac{1}{2}(T_x + T_y)$ and $t = \frac{1}{2}(T_x - T_y)$. Then (5) simplifies to

$$(e/\tau_b)^2 = \frac{(A + s)^2 - t^2}{(A + 2s)^2}. \tag{7}$$

Consider first the partial derivitive of $(e/\tau_b)^2$ with respect to s:

$$\frac{\partial (e/\tau_b)^2}{\partial s} = \frac{2(2t^2 - A^2 - As)}{(A + 2s)^3}. \tag{8}$$

This will be negative except when $t^2 \geq \frac{1}{2}(A^2 + As)$, which occurs only when there is an extreme difference in the marginal dispersions on x and y (to see this, note that these dispersions are given by $U_x = A + T_y$ and $U_y = A + T_x$, respectively). Thus, except for these extreme cases, the ratio $(e/\tau_b)^2$ is a decreasing function of the number of pairs tied on one variable but not the other. In effect, such pairs represent a failure of the data to cluster along the main diagonal in a table, and thus e appears to be more sensitive than τ_b to the extent to which the data actually do cluster around the main diagonal.

These remarks are illustrated in Table 11.4, a two-by-two table for the case of identical marginal dispersions. In both parts of Table 11.4, $\tau_b = \frac{1}{2}$, which would indicate the same degree of association; however, e is smaller in Table 11.4b, which departs further from a symmetrical distribution around the main diagonal than Table 11.4a.

Next consider the partial derivative of $(e/\tau_b)^2$ with respect to t:

$$\frac{\partial (e/\tau_b)^2}{\partial t} = \frac{-2t}{(A + 2s)^2}. \tag{9}$$

Table 11.4. Examples with Equal τ_b's and Different e's.

A. Symmetrical around the diagonal				B. Unsymmetrical around the diagonal			
		x					*x*	
y		*Low*	*High*		*y*		*Low*	*High*
High		9	27		High		24	24
Low		27	9		Low		24	0

NOTE: $\tau_b = 0.5000$, $e = 0.3639$.   NOTE: $\tau_b = 0.5000$, $e = 0.333$.

This is clearly negative when t is positive, which means, in effect, that if two tables have equal values for s and A, the table with the larger t will have the smaller ratio of e to τ_b. Thus, e is more heavily penalized than τ_b for differences in marginal dispersion. For some purposes, this might be viewed as a defect of e in comparison with τ_b, but before accepting this conclusion, one ought to ask what notion of association, and in particular what type of hypothesis, he has in mind for which high association can go along with large differences in marginal dispersions. It may well be an asymmetric hypothesis in which case d_{yx} is the appropriate measure.

In summary, it appears that e may be superior to τ_b as a measure for strict ordinal hypotheses, in that it has a simple interpretation within a coherent model and has properties that one can argue are more suitable than those of τ_b for assessing the fit between data and a strict hypothesis. A definitive assessment, however, would also have to include an investigation of the sampling distribution of e, which is beyond the scope of this chapter (but see Quade, this volume, for relevant developments).

An Example

The appropriate choice of a measure of association is more than merely a purist's concern, for the conclusions reached in the analysis of a given set of data can depend crucially on the measure employed. Thus, since the use of a particular measure implies commitment to a particular type of hypothesis, clarity concerning the type of hypothesis under investigation is essential.

For illustration consider a hypothetical example. Suppose data on educational level, responsibility level, and field of training are gathered in a very large research-and-development organization. The relations between responsibility and education for all fields are given in Table 11.6, and for pure scientists and engineers separately in Table 11.7. But first consider Table 11.5, which presents the values of γ, d_{yx}, and e for the original relation and under the two control conditions. If the researcher begins with a no-reversals hypothesis, γ is the appropriate measure of association. Consequently, looking down the first column of

Table 11.5. Values of γ, d_{yx}, and e for Tables 11.6 and 11.7

Condition	γ	d_{yx}	e
Original relation	0.591	0.401	0.304
Pure science, including mathematics	0.743	0.320	0.143
Engineering	0.743	0.192	0.143

Table 11.6. Responsibility by Education

Responsibility level	Education level		
	B.S.	M.S.	Ph.D.
High*	0	200	55
Medium†	200	100	55
Low‡	55	55	0
Total	255	355	110

NOTE: Data are hypothetical.
*Has served as director or codirector of a project.
†Participates in formulation of projects.
‡All others.

Table 11.5, he will see that γ is relatively high for the bivariate relation between education and responsibility and that it increases when a control for field is introduced. Thus, the researcher can conclude that responsibility is strongly related to education, irrespective of field.

If, however, an asymmetric hypothesis is under investigation, the appropriate measure is d_{yx}. Consequently, inspecting the second column of Table 11.5, the researcher concludes that the effect of education on responsibility is fairly strong among pure scientists, but fairly weak among engineers. This strongly suggests that engineers and pure scientists have different opportunities in the organization, an interpretation directly opposed to what the researcher might conclude on the basis of γ.

Finally, if the researcher is interested in the extent to which differ-

Table 11.7. Responsibility by Education, by Field

Responsibility level	Educational level		
	B.S.	M.S.	Ph.D.
	Pure science, including mathematics		
High	0	200	50
Medium	0	50	5
Low	5	50	0
Total	5	300	55
	Engineering		
High	0	0	5
Medium	200	50	50
Low	50	5	0
Total	250	55	55

NOTE: Data are hypothetical.

ences and similarities in responsibility are explained by differences and similarities in education, he is concerned with a strict hypothesis, and the appropriate measure is e. In this case, although e is moderately high for the sample as a whole, it is quite low when the control for field is introduced. Among pure scientists, then, there is a sizable variation in responsibility that is not attributable to education (in Table 11.7, note particularly those scientists with a middle level of education), even though education has a strong effect. Thus, e drops to 0.143, while d_{yx} drops only to the relatively high value of 0.320. In contrast, among engineers the effect of education is much smaller ($d_{yx} = 0.192$), but much of the existing variation in responsibility is associated with variation in education (this is indicated by the converse asymmetric measure, $d_{xy} = 0.320$). Therefore, although education has a strong effect on responsibility among scientists, and little effect among engineers, it is not a particularly good explanation within either group. Clearly, a more complex set of processes needs to be taken into account if we are to understand what is going on.

Discussion

The foregoing example illustrates the importance of clarity concerning the type of hypothesis under investigation and of selection of an appropriate measure of association. In addition, the discussion of the strict hypothesis stresses the considerable insight gained by taking account of the asymmetric relation and its converse through the use of d_{yx} and d_{xy} as well as e. This is perhaps not surprising, since a strict hypothesis is the logical conjunction, or simultaneous assertion, of an asymmetric hypothesis with its converse. As a general recommendation, then, it appears to be useful to compute d_{yx}, d_{xy}, and e, and the interpretation should take account of the information given by all three. Moreover, γ and τ_b contribute no new information:[2] by elementary algebra it is easy to verify that

$$\frac{1}{\gamma} = \frac{1}{d_{yx}} + \frac{1}{d_{xy}} - \frac{1}{e} , \tag{10}$$

and there is the well-known relation $\tau = \pm (d_{yx}d_{xy})^{1/2}$.

It may be noted that the practice of almost always presenting the percentage tables as well as the measures of association serves as a protection against gross misinterpretation of data resulting from confusion

---

2. As can be seen from equation (10) below, from a mathematical point of view, any three of the four measures γ, d_{yx}, d_{xy}, and e contain all the information. The reason for preferring the last three as a standard set instead of the first three is that asymmetric and strict hypotheses seem to be of the greatest substantive interest.

about the type of hypothesis and from the use of an inappropriate measure of association. For example, no researcher is likely to be misled by the γ's resulting from Tables 11.6 and 11.7 into asserting that pure scientists and engineers fare equally well in the hypothetical organization, since it is obvious from the tables themselves that something else is going on. Such means of avoiding difficulty, however, defeat the very purpose of employing a measure of association in the first place, since in this case the measure is treated, not as representing in a consistent way certain properties of the data relevant to their interpretation, but rather as some sort of window dressing that can be dispensed with whenever convenient. Consequently, if measures of association are to be used at all, they should be chosen with careful attention to the kinds of information they actually represent about the data and the relevance of that information to the interpretations the researcher wishes to make.

Conclusion

A general framework has been proposed for constructing measures of association for bivariate ordinal hypotheses. The fundamental requirement is that the kind of relation concerning which evidence is sought be stated clearly and precisely. Such a formulation is essential for specifying what is to constitute perfect association and what is to count as evidence for and evidence against the hypothesis that a relation of the stated kind exists in the data. For metric data, this requirement is met routinely with the formulation of a numerical algebraic model, the parameters of which are estimated by regression techniques and whose degree of fit is assessed by correlation methods. For ordinal data, numerical algebraic models are unavailable, and so three general types of ordinal relations are identified: no-reversals, asymmetric, and strict. Further, because ordinal variables permit the notion of direction, each type of relation can appear in a positive or a negative form. Association is then measured by taking the difference between the proportion of pairs conforming to the positive form and the proportion conforming to the negative form, among those pairs relevant to the hypothesis, where the relevant pairs are those concerning which the hypothesis makes a prediction but which do not simultaneously conform to both the positive and negative forms. Within this framework, the appropriate measure for each of the three types of ordinal hypotheses is obtained: γ for the no-reversals case, Somers's d_{yx} for the asymmetric case, and a new measure, e, for the strict case. Each of these measures is uniquely suited to its particular application, and the differences among them are such that serious errors of interpretation can result from failure to be clear about the type of relation under investigation. However, because of the logical relation of a strict hypothesis to the corresponding asymmetric hypothesis and its converse, the most reasonable recommendation seems to be that, unless one is specifically interested in a hypothesis of no reversals, one should routinely compute d_{yx}, d_{xy}, and e and employ all three in interpreting the data.

It should be noted that the major difference between the three types of hypotheses concerns the status of ties, but the ties that matter are those occurring on one variable but not on the other. Thus, those pairs tied on both variables, the number of which is T_{xy}, are not relevant to any of the hypotheses considered here. We can in fact state the following theorem:

$$\gamma = d_{yx} \quad \text{if and only if} \quad T_y = 0,$$

and

$$\gamma = d_{xy} \quad \text{if and only if} \quad T_x = 0;$$

$$d_{yx} = d_{xy} = \tau_b \quad \text{if and only if} \quad T_y = T_x; \tag{11}$$

$$\tau_b = e \quad \text{if and only if} \quad T_y = T_x = 0.$$

Thus, it is clear that these measures approach one another in value as the number of pairs tied on one variable, but not on the other, diminishes.

The source of ties is generally held to be measurement error, a notion based on the model of an underlying continuous distribution, for which ties have probability zero. Such a model leads one to expect that, under conditions of comparable measurement precision for both variables and an underlying strict relation between them, two cases so close together on one variable as to appear tied should also be close enough together on the other variable to appear tied. However, if one variable is measured with substantially less precision than the other, a large number of pairs tied on that variable but not on the other will be created, which will reduce the value of e (or τ_b). This suggests that where a strict hypothesis is under consideration, which is probably the usual case when the hypothesis follows from some theory, it might be useful to compare the values of T_y and T_x; for if these differ greatly, it may indicate that one variable has been measured significantly less precisely than the other. In such a case, it is not clear what the best strategy would be, but one suggested by Table 11.2 is the use of d_{yx}, where x is the less precisely measured variable. For it can be seen from the table and equation (2) that pairs tied only on x do not directly affect d_{yx}, and if many of such pairs are the result of imprecise measurement, it may be well to reduce their importance. If the variables are both crudely measured, but equally so, however, it seems inappropriate to disregard ties as irrelevant, because, on the assumption of comparable measurement precision, this would amount to discarding or ignoring evidence against a strict hypothesis.

Finally, a word should be said about the decision to use ordinal variables in the first place. There are sound reasons for avoiding metric techniques when the assignments of numerical scores cannot be justified directly by the measurement procedures, but recourse to ordinal variables is not a fully satisfactory solution. On the one hand, even a strict bivariate ordinal hypothesis does not adequately represent a theoretically formulated relation between two variables (Wilson 1971); and, on the other hand, in contrast with the metric case, where numerical algebraic models are available, no clear formulation of a multivariate ordinal hypothesis in strictly ordinal terms seems to be available. Thus, current proposals for ordinal multivariate analysis, such as those developed in this volume, must be viewed as methodological explorations whose applications to substantive social science research await a clear statement of what relations are under investigation, and a precise, empirically relevant interpretation of the numerical results of the computations.

In sum, until more adequate ordinal models are formulated in strictly ordinal terms, particularly at the multivariate level, or fully adequate and justifiable interval and ratio measurement is attained, ordinal and metric statistical procedures in social science research should be treated as heuristic devices for interpreting social phenomena, devices that must be supplemented by, and cross-checked with, information of other, perhaps more informal though no less valid, sorts. But this is no counsel to abandon intellectual rigor: rather, it is recognition that sound scholarship depends upon recognition and acknowledgment of the methodological limitations of one's data and of one's conclusions.

References

Costner, Herbert L.
    1965. "Criteria for Measures of Association." *American Sociological Review* 30 (June):341-353.
Davis, James A.
    1963. "Notes on Gamma: Interpretations, Computation, Partials, Multiples." Mimeographed.
Goodman, Leo, and William Kruskal
    1954. "Measures of Association for Cross Classifications I." *Journal of the American Statistical Association* 49 (December):732-764.
Leik, Robert K., and Walter Gove
    1969. "The Conception and Measurement of Asymmetric Monotonic Relationships in Sociology." *American Journal of Sociology* 74 (May):676-709.
Morris, Raymond N.
    1970. "Multiple Correlation and Ordinally Scaled Data." *Social Forces* 48 (March):299-311.
Somers, Robert H.
    1962. "A New Asymmetric Measure of Association." *American Sociological Review* 27 (December):799-811.
    1968. "On the Measurement of Association." *American Sociological Review* 33 (April):291-292.
Wilson, Thomas P.
    1969. "A Proportional-Reduction-in-Error Interpretation for Kendall's tau-b." *Social Forces* 47 (March):340-342.
    1971. "Critique of Ordinal Variables." *Social Forces* 49 (March):432-444.

Chapter 12

ORDINAL MEASURES OF ASSOCIATION AND THE GENERAL LINEAR MODEL

DONALD R. PLOCH

Donald R. Ploch is currently Director of the Sociology Program, Division of Social Sciences, National Science Foundation. He received his Ph.D. from the University of North Carolina in 1968. His research interests have centered in the sociology of religion, social stratification, and statistical applications, particularly in the use of ordinal variables to test sociological hypotheses.

Within the last few years much progress has been made in the interpretation and use of measures of association for ordinal data. It is now quite clear that these measures can be used in causal analysis (e.g. Reynolds 1971; and Chapter 14 in this volume) and that they can be considered in the framework of the general linear model (e.g. see Kendall 1962; Somers 1959, 1962a; Quade 1967; Hawkes 1971). It is important to develop the analogy to the general linear model because it will have a pay-off in later research. Once measurement is improved, as it must be, researchers can use results based on ordinal measures of association to anticipate or predict results based on interval levels of measurement. In the meantime, patterns of association between variables, even the flow of causal influence, can be detected and elaborated. Thus this chapter will concentrate on Kendall's tau, Goodman and Kruskal's gamma, Somers's *d*, and derived statistics to show how ordinal measures of association can be used in the framework of the general linear model. A considerable start in this direction has been made by Kendall, Somers (1959), Reynolds, and Hawkes. While some of the results are tentative, enough is known to merit increased use of the general linear model with ordinal measures of association.

343

Spearman's Rho

Spearman's rho (r_s) is a product-moment correlation of the ranks. If one assumes that the ranks can be used as variable scores, then computation of the Pearson product-moment correlation (r) yields r_s. In general this is equivalent to assuming equal intervals; that is, the distance between ranks 1 and 2 is considered the same as that between ranks 3 and 4.

Kruskal (1958) has provided two ways of interpreting r_s that do not depend on rank differences. Both of these involve probabilities of concordance and discordance of direction of rank differences on three observations. Basically he shows that r_s is a measure of net concordance (over discordance) for the two crossed pairs from three observations. The interpretations are more difficult to grasp than the traditional one based on rank differences. Further, if one uses Spearman's rho in order to get a function rule relating rankings on X to those on Y, or, like Quade (1967), to do covariance analysis, one ought to use the traditional interpretation rather than Kruskal's reinterpretation.

The ability to compute r_s with algorithms appropriate to r leads to the temptation to test r_s for significance with procedures based on the distribution of r. If the variable distributions are more or less normal, this is appropriate. If they are not, careful attention to the tests for r_s is in order. Because r_s can be computed with algorithms for r, and because these algorithms are readily available at most computer centers, computation will not be discussed.

Similarities between r_s and r provide a useful framework for interpreting r_s. In general, r_s is a measure of our ability to predict one set of ranks from another. Without modification, the procedure assumes that the function rule relating the sets of ranks will be linear. Thus, given the rank of an observation on X, one predicts its value on Y by means of a linear function rule such as

$$\hat{Y} = a + bX. \tag{1}$$

This is a familiar linear equation. Though it is not generally used with r_s, it is clear that b is the number of ranks shifted by Y relative to a single rank shift of X. The intercept, a, is the predicted rank of Y when the rank of X is zero. If it is not possible for the rank of X to be zero, this interpretation, while meaningful, does not deal with the part of the line segment of interest. Since the whole procedure of measurement and data analysis is an abstraction, this particular extension of the abstraction should not cause any consternation.

Given the analogy to this point, it is apparent that r_s^2 is a coefficient of determination and $1 - r_s^2$ a coefficient of alienation. Thus r_s^2 is a proportional reduction in error (PRE) statistic that tells one how closely the observations cluster about a linear function.

If one is able or willing to assume that ranks can be treated as scores, the possible modifications of r_s depend only on one's imagination. Just as one transforms scores to see if the relationship is some nonlinear function, so can one transform ranks. Mathematically there is nothing to prevent analysis based on, say,

$$\hat{Y} = a + bX + cX^2 \tag{2}$$

or

$$\log \hat{Y} = \log a + b \log X. \tag{3}$$

The fewer the ranks, the less likely it is that one would try these fancy tricks. It must be understood, however, that these tricks are possible and quite meaningful once one assumes that ranks can be treated as measured scores. If one assumes the best possible measurement for his data, one then has access to the most powerful techniques. There are times when either modesty or reality prevails and one seeks measures of association with less stringent measurement assumptions. Such a set of measures is the one based on pair scores.

Measures Based on Pair Scores

In measures based on pairs of observations, the score given the pair identifies the direction of the difference between observations; that is, it identifies the larger but does not specify the magnitude of the difference. While one can no longer concentrate on individual observations as one does when measurement is interval, the use of pairs has some redeeming features. It forces the researcher into an explicit comparative framework. One must speak of a difference between observations. If X can be changed in a certain direction, one gains information about the probability that Y will change in the same direction. There is no doubt or argument that interval-level is better than ordinal-level measurement because it allows us to specify functional relations more completely (see Borgatta 1968 and Wilson 1971 for additional comment). Still, the use of pairs based on ordinal measures of association will allow us to analyze data within the framework of the general linear model. Thus we can anticipate results that should follow once better measurement is available.

By taking a random pair of observations from a sample, say the ith and jth, one can score the pair for the variable X:

$$x_{ij} = \begin{cases} +1 & \text{if} \quad X_i > X_j, \\ 0 & \text{if} \quad X_i = X_j, \\ -1 & \text{if} \quad X_i < X_j. \end{cases} \tag{4}$$

If one does the same for y_{ij} based on Y, a cross-classification such as that shown in Table 12.1 will be an exhaustive cross-partition of the pairs. It is important to bear this table in mind, since all measures of association based on pair scores can be referred to it. Though computing routines use tables of frequencies and are designed so that the information in Table 12.1 is all but invisible to the user, a firm grasp of Table 12.1 is essential. Both association and prediction are between pairs of observations, that is, between rows and columns of Table 12.1. Assuming a positive relationship between occupation and education, and that the statistic used to summarize the relationship is one of the set currently being discussed, then, for a pair of observations drawn at random, if the rank of the first observation is higher than the second on occupation, the rank of the first will be higher than the second on education. Association and prediction are between the direction of difference of two observations. This point cannot be overstressed.

Table 12.1. Cross-Classification of Pairs x_{ij}, y_{ij}

x_{ij} \ y_{ij}	$+$	0	$-$	x_{ij} total
$+$	½ C	½ T_y	½ D	½ Σx_{ij}^2
0	½ T_x	T_{xy}	½ T_x	$x_{ij} = 0$
$-$	½ D	½ T_y	½ C	½ Σx_{ij}^2
y_{ij} total	½ Σy_{ij}^2	$y_{ij} = 0$	½ Σy_{ij}^2	$n(n-1) =$ $C + D + T_{xy} + T_y + T_x$

NOTE: n = number of observations.

In Table 12.1 each of the cells is labeled according to the following scheme:

C = the number of concordant pairs
 = $X_i > X_j$ and $Y_i > Y_j$ $(+\ +)$,
    $X_i < X_j$ and $Y_i < Y_j$ $(-\ -)$;
D = the number of discordant pairs
 = $X_i < X_j$ and $Y_i > Y_j$ $(-\ +)$,
    $X_i > X_j$ and $Y_i < Y_j$ $(+\ -)$;
T_{xy} = the number of pairs tied on both variables
 = $X_i = X_j$ and $Y_i = Y_j$ $(0\ 0)$;

T_y = the number of pairs varying on X but tied on Y
$$= X_i < X_j \quad \text{and} \quad Y_i = Y_j \, (-\, 0),$$
$$X_i > X_j \quad \text{and} \quad Y_i = Y_j \, (+\, 0);$$
T_x = the number of pairs varying on Y but tied on X
$$= X_i = X_j \quad \text{and} \quad Y_i < Y_j \, (0\, -),$$
$$X_i = X_j \quad \text{and} \quad Y_i > Y_j \, (0\, +).$$
Further,

$$C + D + T_{xy} + T_y + T_x = n(n - 1), \tag{5}$$

where n is the number of observations.

Table 12.2. Cross-Classification of Ranks of X and Y

X ranks \ Y ranks	1	2	$\cdots$	J	Total
1	n_{11}	n_{12}	$\cdots$	n_{1J}	$n_1 \cdot$
2	n_{21}	n_{22}	$\cdots$	n_{2J}	$n_2 \cdot$
$\vdots$	$\vdots$	$\vdots$	$\vdots$	$\vdots$	$\vdots$
I	n_{I1}	n_{I2}	$\cdots$	n_{IJ}	$n_I \cdot$
Total	$n_{\cdot 1}$	$n_{\cdot 2}$	$\cdots$	$n_{\cdot J}$	$n_{\cdot \cdot}$

NOTE: The number of columns is $J \geq 2$, the number of rows $I \geq 2$, and i and j range from 1 to I and J, respectively. The dot subscript stands for summation; e.g., $n_2 \cdot$ is the summation over all columns in row 2, $n_{\cdot 1}$ the summation over all rows in column 1, and $n \cdot \cdot$ the summation over all rows and columns.

In a conventional table such as Table 12.2 the pairs are defined:
C = ++, the sum over all cells of the cell frequency times all cell frequencies down and to the right,
plus, −−, the sum over all cells of the cell frequency times all cell frequencies up and to the left;
D = +−, the sum over all cells of the cell frequencies times all cell frequencies down and to the left,
plus, −+, the sum over all cells of the cell frequency times all cell frequencies up and to the right;
T_{xy} = 00, the sum over all cells of the cell frequency times the cell frequency minus 1;
T_y = +0, the sum over all cells of the cell frequency times the sum of all frequencies below it in the same column,
plus, −0, the sum over all cells of the cell frequency times the sum of all frequencies above it in the same column;
T_x = 0+, the sum over all cells of the cell frequency times the sum of all frequencies to the right of it in the same row,
plus, −0, the sum over all cells of the cell frequency times the sum of all frequencies to the left of it in the same row.

Alternatively, T_y and T_x can be defined:

T_y = the sum over all cells of the cell frequency times the column total minus the cell frequency,

T_x = the sum over all cells of the cell frequency times the row total minus the cell frequency.

For the convenience of the computer these pairs can be defined:

$$C = \sum_{i=1}^{I} \sum_{j=1}^{J} n_{ij} \left(\sum_{i'=1}^{i-1} \sum_{j'=1}^{j-1} n_{i'j'} + \sum_{i'=i+1}^{I} \sum_{j'=j+1}^{J} n_{i'j'} \right) ; \qquad (6)$$

$$D = \sum_{i=1}^{I} \sum_{j=1}^{J} n_{ij} \left(\sum_{i'=1}^{i-1} \sum_{j'=j+1}^{J} n_{i'j'} + \sum_{i'=i+1}^{I} \sum_{j'=1}^{j-1} n_{i'j'} \right) ; \qquad (7)$$

$$T_y = \sum_{i=1}^{I} \sum_{j=1}^{J} n_{ij}(n_{i.} - n_{ij}) ; \qquad (8)$$

$$T_x = \sum_{i=1}^{I} \sum_{j=1}^{J} n_{ij}(n_{.j} - n_{ij}) ; \qquad (9)$$

$$T_{xy} = \sum_{i=1}^{I} \sum_{j=1}^{J} n_{ij}(n_{ij} - 1) . \qquad (10)$$

It should be noted that all definitions lead to the same numerical conclusions. The more forbidding set of equations is the more flexible, and the easier to use for giving a computer directions. The verbal description is intended for those who have trouble intuiting the meaning of summation equations. In any case, we are ready for the statistics themselves.

Kendall's Tau

Starting from data in which all observations were ranked and none were tied (a situation I shall call *fully ranked*), Kendall (1962)[1] observed that one could count concordant and discordant pairs and could speak of association between X and Y by the relative magnitudes of these types of pairs. A convenient summary was

$$S = C - D. \qquad (11)$$

But S was not really satisfactory, since its size depends on the number of pairs. The larger the number of pairs (or observations), the larger

1. In general, Kendall counted pairs in one direction only, for example, down and to the right, so that he got ½ C and ½ D. His other counts differ in the same way. Thus definitions of the statistics are equivalent to those given here, though counts of pairs are different.

the S, even if association could be said to be the same. It was desirable to standardize S so that the resulting statistic had the same value for similar association regardless of sample size. Since $n(n - 1)$ was the number of pairs that could be drawn from n observations, and $C + D = n(n - 1)$ (remember, there are no ties), it was appropriate to define tau,

$$\tau = \frac{S}{n(n - 1)} = \frac{C - D}{n(n - 1)} = \frac{C - D}{C + D}. \tag{12}$$

This definition has the further virtue of ranging from $+1$, perfect positive association, to -1, perfect negative association.

Operationally, if one knows the difference of ranks of a pair of observations on X and bets that the difference of rank on Y is the same as that on X, and if the outcome is the winning or losing of a dollar, then τ dollars will be the expected winnings. Put another way, if one predicts direction of difference in occupational status to be the same as direction of difference in educational status (again no tied statuses), then τ is the net proportion of correct predictions from knowing the educational status, and τ times $n(n - 1)$ is the net number of correct predictions. It should be noted that, if τ is negative, the prediction rule used here will yield a negative winning (a loss), or more errors than correct predictions. The obvious solution is to bet discordance if τ is negative.

Costner (1965) has shown that under this operational definition τ is a PRE measure. Without knowledge of a second variable, one's error rate in predicting which of two observations has the larger rank will be .5. If $\tau \geq 0$, and one predicts concordance, the error rate is

$$D/(C + D), \tag{13}$$

and the PRE statistic is

$$\text{PRE} = \frac{.5 - D/(C + D)}{.5} = \tau. \tag{14}$$

If $\tau < 0$, and one predicts discordance, the error rate is

$$C/(C + D), \tag{13a}$$

and the PRE statistic is

$$\text{PRE} = \frac{.5 - C/(C + D)}{.5} = |\tau|. \tag{14a}$$

Alternatively, if one restricts prediction so that one predicts concordance and discordance with a proportion equal to the probability of their occurrence, a new PRE statistic develops. If one does not know a second variable, the error rate for predicting which observation has the higher rank is still .5. If one does know a second variable, one predicts concordance with probability

$$p(C) = C/(C + D),\qquad(15)$$

and discordance with probability

$$p(D) = D/(C + D).\qquad(16)$$

When one predicts concordance, the error rate is the probability of discordance, $p(D)$; when one predicts discordance, the error rate is $p(C)$. Thus one predicts concordance with probability $p(C)$ and expects errors with probability $p(D)$. Since these events are independent, $p(C)p(D)$ is the proportion of time one would expect to predict concordance and be in error. Similarly, one predicts discordance with probability $p(D)$ and expects errors with probability $p(C)$; thus, $p(D)p(C)$ is the proportion of time one would expect to predict discordance and be in error. Since predictions of discordance and concordance are mutually exclusive, the total error rate is the error rate for concordance plus that for discordance, or

$$2p(C)p(D) = 2CD/(C + D)^2.\qquad(17)$$

The PRE statistic is

$$\text{PRE} = \frac{.5 - 2CD/(C + D)^2}{.5} = \tau^2\ .\qquad(18)$$

Thus τ^2 is a PRE statistic if one restricts prediction so that predicted outcomes have the same probability as actual outcomes. Operationally, one would predict concordance with probability $p(C)$ and discordance with probability $p(D)$. For any one pair the decision would be concordant or discordant. For the long run, probabilities would be $p(C)$ and $p(D)$, and PRE would be τ^2.

Tied Ranks

The last example raises the most pressing problem with this statistic. Social science data are full of ties. Though Kendall worked with very small samples and did not anticipate many ties, he did suggest modifications of τ for data with ties. The first of these was

$$\tau_a = \frac{C - D}{n(n - 1)}\ .\qquad(19)$$

In this case $C + D$ does not equal $n(n - 1)$. Ties on either variable are considered errors of measurement, and the statistic is attenuated by including those pairs in the denominator but not in the numerator. In effect, one pays an immediate and visible price for errors. The measure seems most appropriate when one set of observations is known to be ranked without ties and the second set is an attempt to reproduce the first. For example, the ordering of color discs on a green-red continuum as a test for color blindness, or the attempt to predict from the order of birth (multiple births *not* counted as ties) to some other characteristic.

Since these types of situations do not occur frequently for social scientists, the measure does not seem particularly useful. Further, the penalty for ties is excessive when one considers that ties are inevitable in most social scientific problems. If one has 100 observations to be ranked according to five social classes, ties are inevitable. Errors of measurement include, not only aggregation, but also misclassification. It seems appropriate not to penalize for the former, since the researcher ought to know that this error is occurring, nor to directly penalize for the latter, since presumably the researcher has done his best to minimize this. Thus a more appropriate measure is

$$\tau_b = \frac{C - D}{\sqrt{C + D + T_y}\ \sqrt{C + D + T_x}},$$ (20)

where the denominator is the geometric mean of the number of pairs that vary on each variable. There are reasons for this choice that I shall discuss later.

One virtue of τ_b is that it ranges from $+1$ to -1, though it reaches its maximum only for square tables (number of ranks on X = number of ranks on Y). There is no easy operational explanation. Ties on one variable not matched by ties on the other are considered errors. A direct and visible penalty is exacted by including such pairs in the denominator but not the numerator. Wilson (1969) has developed a PRE interpretation of τ_b^2. It is possible to develop a more direct PRE interpretation based on analogy between τ_b and r. This is deferred until the next section.

Because τ_b reaches its maximum only for square tables, it seemed desirable to correct for this deficiency. The logic is that, if one starts with five occupational and four educational statuses, a perfect match is impossible. In effect, to report τ_b is to imply that this difference in number of ranks (or categories) is an error. This is like saying that if the experimental design were better, the ranks would be equal. If on the other hand, the number of ranks is fixed and not subject to experimental control, to report τ_b is to pay a penalty for the arbitrary and

capricious structure of the empirical world. While this is manifestly un-
fair, it seems to be far less a problem than is generally assumed.

The one available correction, called τ_c by Kendall,[2] is to correct τ_a.
The correction causes τ_a to approximate τ_b in size. In a limited range of
experimental results including Kendall's initial work, τ_c seems a quick
and dirty way to arrive at an estimate of τ_b.

On the whole it seems desirable to report the coefficients as they fall
rather than to search for ways to increase their sizes. One suspects that
social science suffers more from the drive to report the highest available measure of association, regardless of its appropriateness, than from
the arbitrary and capricious nature of the empirical world.[3] In addition, τ_b is not difficult to compute and fits the analogy of the general
linear model better than either τ_a or τ_c.

In the years since Kendall published, there have been other modifications of tau proposed. The most popular and enduring of these has
been gamma defined by Goodman and Kruskal (1954):

$$\gamma = \frac{C-D}{C+D}.$$ (21)

Here, all tied pairs are considered nonrelevant. The researcher thus
gets the highest possible measure of association of this type, since he
omits error based on aggregation and that based on certain misclassifi-
cations. One limits prediction to those pairs that vary on both variables.

If one is considering the association between education and occupation, gamma summarizes a hypothesis of no reversals (see the previous
chapter by Wilson). Thus if gamma is positive, and

$$\text{if } X_i > X_j, \quad \text{then} \quad Y_i \geq Y_j.$$ (22)

While tau summarizes a linear relationship between pairs, gamma
summarizes a monotonic one. Tau reaches its maximum value only if
all cases are on the diagonal. Gamma reaches its maximum for this case
and for many others.

Since definitions of τ and γ are identical when tied pairs are ignored
(cf. eq. [12] and [21]), it is apparent that PRE interpretations of τ and
τ^2 hold for γ and γ^2. The difference consists in whether one makes the
most efficient prediction (always predict concordance or discordance)
or whether one predicts outcomes with a probability equal to their oc-
currence. In the former situation PRE is τ or γ; in the latter, τ^2 or γ^2.

---

2. Correction $\tau_c = \left[(n-1)/n\right]\left[m/(m-1)\right]\tau_a$, where n equals the number of cases and m
equals the number of cells in the longest diagonal.

3. This argument parallels that for maximum values of phi given by Costner (1965,
p. 352).

A General Theory of Correlation

All the statistics given above are analogs of the product-moment correlation coefficient in that they are symmetrical (it makes no difference which variable is independent or dependent). The analogy has been pressed in work by Daniels (1944), Kendall (1962) and Somers (1959). Kendall summarized Daniels's work, showing that if one created x_{ij} as the difference between x_i and x_j, different scoring conventions followed by the same mathematics would lead to different measures of association. Thus, if X_i and X_j are interval scores and Y_i and Y_j are the same, defining $x_{ij} = X_i - X_j$ and $y_{ij} = Y_i - Y_j$ leads to

$$\sum_{ij} x_{ij}^2 = 2n\sum_i (X_i - \overline{X})^2 \ , \tag{23}$$

$$\sum_{ij} x_{ij} y_{ij} = 2n\sum_i (X_i - \overline{X})(Y_i - \overline{Y}) \ , \tag{24}$$

and the product-moment correlation is

$$r = \frac{\sum x_{ij} y_{ij}}{\sqrt{\sum x_{ij}^2 \sum y_{ij}^2}} \ . \tag{25}$$

If X_i, X_j, Y_i, and Y_j are ranks for observations, then scoring $x_{ij} = X_i - X_j$ and $y_{ij} = Y_i - Y_j$ yields Spearman's rho,

$$r_s = \frac{\sum x_{ij} y_{ij}}{\sqrt{\sum x_{ij}^2 \sum y_{ij}^2}} \ , \tag{26}$$

or r_s is the analog to r when ranks are used as scores.[4]

Finally if x_{ij} and y_{ij} are scored as in equations (4), that is, $+1$ if $X_i > X_j$, 0 if $X_i = X_j$, -1 if $X_i < X_j$,

$$\tau = \frac{\sum x_{ij} y_{ij}}{\sqrt{\sum x_{ij}^2 \sum y_{ij}^2}} = \frac{C - D}{\sqrt{(C + D + T_y)(C + D + T_x)}} . \tag{27}$$

This is τ_b (20), which reduces to τ in the special case in which the data

4. See Schussler (1971, p. 389) for an alternative derivation of r_s.

are fully ranked. The analogy to r is a principal reason for taking the geometric mean rather than the arithmetic mean of the pairs. The geometric mean will yield the same value as the numerator if association is perfect. The arithmetic mean may not. In fact, use of the arithmetic mean may allow the statistic to exceed the bounds ± 1.

In a variety of articles Somers (1959, 1962*a*, 1968) has expanded this position. He defined the statistic d_{yx} as an analog of b_{yx} (1962*a*), that is, $d_{yx} : \tau :: b_{yx} : r$. Specifically,

$$d_{yx} = \frac{C - D}{C + D + T_y} = \frac{\Sigma x_{ij} y_{ij}}{\Sigma x_{ij}^2},$$ (28)

and

$$\tau_b^2 = d_{yx} d_{xy} = \frac{\Sigma x_{ij} y_{ij}}{\Sigma x_{ij}^2} \cdot \frac{\Sigma x_{ij} y_{ij}}{\Sigma y_{ij}^2}.$$ (29)

Somers's d is an asymmetric measure of prediction.

The analogy between d_{yx} and b_{yx} may help to clarify the meaning of d_{yx}. The term b_{yx} is a function rule. It states the mapping function from X to Y based on units of measurement of X and Y. If either of these units is changed, b_{yx} changes. If one looks back to the coding of x_{ij} and y_{ij} for r and τ_b, one sees that, for τ_b, pair scores are restricted to $+1$, 0, and -1. Thus if d_{yx} is also a mapping function, and if one knows the value of x_{ij}, then d_{yx} is the estimate of the pair score on Y. But pair scores on Y are restricted to -1, 0, and $+1$. Thus, except for these three cases, prediction of d_{yx} is prediction of a score that cannot occur. On the other hand, think of the distribution of Y pair scores as having a mean and variation about that mean. This variation can be seen as composed of two parts: that explained by x_{ij}, and error. The best prediction of y_{ij} is $d_{yx} x_{ij}$ because it will yield the minimum error variation. This is seen graphically in Figure 12.1. Recall from Table 12.1 that the numbers of $(++)$ and $(--)$ pairs are equal, as are the numbers of $(+-)$ and $(-+)$ pairs, of $(+0)$ and (-0) pairs, and of $(0+)$ and $(0-)$ pairs. Means of x_{ij} and y_{ij} are zero. Thus a regression through this set will pass through 0, 0 and its slope will be d_{yx}. Unless marginal distributions are widely variant, pairs $(+0)$, (-0), $(0+)$, and $(0-)$ will have approximately equal frequencies. The slope is determined by relative frequencies of pairs $(+-)$, $(--)$ and $(++)$, $(-+)$. Differences between d_{yx} and d_{xy} are due to relative densities of pairs $(+0)$, (-0), $(0+)$, $(0-)$. Note that this discussion of d_{yx} does not hinge on knowing that $x_{ij} \neq 0$. If $x_{ij} = 0$, the prediction is $y_{ij} = 0$; if $x_{ij} = \pm 1$, the prediction is $y_{ij} = \pm d_{yx}$.

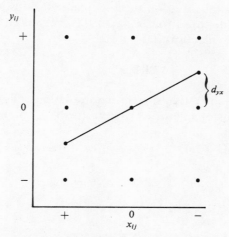

Figure 12.1. Graph of regression of y_{ij} on x_{ij}.

In analogy with b_{yx}, this is the best predictor of y_{ij} in the sense that it minimizes squared deviation about the mean of y_{ij}.

Another contribution of Somers (1959) was to show that if scores for x_{ij}; y_{ij} were seen as a matrix with a row for each pair and a column for each variable, by labeling this matrix XY one would get Σx_{ij}^2, Σy_{ij}^2, and $\Sigma x_{ij}y_{ij}$ from the first moment of XY.

$$(XY)'XY = \begin{bmatrix} \Sigma x_{ij}^2 & \Sigma x_{ij}y_{ij} \\ \Sigma x_{ij}y_{ij} & \Sigma y_{ij}^2 \end{bmatrix} \tag{30}$$

Use of the prediction equation

$$\hat{y}_{ij} = d_{yx}x_{ij} \tag{31}$$

leads to:

$$\text{Variation explained} = d_{yx}^2 \, (C + D + T_y). \tag{32}$$

Substituting equation (28) and manipulating algebraically leads to

$$d_{yx} \, (C - D) = d_{yx} \, \Sigma x_{ij}y_{ij}. \tag{33}$$

This is directly analogous to the ordinary least-squares estimator of the sums of squares due to regression. A PRE statistic would be

$$\text{PRE} = \frac{d_{yx} \, \Sigma x_{ij}y_{ij}}{\Sigma y_{ij}^2}, \tag{34}$$

where Σy_{ij}^2 is the total variation to be explained. Substitution of equation (28), and the identities for $\Sigma x_{ij}y_{ij}$ and Σy_{ij}^2 from equation (27), will show with very little algebra that

$$\text{PRE} = \tau_b^2. \tag{35}$$

It is a short step to show that matrix manipulation will yield τ_b and d_{yx}. Given X^* as a vector of x_{ij} and Y^* as a vector of y_{ij}, then

$$d_{yx} = X^{*\prime}Y^*(X^{*\prime}X^*)^{-1} \tag{36}$$

and

$$\tau_b^2 = d_{yx}X^{*\prime}Y^*/Y^{*\prime}Y^*$$

$$= X^{*\prime}Y^*(X^{*\prime}X^*)^{-1}X^{*\prime}Y^*/Y^{*\prime}Y^*. \tag{37}$$

Hawkes (1971), combining this with work done by Somers for partial $d_{yx.z}$ (1968), Kendall (1962) for partial $\tau_{yx.z}$, and Moran (1951) for multiple $\tau_{y.xz}$, has urged matrix manipulation for all these statistics. The argument presented below parallels that given by Hawkes.

Kendall showed that

$$\tau_{yx.z} = \frac{\tau_{yx} - \tau_{yz}\tau_{xy}}{\sqrt{(1 - \tau_{yz}^2)(1 - \tau_{xy}^2)}}, \tag{38}$$

which parallels the definition of partial $r_{yx.z}$.

Moran showed that

$$(\tau_{y.xz})^2 = \frac{\tau^2_{yz} + \tau^2_{yx} - 2\tau_{yx}\tau_{yz}\tau_{xz}}{1 - \tau_{xz}^2}, \tag{39}$$

which parallels multiple $(R_{y.xz})^2$.

Kendall thought that the parallel was coincidental, and this view seems to have prevailed. However, if one defines a matrix, X^*, with rows for pairs and columns for $x_{ij}, \cdots, x_{ij(p)}$, and a vector, Y^*, for pairs y_{ij}, then a vector of partial Somers's d_{yx} is

$$\hat{D} = (X^{*\prime}X^*)^{-1}X^{*\prime}Y^*. \tag{40}$$

The case with two independent variables was discussed by Somers

(1968). In addition, if one takes $Y^{*\prime}Y^*$ as the variation to be explained, then variation explained by a function rule (an analog of regression) is

$$V_{\text{reg}} = \hat{D}' \ (X^{*\prime}Y^*) \tag{41}$$

and

$$\tau_b{}^2 \text{ (multiple)} = V_{\text{reg}}/Y^{*\prime}Y^*. \tag{42}$$

It is clear that analogies between τ_b and r are not coincidental. Multiples and partials are defined by the same mathematical procedures but from different starting points. We should expect completely parallel structures.

A New Step

It seems evident that one can carry the analogy further. For the product-moment, standard equations are defined where the coefficient b^*_{yx} is equal to r_{yx} in the bivariate case. In the multivariate case partial $b^*_{yx.z}$ compared to $b^*_{yz.x}$ is an indicator of the relative strengths of X and Z in explaining variation in Y. Specifically,

$$\hat{B}^* = C^{-1}R \ , \tag{43}$$

where C is a matrix of correlation coefficients for all independent variables, R is a vector of correlation coefficients between independent and dependent variables, and $\hat{B}^*$ is a vector of estimated standard coefficients.

If C^{-1} and R are composed of τ_b's, then

$$\hat{D}^* = C^{-1}R \tag{44}$$

and $\hat{D}^*$ are estimated standard Somers's d. If C^{-1} and R are composed of r_s's, then

$$\hat{B}^*_s = C^{-1}R \tag{45}$$

and $\hat{B}^*_s$ are estimated standard coefficients not yet named. In each case the coefficients estimate the relative effects of all the independent variables in the same equation.

Some researchers (Boyle 1970; Klatzky and Hodge 1971) have argued that using marginal frequencies to standardize categorical data is improper because standardization then depends on marginal distributions. But it is clear from the analogy that standardization is the same for categorical or interval data. In both cases the coefficients are standardized for differences in variation; in both cases this variation is a function of marginal distributions. It is just that in the interval case we rarely look at marginal distributions; so we are less aware of their influence.

There is nothing to prevent application of multivariate measures to these statistics. A matrix of τ_b's or r_s's could be factor analyzed to determine clusters or reduction of dimensions. Or one could use such a matrix to test path-analysis models.

Insofar as these techniques refer to presence or absence of association, there is no problem. Where they estimate relative strengths of associations, there is no problem. And if one exercises reasonable restraint, there is little problem in discussing forms of relationships. One must be aware that statistics for ordered sets are insensitive to ordinal transformation of the variables; therefore, no metric inferences can be made.

On the positive side, if $\tau_b = 0$, the researcher screens out more forms of relationships between X and Y than he does if $r = 0$. When $r = 0$ there is no linear relationship between X and Y. But r may not be equal to zero if either X or Y or both are transformed to alter the metric, but not the order, of observation. If $\tau_b = 0$, it will be zero for all transformations which change metric, or distance between categories, but not order. In addition, presence of association, indicated by r, is restricted to the metric in hand, and one should test to see if some other theoretically acceptable metric (e.g., log transform) will yield a higher r. Conversely, no ordinal transformation will increase the value of τ_b.

A Worked Example

For purposes of this example 100 observations on four variables were created from random normal deviates generated by the IBM subroutine Gauss. They were defined as

$$\begin{aligned} X_2 &= .8X_1 + .6e_2, \\ X_3 &= .8X_2 + .6e_3, \\ X_4 &= .8X_3 + .6e_4, \end{aligned} \tag{46}$$

where X_1, e_2, e_3, and e_4 were generated from Gauss. All variables have expected mean of zero and variance of one. In addition, each variable was trichotomized with the cutpoints

1. $-\infty < L \leq -.67$,
2. $-.67 < M < .67$,
3. $.67 \leq H < +\infty$.

The expected distribution for 100 observations is 25, 50, 25. Table 12.3 lists sample means, sample variances, and matrices of r and τ_b. The question is: Are these matrices equally efficient in evaluating the path model? The system is recursive:

$$
\begin{aligned}
X_1 &= e_1, \\
X_2 &= p_{21}X_1 + e_2, \\
X_3 &= p_{31}X_1 + p_{32}X_2 + e_3, \\
X_4 &= p_{41}X_1 + p_{42}X_2 + p_{43}X_3 + e_4.
\end{aligned}
\tag{47}
$$

Table 12.3. Measures of Association between Four Variables, r in Upper Triangle : τ_b in Lower, Computer-generated Data

	1	2	3	4
1		.815	.597	.442
2	.650		.784	.633
3	.426	.638		.842
4	.376	.483	.702	

Variable	Mean	Standard deviation	Distribution		
			H	M	L
1	+ .010	1.091	30	44	26
2	− .037	1.006	21	54	25
3	+ .050	1.021	28	48	24
4	+ .104	0.951	27	50	23

But knowing construction, we expect that $p_{31} = p_{41} = p_{42} = 0$; that $e_2 = e_3 = e_4 = .6$; and that $p_{21} = p_{32} = p_{43} = .8$. Figure 12.2 shows the results.

Notice that though the coefficients for τ_b are smaller than those for r, the pattern is the same. The relationship is attenuated, but the structure is clear. For larger samples the parallelism would be more striking (see Reynolds 1971 and his chapter in this volume for more extensive experimental results). Though I have done little experimental work, I do have results from twenty tests of these data. All are more or less the same.[5] This is clearly not enough work to warrant putting forward a recommendation without reservation. Yet it is strong support. I hope that enough comparative analyses will be carried out to make the value of the procedure well known.

Sampling Distribution

As the number of observations approaches infinity, all sampling distributions tend to normality, with mean equal to the population value

5. The interested reader can secure copies of the results by writing to the author.

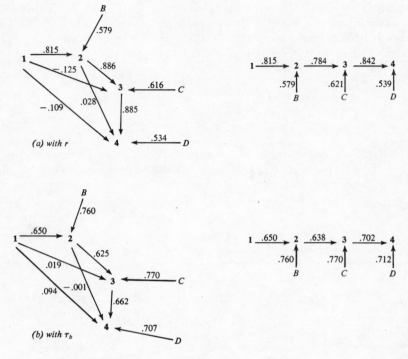

Figure 12.2. Path analyses.

being estimated, and variance that can be estimated by formulas given by Goodman and Kruskal (1963) and Quade (1971; summarized in this volume). Quade's formula can be extended to d_{yx}, d_{xy}, and τ_a by a very simple alteration.

In addition, variances computed from population cell proportions are functions of each other. In general,

$$\sigma_i^2 = \sigma_j^2 H_j^2 / H_i^2 , \qquad (48)$$

where H_j and H_i are denominators for the appropriate statistic. Equation (48) can be used to estimate the variance of τ_b.

$$s_{\tau_b}^{\ 2} = (s_{d_{yx}})^2 (C + D + T_y)/(C + D + T_x) . \qquad (49)$$

Because the estimated variances are functions of the sample statistics, and because the statistics will always be in the order $|\gamma| \geq |d_{yx}, \tau_b, d_{xy}| \geq |\tau_a|$, the estimated variances are not exact functions of each other. In general, d_{yx} will be close enough to τ_b to allow use of $s_{d_{yx}}^{\ 2}$ to estimate $s_{\tau_b}^{\ 2}$.

Though multivariate sampling distributions are not known, there does not appear to be a problem. Social science samples are generally large—200 or more. If they are reasonably well drawn, values of statistics indicating effects of practical significance will probably be statistically significant.[6] The problem is to find nontrivial effects; one need not worry about the statistical significance of trivial ones.

Analysis of Covariance

Frequently, social scientists want to test hypotheses such as: the relationship between education and occupation is different for different values of racial-ethnicity; or more generally that the relationship between two (or more) covariables depends on the value of a categorized control variable. A more extended discussion can be found in Blalock (1972, chap. 20) and Schuessler (1969). For now we can be content with working out an example with data from Table 12.4.

An alternative method based on Spearman's rho was suggested by Quade (1967). His method and mine diverge at several points. Most notably, he is more interested in the location of means once an adjustment is made for a covariable. In my case the mean of a pair of scores, before and after adjustment, is zero. Consequently, I am interested in parallelism of regression lines between samples, and the use of samples to reduce variation or dispersion of dependent variable scores. Thus my attention centers on interaction and the proportion of variation explained.

To begin, recall that equations (23) and (24) showed that the procedure we are using would overestimate the variation and covariation by factors of $2n$ (n = number of observations). Since all previous cases dealt with the same sample, no correction was called for. In this application, each category of the nominal variable is treated as a separate sample; therefore, some correction is necessary. Each element of the statistics is divided by $2n$. Thus from equations (6)-(10), one derives corrections:[7]

$$C' = \frac{1}{2n}C \qquad \text{(from 6),} \qquad (50a)$$

$$D' = \frac{1}{2n}D \qquad \text{(from 7),} \qquad (50b)$$

$$T'_y = \frac{1}{2n}T_y \qquad \text{(from 8),} \qquad (50c)$$

$$T'_x = \frac{1}{2n}T_x \qquad \text{(from 9),} \qquad (50d)$$

$$T'_{xy} = \frac{1}{2n}T_{xy} \qquad \text{(from 10).} \qquad (50e)$$

6. See Crocker (1972) for a concise discussion of practical vs. statistical significance.

7. Hawkes (1971) suggests correcting by the same figure. Since he derives his statistics differently and uses variance-covariation instead of variation-covariation, there is an apparent difference.

Table 12.4. Occupation by Education by Racial-Ethnicity

Racial-ethnicity	Education	Occupation			
		High	Medium	Low	Total
Old American*	High	55	25	6	86
	Medium	48	48	32	128
	Low	7	15	24	46
	Total	110	88	62	260
Rapidly Assimilating†	High	35	24	5	64
	Medium	35	49	14	98
	Low	10	16	44	70
	Total	80	89	63	232
Other‡	High	41	30	6	77
	Medium	63	59	47	169
	Low	6	32	63	101
	Total	110	121	116	347
Total	High	131	79	17	227
	Medium	146	156	93	395
	Low	23	63	131	217
	Total	300	298	241	839

SOURCE: Ploch 1968, where definitions are given for occupational and educational categories. Education is controlled for age.

*Third-generation American regardless of nationality identification.

†Less than third-generation Americans with nationality identification—English, Canadian, Irish, German, French, other British Isle, Low Countries.

‡All Jews and nonwhites as well as Latin Americans, Southern and Eastern Europeans.

Henceforth the primes will be dropped for convenience, but all reference to these terms or their derivatives will assume division by $2n$.

As in parametric analysis of covariance the task is to compute associations between covariates, in this case occupation and education, to see if they are different for different values of a categorized variable, in this case racial-ethnicity. This means computing Σx_{ij}^2, $\Sigma x_{ij} y_{ij}$, and Σy_{ij}^2 for each category and using them to form d_{yx}; then computing the variation explained by X, and the residual (unexplained by X). Table 12.5 gives the results of these computations. It happens that there is no interaction.

If the interaction term were larger, one could test for statistical significance by forming a summary statistic, W^2, whose asymptotic distribution (as $n_k \to \infty$) approaches the chi-square distribution with

Table 12.5. Analysis of Covariance for Education and Occupation Within Categories of Racial-Ethnicity

(1) Racial-Ethnic Classification A	(2) n_k	(3) Variation in Occupation Σy^2	(4) Variation in Education Σx^2	(5) Covariation Σxy	(6) $d_{yx} = \dfrac{\Sigma xy}{\Sigma x^2}$	(7) Explained by X $d_{yx}\Sigma xy$	(8) Unexplained by X $\Sigma y^2 - d_{yx}\Sigma xy$	(9) $r_b = (7)/(3)$	(10) r_b
Old American	260	84.4	80.2	30.2	.376	11.4	73.1	.134	.367
Rapidly Assimilating	232	76.6	75.9	32.2	.424	13.7	62.9	.178	.422
Other	347	115.6	109.1	46.3	.425	19.7	95.9	.170	.412
Sum	839	276.6	265.2	108.7		45.8	231.9		
Total	839	278.3	267.7	110.8	.414	45.8	232.5	.165	.406
Between Class		1.7	2.5						
Within Class		276.6	265.2	108.7	.410	44.5	232.1	.161	.401

$K - 1$ degrees of freedom (K is the number of categories). If $n_k \geq 50$, there is no problem (see Rosenthal 1966). The statistic is defined:

$$W^2 = \sum_{k=1}^{K} \left(\frac{d_{yx|z_i} - d_{yx|z}}{s_{d_{yx|z_i}}} \right)^2 , \qquad (51)$$

where K = the number of categories (in this case 3), $d_{yx|z_k}$ is Somers's d_{yx} within the kth category, and $d_{yx|z}$ is the average within class Somers's d_{yx}. Analogous statistics have been defined for gamma by Davis, but he has called them conditional and partial, respectively. While this accents the connection to probability theory, it obscures the covariance analogy. Thus I changed terminology to accent the covariance analogy. To return to W^2, it is computed:

$$W^2 = \left(\frac{.376 - .410}{.0489} \right)^2 + \left(\frac{.424 - .410}{.0532} \right)^2 + \left(\frac{.425 - .410}{.0373} \right)^2$$

$$= .483 + .069 + .162 = .714 .$$

When this is compared with chi square for two degrees of freedom, the probability of W^2 this large or larger is .70 ($X_{(2,.70)}^2 = .713$). Standard errors were computed for each class by use of an equation modified from those given by Quade (1971). The form used here accents the relationship to chi square, since each of the summation elements of W^2 is asymptotically unit-normal as $n_k \to \infty$. In addition, there are K elements, but only $K - 1$ of them are independent of each other. This test follows the rationale for interaction tests given by Goodman and Kruskal (1963).

Since there is no interaction, main effects can be evaluated. The effect of education net of ethnicity is determined from the row of average within class statistics (labeled "within" in Table 12.5). What of the effect of ethnicity net of education, and the zero-order effect of ethnicity on education and occupation? One can form a PRE statistic similar to Goodman and Kruskal's tau (T'), (Somers 1962b; Leik and Gove 1969). For the effect of ethnicity, R, controlled for education, E, use data from Table 12.5, column 8.

$$T'_{OR.E} = \frac{\text{Total} - \text{Within}}{\text{Within}} = \frac{\text{Between}}{\text{Within}}$$

$$= \frac{232.5 - 232.1}{232.1} = \frac{.04}{232.1} = .0002 .$$

Zero-order effects of ethnicity on occupation, O, are

$$T'_{OR} = \frac{1.7}{276.6} = .006 \ .$$

On education they are:

$$T'_{ER} = \frac{2.5}{265.2} = .009 \ .$$

Had interaction been significant, the partial should not have been computed, since the effect of education on occupation would have varied according to ethnicity classification.

Summary

I have attempted to put measures of association for ordinal data into the framework of the general linear model, to accent their utility for data analysis. It seems clear that Kendall's τ_b and Somers's d_{yx} are the best statistics to use for this purpose. It also seems appropriate to take standardized Somers's d_{yx} as an analog of a path coefficient. This enables one to carry through a rather complex multivariate analysis without assmmptions of metric or distribution.

Whenever comparisons have been made, it is known that these statistics have an asymptotic relative efficiency of .95 compared to product-moment statistics as $n \to \infty$ and the conditions for the product-moment statistics are met. For practical purposes this efficiency is reached when $n \geqslant 100$. Certainly if $n \geqslant 500$ there is little basis on which to choose between r, r_s, and τ_b from the standpoint of efficiency. At the same time, τ_b is invariant under ordinal transformations of any or all the variables; whereas r is not (see Reynolds 1971; and his chapter in this volume). Thus τ_b will be sensitive to a wider range of associations, while r will give more precise information about the form.

The fact that the sampling distributions of some statistics are unknown should not be a deterrent to their use. In the first place, it does not affect their ability to describe and summarize data. Nor does it affect our ability to interpret data with their aid. Second, with samples of 100 to 500 or more, any statistic indicating socially important relationships in the bivariate case will be statistically significant. Rather than worry about tests of significance and the computation of confidence limits, we should develop consensus about those statistics whose size indicates socially significant processes. This is another way of saying that variance explained is more important than statistical significance. One can increase sample size until any trivial relationship is significant. Even so, it continues to be trivial, and the discipline would be better off if we recognized the fact.

The use of the general linear model also helps to explain why these statistics can be zero even when there is a stochastic dependence between the variables. Just as the product-moment, r, can be zero when the stochastic dependence is nonmonotonic, so the statistics discussed above can be zero when the stochastic dependence is nonmonotonic. There is no mystery here. The statistics are sensitive to a limited range of forms. Outside that range they are no more or no less sensitive than r outside its proper range.

Comparison and analogy with the product-moment coefficient are important for pointing up both the strengths and the weaknesses of these statistics. There is no substitute for improved measurement so that researchers can get precise statements of the forms of relationships. At the same time it is foolhardy to put off all sophisticated analysis until the perfect methodology is devised. We have well-defined ordinal data in hand. Why not exploit them to the full while we await a better day? Although it is true that we await the future to see the fine details of our work, our present procedures will reveal gross outlines.

All of this must be said with some caution. We know that ordinal measures of association are generally lower than product-moment coefficients computed from continuous variables. How much loss is due to grouping, and how much to change in level of measurement, is unknown. We are also unsure of the mathematics underlying much of the expansion of ordinal measures of association into the general linear model. Sampling distributions are unknown. Work by Reynolds, as well as that reported above, is more suggestive than conclusive. There are reasonable grounds for continuing and expanding usage; however, this cannot be done thoughtlessly. We must press the comparison of certain techniques derived from the product-moment correlation to the evaluation of the relative efficiency of each. Increased use of dummy variables along with multivariate techniques such as canonical correlations could provide viable alternatives to the exposition given above. This is clearly a pressing area for future research.

References

Blalock, Hubert M.
   1972. *Social Statistics.* 2nd ed. New York: McGraw-Hill.
Borgatta, Edgar F.
   1968. "My Student the Purist: A Lament." *Sociological Quarterly* 9:29-34.
Boyle, Richard P.
   1970. "Path Analysis and Ordinal Data." *American Journal of Sociology* 4 (January):461-80.
Costner, Herbert L.
   1965. "Criteria for Measures of Association." *American Sociological Review* 30:341-53.
Crocker, Douglas C.
   1972. "Some Interpretations of the Multiple Correlation Coefficient." *American Statistician* 26, no. 2 (April):31-33.
Daniels, H. E.
   1944. "The Relation between Measures of Correlation in the Universe of Sample Permutations." *Biometrika* 33:129-35.
Davis, James A.
   1967. "A Partial Coefficient for Goodman and Kruskal's Gamma." *Journal of the American Statistical Association* 62:189-93.
Goodman, Leo A., and William H. Kruskal
   1954. "Measures of Association for Cross Classifications." *Journal of the American Statistical Association* 49:732-64.
   1963. "Measures of Association for Cross-classifications, III, Approximate Sampling Theory." Ibid. 58:310-64.
Hawkes, Roland K.
   1971. "The Multivariate Analysis of Ordinal Measures." *American Journal of Sociology* 76 (March):908-26.
Kendall, Maurice G.
   1962. *Rank Correlation Methods.* 3d ed. London: Griffin.
Klatzky, S. R., and R. W. Hodge
   1971. "A Canonical Correlation Analysis of Occupational Mobility." *Journal of the American Statistical Association* 66 (March):16-22.
Kruskal, William H.
   1958. "Ordinal Measures of Association." *Journal of the American Statistical Association* 53 (December):814-61.
Leik, Robert K., and Walter R. Gove
   1969. "The Conception and Measurement of Asymmetric Monotonic Relationships in Sociology." *American Journal of Sociology* 74:696-709.
Moran, P. A. P.
   1951. "Partial and Multiple Rank Correlation." *Biometrika* 38:26-32.
Ploch, Donald R.
   1968. "Status Inconsistency: A Method of Measurement and Substantive Evaluation." Ph.D. dissertation, University of North Carolina.
Quade, Dana
   1967. "Rank Analysis of Covariance." *Journal of the American Statistical Association* 62:1187-1200.
   1971. "Nonparametric Partial Correlation." Report SW 13/71. Amsterdam: Mathematisch Centrum.

Reynolds, H. T.
1971. "Making Causal Inferences With Ordinal Data." Working Papers in Methodology, no. 5. Chapel Hill: University of North Carolina.
Rosenthal, I.
1966. "The Distribution of the Sample Version of the Measure of Association, Gamma." *Journal of the American Statistical Association* 61:440-54.
Schuessler, Karl
1969. "Covariance Analysis in Sociological Research." Chapter 7 in Edgar F. Borgatta, ed., *Sociological Methodology*. San Francisco: Jossey-Bass.
1971. *Analyzing Social Data*. Boston: Houghton Mifflin.
Somers, Robert H.
1959. "The Rank Analogue of Product-Moment Partial Correlation and Regression, with Application to Manifold, Ordered Contingency Tables." *Biometrika* 46 (June):241-46.
1962a. "A New Asymmetric Measure of Association for Ordinal Variables." *American Sociological Review* 27:799-811.
1962b. "Similarity between Goodman and Kruskal's Tau and Kendall's Tau, with a Partial Interpretation of the Latter." *Journal of the American Statistical Association* 57:804-12.
1968. "An Approach to Multivariate Analysis of Ordinal Data." *American Sociological Review* 33 (December):971-77.
Wilson, Thomas P.
1969. "A Proportional-Reduction-in-Error Interpretation for Kendall's Tau-b." *Social Forces* 47 (March):340-42.
1971. "A Critique of Ordinal Variables." Ibid. 49 (March):432-44.

Chapter 13

NONPARAMETRIC PARTIAL CORRELATION

DANA QUADE

Dana Quade is Professor of Biostatistics in the School of Public Health of the University of North Carolina, Chapel Hill. He received his Ph.D. in Statistics from the University of North Carolina in 1960. Dr. Quade's main research interests lie in the area of nonparametric statistics and he has published many important articles in a variety of mathematical and statistical journals.

It is often considered desirable to measure the correlation between two variables, say, X and Y, controlled for a third variable, say, Z, given a sample of observations (X_i, Y_i, Z_i) for $i = 1, 2, \cdots, n$. Any such measure may be called a *partial correlation*, written $C(X, Y|Z)$, where C indicates *correlation* and $(|)$ indicates *controlled for*. The varying interpretations of these two concepts form a basis for distinguishing among the indices proposed in the literature; I shall began this chapter by briefly reviewing these concepts and the indices derived from them. Afterward I shall propose a new index of partial correlation based on matching, for which I provide sampling theory, examples, and discussion.

Concepts of Correlation

Ignoring Z for the present, suppose we have two variables X and Y, both of which must be measured on at least an ordinal scale, and let us consider as a concept the correlation between them. In general terms we may say that X and Y are positively correlated if there is a tendency for high values of X to occur together with high values of Y, and low

Supported by National Institutes of Health Research Career Development Award no. GM-38906.

values of X with low values of Y; they are negatively correlated if high values of X tend to occur with low values of Y, and low X with high Y. And correlation per se means either positive or negative correlation.

Quantitative indices of correlation are generally defined so as to satisfy certain conditions. For example, we *standardize* them so that

$$-1 \leqslant C(X, Y) \leqslant 1 \qquad \text{or} \qquad 0 \leqslant C(X, Y) \leqslant 1,$$

where the values $+1$ and -1 are attainable in case of extreme or *perfect* positive or negative correlation (the second set of inequalities applies to indices which do not distinguish between the two directions) and the value 0 indicates complete lack of correlation. In addition, we require any index to be *symmetric under interchange* of the variables, so that

$$C(X, Y) = C(Y, X) \, ;$$

and also *symmetric under reversal* of the variables, so that

$$C(X, Y) = -C(-X, Y) = -C(X, -Y) = C(-X, -Y)$$

if the index distinguishes between the directions, and otherwise

$$C(X, Y) = C(-X, Y) = C(X, -Y) = C(-X, -Y) \, .$$

Furthermore, we prefer that a quantitative index exhibit some form of *invariance under transformations*, which means in general terms that if X and Y are separately transformed to new variables $X' = f(X)$ and $Y' = g(Y)$, where f and g are taken from a suitable class of functions, then

$$C(X', Y') = C(X, Y).$$

In particular, *linear invariance* obtains if $C(X',Y') = C(X,Y)$ whenever $f(X) = a_X + b_X X$ and $g(Y) = a_Y + b_Y Y$ with $b_X b_Y > 0$. The more restrictive condition of *monotonic invariance*, which is required if the index is to be suitable for ordinal data, obtains if $C(X', Y') = C(X, Y)$ whenever f and g are both monotonic increasing functions. Finally, it has been argued (see Costner 1965) that all indices of association should have a *proportional reduction in error* interpretation, as explained below.

The first and best-known index is undoubtedly the classical *product-moment correlation* of Pearson, which may be defined by the formula

$$r(X, Y) = \frac{\text{(covariance of } X \text{ and } Y)}{\text{(standard deviation of } X) \cdot \text{(standard deviation of } Y)}.$$

It is difficult to provide any interpretation of this index unless X and Y are both at least interval-scale variables. In that case r indicates the tendency of the sample to be concentrated on a straight line; in fact r may well be called, as it has been by some authors, the coefficient of linear correlation. We have perfect positive (or negative) correlation if the entire sample lies exactly on a straight line of positive (or negative) slope.

A rival concept of correlation, which requires no more than ordinal measurement of X and Y, is based on consideration of pairs of observations, for example (X_1, Y_1) and (X_2, Y_2). Such a pair is called *concordant* if $X_1 < X_2$ and $Y_1 < Y_2$ or if $X_1 > X_2$ and $Y_1 > Y_2$; that is, if the observation with the smaller value of X also has the smaller value of Y, and the one with the larger X has the larger Y—or, to put it another way, if the ordering of the pair is the same with respect to both variables. The pair is *discordant* if $X_1 < X_2$ and $Y_1 > Y_2$ or if $X_1 > X_2$ and $Y_1 < Y_2$; that is, if the observation with the smaller X has the larger Y and the one with the larger X has the smaller Y, or if the ordering of the pair given by one variable is the opposite of the ordering given by the other. If $X_1 = X_2$ or $Y_1 = Y_2$, or both, the pair is *tied* (at this point we need not distinguish among the various kinds of ties.) In a sample of n observations there will be $N = n(n-1)/2$ pairs of observations; of these let $C, D,$ and T be the number concordant, discordant, and tied, respectively. Then, a possible index of correlation is *Kendall's* (1962) *tau$_a$*, defined as

$$\tau_a(X, Y) = \frac{C - D}{C + D + T} = \frac{C - D}{N}.$$

This may be interpreted as the difference between the proportions of sample concordant pairs and discordant pairs; we have perfect positive (or negative) correlation if all sample pairs are concordant (or discordant), as is the case when the entire sample lies on some monotonically increasing (decreasing) curve. Note, however, that if ties occur—for example, with categorized variables—then τ_a cannot reach the limits $+1$ and -1. Such an infelicity can be avoided by using a variation on the same theme, namely, the *Goodman-Kruskal* (1954) *index*

$$\gamma(X, Y) = \frac{C - D}{C + D} = \frac{C - D}{N - T},$$

which may be interpreted as the difference between the conditional proportion of sample concordant pairs, and the conditional proportion of discordant pairs, given that they are not tied; we now have perfect positive (or negative) correlation if there are no discordant (or no concordant) pairs, whether tied pairs occur or not—unless all pairs are tied, in which case γ is undefined. Another well-known variant, *Kendall's* (1962) *tau$_b$*, may be defined as follows: Let T_x be the number of pairs tied on X only, and similarly, let T_y be the number of pairs tied on Y only. Then,

$$\tau_b(X,\ Y) = \frac{C - D}{\sqrt{C + D + T_x}\ \sqrt{C + D + T_y}}.$$

This index, though often used, has no simple interpretation; its advantages are more theoretical in nature. It is not difficult to see that τ_b always lies between τ_a and γ—usually it is very nearly halfway between them—so that $0 \leqslant \tau_a \leqslant \tau_b \leqslant \gamma \leqslant 1$ or $-1 \leqslant \gamma \leqslant \tau_b \leqslant \tau_a \leqslant 0$. Note that the only difference among these indices (and other variants appearing in the literature) lies in their treatment of tied pairs: in fact, if $T = 0$ they all coincide.

A third basic concept of correlation views it not as a description of the sample, but operationally, as a measurement of the value of knowing something about one variable when one needs to know something about the other. For example, suppose we are asked to guess the component Y of some observation $(X,\ Y)$ taken at random from the sample, and suppose that if our guess is Y_1 when the true value is Y_2 we suffer some nonnegative *loss* $L(Y_1,\ Y_2)$. Consider two situations: (1) we are given no further information before we must guess Y; and (2) we are first told the value of X. Let R_1 and R_2 be the expected losses, or *risks*, in the two situations. Then, an index of the value of knowing X is the *proportional reduction in risk* (PRR) of situation 2 as compared with situation 1, or

$$\text{PRR}(X,\ Y) = 1 - \frac{R_2}{R_1}.$$

Since it is clear that R_2 can be no greater than R_1, we have $0 \leqslant \text{PRR} \leqslant 1$; the value 1 is attained if $R_2 = 0$, that is, if knowledge of X reduces the risk to zero; and $\text{PRR} = 0$ if $R_2 = R_1$, that is, if knowledge of X is of no value whatever for the purpose of guessing Y. Note that the direction of the correlation between X and Y is ignored, and indeed it is irrelevant; with this concept an index of association can be constructed even for unordered variables X and Y. As just defined,

PRR is not symmetric under interchange of X and Y, but this can be corrected as follows: Suppose we are as likely to be asked to guess Y as to guess X; and suppose that in situation 1 we are given no further information, but that in situation 2 we are told the value of one variable before we must guess the value of the other. Then, R_1 and R_2, and hence PRR, can be redefined in an obvious manner. In this generality the present concept was first formalized by Goodman and Kruskal (1954); a somewhat less general version is well known as the *proportional reduction in error*, or PRE. All the above may be further generalized, of course, by replacing the requirement to "guess Y" by more general situations than this simple prediction.

Many of the indices originally based on other concepts of correlation can also be given PRE interpretations. For example, the well known PRE interpretation of the product-moment correlation proceeds as follows: Suppose we must guess Y when the loss will be equal to squared error. In situation 1 the minimum risk is achieved by using the mean of Y and is equal to the variance, say, $s^2(Y)$; in situation 2 it is achieved by using the conditional mean of Y given X and is equal to the conditional variance, say, $s^2(Y|X)$. The proportional reduction in risk is then equal to $1 - s^2(Y|X)/s^2(Y)$; but this is just $r^2(X, Y)$ if the conditional mean is a linear function of X. As another example, suppose two observations (X_1, Y_1) and (X_2, Y_2) are to be chosen, and we are required to guess whether $Y_1 < Y_2$ or $Y_1 > Y_2$. If we guess correctly we lose 0, and if incorrectly, 1, except that if $Y_1 = Y_2$ (but we are not permitted to make this our guess), we lose the amount 1/2. If we are given no information about X_1 and X_2 our risk is $R_1 = 1/2$ no matter what strategy we adopt for guessing the ordering of Y_1 and Y_2; we may as well toss a coin. But if we are told the ordering of X_1 and X_2, we may adopt the following minimum-risk guessing scheme: for $X_1 = X_2$ toss a coin anyway; but otherwise guess the ordering of Y_1 and Y_2 so as to make the pair concordant (discordant) if τ_a is positive (negative). Then, $R_2 = \min (C/N, D/N) + (T/2N)$, and PRR $= |\tau_a|$. For a PRE interpretation of Goodman and Kruskal's gamma, see Costner (1965), and for τ_b—this one being rather strained—see Wilson (1969).

There are of course many other concepts of correlation, yielding, for example, the familiar Spearman's rho, various form of median and quadrant correlation, and more; but since these do not yet seem to have been used in measuring partial correlation I shall not treat them here. For further discussion see the papers by Goodman and Kruskal (1954, 1963).

Concepts of Control

Let us now consider what it means to control for the variable Z. It seems possible to distinguish at least four different concepts in the literature, of which the most basic may be called *holding Z constant*. The usual technique here is to partition the sample into strata within each of which Z is indeed constant, at least approximately. Contingency tables are then displayed, or summary statistics—in particular, measures of correlation, which may be called *conditional correlations*—are provided, for each of the strata. Of course, reducing the variation in Z to a reasonable range often requires so many strata that the mind cannot comprehend them all, and some may occur so rarely that, with any realistic total number of observations, sampling variation will hide the relationships they should show. One way out, suggested by Rosenberg (1962), is standardization: we might call the correlation in the standardized sample the partial correlation. Alternatively, we may define the partial correlation as an average conditional correlation. This approach was formalized by Goodman and Kruskal (1954), who applied it there to their coefficient λ, an index most appropriate when X and Y are purely nominal.

An important index obtained by holding Z constant is Davis's (1967) partial correlation coefficient based on Goodman and Kruskal's gamma. Davis considers the case where X, Y, and Z are all categorized, so that the sample might be displayed as a three-way contingency table. Let C_i (or D_i) be the number of pairs tied on Z at its ith value that are also concordant (or discordant) with respect to X and Y. Davis then defines his index of partial correlation as

$$\gamma(X, \ Y|Z) = \frac{\Sigma C_i - \Sigma D_i}{\Sigma C_i + \Sigma D_i} \ ,$$

where ΣC_i (or ΣD_i) is the total number of pairs tied on Z and concordant (or discordant) with respect to X and Y. Thus γ is the difference between the proportion of those pairs tied on Z but not on X or Y which are concordant with respect to X and Y, and the proportion which are discordant. But if we write γ_i for the conditional Goodman-Kruskal correlation between X and Y at the ith level of Z, that is,

$$\gamma_i = \frac{C_i - D_i}{C_i + D_i} \ ,$$

we see that the partial correlation can be reexpressed as

$$\gamma(X, \ Y|Z) = \frac{\Sigma(C_i + D_i)\gamma_i}{\Sigma(C_i + D_i)} \ ;$$

that is, γ is a weighted average of the conditional correlations in which the weight given to the ith correlation is proportional to the number of pairs of observations tied on Z at its ith value but not tied on X or Y.

When considered as a weighted average, Davis's γ may seem to use rather unusual weights. Goodman and Kruskal (1954) suggested that it might seem natural to use weights proportional to the numbers of observations at the various levels of Z. Another reasonable approach might be to use equal weights for all strata. Davis's weights are somewhat simpler in this context, however, and they are intuitively reasonable in view of his original definition. Furthermore, as he states, and as was verified empirically in considerable Monte Carlo experimentation by Reynolds (1971; summarized in the next chapter), the three weighting schemes do not differ appreciably in typical research situations.

The second major concept of control may be called *adjusting for Z*. To do this we proceed as follows: Let f be a suitable function to use in predicting X from Z, in that the *residual* $X' = X - f(Z)$ is concentrated about zero as closely as possible according to some reasonable criterion. Similarly, let g be suitable for predicting Y from Z, with $Y' = Y - g(Z)$ the corresponding residual. Then let the index of partial correlation $C(X, Y|Z) = C(X', Y')$, the total correlation between the residuals. (To correlate what might more properly be called *adjusted values*, obtained perhaps by adding the respective means of X and Y to X' and Y', is of course equivalent when the index used is linearly invariant.) If, in particular, the criterion of concentration is variance, f and g are the *regression functions*, the conditional means of X and Y when Z is given. And if product-moment correlation is used, we obtain the classical product-moment partial correlation coefficient, $r(X, Y|Z)$. If, furthermore, it happens that the regression functions are linear in Z, and that the conditional variances do not depend on Z, the same result can also be obtained directly from the familiar *partial correlation formula*:

$$r(X, Y|Z) = \frac{r(X, Y) - r(X, Z)r(Y, Z)}{\sqrt{1 - r^2(X, Z)}\sqrt{1 - r^2(Y, Z)}},$$

which is even used as a definition of partial correlation by some authors. The formula can of course be generalized in the well-known manner to allow for multiple and curvilinear regression. In principle it would seem possible to implement the concept of adjustment by using different methods of prediction, different indices of correlation, or both, but I have not yet seen any other partial correlation measures of this type in the literature.

Although there may be no problem in holding constant a categorical

Z, Somers (1966, p. 972) claims that, with a continuous Z, methods derived from that concept "would be inapplicable, except by approximation, since each subgroup on the control variable would have no more than one observation." It must be admitted that in such a case the hypothetical population-average conditional correlation generally cannot be estimated without some bias. This bias, however, can be made negligible in practice, by using the technique proposed later. A more important objection is that a summary average may have no useful interpretation without the assumption, so far implicit, that the conditional correlations being averaged are not substantially different. For discussion of this point see Ploch (1969). The corresponding difficulty with methods based on the concept of adjustment, of course, is the need for structural assumptions, that is, for knowledge of the functional form of the relationships of X and Y to Z. For example, the product-moment partial correlation as found from the simple formula is entirely inappropriate unless both X and Y have linear regressions on Z.

The two basic concepts of control discussed so far are often confused in the literature because of the importance of one special case in which they are entirely equivalent: when X, Y, and Z have a joint normal distribution. In a normal population the conditional correlations between X and Y, given $Z = z$, are the same for every z, and hence also the same as their average. In addition, the conditions for applying the simple partial correlation formula hold, and the measure of partial correlation so obtained turns out to be identical with the constant conditional correlation. But since such a situation obviously cannot be expected in general, it seems best always to keep clearly in mind what is to be meant by controlling for Z before attempting to choose an appropriate measure of partial correlation.

A third concept of control is employed in constructing Kendall's (1962) partial correlation coefficient. Suppose X, Y, and Z are all at least ordinal, and to simplify matters assume for the moment that there are no ties. Each pair of observations can then be classified according as it shows X and Y concordant or discordant with Z. The results are arranged as in a fourfold table (see Table 13.1). Specifically N_0 is the number of *non-discordant* pairs, meaning that $(X_1 - X_2)(Z_1 - Z_2) > 0$ and $(Y_1 - Y_2)(Z_1 - Z_2) > 0$, which imply that $(X_1 - X_2)(Y_1 - Y_2) > 0$ also; N_X is the number of *X-discordant* pairs, meaning that $(X_1 - X_2)(Z_1 - Z_2) < 0$ but $(Y_1 - Y_2)(Z_1 - Z_2) > 0$, and hence $(X_1 - X_2)(Y_1 - Y_2) < 0$, and similarly, N_Y and N_Z are the numbers of *Y-discordant* and *Z-discordant* pairs. Note that, with respect to X and Y, non-discordant and Z-discordant pairs are concordant, while X- and Y-discordant pairs are discordant; hence $C = N_0 + N_Z$ and $D = N_X + N_Y$. According to Somers (1966, p. 974), Kendall (1962) argues, in effect, that if the non- and Z-discordant pairs predominate

Table 13.1

Y, Z ⟍ X, Z	Concordant	Discordant
Concordant	N_O	N_X
Discordant	N_Y	N_Z

over the X- and Y-discordant pairs the partial correlation tends to be positive, whereas if the X- and Y-discordant pairs predominate it tends to be negative; and "if they are proportionately the same, then the partial is zero, that is, if the fourfold table exhibits statistical independence". This is because the non- and Z-discordant pairs show X and Y "rising and falling together, regardless of the change in the control variable," while the X- and Y-discordant pairs show X and Y "moving consistently in opposite directions, regardless, again, of the behavior of the control variable." Kendall proposed using as an index of partial correlation the well known ϕ-coefficient computed from the table: that is,

$$\phi(X, Y|Z) = \frac{N_O N_Z - N_X N_Y}{\sqrt{(N_O + N_X)(N_Y + N_Z)(N_O + N_Y)(N_X + N_Z)}}.$$

He also made the surprising discovery that the same result is obtained if one substitutes the Kendall total correlations into the partial correlation formula. This apparent coincidence was first explained by Somers (1959). Further development by Hawkes (1971), in terms of a formal "regression of pairwise differences," suggests that the partial correlation formula is still valid if ties occur—and can even be extended to more than one control variable—provided the tau_b version is used for the total correlations; Somers (1966), however, prefers to discard the ties and calculate the ϕ-coefficient from only the untied pairs.

A somewhat different line of development is pursued by Goodman (1959). For any positive integer $k < n$, let a fourfold table be constructed which classifies the $(n - k)$ pairs in which the ranks of the two values of Z differ by exactly k. The index of association in such a table may be regarded as a partial index of partial association. Note that if k is very small the table includes only pairs in which Z is approximately constant.

A final concept of controlling for Z extends to partial correlation the proportional reduction in error concept of total correlation. In general terms, suppose we are asked to make a statement about Y, subject to specified losses in case of error, in one of two situations: (1) we are given information about Z but not about X; (2) we are given information about both Z and X. The proportional reduction in expected loss for the second situation, as compared with that for the first, may then be taken as a measure of partial correlation. Several of the indices of partial correlation presented previously can also be given such PRE interpretations. For example, the product-moment partial correlation can be obtained just as the total correlation is obtained—by specifying the loss as the squared error in predicting Y. Also, a PRE interpretation of the Davis coefficient follows from that of Goodman and Kruskal's gamma if the statement we must make is a prediction of the ordering on Y of two random observations having the same value of Z, and in situation 1 we are told only the common value of Z, but in situation 2 we are also told the ordering on X. It should again be noted that the PRE concept cannot produce an index which distinguishes positive from negative correlation.

An interesting little example presented by Somers (1966) illustrates beautifully several of the concepts discussed above. Consider the sample of six observations listed in Table 13.2. Holding Z constant, we immediately produce three subgroups of two observations each, namely, (a and b), (c and d), and (e and f). Within each of these subgroups we see perfect positive correlation, and hence without further ado we put the partial correlation, viewed as average conditional correlation, equal to $+1$. Attempting to adjust for Z by means of linear regression—although Somers presented his example as involving strictly ordinal variables—we calculate total product-moment correlations $r(X, Z) = r(Y, Z) = 0$; hence, from the partial correlation formula, $r(X, Y|Z) = r(X, Y) = 1/17$. However, plots of X and Y against Z suggest that linear regression is not appropriate; and on fitting quadratic functions instead, we find perfect positive correlation between the residuals, in agreement with the previous result.

Table 13.2

Observation identification	X	Y	Z
a	1	2	1
b	2	3	1
c	2	1	2
d	3	2	2
e	1	2	3
f	2	3	3

A complete listing of the fifteen possible pairs of observations is given in Table 13.3. With respect to X and Z there are four concordant and four discordant pairs, and similarly with respect to Y and Z; so $\tau_b(X, Z) = \tau_b(Y, Z) = 0$. Hence, if we use the standard formula to produce an index of partial correlation, as suggested by Hawkes, we have $\tau_b(X, Y|Z) = \tau_b(X, Y)$. Now with respect to X and Y we find five concordant and four discordant pairs, and also four tied on X and four on Y (including two tied on both X and Y); thus the result is $(5 - 4)/(15 - 4) = 1/11$. Somers himself—and this is his example —constructs the fourfold table based only on pairs not tied on any variable (see Table 13.4) and hence obtains a phi-coefficient equal to $-1/3$. He remarks (1966, p. 976) that this is an "example from which most investigators, using subgroup analysis, would draw an erroneous conclusion." The reader will have to judge for himself. At any rate, one may well agree with his further remark that "partial association among ordinal variables is not a simple notion that can be easily summarized in a single statistic."

Table 13.3

| | Classification with respect to: | | | | | | |
| Pair | One variable at a time | | | Two variables at a time | | | All three variables |
	X	Y	Z	XY	XZ	YZ	XYZ
ab	U	U	T	C	T	T	T
ac	U	U	U	D	C	D	Y-discordant
ad	U	T	U	T	C	T	T
ae	T	T	U	T	T	T	T
af	U	U	U	C	C	C	non-discordant
bc	T	U	U	T	T	D	T
bd	U	U	U	D	C	D	Y-discordant
be	U	U	U	C	D	D	Z-discordant
bf	T	T	U	T	T	T	T
cd	U	U	T	C	T	T	T
ce	U	U	U	D	D	C	X-discordant
cf	T	U	U	T	T	C	T
de	U	T	U	T	D	T	T
df	U	U	U	D	D	C	X-discordant
ef	U	U	T	C	T	T	T

NOTE: C = concordant, D = discordant, T = tied, U = untied.

Sampling Theory and Statistical Inference

So far, I have considered only the descriptive and operational interpretations of measures of partial correlation, in the light of the basic concepts involved; there now follow a few remarks on the sampling theory, for lack of which inference in this area is fraught with difficulties.

A statistic derived from holding Z constant, namely, an average conditional correlation, is likely to be approximately normally distributed

Table 13.4

X, Z Y, Z	Concordant	Discordant
Concordant	1	2
Discordant	2	1

simply because it is an average. Hence only an estimate of variance is needed, and for this it suffices to have the first two moments of the conditional correlations. For example, Goodman and Kruskal (1963) have given suitable estimates of the moments of their index gamma, and thence an approximation to the distribution of Davis's (1967) coefficient might be obtained. This line of thought does not seem to have been pursued, however, and Davis reported himself unable to obtain a sampling theory. The distribution of the product-moment partial correlation coefficient is known exactly if the conditions for applying the simple partial correlation formula hold, and if in addition X and Y are conditionally jointly normal, given Z. Although this last assumption is unnecessary for an asymptotic result, it is clear that strong assumptions are still required, and little is known of the effects of departures from them. For the Kendall type of measures of partial correlation there are a few results in large-sample theory, but nothing of any value in practice other than Goodman's (1959) asymptotic "partial tests" for his partial indices, and even those require fairly strong structural assumptions. Thus the sampling theory for indices of partial correlation, as reported in the literature, is in a most unsatisfactory state.

But in fact, a quite adequate asymptotic sampling theory is available for a very large family of measures including many correlation indices. Let there be established some definition by which it can be decided whether or not any pair of observations is *relevant*; then consider all indices of the form

$$\theta = \frac{C_R - D_R}{R},$$

where R is the number of relevant pairs, and C_R and D_R are the numbers among these which are concordant and discordant, respectively. Note that all members of this family are standardized: clearly, $-1 \le \theta \le 1$, with $\theta = 1$ if the relevant pairs are all concordant, $\theta = -1$ if they are all discordant, and $\theta = 0$ if there are equally as many concordant as discordant relevant pairs. (If a particular sample should fail to contain any relevant pairs, θ might be arbitrarily set equal to zero for that sample.)

Whether θ satisfies the other conditions stated earlier for indices of correlation depends on the definition established for "relevant," which is quite arbitrary in this context: every different definition of "relevant" produces another index in the family. Some examples follow. If we say that "all pairs are relevant," $R = N$, $C_R = C$, and $D_R = D$; and the total correlation index tau_a is produced. If we say that "pairs are relevant unless they are tied," R is reduced to $C + D$, but again $C_R = C$ and $D_R = D$; so we have Goodman and Kruskal's gamma. If "pairs are relevant unless they are tied on X," we obtain the asymmetric index d_{yx} of Somers (1962). If "pairs are relevant unless they are tied on both X and Y simultaneously," we obtain the measure e proposed by Wilson in this volume. And finally, of greater interest for our present purposes, stipulating that "pairs are relevant if they are tied on the control variable Z but not tied on X or on Y" produces Davis's partial correlation coefficient.

Now, for each $i = 1, 2, \cdots, n$, let R_i be the number of relevant pairs which include the particular observation (X_i, Y_i, Z_i); and let W_i be the number of these pairs which are concordant, less the number which are discordant, so that $-R_i \le W_i \le R_i$. Then, $\Sigma R_i = 2R$: the factor 2 appears because each relevant pair is counted twice (e.g., the relevant pair consisting of the ith and jth observations, say, is counted as part of R_i and also as part of R_j). Similarly, $\Sigma W_i = 2(C_R - D_R)$. Hence we have the alternative formula

$$\theta = \frac{\Sigma W_i}{\Sigma R_i},$$

where the factor 2 has canceled from both numerator and denominator. This method of computation leads to a convenient formula for the asymptotic standard error of θ, namely,

$$s_\theta = \frac{2}{(\Sigma R_i)^2} \sqrt{(\Sigma R_i)^2 \Sigma W_i^2 - 2\Sigma R_i \Sigma W_i \Sigma R_i W_i + (\Sigma W_i)^2 \Sigma R_i^2}.$$

It can also be shown that, as the sample size n increases, the sampling distribution of θ becomes normal; that is, for large n the quantity

$$\frac{\theta - E[\theta]}{s_\theta}$$

is approximately a standard normal variable. The only assumptions required for this, other than that sampling is random, are that relevant concordant and discordant pairs must both have nonzero probability of occurrence, and that the limiting value of s_θ must not be zero. It appears that the possibility of this latter condition's taking place may safely be ignored in practice; it is similar to the condition described by Goodman and Kruskal (1963, p. 364) which they suggest "is an unlikely state of affairs in most applications." Details regarding the derivation of these asymptotic results may be found in my monograph (Quade 1971).

Since the sampling theory just presented is strictly asymptotic, you may well ask for the distribution of θ in small samples, or at least for the proper definition of "small" in this context. Although I can give no really satisfactory answer at this stage, I offer the following speculation: It seems reasonable that the validity of the asymptotic results in finite samples will depend most directly on C_R and D_R, the numbers of concordant and discordant relevant pairs. One special case of θ has been extensively studied: the Goodman and Kruskal index γ. Sampling experiments by Rosenthal (1966) for 5×5 cross-classifications over a wide range of the population value γ_0 showed the distribution of $(\gamma - \gamma_0)/s_\gamma$ to be reasonably close to the standard normal in samples of $n = 50$ for $|\gamma_0| < .50$. The probability of a tie in a 5×5 cross-classification cannot be less than .20, and in the representative examples presented by Rosenthal it varies from about .25 to more than .40. Since the total number of pairs at $n = 50$ is $N = 1,225$, it appears that her experiments must typically have involved some 800 untied pairs. With $|\gamma_0| < .50$, at least 200 of these would have been concordant and at least 200 discordant. Thus it appears safe to rely on the asymptotic theory if C_R and D_R are both as great as 200. In smaller samples Rosenthal found a tendency for the standard error formula to underestimate. An extreme example of this is that $s_\theta = 0$ if the relevant pairs are all concordant, all discordant, or all tied, and this is not unlikely in very small samples. Note, however, that these cautions do not in any way detract from the usefulness of indices of the form θ as meaningful descriptive statistics in samples however small.

Statistical inference based on any index of the form θ is thus possible, at least in large samples. Let Q_α be the critical value for a normal deviate Q, so that $P\{|Q \geq Q_\alpha\} = \alpha$. Then, for example, a two-sided confidence interval with confidence coefficient $100(1 - \alpha)$ percent is $(\theta - s_\theta Q_\alpha, \theta + s_\theta Q_\alpha)$, and the hypothesis that the population value of θ is θ_0, say, can be rejected in favor of a two-sided alternative if the value θ_0 lies outside this confidence interval. One-sided tests and confidence intervals can also be constructed, in an obvious manner. As a special case, the hypothesis that the population value is zero might be rejected if $|\theta/s_\theta| \geq Q_\alpha$. For this null hypothesis, however, a simpler test involving only the W's and not the R's may be preferable: namely, reject if

$$\frac{\overline{W}\sqrt{n}}{2\sqrt{\Sigma(W_i - \overline{W})^2}} \geq Q_\alpha \, ,$$

where $\overline{W} = \Sigma W_i/n$. (Do not neglect the factor 2, which may give this formula an unfamiliar look.)

It appears that a suitable upper bound for the true standard deviation of the asymptotic distribution of θ is

$$\sigma_\theta \leq \sqrt{\frac{2(1 - \theta_0^2)}{np_R}}$$

where θ_0 is the population value and p_R is the probability that a randomly chosen pair will be relevant. Suppose relevant pairs cannot be tied on X or Y, as, for example, when X and Y are continuous, or when ties are simply excluded in the definition of relevance. Then the bound may be proved valid by using exactly the argument of Goodman and Kruskal (1963, p. 363), but interpreting their subscript s as indicating "concordant and relevant", d as "discordant and relevant", and t as "not relevant." The bound is also easily shown to hold if $\theta_0 = 0$ whether or not relevant pairs can be tied. Unfortunately, I have not been able to prove it in the remaining case (relevant tied pairs possible, $\theta_0 \neq 0$), although obviously it must hold at least approximately if such ties are unlikely or θ_0 is small.

One use for such a bound, as Goodman and Kruskal indicate, is to allow the possibility of "conservative" inference procedures in situations where use of an asymptotic standard error seems unjustified or its calculation is inconvenient. Then, for example, a "conservative" $100(1 - \alpha)$ percent confidence interval for θ_0 is formed by the set of values θ_0 which satisfy the quadratic inequality

$$nR(\theta - \theta_0)^2 \leq 2N(1 - \theta_0^2)Q_\alpha^2,$$

where the unknown value of p_R in the bound has been estimated by R/N. A second use for the bound is to show, at least qualitatively, how the sample variance of θ decreases to zero as the population value of θ approaches $+1$ or -1 and increases as the probability of obtaining a relevant pair decreases.

We thus see that the sampling theory just presented for indices of form θ provides a unified treatment for a large number of correlation indices already in the literature. The results agree completely with those obtained previously: for example, those given by Kendall (1962) for his tau$_a$, and by Goodman and Kruskal (1963, 1972) for their gamma and for Somers's asymmetric measure. And the family also includes other indices for which sampling theory has not previously been published, in particular the general measures of partial correlation developed below.

Partial Correlation Based on Matching

I shall now present a general index of partial correlation between X and Y, given Z, based on the concept of correlation in terms of the concordance and discordance of pairs of observations with respect to X and Y, and on the concept of partialing out Z by holding it constant, or, more precisely, in terms of the concept of *matching*. Two observations are intuitively considered matched if their values of Z are "practically" equal. For what follows, however, it it sufficient if there has been established any specific rule whatever by which it can always be decided whether two observations are matched or not. A reasonable way of measuring the partial correlation, then—in wording imitating that used by Goodman and Kruskal (1954) in defining their correlation index gamma—is to find out how much more probable it is to get like than unlike orders with respect to X and Y when pairs of observations matched on Z are chosen at random from the sample. More specifically, let M be the number of sample pairs matched on Z; and let C_M and D_M be the number of these pairs which are concordant and discordant, respectively, with respect to X and Y. I now propose a *matched partial correlation coefficient*

$$\tau_a(X, Y|Z) = \frac{C_M - D_M}{M},$$

the difference between the proportions of concordant and discordant matched pairs. It is easy to see that such a coefficient satisfies all the conditions suggested for indices of correlation, and also that it belongs to the family described earlier, since we can say that "pairs are relevant if they are matched on Z." Thus the asymptotic results derived for the family all apply. A closely related matched partial correlation coefficient,

$$\gamma(X, Y|Z) = \frac{C_M - D_M}{C_M + D_M},$$

results if we say that "pairs are relevant if they are matched on Z and not tied on X or on Y." I am using the same notation here that I used for Davis's coefficient, since his is a special case—namely, the case where the variable Z is discrete and "matched" is interpreted as meaning "tied." But these coefficients are far more general, since they can be applied to any control variable Z whatever, not just to discrete ones.

Suppose, in particular, that Z is measured on an interval scale. It is convenient to define matching in terms of the *tolerance*, the maximum discrepancy allowed between two observations before they must be declared unmatched. That is, if a tolerance ϵ is set, two observations (X_1, Y_1, Z_1) and (X_2, Y_2, Z_2) are declared matched if $|Z_1 - Z_2| \leq \epsilon$. (Setting $\epsilon = 0$ corresponds to interpreting "matched" as "tied.") Such a definition avoids the anomalies which can result from grouping on Z. For example, suppose we are trying to control for age. If we form matches by using, say, 10-year age intervals 20-29, 30-39, and so on, a person at age 30 will be declared matched with one at age 39, but not with one at age 29. But if we form matches by setting a tolerance $\epsilon = 5$ years (half the width of the age intervals) we will obtain about the same number of matched pairs while maintaining a more logical pattern. It may be noted that, unlike the grouping method, matching by using a tolerance does not produce *transitivity:* thus, given that persons at age 20 are matched with those at age 25, and that those at age 25 are matched with those at age 30, it does not follow that persons at age 20 are matched with those at age 30. This phenomenon is accounted for, however, in the standard error formula. It may also be useful to point out that it is often better to match only after first transforming the variable Z. For example, one might hesitate to designate a match on age as "within a tolerance of ϵ years," on the grounds that the same difference in age means more for young individuals than for old ones. This could be handled easily, however, by transforming Z to $\log Z$, say, instead of using Z directly.

Now suppose we wish to match on several control variables, so that Z is of the form

$$Z = (Z^{(1)}, Z^{(2)}, \cdots, Z^{(m)})'.$$

The simplest treatment is to define matches on each component of Z separately, and to declare two observations matched if they are matched on all components simultaneously. But more generally, we may want to balance off the discrepancies due to the various components of Z, so that two observations may be called matched if they differ little on the average, though they may differ more on some components if they are particularly close on others. This can be accomplished conveniently by defining a sort of *distance* function—though it need not have all the properties which mathematicians imply by use of that term—to measure the discrepancy between any two points in the sample space, and then setting a tolerance on the distance. Two observations are then declared matched only if the distance between them is no greater than the tolerance. It is often suitable to use distance functions of the form

$$D((X_i, Y_i, Z_i), (X_j, Y_j, Z_j)) = (Z_i - Z_j)'W(Z_i - Z_j),$$

where W is a matrix of weights. If $W = V^{-1}$, where V is the sample variance matrix of Z, then D becomes the *Mahalanobis distance* which gives each component of Z equal importance in determining a match.

By this time it should be clear that infinitely many matched partial correlation coefficients may be possible for a given situation, these being distinguished from one another by their definitions of matching. All these, however, are of the form θ as described above, and hence they can be used for statistical inference as indicated.

Examples

The first example, which will illustrate the method of computation in some detail, is based on Table 13.5, which gives (fictitious) data on $n = 25$ fourth graders. Let X be the result of a certain examination, an ordinal variable recorded as A, B, C, D, or F; and let Y be the variable height, recorded in inches. The variable to be controlled for is a bivariate Z of which the first component is the dichotomy sex (Z_1) and the second component is IQ (Z_2). Two children will be declared matched on sex if they are of the same sex (tolerance 0 on Z_1) and matched on IQ if they differ in IQ by no more than 10 units (tolerance 10 on Z_2).

The matched partial correlation coefficient $\tau_a(X, Y|Z_1, Z_2)$ between examination result and height controlled for both sex and IQ, where all pairs matched on both control variables simultaneously are considered relevant, is obtained by means of the values of R_i and W_i shown in the last section of the table. One can easily verify that the first child, for instance, is matched with exactly two others, namely, the second and third (for convenience in hand computation the data have been sorted on the variables to be controlled for), and hence $R_1 = 2$; and he is concordant with both of them—in particular, he is the shortest of the three and also received the lowest grade—hence $W_i = 2$ also. The values of R_i and W_i for the other 24 children can be checked similarly. One may then compute $\Sigma R_i = 96$, which indicates that there are 48 matched pairs of children; and $\Sigma W_i = 10$, which indicates that there are 5 more concordant pairs than discordant; hence the matched partial correlation coefficient is

$$\tau_a(X, Y|Z_1, Z_2) = \Sigma W_i/\Sigma R_i = 10/96 = .104.$$

Table 13.5. Sex, IQ, Height, and Final-Examination Results for a Class of Fourth-Grade Children

i	Result of exam.	Height (in.)	Sex	IQ	Without matching		Matching on sex only		Matching on IQ* only		Matching on sex and IQ*	
	X	Y	Z_1	Z_2	R	W	R	W	R	W	R	W
1	F	50	M	85	24	+19	12	+9	4	+3	2	+2
2	D	58	M	92	24	−12	12	−3	9	−4	5	−1
3	D	54	M	93	24	+2	12	+5	10	+2	6	+5
4	A	56	M	96	24	+9	12	+1	10	+2	5	−1
5	C	55	M	100	24	+3	12	+6	10	+2	6	+2
6	C	58	M	102	24	−1	12	+1	11	0	6	−1
7	B	57	M	103	24	+7	12	+2	10	+3	5	+1
8	C	53	M	109	24	+3	12	+2	10	+1	5	+1
9	F	54	M	115	24	+1	12	+4	9	−3	4	−2
10	B	57	M	118	24	+7	12	+2	8	+3	5	+2
11	A	49	M	120	24	−21	12	−11	7	−6	4	−4
12	D	52	M	123	24	+7	12	+6	7	0	4	0
13	B	60	M	128	24	+12	12	+6	6	+1	3	0
14	C	51	F	83	24	0	11	0	4	−2	1	−1
15	B	50	F	86	24	−13	11	−6	5	−2	1	−1
16	C	52	F	98	24	+1	11	0	9	−2	3	−2
17	D	57	F	99	24	−9	11	−9	10	−3	3	−1
18	F	53	F	105	24	+6	11	0	11	−6	5	+2
19	C	53	F	106	24	+3	11	+1	11	+1	5	0
20	A	54	F	111	24	+2	11	+5	10	0	4	+2
21	C	55	F	114	24	+3	11	−3	9	+2	4	0
22	C	51	F	121	24	0	11	0	8	0	3	+1
23	C	52	F	131	24	+1	11	0	5	+3	3	+2
24	A	55	F	135	24	+7	11	+7	3	+1	2	+2
25	B	54	F	140	24	+5	11	+5	2	+2	2	+2

NOTE: Data are fictitious.

*Within a tolerance of 10 units.

(In actuality, 22 of the matched pairs are concordant, 17 discordant, and 9 tied; without modification, however, the computational scheme here presented does not provide these numbers.) Having calculated $\Sigma R_i^2 = 422$, $\Sigma R_i W_i = 50$, and $\Sigma W_i^2 = 90$, one may substitute these into the standard error formula and obtain

$$s_a = \frac{2}{(96)^2}\sqrt{(96)^2(90) - 2(96)(10)(50) + (10)^2(422)} = .191.$$

Thus the coefficient is smaller than its standard error and certainly is not significantly different from zero in the statistical sense. If this sample could be regarded as large, $\tau_a/s_a = .545$ could be taken as a normal deviate in making such a test, and the 95 percent (say) confidence interval $\tau_a \pm 1.96s_a$, or $(-.270, +.469)$, could be produced for the population index. However, with only 25 observations and 48 matched pairs—which are not independent of each other—it is best to be somewhat restrained in making such inferences.

The first section of Table 13.5, labeled "without matching," shows the ingredients for computing the total correlation $\tau_a(X, Y)$. This can be obtained by declaring all pairs relevant, so that $R_i = n - 1 = 24$ for all i. We then have $\Sigma R_i = 25(24) = 600$, which indicates that there are $R = 300 (=N)$ relevant pairs; and $\Sigma W_i = 42$, which indicates that of these pairs there are 21 more concordant than discordant (actually, there are 122 concordant, 101 discordant, and 77 tied pairs) and hence the index takes the value

$$\tau_a(X, Y) = \Sigma W_i/\Sigma R_i = 42/600 = .070.$$

Its standard error can be computed by the same formula, and it turns out to be $s_a = .136$. Again the correlation is not significant.

The other two sections of Table 13.5 show the values of R_i and W_i where matching has been performed on only one of the two variables, either sex or IQ; the computations proceed in exactly the same manner (results are summarized in Table 13.6). Note that the conditional correlations for the two sexes are obtainable almost as by-products of the computation for the partial correlation when sex is given: to obtain the

Table 13.6

Correlation	Pair (i, j) matched if:	ΣR_i	ΣW_i	ΣR_i^2	$\Sigma R_i W_i$	ΣW_i^2	τ_a	s_a
Total	(always)	600	42	14,400	1,008	1,726	.070	.136
Partialling out sex	$Z_{1i} = Z_{1j}$	288	30	3,324	360	600	.104	.165
Conditional on male	$Z_{1i} = Z_{1j} = $ "male"	156	30	1,872	360	374	.192	.224
Conditional on female	$Z_{1i} = Z_{1j} = $ "female"	132	0	1,452	0	226	.000	.228
Partialling out IQ*	$\lvert Z_{2i} - Z_{2j} \rvert \leqslant 10$	198	10	1,744	88	178	.051	.133
Partialling out sex and IQ*	$Z_{1i} = Z_{1j}$ and $\lvert Z_{2i} - Z_{2j} \rvert \leqslant 10$	96	10	422	50	90	.104	.191

*By matching with a tolerance of 10 units.

conditional correlation among males, take R_i and W_i as identical with those used in obtaining the partial correlation if the ith student is male, and take $R_i = W_i = 0$ if the ith student is female; and to obtain the conditional correlation among females, do the reverse. The values of ΣR_i, ΣW_i, ΣR_i^2, ΣW_i^2, and $\Sigma R_i W_i$ for the partial correlation indices are equal to the sums of the corresponding values for the two conditional correlation indices. A similar situation will obtain whenever the variable being controlled for is discrete.

Now let us consider an example in which the underlying population distribution is known. For $i = 1, 2, \cdots, 50$, let C_{1i}, C_{2i}, and C_{3i} be the entries in columns 01, 02, and 03 of the random normal deviates given by Dixon and Massey (1969, Table A-2), and for $i = 51, 52, \cdots, 100$ continue with columns 11, 12, and 13. Define $X_i = C_{1i} + C_{3i}$, $Y_i = C_{2i} + C_{3i}$, and $Z_i = C_{3i}$ for $i = 1, 2, \cdots, 100$. Simple considerations will then show that the total product-moment correlation for the population is $\rho(X, Y) = 1/2$, with partial correlation $\rho(X, Y|Z) = 0$; the corresponding sample values happen to be $r(X, Y) = .533$ and $r(X, Y|Z) = -.009$. If two observations (X_i, Y_i, Z_i) and (X_j, Y_j, Z_j) are defined to be matched if $|Z_i - Z_j| \leqslant \epsilon$, then with X, Y, and Z as specified it can be shown (see Quade 1971) that the limiting value of the matched partial correlation coefficient, considered as a function of ϵ, is

$$\theta_0(\epsilon) = \frac{1}{3} P(|Q| \leqslant \frac{\epsilon}{\sqrt{2}})^2 \ ,$$

where Q is a normal $(0, 1)$ variable. Note that for an infinite tolerance, corresponding to declaring all pairs matched, we have $\theta_0(\epsilon) = 1/3$, which is the value of the Kendall total correlation in the population. As ϵ decreases to zero, $\theta_0(\epsilon)$ decreases to zero also, thus behaving exactly as the population product-moment correlation. Results of computing the matched partial correlation coefficient from the sample for decreasing values of the tolerance are shown in Table 13.7, and these show a similar steady decrease. Note also that as the tolerance decreases, and the number of matched pairs decreases correspondingly, the standard error increases; this would be expected, of course, on intuitive grounds, and also from the form of the upper bound given earlier; but the apparent increase is not drastic until a very small tolerance has been reached.

As a third example, consider the data of Angell quoted by Blalock (1972) for $n = 29$ non-Southern cities of 100,000 or more. Here Y is an index of moral integration "derived by combining crime-rate indices with those for welfare effort," X is an index of heterogeneity "meas-

Table 13.7

Tolerance for matching on Z* (ϵ)	Number of matched pairs (R)	Population index (θ_0)	Sample index (τ)	Standard error (s)
∞	4,950	.333	+.363	.053
3.00	4,804	.311	+.343	.052
2.00	4,164	.237	+.261	.053
1.50	3,486	.168	+.179	.055
1.00	2,514	.090	+.086	.060
0.75	1,942	.055	+.049	.063
0.50	1,308	.026	+.040	.069
0.25	674	.007	−.003	.078
0	0	.000		

*The true standard deviation of Z is $\sigma_Z = 1.000$, with $s_z = .997$.

ured in terms of the relative numbers of nonwhites and foreign-born whites in the population," and Z is "a mobility index measuring the relative numbers of persons moving in and out of the city." The product-moment total correlations are $r(X, Y) = -.156$, $r(X, Z) = -.456$, and $r(Y, Z) = -.513$, with partial correlation $r(X, Y|Z) = -.511$. Results for the matched partial correlation are summarized in Table 13.8, and as in the previous example they agree nicely with those found by the more standard method. In this example the matched partial correlation increases in absolute value as the tolerance is reduced, and since any correlation is the more accurately determined the farther it is from zero, this has to some extent canceled out the otherwise-expected increase in standard error. It is encouraging to note the regularity of the pattern of results as the tolerance for matching is reduced to ever smaller values and the number of matched pairs drops far below that recommended for reliance on the asymptotic theory.

Table 13.8

Tolerance for matching on Z* (ϵ)	Number of matched pairs (R)	Index of matched correlation (τ)	Standard error (s)
∞	406	−.138	.100
20	349	−.209	.090
15	286	−.294	.079
10	215	−.349	.085
5	125	−.488	.103
2	47	−.532	.134
1	24	−.583	.165

*The standard error of Z is $s_Z = 9.66$.

The last example uses the data of Hajda quoted by Davis (1967), which were obtained from a sample survey of $n = 1,850$ Baltimore women. Here X is a dichotomy, taking the value "high" (or "low") if the respondent was above (or below) 45 years of age; Y is another dichotomy, taking the value "high" (or "low") if she had (or had not) recently read a book; and Z distinguishes three categories of educational attainment, "college", "high school," and "less than high school." A pair of observations will be declared matched if it is tied on Z. Two versions of the matched partial correlation coefficient will be discussed: $\tau_a(X, Y|Z)$, in which all matched pairs are considered relevant; and Davis's coefficient $\gamma(X, Y|Z)$, in which only those matched pairs not tied on X or on Y are considered relevant. Since it may be instructive to follow the calculations for a problem involving categorical data, Table 13.9 shows them in some detail. The twelve possible values of (X, Y, Z) are listed first, and the frequency (labeled F) with which each occurs in the sample follows. Next are shown how many of the observations matched with those at any given value are also concordant, discordant, and tied with them; these numbers are labeled C, D, and T, respectively. Then, $W = C-D$ is given. Finally, for τ_a we have

Table 13.9

Age (X)	Book reading (Y)	Education (Z)	Frequency (F)	C	D	T	W	R_a	R_γ
High	High	College	104	46	0	302	+46	348	46
High	Low	College	36	0	163	185	−163	348	163
Low	High	College	163	0	36	312	−36	348	36
Low	Low	College	46	104	0	244	+104	348	104
High	High	High school	159	327	0	627	+327	954	327
High	Low	High school	179	0	290	664	−290	954	290
Low	High	High school	290	0	179	775	−179	954	179
Low	Low	High school	327	159	0	795	+159	954	159
High	High	Less than high school	54	133	0	412	+133	545	133
High	Low	Less than high school	335	0	24	521	−24	545	24
Low	High	Less than high school	24	0	335	210	−335	545	335
Low	Low	Less than high school	133	54	0	491	+54	545	54

$R_a = C + D + T$, and for γ we have $R_\gamma = C + D$. In either case the matched partial correlation coefficient is calculated as $\Sigma FW/\Sigma FR$, and its standard error, specializing to categorical data the formula given previously, is

$$\frac{2}{(\Sigma FR)^2} \sqrt{(\Sigma FR)^2 \Sigma FW^2 - 2\Sigma FR \Sigma FW \Sigma FRW + (\Sigma FW)^2 \Sigma FR^2}.$$

In the second case only, an equivalent formula for the standard error in terms of the C's and D's might also be used; in grouped-data form this is

$$s_\gamma = \frac{4}{(\Sigma FC + \Sigma FD)^2} \sqrt{\Sigma FC^2 (\Sigma FD)^2 - 2\Sigma FC \Sigma FD \Sigma FCD + (\Sigma FC)^2 \Sigma FD^2}$$

For the example, $\Sigma FW = -3{,}718$ and $\Sigma FW^2 = 55{,}729{,}114$. For the first definition of matching, $\Sigma FR = 1{,}330{,}092$, $\Sigma FR^2 = 1{,}073{,}601{,}726$, and $\Sigma FRW = -1{,}531{,}320$, and thus the partial correlation $\tau_a = -.0028$ with $s_a = .0112$. For the second definition, $\Sigma FR = 259{,}554$, $\Sigma FR^2 = \Sigma FW^2$ (this equality holds when X and Y are both dichotomous, but not in general), and $\Sigma FRW = -1{,}070{,}650$, and thus Davis's coefficient $\gamma = -.0143$ with $s_\gamma = .0581$. Note that γ, in which the ties are discarded, is about five times larger than τ_a, in which they are retained, but s_γ is also five times larger than s_a, so the critical ratio for testing the null hypothesis of no partial correlation is about the same, namely, $-.25$, in both cases. The simpler test for this null hypothesis would of course be identical for the two coefficients, since it depends only on the W's; it gives a critical ratio of $-.006$. Although a number of shortcuts could have been taken in the calculations for this rather simple example, a general computer program would probably best proceed from the formulas as given.

In this same example the total correlation between age (X) and book reading (Y) is $-.0596$ as measured by τ_a, or $-.2412$ as measured by γ, which is significantly different from zero at $\alpha < .01$; and holding education constant has reduced the correlation by substantially more than 90 percentage points, to a clearly insignificant value. On the other hand, using the partial correlation formula with τ_b as suggested by Hawkes, we calculate $\tau_b(X, Y) = -.1206$, $\tau_b(X, Z) = -.2442$, and $\tau_b(Y, Z) = .4139$; hence $\tau_b(X, Y | Z) = -.0221$, for a reduction of only 82 percentage points. And if we adopt Somers's method, we have a fourfold table (see Table 13.10), from which $\phi = -.0674$; this again illustrates the difference in results which can arise from different concepts of control.

Table 13.10

Y, Z \ X, Z	Concordant	Discordant
Concordant	68987	180932
Discordant	15600	27456

Discussion

Definition of Matching

In the preceding development, I have implicitly assumed that the definition of matching is to be based on substantive considerations, and as a statistician I might take the attitude that this is not really a statistical question at all. Yet I may still offer some suggestions. If ties on Z are plentiful, it will nearly always be satisfactory to let them serve as the set of matched pairs. But suppose, for example, that Z is continuous, so that no ties occur. One wants to choose the tolerance very small, since logically that choice most nearly achieves the complete partialling out of the control variable. (Recall that, at the opposite extreme, allowing an infinite tolerance produces a completely unpartialled total correlation index.) But, in finite samples, as the tolerance decreases the number of matched pairs decreases also. This leaves a smaller and smaller basis for the estimate, whose variance accordingly increases. Thus the optimal tolerance for estimating a partial correlation is a compromise: a large value may have too much bias, a small value too much variance. Presumably the investigator will first propose a definition of matching based on totally nonstatistical substantive grounds. If this definition implies too few matched pairs for reliance on asymptotic theory, a relaxation might be suggested. And if the proposed definition implies a very large number of matched pairs, it might be tightened to reduce possible bias.

A related question of interest to the mathematical statistician is, What happens asymptotically as the sample size increases, if the definition of matching is simultaneously tightened? Presumably a consistent result could be obtained in this manner, but the theory has not yet been worked out. Similar questions arise if the definition of matching is made relative rather than absolute: for instance, one might decide to pair each observation with the k others most closely matched to it, or simply to use the K most closely matched pairs out of the total N. Such a decision would confer the advantage of making the number of matched pairs fixed instead of random; but both practical and theoretical problems are raised in attempting to order pairs of observations according to closeness of matching.

Some researchers might prefer a measure of partial correlation in which pairs are not simply classified as "matched" (and hence used) or "not matched" (and hence discarded) but are weighted according to their closeness with respect to the control variable. Thus if $D((X_1, Y_1, Z_1), (X_2, Y_2, Z_2))$ is the distance, or discrepancy, between any two observations (X_1, Y_1, Z_1) and (X_2, Y_2, Z_2), one might, for example, want to give a pair of observations with discrepancy D the weight $f(d) = 1/D$, or $\exp(-D)$. Although more complicated, this is still entirely feasible. Let

$$R_i = \sum_{j \ne i} f\{D[(X_i, Y_i, Z_i), (X_j, Y_j, Z_j)]\}.$$

for $i = 1, 2, \cdots, n$; and similarly let W_i be the difference between weighted sums of concordant and discordant pairs. Then define a generalized matched partial correlation coefficient $\theta = \Sigma W_i / \Sigma R_i$ as before. It can be shown that the entire asymptotic sampling theory, including the standard error formula, applies also to such generalized coefficients.

Relevance of Ties

In constructing an index of correlation based on the notion of concordant and discordant pairs, should tied pairs be included or not? The theory presented here is sufficiently general that one may have it either way, and the choice is to some extent a matter of taste. For one thing, exclusion of tied pairs often simplifies computations, at least hand computations, if only by diminishing the numbers involved; and the indices thus produced may be more satisfying, since they are greater in magnitude. On the other hand, the theory is perhaps more elegant when relevance can be defined in terms only of matching on the control variables. Also, Wilson has argued that the decision should depend on the type of hypothesis to be tested.

But suppose we take the point of view that X and Y, even if not continuous as recorded, usually represent underlying continuous variables, with ties occurring only because the measurements are imprecise or because they are grouped afterward. It is then a reasonable goal to determine the correlation in the underlying continuous population. (For simplicity, consider only the total correlation at present.) We may begin by asking how many of the tied pairs we observe would be found concordant, and how many discordant, if they could be properly resolved. This requires guessing the correlations within subpopulations where the range of X and/or Y is restricted. One ordinarily expects such subcorrelations to be smaller, on the whole, than the correlation for unrestricted X and Y. As an extreme case, set them all equal to zero. This can be effectively accomplished in the sample by adjusting the data so that half the tied pairs are counted as concordant and half as discordant. Thus $C' = C+(T/2)$ and $D' = D+(T/2)$, where C, D, and T are the numbers of concordant, discordant, and tied pairs in the data as recorded, while C' and D' are the numbers of concordant and discordant pairs after adjustment. But $(C' - D') = (C - D)$, so the adjusted correlation index is $(C' - D')/N = (C - D)/N = \tau_a$ (the denominator for the adjusted data is unequivocally N, since there are now no ties); that is, we get the same result we would have gotten had we calculated τ_a from the original data. For the opposite extreme case, set the subcorrelations equal to the total correlation. In the sample this amounts to allocating the tied pairs in the same proportions as the untied ones. Then

$$C' = C + (\frac{C}{C+D})T = \frac{CN}{C+D}, \qquad D' = D + (\frac{D}{C+D})T = \frac{DN}{C+D},$$

and the adjusted correlation index is

$$\frac{C' - D'}{N} = \frac{\dfrac{CN}{C+D} - \dfrac{DN}{C+D}}{N} = \frac{C-D}{C+D} = \gamma \; ;$$

that is, the result is now the same as that a calculation of γ from the original data would have yielded. In general, those measures which include ties may be regarded as conservative, or pessimistic, since they tend to underestimate the strength of any underlying correlation; whereas those which discard ties are optimistic, since they tend to overestimate its strength. Probably in most contexts underestimation would be preferable to overestimation, which suggests that tied pairs be retained.

On the other hand, it is possible to compromise. My personal impression, admittedly based on a rather limited number of cases, is that imposing a grouping on an underlying continuous population almost always increases the correlation as measured by γ but decreases the correlation as measured by τ_a. Since the effect on the former measure is usually much the greater, τ_a tends to declare the correlation somewhat too weak, while γ makes it much too strong. Thus τ_b, which always falls between them, might well be a good overall estimator for realistic cases, although peculiar populations can be invented to favor any of the three indices. (It might also be mentioned that numerical work reported by Reynolds in the next chapter also suggests that γ is inferior to τ_a, and especially to τ_b, for a somewhat different purpose but perhaps for the same reasons.) Of course, τ_b is more difficult to interpret in terms of the measurements actually at hand, and it is certainly much more difficult to work with, both numerically and theoretically, since it is not a member of the family of indices of form θ. Another possibility is the measure e proposed by Wilson, which also falls between τ_a and γ: in fact, between τ_a and τ_b. Further work is required to settle this question.

Computational Matters

It is perhaps a disadvantage that the calculation of a matched partial correlation must always begin from scratch, since there is no formula by which it can be determined from total correlations. Yet the partial correlation formula is sometimes deceptively easy, since its numerical instability in the presence of highly correlated variables is not always obvious. This is not so with matched correlations, where any instability is always clearly indicated, if not by the asymptotic variance formula, then certainly by a paucity of matched pairs. Of course, any statistic requiring individual consideration of all pairs of observations is tedious to calculate; even on the computer, although a matched-correlation program may be simple and short, the time it requires may be long. This computational problem can be avoided by grouping the data, but unfortunately the resulting ties reduce the precision of the estimate. For large numbers of observations it may be preferable to consider only a sample of the possible pairs; but inference procedures would have to be modified accordingly.

Summary

Let me review the comparison of the matched partial correlation coefficient between X and Y, given Z, with its major competitors. Since Davis's coefficient is not a competitor, but instead is a special case of matched correlation, the main rivals appear to be the product-moment partial correlation and the Kendall-Somers-Hawkes measures. Of these, the former is inapplicable, or at any rate difficult to interpret, unless X and Y are at least interval-scale variables; the latter require Z to be at least ordinal. Small-sample theory for the product-moment partial correlation is available, but only under strong assumptions including normality, and even for asymptotic results the form of relationship of X and Y to Z must be known; for the Kendall type of measures, sampling theory is practically nonexistent. On the other hand, the proposed new index has the following clear advantages:

    1. The *applicability* of matched correlation is almost unlimited. It may be used to control for a completely arbitrary variable Z, even a multivariate Z in which the scale of each component separately may be interval, ordinal, or purely nominal, provided only that a definition of matching can be supplied. And the variables X and Y need be no more than ordinal, including ordered-categorical.

2. The *interpretation* of matched correlation is based on two very simple concepts: determining whether two observations are matched or not, and whether they are concordant or discordant with respect to X and Y. The index may then be defined as the probability that a randomly chosen matched pair will be concordant, minus the probability that it will be discordant. (A slight modification is required if tied matched pairs are irrelevant.)

3. Asymptotic *sampling theory* for matched partial correlation coefficients is available, without restrictive assumptions, and hence statistical inference is possible, at least in large samples.

References

Blalock, Hubert M., Jr.
  1972. *Social Statistics*. 2nd ed. New York: McGraw-Hill.
Costner, Herbert L.
  1965. "Criteria for Measures of Association." *American Sociological Review* 30:341-53.
Davis, James A.
  1967. "A Partial Coefficient for Goodman and Kruskal's Gamma." *Journal of the American Statistical Association* 62:189-93.
Dixon, Wilfrid J., and Frank J. Massey, Jr.
  1969. *Introduction to Statistical Analysis*. 3d ed. New York: McGraw-Hill.
Goodman, Leo A.
  1959. "Partial Tests for Partial Taus." *Biometrika* 46:425-32.
Goodman, Leo A., and William H. Kruskal
  1954. "Measures of Association for Cross Classifications." *Journal of the American Statistical Association* 49:723-64.
  1963. "Measures of Association for Cross Classifications," III, "Approximate Sampling Theory." Ibid. 58:310-64.
  1972. "Measures of Association for Cross Classifications," IV, "Simplification of Asymptotic Variances." Ibid. 67:415-21.
Hawkes, Roland K.
  1971. "The Multivariate Analysis of Ordinal Measures." *American Journal of Sociology* 76:908-26.
Kendall, Maurice G.
  1962. *Rank Correlation Methods*. 3d ed. New York: Hafner.
Ploch, Donald R.
  1969. "An Interaction Test for Goodman and Kruskal's Gamma." Manuscript. New Haven, Conn.: Yale University.
Quade, Dana
  1971. "Nonparametric Partial Correlation." Report SW 13/71. Amsterdam: Mathematisch Centrum.
Reynolds, H. T.
  1971. "Making Causal Inferences with Ordinal Data" Working Paper no. 5. Chapel Hill, N.C.: Institute for Research in Social Science.
Rosenberg, Morris
  1962. "Test Factor Standardization as a Method of Interpretation." *Social Forces* 41:53-61.
Rosenthal, Irene
  1966. "Distribution of the Sample Version of the Measure of Association, Gamma." *Journal of the American Statistical Association* 61:440-53.
Somers, Robert H.
  1959. "The Rank Analogue of Product-Moment Partial Correlation and Regression, with Application to Manifold, Ordered Contingency Tables." *Biometrika* 46:241-46.
  1962. "A New Asymmetric Measure of Association for Ordinal Variables." *American Sociological Review* 27:799-811.
  1966. "An Approach to the Multivariate Analysis of Ordinal Data." Ibid. 31:971-77.
Wilson, Thomas P.
  1969. "A Proportional-Reduction-in-Error Interpretation for Kendall's Tau-b." *Social Forces* 47:340-42.

Chapter 14

ORDINAL PARTIAL CORRELATION AND CAUSAL INFERENCES

H. T. REYNOLDS

H. T. Reynolds, who received his Ph.D. from the University of North Carolina in 1971, is currently Assistant Professor of Political Science at the University of Delaware. In addition to his interests in methodology, he is concerned with political behavior; on this subject he is presently completing a book, as well as undertaking an analysis of voting behavior.

The only available scales for studying many political and social problems are nominal and ordinal. These scales pose difficulties for the social scientist because many of the most popular and versatile statistical procedures require interval data. There are, of course, sophisticated techniques for analyzing nominal and ordinal data, but for several reasons researchers prefer to use methods such as correlation and regression. Often, in taking advantage of "parametric" statistics, an investigator will ignore the level of measurement and will make calculations directly on category scores.

In causal analysis (Blalock 1964), the problem can be especially acute. Suppose one wished to study the relationship between political efficacy and political involvement. He might suspect that any observed correlation between these two variables could be created by education. It would be a simple matter to test for spuriousness if interval level data were available—assuming the necessary assumptions could be made. But quite frequently the investigator only has survey data involving, at best, order categories. As we will see in the next section, making causal tests is difficult in this situation.

I should like to thank Hubert M. Blalock and Dana Quade for their comments on earlier drafts of this chapter.

One can make analyses of the causal type with nominal and ordinal data—"test factor stratification" (Lazarsfeld 1955; Hyman 1955; Rosenberg 1968) is one way—but the methods for doing so tend to be cumbersome and imprecise. The Lazarsfeld approach, for example, requires a relatively large sample size in order to compute meaningful percentages. Also, it is hard to tell whether a controlled relationship has increased or decreased and by how much. For these reasons, many people apply product-moment correlation formulas directly to category scores, even if the scores represent convenience rather than information about the true numerical values of the observations.

Since causal analysis is helpful to us for both heuristic and practical reasons, however, it is worthwhile to develop ways of handling lower levels of measurement in testing causal models. My purpose in this chapter is to argue that we can make causal analyses with ordinal data. I shall first describe two procedures for doing so and then apply them to various models and measurement conditions. One of these techniques, ordinal partial correlation (see Quade's chapter in this volume), is a very satisfactory and flexible method which contains several desirable properties. The other, treating interval data as though they were ordinal, "works" in a number of situations but does not have many of the advantages of Quade's procedure. For testing causal models, neither of the methods is as sensitive and accurate as "parametric" statistics applied to interval data. Nevertheless, they are an improvement over what is currently available, and, if used in conjunction with other techniques, they should allow us to squeeze quite a bit of information from data.

Ordinal Partial Correlation

A study conducted by Bell (1969) illustrates some of these points. He sought to develop a causal model which would explain "psychological involvement in politics," but he had only categorical data drawn from the Survey Research Center's (SRC) 1964 election survey. That the level of measurement troubled him is evident:

> The measures of correlation which are central to the prosecution of the technique [i.e., causal analysis] require interval-level measurement of variables. Reference to the Appendix will reveal that the data in this essay are not measured at the interval level; indeed, it requires a warm and optimistic personality to regard some of them as even ordinal level. It does not follow from all of that, however, that the results shown in this essay are worthless. It does follow, I believe, that the value of this exercise will be idiosyncratic; some readers will find it helpful, while others will not. [P. 241]

Bell's solution to the problem was to substitute category scores into correlation and partial correlation formulas, which, in effect ignored the level of measurement. One model he tested is depicted in Figure 14.1. It shows a spurious correlation between political involvement and political efficacy due to education. As is apparent, the data do not fit the model; so he concluded that another model must be operative. What is of interest here is whether or not the level of measurement leads to an incorrect substantive interpretation.

Using ordinal data in this manner to test causal models seems to be a common practice, a practice which—despite objections from some investigators (e.g., Wilson 1971)—may in fact produce accurate inferences, especially if the number of categories is large (Labovitz 1967, 1970; Boyle 1970). Still, the adequacy of this approach has not received much systematic study. We do not know, for example, the seriousness of errors introduced by using dichotomies and trichotomies in making causal inferences. One of my goals in this chapter is to examine the advantages and disadvantages of employing ordinal data in correlation and regression formulas in the context of causal analysis.

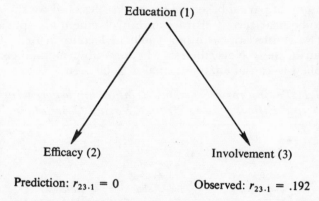

Education (1)

Efficacy (2)   Involvement (3)

Prediction: $r_{23.1} = 0$ Observed: $r_{23.1} = .192$

Figure 14.1. A test for spurious correlation between political involvement and political efficacy. (Data here and in Table 14.1 based on Bell's [1969] analysis; data from Survey Research Center, University of Michigan, Study no. 473, "1964 Election Study.")

There is, however, an alternative approach: ordinal partial correlation. Goodman and Kruskal (1954) suggest computing a weighted average of contingent measures of association, the average being interpreted as a partial correlation coefficient. Suppose, for example, a set of observations is divided into K strata, with each observation assigned on the basis of its score on a test or control variable (say, Z) which may be multivariate. Within each stratum we can compute a *contingent*, or *conditional*, measure of association between two other variables—say, X and Y. These measures (e.g., tau$_b$, gamma) are usually computed from cross-classifications of X and Y. A definition of ordinal partial correlation is thus:

$$\theta_{xy.z} = \frac{\sum\limits_{i=1}^{K} (w_i \theta_i)}{\sum\limits_{i=1}^{K} w_i},$$

where w_i and θ_i are, respectively, the weight and measure of association in the ith stratum.

For illustrative purposes I have reanalyzed Bell's data, using tau$_b$, tau$_c$, gamma, and Somers's d_{yx} and weighting by the number of *pairs* of observations in each stratum. That is, I cross-classified efficacy with political involvement within each level of education and computed the indices of association. Weighted averages of these measures form the ordinal partials. Presumably, this type of partial behaves like the product-moment partial based on interval scales, and we should expect its value to be near zero if efficacy and involvement are spuriously correlated. The results appearing in Table 14.1 confirm Bell's finding: a lack of spuriousness. Nevertheless, whether either method can be accurately applied to causal analysis remains to be seen.

Table 14.1. Testing for a Spurious Relationship between Involvement and Efficacy Using Ordinal Partial Correlations

Measure of asso- ciation	Total correlation between involvement and efficacy	Ordinal partial controlling for education	Difference	Percentage reduction
t_b	.231	.149	.082	35.50
t_c	.233	.146	.087	37.34
g	.286	.188	.098	34.27
d_{yx}	.238	.156	.082	34.45

Even though ordinal partial correlation as defined above is a simple and potentially useful idea, surprisingly few social scientists have taken advantage of it. In the previous chapter, Quade has proposed an index of matched correlation which is a more general approach encompassing the idea of the ordinal partial correlation and putting it on a sound theoretical footing. I shall elaborate on his description only to the extent of making a few points related to the application of this technique to causal analysis.

First, note that the computation of a weighted average of conditional correlations does not necessarily require a large sample size. Quade's work makes it clear that one is really only counting different kinds of pairs of observations; it is not even necessary to form contingency tables to calculate the index. Many investigators avoid contingency-table analysis partly because of the need for a large N. This problem is not completely overcome with ordinal partial correlation, but it is reduced by having a single index which pools much of the information in the sample into one number. (As Somers [1968] points out, however, there may be other reasons for preferring tables to a single index.)

The second point emphasized by Quade's approach is that the controlling operation can be defined in many ways. The control variable may be interval, ordinal, or nominal; it may be multivariate, or it may not even involve a random variable. All the method requires is some way to decide which observations are tied. The generality of the ordinal partial gives the investigator some flexibility in selecting controls. Which approach he selects will depend on his requirements and on the research situation.

The fact that different controlling procedures are possible leads to the third conclusion, namely, that the partial as defined in equation (1) is really a family of indices, each of which depends on a choice of measure of association (θ) and a weight (w). This point is amply demonstrated by Quade, who shows that different definitions of "matching" lead to different coefficients. In this chapter, I shall consider weighted (by the number of pairs) averages of tau_a, tau_b, tau_c, gamma, and Somers's d_{yx}. Other measures, though, are possible.

Finally, if tau_a, d_{yx}, or gamma is used and the weight factor is the number of pairs of observations, it is possible to find the asymptotic standard error of the ordinal partial, which makes possible statistical inferences, at least for large samples.

The indices of ordinal partial correlation thus appear to be advantageous because (1) they have reasonably straightforward interpretations, (2) they are easily computed even for small samples, and (3) in some cases they have known sampling distributions and standard errors. We, of course, need to ascertain their utility in causal modeling: Do they behave analogously to product-moment partial correlations based on interval data?

Before answering that question I should mention other limitations of this approach. First, these partials can be meaningfully interpreted only if there is minimal interaction (i.e., if each of the conditional relationships has roughly the same form). Yet, interaction will probably be encountered in many studies. Of course, other techniques do not avoid this problem, although they may have greater flexibility in handling it. Next, this approach to partialling ignores the ordinality of the control variable, a fact troubling to Somers (1968), who feels that these partials can be very misleading. Nevertheless, the ability to use nominal control variables does have advantages, and the technique is applicable even when the control variable is not ordinal. Another criticism, also expressed by Somers (1968), is that since a "partial correlation" is a complex notion it may not be advisable to summarize such a relationship with a single index. Indeed, it may be better to present and discuss an entire series of tables than to mechanically calculate a single descriptive measure.

In spite of these shortcomings, ordinal partial correlation may supply a reasonable analogue to the product-moment system. It remains to be seen whether this approach can be effectively applied to the analysis of causal models and, if so, under what conditions.

Method

In order to answer these questions, I have made use of a computer simulation. Data with known characteristics are created in such a way as to reflect many widespread assumptions about causal models, underlying distributions, the operation of error terms, intercorrelations among variables, and the like. Using these data, we can see how well the two approaches—treating ordinal data as interval, and ordinal partial correlation—work in helping us make causal inferences.

The same general procedure is followed in generating all the data. First, a model is specified. The data generated on the basis of this model are continuous and, for convenience, are called "true scores." Sample sizes are $N = 600$. Next, the predictions are tested, and since the model is generated according to predetermined specifications, they should be borne out except for sampling errors.

After the model is tested in this fashion, the scores are grouped into ordered categories. Each category is assigned an integer, with "1" for the first. Two more tests are then made: first, the new scores are treated as interval scores, and ordinary r's and partial r's are computed (these r's are denoted by $\bar{r}$); second, ordinal partials are computed by taking weighted (by number of pairs) averages of five measures of correlation, tau_a, tau_b, tau_c, gamma, and Somers's d_{yx}. The results of these two tests are then compared with those of the original test. In addition to seeing whether ordinal data "work" (and under what conditions), it is also possible to see which general approach—ordinal partialling or treating ordinal as interval data—does the best job.

In most instances three numbers of categories, three, five, and ten, are used to study the effect of categorization. In other words, a particular model is first tested with trichotomous variables, then with variables having five categories, and finally with variables having ten categories. Initially, the range of each variable is cut into equal-sized intervals, but this procedure is later modified to see what happens with different-sized intervals. (Note, however, that each analysis comes from separately and independently generated data.) With one exception, all the variables in a model always have the same number of categories. In addition, there are three levels of correlation. The values depend on the particular situation and are arbitrarily labeled low, medium, and high.

Hence, with three degrees of intercorrelation and three levels of categorization given, nine combinations are simulated. To estimate the variability of the procedures, each particular combination is replicated ten times, with the results averaged across the ten replications. All the data reported below are based on averages of the ten replications.

The models themselves are usually simple spurious correlations (the one exception is a developmental sequence). They are based on simple recursive systems in which the error terms have means of zero and the variances depend on the correlation level used. None of the models involve confounding factors such as interaction, correlated error terms, and reciprocal causation. I begin with an examination of two models, a spurious correlation and a developmental sequence, and then go on to look at the effects of nonlinearity and changes in categorization. The changes in categorization include using different numbers of cutpoints and making a normally distributed variable appear to be skewed.

By relying on data with known characteristics and by systematically varying their properties I hope to show the extent to which ordinal data can be adapted to formal causal analysis. Although innumerable models and conditions could be generated, only a limited set is reported here. A more complete report may be found in Reynolds (1971).

Results

Spurious Correlation

The first model, a simple spurious correlation, predicts $r_{23.1} = 0$. Tables 14.2, 14.3, and 14.4 show how well this prediction has been met. Table 14.2 displays mean values of the average total and partial correlations and percentage reductions in the total correlations. That is, for a particular statistic the relevant data in each of the nine different conditions are averaged. Since each of the nine numbers is itself an average of the ten replications, Table 14.2 really contains averages of averages. Table 14.3 gives averages in the three different category levels (e.g., statistics in the $3 \times 3 \times 3$ high, medium, and low conditions are averaged) and Table 14.4 provides averages for each of the correlation levels (e.g., statistics in $3 \times 3 \times 3$, $5 \times 5 \times 5$, and $10 \times 10 \times 10$ high conditions are averaged). Space limitations do not allow me to present more detailed tables, but taken together, this information should reveal how closely the two nonparametric approaches come to the theoretical prediction.

In testing for spuriousness, both techniques—the partial $\bar{r}$'s and the

Table 14.2. Mean Total and Partial Correlations and Percentage Reductions for a Spurious Correlation

	Total correlation	Partial	Percentage reduction
r	.5010	.0086	98.75
t_a	.2609	.0388	85.26
t_b	.3753	.0771	82.10
t_c	.3271	.0540	84.59
g	.5319	.1604	70.71
d_{32}	.3740	.0781	81.94
$\bar{r}$	.4398	.0853	79.81

NOTE: Means calculated by averaging across all nine conditions.

ordinal partials—work reasonably well, although both must be used with care. Except for gamma, most of the partials are close to zero, and the percentage reductions are large (see Table 14.2). If this model underlies a set of data, the ordinal partials should generally be sensitive enough to detect it.

Unfortunately there are annoying exceptions. Even though the original relationships always decline substantially, a few of the partials stay considerably larger than zero; some are greater than .2. The explanations for these exceptions lie in the number of categories and in the intercorrelation among the variables.

Consider the number of categories. It is well known that random errors in a control variable of a spurious correlation will confuse causal

Table 14.3. Effects of Different Numbers of Categories on Total and Partial Correlations and Percentage Reductions for a Spurious Correlation

	Ten categories			Five categories			Three categories		
	Total	Partial	% reduction	Total	Partial	% reduction	Total	Partial	% reduction
r	.5003	.0089	99.22	.4943	.0021	99.94	.5077	.0146	97.10
t_a	.3211	.0210	95.78	.2693	.0435	86.46	.1924	.0520	73.54
t_b	.3806	.0277	95.34	.3837	.0768	83.60	.3616	.1269	67.35
t_c	.3571	.0247	95.45	.3362	.0585	85.50	.2881	.0788	72.83
g	.4469	.0366	91.96	.5269	.1347	79.32	.6220	.3100	53.67
d_{32}	.3735	.0277	95.16	.3834	.0767	83.52	.3653	.1300	67.15
$\bar{r}$	.4867	.0366	91.56	.4458	.0900	81.38	.3868	.1332	66.49

NOTE: Means calculated by averaging across the three different correlation levels.

Table 14.4. Effects of Different Levels of Correlation on Total and
Partial Correlations and Percentage Reductions for a Spurious
Correlation

| | CORRELATION LEVEL | | | | | | | | |
| | High | | | Medium | | | Low | | |
	Total	Partial	% reduction	Total	Partial	% reduction	Total	Partial	% reduction
r	.6955	.0000	100.01	.4993	.0214	96.13	.3082	.0043	100.02
t_a	.3753	.0611	82.41	.2549	.0432	81.42	.1525	.0123	91.95
t_b	.5347	.1265	76.06	.3694	.0817	78.08	.2217	.0232	92.16
t_c	.4709	.0854	81.37	.3188	.0596	80.71	.1916	.0170	91.71
g	.7293	.2664	62.15	.5356	.1628	72.62	.3308	.0520	89.83
d_{32}	.5363	.1261	76.17	.3712	.0829	77.87	.2146	.0255	91.59
$\bar{r}$	.6118	.1281	75.14	.4356	.0884	78.40	.2686	.0403	85.90

NOTE: Means calculated by averaging across the three categorization levels.

tests because the partial will not normally be near zero. The distortions introduced by categorizing data apparently have the same effect. Furthermore, as the crudity of the measurement increases, the errors, and hence the difficulty of making accurate inferences, also increase.

Table 14.3 shows that the average partials are higher in the trichotomous than in the $5 \times 5 \times 5$ case, while partials based on variables having ten categories are best because they are nearly always close to zero. This conclusion holds in spite of the fact that in the lower levels of measurement the *total* correlations are smaller. Note in particular that the relative declines are smaller in the $3 \times 3 \times 3$ case than in the $5 \times 5 \times 5$ and $10 \times 10 \times 10$ cases. In short, it appears that, for either method, having at least five categories for each variable will be sufficient, though if the correlation between X_2 and X_3 is not large even trichotomies will do. As I shall mention later, inferences based on dichotomous variables can be even more misleading (for results on the dichotomous case, see Reynolds 1971).

These findings, then, support the rule that one should avoid "collapsing," or combining, categories in order to build up the N's in each contingency table. As pointed out before, one does not need large N's to compute the ordinal partials. The collapsing of categories may result in the loss of information (in the sense of added measurement error) to such an extent that any test of the model becomes indeterminate.

The degree of intercorrelation among the variables also limits the sensitivity and precision of the nonparametric partials: the higher the initial correlation between X_2 and X_3, the larger the partials and the less likely that one will accept the true model (see Table 14.4.) Apparently, the categorization process loses so much information that, unless X_2 and X_3 are moderately or weakly correlated to begin with, the introduction of a control is not powerful enough to reduce the relationship to near zero. Consequently, it seems easier to show spuriousness if the "true" correlation of X_2 with X_3 is, at most, moderate—say, less than .5. If the variables are more strongly correlated it will be harder to detect a spurious correlation, even if it exists. Naturally, this is a serious drawback, but it can be partly overcome by having as many categories as possible. Ten or more should almost always be adequate. Also, some measures of association are less sensitive than others, a point to be pursued in detail toward the end of this chapter.

In short, it seems that we can safely and profitably turn to ordinal partial correlation for causal analysis, provided that we have at least five intervals for each variable. We must realize, however, that the absolute values of these partials are sometimes greater than zero—particularly when X_2 and X_3 are highly correlated—and hence we may confuse spurious correlation with other models. But even this possibility may not be serious, as we see in the next section.

Developmental Sequence

Controlling for X_1 in a developmental sequence $X_1 \rightarrow X_2 \rightarrow X_3$ gives the prediction $|r_{23.1}| \leq |r_{23}|$. This is the same prediction we get in the spurious correlation model $X_2 \leftarrow X_1 \rightarrow X_3$ if there is random measurement error in X_1 (Blalock 1965). Since the same problem may arise with categorized data, it seems worth asking if we can distinguish a developmental sequence from a spurious correlation with only categorical data given.

To answer this question, I have generated data based on a developmental sequence in which X_1 causes X_2, which in turn causes X_3. The procedure follows the previous pattern: there are three sets of categories and three levels of correlation, and the models are tested as before. Here the prediction is simply that the controlled relationship (e.g., $r_{23.1}$) will be *smaller* than the original one. How much smaller depends on the intercorrelation among the variables. Therefore, we have a less precise standard for judging a procedure's adequacy, but we should still be able to tell whether it is working.

Data appearing in Tables 14.5 and 14.6 demonstrate the effects of variations in categorization and strengths of intercorrelations. It does not make sense in this model to compute averages across all nine conditions, since there is no standard against which to judge them. In other respects, the organization of these tables resembles that of Tables 14.2, 14.3, and 14.4.

On the whole, both methods again give correct inferences: most of

Table 14.5. Effects of Different Numbers of Categories on Magnitudes of Differences between Total and Partial Correlations and Percentage Reductions in a Developmental Sequence

	MEAN REDUCTIONS			MEAN PERCENTAGE REDUCTIONS		
	Number of categories			Number of categories		
	10	5	3	10	5	3
r	.0788	.0750	.0767	10.62	11.16	11.38
t_a	.0726	.0660	.0557	14.29	16.63	20.52
t_b	.0682	.0643	.0635	11.79	11.85	12.74
t_c	.0669	.0756	.0771	12.16	15.46	19.34
g	.0607	.0438	.0327	9.20	6.68	4.82
d_{32}	.0614	.0515	.0442	10.69	9.40	8.87
$\bar{r}$	.0778	.0770	.0682	10.63	12.79	12.99

NOTE: Means calculated by averaging across the three different correlation levels; reductions represent magnitudes of differences between total and partial correlations.

Table 14.6. Effects of Different Levels of Correlation on Magnitudes of Differences between Total and Partial Correlations and Percentage Reductions in a Developmental Sequence

	MEAN REDUCTION			MEAN PERCENTAGE REDUCTION		
	Correlation level			Correlation level		
	High	Medium	Low	High	Medium	Low
r	.1742	.0490	.0073	20.95	9.50	2.76
t_a	.1546	.0339	.0048	34.30	13.03	4.12
t_b	.1508	.0391	.0061	22.70	10.30	3.38
t_c	.1737	.0404	.0056	30.69	12.44	3.83
g	.0910	.0385	.0079	10.54	7.29	2.87
d_{32}	.1200	.0324	.0047	17.80	8.44	2.72
$\bar{r}$	.1708	.0456	.0066	23.10	10.34	2.97

NOTE: Means calculated by averaging across the three categorization levels; reductions represent magnitudes of differences between total and partial correlations.

the time the partials are smaller than the total correlations. The techniques work well partly because the standard for judgment is so loose, but nonetheless, both methods seem workable.

More important, notice the amounts and percentage reductions in the original relationships. These declines are considerably smaller than corresponding declines for the spurious correlation. Take some examples: Suppose one has a total tau$_b$ of .25 and an ordinal-partial tau$_b$ of .13. Suppose also that each variable has five categories. These data suggest a developmental sequence. On the other hand, if the partial is .06, one suspects spuriousness. For this reason, Bell's data as reported in Table 14.1 might indicate a developmental sequence rather than a spurious correlation. Now suppose the total tau_b is .60. A partial of .40 then indicates a developmental sequence; a partial of .20, a spurious correlation. As the number of categories increases, the sensitivities of both methods should also increase.

My point is that with a spurious correlation one can expect substantial reductions in the X_2 with X_3 relationships, and only moderate reductions with a developmental sequence. Although these conclusions are tentative, and further research is needed to establish more precise rules, it does seem to me that one will be able to distinguish the two models. Of course, there are still other models with which these could be confused. But I have examined some of them elsewhere and my conclusion remains the same (Reynolds 1971).

As expected, the amounts and percentage reductions in the original relationships depend upon the correlation between X_1 and X_2: the higher this correlation, the greater the difference between the total and partial relationships. Occasionally a partial will exceed the total correlation. This occurs mainly in the low-correlation condition and with trichotomous variables. Since the two correlations, the partial and the total, are expected to have nearly the same values anyway, it appears that these inconsistencies stem mostly from the combination of sampling error and the crudity of the measurement. Whatever the explanation, if one has weakly correlated variables (say, less than .3), one cannot always expect the partial to be smaller than the uncontrolled relationship. In a way this is a propitious finding; in some cases it may help one to distinguish a developmental sequence from a spurious correlation.

The number of categories plays a less significant role in this model. One sees more inconsistencies in the $3 \times 3 \times 3$ levels than elsewhere, but even so, both kinds of partials generally work well with trichotomies. Once again there are differences in the statistics, which will be discussed later.

On the whole, the partial $\bar{r}$ and the ordinal partials do a reasonable job of making these tests. This in turn gives us added confidence in their general utility.

Nonlinearity

One of the most demanding and yet most common assumptions in data analysis is *linearity*. Researchers frequently assume that the relationship between variables is linear. Sometimes the assumption represents convenience; at other times it stems from statistical necessity. But what may be convenient or necessary is not always warranted. In fact, many persons assume linearity in the face of contrary evidence or without justification, and still others do not even recognize or discuss the question.

Of course, there are data transformations and statistical methods available for handling nonlinear but monotonic relationships. But, when one has only categorical data, he may not be able to take advantage of these possibilities. What can be done?

If one believes that his variables are monotonically but not necessarily linearly related, he can use ordinal measures of correlation. If a nonlinear relationship is monotonic, ordinal correlation is appropriate, whereas product-moment correlation is not.

To demonstrate the flexibility of the ordinal partial correlations, and the inappropriateness of r, a separate and independent model is generated to assess the consequences of nonlinearity. The model is again a spurious correlation, with most of the properties of the previous one. The main difference is that X_1 is monotonically, but nonlinearly, related to both X_2 and X_3. Hence r is obviously not an appropriate measure. Partial r's—whether calculated on the basis of the true or the category scores—will not be close to zero except by chance. Nevertheless, in terms of the substance of the model, the ordinal partials should come close to zero. After all, the control variable is creating a spurious association between X_2 and X_3.

The results appearing in Tables 14.7, 14.8 and 14.9 show that the ordinal partials do indeed provide a better test of the model than does either of the r's. The ordinal partials come close to zero and involve substantial percentage reductions. They are adversely affected by the same two factors we noted in connection with the simple spurious correlation—namely, the categorization level and the degree of intercorrelation (see Table 14.8). Table 14.9 indicates that the correlation

Table 14.7. Mean Total and Partial Correlations and Percentage Reductions for a Spurious Correlation in Which X_1 Is Monotonically But Nonlinearly Related to X_2 and X_3

	Total correlation	Partial	Percentage reduction
r	.7028	.5228	29.46
t_a	.2328	.0263	88.83
t_b	.3500	.0669	87.23
t_c	.2945	.0379	87.80
g	.4919	.0768	85.55
d_{32}	.3493	.0407	87.40
$\bar{r}$	.4728	.2037	60.38

NOTE: Means calculated by averaging across all nine conditions.

Table 14.8. Effects of Different Numbers of Categories on Total and Partial Correlations and Percent Reductions for a Spurious Correlation in Which X_1 Is Monotonically but Nonlinearly Related to X_2 and X_3

	Ten categories			Five categories			Three categories		
	Total	Partial	% reduction	Total	Partial	% reduction	Total	Partial	% reduction
r	.7028	.5221	28.27	.7087	.5391	28.68	.6970	.5071	31.43
t_a	.2676	.0203	89.80	.2327	.0368	87.15	.1981	.0218	89.54
t_b	.3462	.0293	89.17	.3581	.0658	85.41	.3457	.0461	87.10
t_c	.2968	.0255	89.06	.2904	.0528	85.32	.2963	.0353	89.02
g	.4352	.0399	88.41	.5092	.1053	-83.46	.5313	.0853	84.77
d_{32}	.3458	.0293	88.89	.3576	.0660	85.39	.3436	.0456	87.80
$\bar{r}$	.4435	.2345	53.87	.4734	.2037	59.71	.3708	.1097	70.43

NOTE: Means calculated by averaging across the three different correlation levels.

level has the same impact: the magnitudes of the partials decline as the correlations between X_2 and X_3 drop. But overall, we should be able to make an adequate test of this model with the ordinal partials.

The most interesting statistic to examine is partial $\bar{r}$. Although it fares somewhat better than the "true" r, it gives somewhat worse results than the ordinal indices. Given $\bar{r}$ alone, one would almost always reject spuriousness. Ironically, in the trichotomous case $\bar{r}$ behaves most like the ordinal coefficients and is least like the r based on the true scores. Trichotomizing the variables apparently neutralizes the effects of nonlinearity.

Table 14.9. Effects of Different Levels of Correlation on Total and Partial Correlations and Percentage Reductions for a Spurious Correlation in Which X_1 Is Monotonically but Nonlinearly Related to X_2 and X_3

	CORRELATION LEVEL								
	High			Medium			Low		
	Total	Partial	% reduction	Total	Partial	% reduction	Total	Partial	% reduction
r	.9177	.8078	12.00	.7391	.5201	30.05	.4517	.2404	46.37
t_a	.3268	.0397	87.95	.2327	.0247	89.47	.1389	.0145	89.08
t_b	.5265	.0751	85.98	.3349	.0438	87.58	.1886	.0223	88.13
t_c	.4133	.0604	85.41	.2945	.0345	88.88	.1757	.0186	89.11
g	.7487	.1223	83.63	.4704	.0738	85.63	.2566	.0343	87.39
d_{32}	.5251	.0752	85.92	.3338	.0435	87.36	.1882	.0223	88.80
$\bar{r}$	.6823	.5059	54.05	.4776	.1919	61.54	.2586	.0904	64.54

NOTE: Means calculated by averaging across the three levels of categorization.

Incidentally, one way of removing the effects of nonlinearity on the $\bar{r}$'s is to compute a weighted average of the contingent $\bar{r}$'s. Although the data are not displayed, the average $\bar{r}$'s look very much like average tau_b's and d_{yx}'s and give more satisfactory results than the formula $\bar{r}$'s.

Thus, the ordinal partials are preferable to the partial $\bar{r}$'s unless the nonlinearity can be corrected. In a sense, the ordinal methods are more general because, as we have seen so far, they do *at least* as well as the $\bar{r}$'s and in this case are far superior. In other words, it appears that the advantages of product-moment correlation are lost once it is applied to categorized data. For this reason I feel that social scientists will be safer in adopting the ordinal partial correlations.

Variations in the Number of Categories

My purpose in this section is to describe the effect of varying the number of a variable's categories. Models incorporating this practice are obviously more common and more realistic than the "symmetrical" models considered earlier.

I am especially concerned with the measurement of the control variable. Specifically, one can hypothesize—on the basis of the previous findings—that, for a fixed categorization of X_2 and X_3, the ordinal partials and partial $\bar{r}$ will more closely approximate the partial based on true scores as the number of categories of the control variable, X_1, increases. For example, in a spurious correlation in which X_2 and X_3 have three categories, a control variable (X_1) with five or ten categories will yield a lower partial than one with only two or three intervals, other things being equal. This hypothesis rests on common sense, but it is still instructive to see to what extent refinements in the control variable improve the accuracy of the tests.

It will also be valuable and interesting to know what happens in the opposite instance, when X_2 and X_3 have five or ten intervals and the control factor is a dichotomy or a trichotomy. Does the refinement in X_2 and X_3 outweigh the crude measurement of X_1? This is an important question. Many investigators devote much of their time and effort to obtaining accurate measures of the dependent and independent variables of major interest—often to the neglect of control variables. Consequently, many controlling operations involve an imbalance, with the control factor measured the least accurately.

Another set of data was generated so that these conditions could be studied. The model is again a spurious correlation with most of the properties of the model described in the first section. There are also three levels of correlation. In the first series of tests, X_2 and X_3 are categorized into five levels, and the control variable, X_1, is first dichotomized and then trichotomized. This categorization generates $5 \times 5 \times 2$ and $5 \times 5 \times 3$ tables. Next, the dependent variables are cut into three levels while X_1 is successively measured with five and ten levels; the result is $3 \times 3 \times 5$ and $3 \times 3 \times 10$ tables. As before, each combination is replicated ten times. For this set of analyses, only one correlation level, "medium," was used. In all these treatments, the ranges of the variables are divided into equal-sized intervals.

The results of the simulation, briefly summarized in Table 14.10, support the two hypotheses. Note first, however, the sizes of the total correlations: they are smaller when X_2 and X_3 are trichotomies than when these variables have five levels. Hence, controlling for a variable in the 3×3 case is not completely comparable to controlling for a variable in the 5×5 case. In the former, the test factor has less work to do, and, one might think, the partial should come closer to zero. Yet what emerges is quite revealing.

The number of levels in the control does make an important difference. The top part of Table 14.10 clearly shows that the partials are large and that the percentage reductions are small. Although it is not possible to report all the data, partials in the $5 \times 5 \times 2$ and $5 \times 5 \times 3$

Table 14.10. *Effects of Varying Number of Categories in Control Variable on Total and Partial Correlations and Percentage Reductions for a Spurious Correlation*

	Total	Partial	% reduction	Total	Partial	% reduction
	Control: Dichotomous X and Y: 5 categories			Control: Trichotomous X and Y: 5 categories		
r	.4730	−.0041	101.24	.4981	.0176	96.97
t_a	.2534	.1239	51.75	.2543	.0318	87.54
t_b	.3735	.2033	47.65	.3432	.0501	85.48
t_c	.3165	.1615	49.48	.3173	.0432	86.45
g	.5365	.3117	42.45	.4584	.0758	83.51
d_{32}	.3744	.1977	47.69	.3465	.0471	86.44
$\bar{r}$	.4309	.2255	48.03	.4458	.1008	77.42
	Control: 5 categories X and Y: Trichotomous			Control: 10 categories X and Y: Trichotomous		
r	.4845	.0013	99.79	.4881	.0178	96.41
t_a	.1670	.0163	90.23	.1778	.0170	90.58
t_b	.3407	.0335	90.17	.3458	.0371	89.46
t_c	.2501	.0277	88.94	.2663	.0251	90.74
g	.6316	.0617	90.24	.6315	.0662	89.68
d_{32}	.3418	.0337	90.18	.3509	.0377	89.41
$\bar{r}$	.3624	.0655	81.96	.3710	.0324	91.39

NOTE: Data based on one correlation level; nature of categories given by labels in table.

cases are also larger than partials in similar $5 \times 5 \times 5$ tables (see Reynolds 1971). The partials in the lower half of Table 14.10, on the other hand, lie very close to zero and involve substantial percentage reductions. Increasing the refinement in the control variable, even at the expense of lost accuracy in the dependent variables, X_2 and X_3, apparently adds to the accuracy of the nonparametric techniques. For example, the $3 \times 3 \times 5$ and $3 \times 3 \times 10$ partials are lower than the corresponding ones in $3 \times 3 \times 3$ cases and are comparable to $5 \times 5 \times 5$ partials.

Despite the limitations in the method and content of the preceding analysis, it does raise interesting and important points. For one: assuming the underlying variables are continuous, the greater the number of intervals used in measuring the control variable (for a fixed level of measurement in the remaining variables), the more likely the data can fit the model. Furthermore, a dichotomous control is not very satisfactory even when the two other variables contain more than three categories. Hence, one should not be casual in choosing his test variables. Blalock (1964) has already shown that if one too loosely interprets the dictum, "control for all relevant variables", he can make serious mistakes such as controlling for dependent variables. We now have evidence that lack of attention to control variables can cause problems of a different nature.

In fact, consider the general rule: Whenever possible, maintain at least as much refinement in the control factors as in the independent and dependent variables of primary concern. One argument for grouping observations into a small number of categories has been that one can retain sufficient N's to compute reliable percentages. If there are too many levels in the control variable, it was thought, none of the tables will have enough cases for computing percentages and making comparisons across tables. Recall, however, that the ordinal partials can be calculated directly from a data matrix with relatively few observations. Therefore, in theory at least, there is no obstacle to using even a continuous control variable, since all one needs is a definition of tied or matched pairs (see Quade's chapter in this volume).

Variations in the Choice of Cutpoints

How scores are assigned to categories is obviously a crucial aspect of the study of categoric data. So far, only the simplest form of categorization has been employed: the range of each variable has been divided into roughly equal-sized intervals. Although grouping data in this way creates both random and nonrandom errors, the nonrandomness is probably not serious. Blalock (1970) argues that a random-error model can be justified (1) if the variables have many intervals, and (2) if the extreme categories involving the greatest distortions have relatively few observations. Otherwise, the relationship of the errors to the true scores will be more complex, particularly if the intervals do not have the same number of cases.

A social scientist rarely knows how the observed category scores relate to the underlying values. Thus, in order to see how nonrandomness can affect the nonparametric methods, I have systematically varied the categorization process. With this additional analysis, I hope to accomplish two related goals: first, and perhaps most important, to increase the generality of the previous findings by showing the adequacy of the techniques under new conditions; second, to add "realism" by applying the partials to the types of data most commonly found in actual research.

There are many ways to divide a continuum into categories. To make the analysis manageable, I have settled on the following plan: Continuing with a spurious correlation, the normally distributed scores are categorized so as to produce *skewed* marginal distributions. Only the variables X_2 and X_3 are affected. The control variable, X_1, is categorized, as before, into equal-sized intervals. Three combinations are considered. First, only one variable, X_2, is skewed; next, X_2 and X_3 are skewed in the same direction; and finally, they are skewed in opposite directions. I further reduce the analysis by using only two correlation levels, "medium" and "low," and two numbers of categories, three and five. These limitations are made in view of the fact that the effects of the number of categories and the correlation level are, by now, well known, and it is necessary to concentrate on unequal category sizes. For this purpose I have taken data from my monograph (Reynolds 1971).

Before examining the results of the simulation, consider the rationale behind the skewed distributions. Variables with skewed marginals are common in the social sciences; they arise from a variety of sources. That many of them come from mismeasurement can be seen in attitude research. One obvious example is the reactive, or "loaded," question. Through faulty wording, a question (or series of questions) may classify the majority of respondents in a sample into one or two large intervals at one end of the scale. This creates the picture of skewness, when in fact the observations may be, say, normally distributed.

What effect will the skewed marginals have on the ordinal statistics? It is difficult to predict. Contingent relationships themselves will be affected to some extent, and the partials will therefore also be affected. But there are no guideposts for stating just how this occurs (see the following chapter by Blalock for additional information on these points). Since for each skewed variable one large open-ended category is created, the product-moment $\bar{r}$'s may be distorted. Again, by how much is an open question.

Tentative answers are given in Table 14.11. Like Table 14.10, Table

Table 14.11. *Effects of Variations in Choice of Cutpoints on Total and Partial Correlations and Percentage Reductions for a Spurious Correlation*

| | X_2 "skewed"; X_3 "normal" | | | X_2, X_3 "skewed" in same direction | | | X_2, X_3 "skewed" in opposite directions | | |
	Total	Partial	% re-duction	Total	Partial	% re-duction	Total	Partial	% re-duction
r	.383	.014	97.14	.370	.010	94.56	.360	−.024	108.21
t_a	.147	.028	83.69	.150	.037	75.64	.133	.025	87.81
t_b	.248	.051	82.46	.254	.067	75.33	.219	.047	87.44
t_c	.200	.039	83.22	.203	.052	75.62	.180	.036	87.83
g	.413	.092	81.08	.399	.110	75.02	.374	.090	87.50
d_{32}	.243	.042	84.93	.254	.068	75.25	.217	.047	87.54
$\bar{r}$	.280	.065	79.61	.292	.102	64.85	.226	.013	96.41

SOURCE: Reynolds 1971, p. 219.

14.11 summarizes the results of the simulation. It contains averages of the coefficients across both categories (i.e., $3 \times 3 \times 3$ and $5 \times 5 \times 5$ tables) and the two correlations (i.e., medium and low).

The most surprising finding is that this set of cutpoints does not change the accuracy and effectiveness of either of the techniques. For the most part, the partials are low and are accompanied by substantial percentage reductions. Some of the partials are a bit high, but no higher than those under the previous conditions. Contrary to expectations, $\bar{r}$ is not noticeably affected. Furthermore, the skewing of two variables causes no greater difficulty than the skewing of only one, and the direction of the skewness seems to have no impact. Finally, the level of categorization again appears to be the most important consideration: with five categories rather than three, one's chances of adequately testing the model are improved.

This last point leads to an important generalization. On the basis of both these data and those in my monograph (Reynolds 1971), I conclude that *how* the scores are categorized is less important than the fact that they were categorized in the first place. Undoubtedly, there are transformations which will completely alter an original relationship, but many of the commonly assumed categorization schemes probably will not cause substantial problems—though there is no way of knowing this for sure. The "robustness" is noteworthy because it means that they will provide accurate tests of causal models—subject to the limitations discussed above—even with different categorical data. So, if interval-level measurement is not available, one can still achieve reasonable results with ordinal data, though he should strive for as many cutpoints as possible.

Differences Among Statistics

So far, I have been referring to the ordinal partials as a homogeneous group. Obviously, however, there is a great deal of variation in their performances. When used in the averages, some statistics give better results than others.

Superficially, tau_a is best for testing for spurious correlation. Its partials are lower, and its percentage reductions are higher, than those of the other measures. The catch is that the total, or original, correlations also tend to be low, sometimes so low as to be misleading. If tau_a is computed from a contingency table, the denominator will generally contain a large number of tied pairs. These ties can decrease the magnitude of the coefficient, even if the "true" correlation is sizable. Consequently, tau_a will be closer to zero if the number of ties is large. Because it is biased in this sense, applying a control variable may produce the appearance of spuriousness where it does not exist. At any rate, since tau_a involves a smaller initial correlation, control variables have less work to do.

Partials based on gamma, on the other hand, are too high. Since all tied pairs are excluded from its computation, its numerical value is larger than other statistics. It often overstates the true relationship (i.e., the relationship based on ungrouped scores), especially if the variables are trichotomies. In many cases the magnitude of gamma is so large that the partialling techniques do not reduce the total correlation close enough to zero to produce an unambiguous test for spuriousness. Testing for other models creates similar types of problems. Thus, I recommend that gamma not be used for causal analysis except possibly in conjunction with other measures of association. This conclusion is, of course, disappointing, because we are now beginning to learn much about its behavior and because it is a popular and easily computed measure of association. Nevertheless, there seem to be more satisfactory statistics available.

Tau_b, tau_c, and d_{yx} are most acceptable from the standpoint of their *empirical* behavior in the data sets presented here. They work in the widest variety of circumstances. In the spurious correlation case, tau_c partials are smaller than the others, but like tau_a, its original correlations are also small. (Of course, note that I have considered only symmetric $r \times r$ tables. The effect of changing table dimensions is yet to be explored.) In addition, tau_c has an awkward interpretation. It is easier to interpret d_{yx}, although its partials are a little higher in the spurious correlation case. Tau_b lies between tau_c and d_{yx} in these respects. All three coefficients generally allow one to make reasonably accurate tests, if allowance is made for the limitations cited above. Combined with the investigator's substantive knowledge of a problem, ordinal partials based on these measures should provide useful tools for testing causal models. Which of them is selected will probably depend on theoretical properties (see Wilson's chapter in this volume) or on personal taste and computational convenience. In most circumstances it will be advisable to report several of them and to display at least some of the data upon which they are based.

This leaves $\bar{r}$, the product-moment r based on category scores. The results reported above show that partial $\bar{r}$'s are usually about the same size as tau_b and d_{yx}. In spite of the similar performance, I believe, for several reasons, that most researchers will come to prefer the ordinal partials. First, they give as accurate results as $\bar{r}$ under the conditions studied herein, and I see no other meaningful data transformations that will alter this conclusion. In other words, if one has categorical data to begin with, the advantages of the interval system are already lost, and trying to go back to it will probably not be any more advantageous than using ordinal measurement. And, in addition, $\bar{r}$ is sometimes not appropriate where the nonparametric partials are. In the example given above, the nonlinear but monotonic relationships, $\bar{r}$ produced very misleading results, whereas the nonparametric statistics were quite satisfactory. Hence, the ordinal alternatives seem more general. The use of $\bar{r}$ also involves the violation of several assumptions. Since there are good alternatives available, why bother to ignore or stretch assumptions? Finally, as mentioned before, if certain combinations of statistics and weights are selected, it is possible to compute their standard errors and make tests of significance. That one is able to test them for significance certainly adds to their usefulness. For all these reasons, then, I recommend that social scientists use ordinal partials when categorical data, only, are available.

Discussion

I have argued that ordinal partial correlation provides a reasonably satisfactory way to test causal models with categorical data. The argument rests on limited evidence, however; only a small portion of the possible models and conditions has been discussed. To obtain greater confidence in the methods we should look at as many situations as possible.

Additional work has been done in this area, the results of which are reported elsewhere (Reynolds 1971). In a chapter of this length it is not possible to describe all these findings, but it may be helpful to describe some of the more pertinent ones.

Additional Models

I have considered additional causal models. One, a "double spurious correlation," predicted that controlling for X_1 and X_2 would cause the relationship between X_3 and X_4 to vanish (X_1 and X_2 were themselves uncorrelated). It turned out, however, that for this model the total (uncontrolled) correlations between X_3 and X_4 were often quite large —even when measured by ordinal statistics such as tau$_a$ (in the high-correlation situation the taus were sometimes greater than .75). Consequently, both the ordinal partials and partial $\bar{r}$ were frequently much greater than zero. The problem was most serious, of course, when X_2 and X_3 were highly correlated. Therefore, when applying these data to categorical data one must pay attention to the magnitude of the original correlation. If it is large (say, greater than .75), he should not expect the partial to be much less than .25. Needless to say, this result is somewhat unfortunate, because a double spurious correlation might be confused with a model predicting, simply, $|r_{34.12}| \leq |r_{34}|$. However, by looking at the sizes of the present reductions, which should be at least 65 percentage points, and by cutting the variables into as many levels as possible, the researcher will avoid some confusion.

Another model was called "independent" causes. Two uncorrelated variables, X_1 and X_2, produced variations in X_3. Controlling for X_1 gave the prediction $|r_{23.1}| \geq |r_{23}|$. Even with interval-level data, the size of the difference between the partial and the total correlation will be a function of the magnitude of the correlation between X_1 and X_3. When this correlation is small, the difference will be small. Both partial $\bar{r}$ and the ordinal partials generally lead to correct inferences. Discrepancies arise mostly where the correlation between X_1 and X_3 is small. Keeping as many categories as possible helps to improve the sensitivity of both methods. These conclusions hold for a similar model, in which X_1 and X_2 were correlated.

In summary, the two techniques worked satisfactorily in testing a variety of models. It seems reasonable to expect that the ordinal partials can be effectively applied to more complex situations.

Weighting Procedures

For the ordinal partials analyzed in this chapter I have weighted by the number of *pairs* of observations in each stratum or table. Quade's chapter makes clear the statistical advantages of this weighting scheme. But it is possible to conceive of others. I have examined the effects of using a simple average and a weighted average based on the *number* of observations. For the types of situations I considered, it made no practical difference which averaging procedure was used. Although simple averages of the coefficients are easier to compute, most investigators will probably want a weighted average. Weighted averages may reduce the effects of sampling errors by reducing the impact of those strata comprising small numbers of cases. Also, the scheme of weighting by the number of pairs has nice mathematical properties—at least for gamma and tau$_a$—as noted above.

Additional Measures of Association

In addition to the measures reported herein, I considered Spearman's rho corrected for ties (Siegel 1956). Spearman's rho is not suitable for the analysis of categorical data, but rho corrected for ties behaves very much like tau$_b$ and $\bar{r}$. It is not especially convenient to compute, since the data must be ranked, but it is interesting to note that this kind of measure works quite satisfactorily in testing causal models.

Davis (1967) has proposed a partial gamma similar to the one used in this chapter. His coefficient is equivalent to a weighted average of the conditional gammas, with the weight proportional to the total pairs differing on X and Y but tied on Z. The behaviors of Davis's partial gamma and the gamma reported above are very similar; there are few practical differences. For the reasons already cited, neither one works well in testing for spuriousness.

Number of Categories

Finally, I have explored in more detail than is reported in this chapter the effect of differing numbers of categories. In particular, I have examined the effects of dichotomous variables. These variables behave much like trichotomies. Since dichotomizing increases measurement error, it is difficult to make accurate tests, especially when, as in a spurious correlation, the ordinal partials may be sensitive to the level of intercorrelation.

Dichotomous variables frequently crop up in social science research. In some cases, they are a "natural" consequence of a classification (e.g., sex). All too often, however, dichotomies result from crude measurement or from collapsing categories. Insofar as possible, the investigator should make every effort to avoid "unnecessary" dichotomies, since they can produce quite misleading results.

Conclusion

One point is clear: the results reported in this chapter are tentative. The two methods—treating ordinal data as though they were interval, and ordinal partial correlation—seem to provide a satisfactory approach to making inferences with ordinal data. But for us to have more confidence in these approaches, we need to study systematically the effects of different conditions (e.g., choice of cutpoints, interactions) which might affect the results. Wilson (1971) convincingly argues that, since one never knows the underlying measurement of the variables, one cannot be certain that his data belong to the class of data for which the methods have been shown to be valid. This, of course, is true. If we examine many types of situations, however, we may achieve a *practical* confidence in these techniques. Achieving this confidence is important because it appears that in the short run, at least, the level and quality of most social science measurement are not going to improve dramatically.

As the chapters in this volume by Blalock and Ploch indicate, our knowledge of ordinal measures and ordinal data is rapidly increasing. In this spirit, I hope the results of this simulation will help those who wish to test simple causal models with ordinal data. More important, I hope this research will encourage additional efforts in these areas.

References

Bell, Roderick
  1969. "The Determinants of Psychological Involvement in Politics: A Causal Analysis." *Midwest Journal of Politics* 8:237-53.
Blalock, Hubert M., Jr.
  1964. *Causal Inferences in Nonexperimental Research*. Chapel Hill: University of North Carolina Press.
  1965. "Some Implications of Random Measurement Error for Causal Inference." *American Journal of Sociology* 71:37-47.
  1970. "A Causal Approach to Nonrandom Measurement Errors." *American Political Science Review* 64:1099-11.
Boyle, Richard P.
  1970. "Path Analysis and Ordinal Data." *American Journal of Sociology* 75:461-80.
Davis, James A.
  1967. "A Partial Coefficient for Goodman and Kruskal's Gamma." *Journal of the American Statistical Association* 62:189-93.
Goodman, Leo A., and William H. Kruskal
  1954. "Measures of Association for Cross Classifications." *Journal of the American Statistical Association* 49:732-64.
Hyman, Herbert H.
  1955. *Survey Design and Analysis*. New York: Free Press.
Labovitz, Sanford
  1967. "Some Observations on Measurement and Statistics." *Social Forces* 46:151-60.
  1970. "The Assignment of Numbers to Rank Order Categories." *American Sociological Review* 35:515-25.
Lazarsfeld, Paul F.
  1955. "Interpretation of Statistical Relations as a Research Operation." In Paul F. Lazarsfeld and Morris Rosenberg, eds., *The Language of Social Research*. New York: Free Press.
Reynolds, H. T.
  1971. "Making Causal Inferences with Ordinal Data." Working Papers in Methodology, no. 5. Chapel Hill: University of North Carolina.
Rosenberg, Morris
  1968. *The Logic of Survey Analysis*. New York: Basic Books.
Siegel, Sidney
  1956. *Nonparametric Statistics*. New York: McGraw-Hill.
Somers, Robert
  1968. "An Approach to the Multivariate Analysis of Ordinal Data." *American Sociological Review* 33:971-77.
Wilson, Thomas
  1971. "A Critique of Ordinal Variables." *Social Forces* 49:432-44.

Chapter 15

BEYOND ORDINAL MEASUREMENT: WEAK TESTS OF STRONGER THEORIES

H. M. BLALOCK, JR.

H. M. Blalock, Jr., is Professor of Sociology, University of Washington. He received his Ph.D. in Sociology from the University of North Carolina, Chapel Hill, in 1954. Professor Blalock's main interests are in general methodology, applied statistics, theory building, race relations, and social power, and he is the author of many publications on these subjects.

The previous chapters in this section have dealt with a number of ordinal measures, methods of partialling or controlling, and the empirical behavior of these several measures and methods under various models and assumptions. The results are not at all discouraging, and they clearly imply that ordinal procedures may safely be used under a variety of circumstances. Nevertheless, I believe it would be a serious mistake for social scientists to rest content with ordinal techniques and with measurement procedures that yield, at best, ordinal scales. We should always strive to improve our measurements and to achieve ordered-metric, interval, or ratio scales whenever possible. But since it will be generally difficult to utilize measurement procedures that meet the very strict criteria for interval and ratio scales, it seems wisest to develop the habit of analyzing one's data by several different methods and to check for consistency of the conclusions reached. In this chapter I shall be concerned with some very weak tests involving ordinal measures of association that can be used to make inferences concerning underlying frequency distributions, nonlinearity, nonadditivity, or homo-

I am grateful to Robert Leik, Donald Ploch, Henry Reynolds, Robert Somers, and Thomas Wilson for their comments on an earlier draft of this chapter.

scedasticity and that may make it possible to transform the ordinal data into crude interval scales.

To motivate the discussion that follows, let us consider certain basic differences between the general formulation of linear models and the way we have conventionally looked at measures of ordinal association. In regression theory the equation

$$Y = \alpha + \beta_1 X_1 + \beta_2 X_2 + \cdots + \beta_k X_k + \epsilon$$

becomes an extremely flexible and powerful tool because of the fact that the X_i may be transformed so as to handle numerous specific forms of nonlinearity (e.g., logarithmic, exponential, and polynomial models), nonadditivity (e.g., multiplicative or more complex interaction terms), and nominal scales (through the use of dummy variables). One may also distinguish between the unstandardized regression coefficients, which tell us how much the dependent variable will change with *hypothetical* changes in the X_i, and standardized regression coefficients such as beta weights or path coefficients. This distinction is fundamental whenever one wishes to make comparisons across populations or time periods in order to infer the nature of causal laws. A similar distinction can be made between the unstandardized asymmetric regression coefficients and standardized symmetric correlation coefficients, which are also functions of the actual variation in the X_i relative to that of the disturbance term ϵ. For example, the numerical values of correlation coefficients will shift whenever the original units are aggregated in simple ways (Blalock 1964) because aggregation will generally change the ratio of the variances in the X_i relative to that of the disturbance term.

Furthermore, in regression analyses explicit assumptions are made about the behavior of the disturbance terms. The usual assumptions are that $E(\epsilon) = 0$, that Cov $(X_i, \epsilon) = 0$ for all X_i, and that σ_ϵ^2 is a constant and therefore not a function of X or any other variable in the system. For conventional F tests one also makes the assumption that the disturbance terms are approximately normally distributed. The crucial assumption that Cov $(X_i, \epsilon) = 0$ must be modified for nonrecursive simultaneous-equation models involving reciprocal causation, and it then becomes necessary to find alternatives to ordinary least squares in order to obtain consistent estimates of the structural parameters.

There is no need to elaborate further on these assumptions. The main point is that many of these important assumptions and issues become blurred or only implicit when we shift to ordinal measures of association. Although a number of authors, such as Somers (1962), Leik and Gove (1969, and 1971), Hawkes (1971), and Ploch (this section), have shown important parallels between ordinal and regression formulations, in practice there are still certain basic difficulties with ordinal formulations. The most important of these, for present considerations, are: (1) the lack of explicit attention given to assumptions about disturbance terms, particularly the assumed lack of correlation between the disturbance and independent variables and the homoscedasticity assumption; (2) the fact that ordinal measures, like correlation coefficients, focus on how *well* we can predict (e.g., PRE) which is a function of the relative magnitudes of variances and is therefore population specific; (3) the lack of attention given to the difference between unstandardized and standardized coefficients; and (4) the lack of ordinal tools comparable to those developed to handle reciprocal causation (e.g., two-stage least squares and three-stage least squares). In fact, since only the ordering of cases is used, ordinal procedures in effect "force" a uniform dispersion on the data because ranks must always be 1, 2, 3, $\cdots$, N if ties are excluded. Therefore in cross-population comparisons possible differences between the behaviors of unstandardized and standardized measures will be obscured. For example, taus or gammas may differ across populations because of fundamentally different values of structural parameters, because of differences between the relative magnitudes of variances of independent variables and disturbance terms, or because of differences between categorization procedures.

On the theory side of the coin, it is undoubtedly true that current theory in sociology, political science, and most of the other social sciences is still in the stage for which rather crude, qualitative statements of the form "The greater the X, the greater the Y" or "If X increases, Y will increase" tend to predominate. Sometimes it is possible to predict that a given slope or correlation will be less than, equal to, or greater than another slope or correlation, but it is extremely rare that a specific numerical value (other than zero) can be predicted a priori from the theory. The potentially useful distinction between unstandardized regression coefficients and correlations is also seldom made. For example, one may simply theorize that the relationship between X and Y will be "stronger" in one context than in another, without specifying whether the intended comparison is between slopes or correlation coefficients, the latter being functions of both slopes and relative variances. Whenever theories are in this crude form, ordinal measures will suffice as well as regression analyses and—as Reynolds's findings with regard to nonlinear but monotonic models suggest—may even be less misleading.

I am assuming, however, that we shall wish to formulate our theories much more precisely whenever possible. Obviously, if interval- or ratio-level measurement of all variables were possible, empirical investigations would be directly useful in sharpening these theories in numerous ways. But in the absence of interval and ratio scales, what can we do? The suggested strategy in this chapter is that of attempting to move our theoretical formulations a bit ahead of our measurement limitations so as to take advantage of properties analogous to those of interval-level models, thereby making possible predictions about the behavior of ordinal measures of association.

We are thus arguing that it is highly desirable to move beyond ordinal measurement. One approach, exemplified by the work of Coombs (1964), as reported by Long and Wilken, is to collect the data in such a way that one can infer metric properties from response patterns and thereby construct either ordered-metric or crude interval scales from the data. Another approach is to attempt ratio-scale measurement following the lead of psychophysicists, as explored by Hamblin and Shinn. Certainly these improved data-collection techniques are to be recommended whenever they are feasible. Obviously, the data-*collection* stage is the most crucial stage in developing these improvements. Nevertheless, it is also important to find ways of squeezing as much information as possible from whatever data have been collected. In this instance, we shall be concerned with inferring metric properties from data that directly yield nothing stronger than ordinal measures of association. We thus take relatively crude data-collection procedures as given and attempt to make weak predictions concerning the magnitudes of ordinal measures under varying assumptions that may be generated by stronger theories. The implication is that theorists may attempt to *think* in terms of interval and ratio scales even where they anticipate that data-collection procedures will yield ordinal scales at best. In this way, they may provide an incentive to improve existing data-collection techniques so as to permit stronger tests as well as estimates of specific parameters.

The kind of advice one gives concerning the analyzing of ordinal data is likely to depend upon on one's stance regarding the violation of the assumptions required by parametric procedures. What makes the situation particularly confusing, and frustrating, is that it is practically always difficult, if not impossible, to assess the degree to which parametric assumptions are being violated in actual applications. To do so ordinarily requires one to make very specific assumptions regarding the nature of the underlying reality that has yielded the ordinal measurements. For example, does it make sense to conceive of an underlying metric that, if "discovered," would yield an interval or a ratio scale? If so, what would one assume about the underlying frequency distribution? If normality (or any other specified form such as chi-square) could be assumed, for example, it would then be a simple matter to convert the rankings into an interval scale. But without the proper operational procedures, such an assumption of underlying normality becomes an untestable assumption which many persons are unlikely to want to make.

Ordinal Measurement and Theoretical Conceptualization

In the present context, the problem of linking our mathematical or statistical operations with the real world can be stated in roughly the following manner: We have a number of possible mathematical operations, called transformations, that all preserve the same ordering (including ties) among the scores for each variable. In effect, this means that a particular measure of ordinal association will be invariant under these transformations. But it also implies that if we are given knowledge about the numerical values of these ordinal coefficients we cannot infer anything about the "correct" values of the true scores apart from these orderings. The mathematical operations are thus very flexible, and our problem becomes that of deciding whether or not the "real world"—or, more correctly, our theory about the real world—imposes any restrictions on these transformations. If, for example, our theory implies that the distribution of X must be normal, rather extreme conditions will be imposed on the permissible transformations. If it merely imposes some conditions on the ordering of the distances between scores (e.g., $\overline{AB} < \overline{BC}$), some but not all transformations will be allowable.

As a simple illustration suppose we begin with the equation $Y = X + e$, where X and e are independently and normally distributed. This implies that Y is also normally distributed. We may transform X into X', preserving the ordering among all X_i, by a function f such that $X' = f(X)$; then transform back from X' to X through the inverse function f^{-1} so that we may rewrite the equation for Y as $Y = X + e = f^{-1}(X') + e$. Suppose X is transformed from a normal distribution to a highly skewed one, or perhaps to an approximately rectangular distribution. Clearly, this does not affect the distribution of Y, which remains normal. In effect, if we wish to write Y as a function of the nonnormal X' values, the equation $Y = f^{-1}(X') + e$ specifies that we must first normalize these X' values. But we might write two (or more) other equations for the dependent variable in such a way that the ordering of the Y_i is also preserved. In the first procedure, we take Y' as a linear function of the transformed X values, using the equation $Y' = X' + e$. If X' is rectangular but e is normal, Y' is neither rectangular nor normal but something in between. But we might also transform Y directly into Y'' through the function $Y'' = g(Y)$ in such a way that Y'' has exactly the same frequency distribution (say, rectangular) as X'. If e remains normally distributed, Y'' cannot be taken as a simple linear function of the (rectangular) X' and the normally distributed e. Obviously, the three quantities Y, Y', and Y'' are not identical, even within simple transformations. The fact that there is an error term (with its own distribution) has complicated the picture.

These examples illustrate the more general point that we can rather easily play around with mathematical transformations at our own convenience, though we shall practically always want to impose *some* restrictions on the nature of these transformations. Our theoretical problem then becomes that of providing empirically based restrictions so as to make these mathematical transformations conform in some manner to the real world. Suppose, for example, that Y refers to some type of performance level, and X to an ability or skill presumed to affect performance. To come to grips with the question of which mathematical transformations are allowable, we must ask how performance and ability are to be measured and, when measured, how their empirical frequency distributions will look. Are the criteria for evaluating performance completely relativistic in the sense that it is *only* possible to rank order the performers? Or are they being implicitly or explicitly rated or scored according to (possibly crude) absolute standards that imply judging *how much* better A does than B? Does the mere fact that judges are able to rank the performers imply that there are some implicit absolute standards? How, for example, can judges select a most valuable player in a sports contest? Suppose several baseball players are judged according to their batting performances. If A has only a very slightly higher batting average than B, but many fewer runs batted in, B is probably given a higher rating than A. Implicit in this kind of "forced ordering" of partially ordered scales is at least a crude effort to judge distances through the use of standards that are not completely relativistic. And if such standards do exist, it then becomes meaningful to ask questions about forms of frequency distributions as well as questions about relative rankings.

Our difficulties here are *both* theoretical-conceptual and empirical. Obviously, if the actors in a social system are making judgments that *only* imply rankings and nothing else, social scientists who attempt to impose a stronger set of assumptions than reality warrants can fully expect to raise a set of empirically unanswerable questions. But if they impose a set of excessively weak assumptions, their theories and the deductions from these theories will be much more weak than necessary. It appears that in many areas of social science we have reached an impasse in connection with conceptualization and measurement at precisely this point between the ordinal and interval levels. Many authors, for example, formulate propositions of the type "The greater the X, the greater the Y" without ever stopping to ask whether or not it is also meaningful to say something about possible nonlinearities, nonadditive functional relationships, or shapes of frequency distributions. It may be not so much a matter of reality's making such questions meaningless as a matter of our not having even considered the possibility of asking the questions or of attempting more precise measurement.

To justify the general strategy used in the remainder of this chapter it will be necessary to argue that many of our variables now treated as ordinal scales can be conceived at somewhat better than an ordinal level, perhaps that of an ordered-metric scale for which distances between points can be ordered. To do this, I shall list and discuss briefly what appear to be some of the most important kinds of variables often treated at the ordinal level.

It seems as though the apparent necessity of working with ordinal measures stems from one or more of three interrelated sources: (1) the lack of clarity of both our theoretical conceptualizations and real-world situations, (2) the indirectness of many of our measurement procedures, and (3) the inadequacy of our data-collection resources. First, consider the question of clarity. It is obvious that many of our theoretical definitions of concepts do not specify or directly imply any particular metric or research operation capable of yielding such a metric. In one sense, then, they are indifferent with respect to choice of metric (e.g., X versus $\log X$ versus e^X), and hence matters of linearity or nonlinearity cannot be handled at the theoretical level. But do these conceptualizations imply *only* ordinal measurement at best? The answer seems to be yes, if the *definition* of the concept implies that it is theoretically meaningless to imagine any statements comparing the distances between any two individuals. For example, if $A > B > C$ it may be inconceivable that one could attach any meaning to the statement that B is closer to A than to C, except in the sense that there may be fewer cases intervening between A and B than between B and C (e.g., scores may be in the order C, K, B, L, M, N, A rather than in the order C, K, L, M, N, B, A). If statements about relative distances are reasonable, however, by implication it makes sense to attempt measurement at the level of an ordered metric or higher.

The case of attitude measurement has been carefully studied, and it seems clear that attitudes, values, abilities, and most other postulated internal states *can* be measured at the ordered-metric level or better and that it does make sense to assert that B may be closer to A than C with respect, say, to level of prejudice. But suppose one is concerned with relative power or with relative prestige in some small group. If A can dominate B, who in turn can dominate C, does it make sense to attempt to delineate a power continuum on which B may be located closer to either A or C? If not, coalition theories such as those of Caplow (1956) and Gamson (1961), which require assumptions about the relative magnitudes of A and $B + C$ (e.g., $A > B + C$), are not only difficult to test but are also theoretically meaningless. Likewise, is one prepared to claim that it is theoretically meaningless to compare the differences between the prestige scores of, say, the top two members of a group and those between scores of adjacent members closer to the median or near the bottom of the prestige hierarchy?

Such questions are often difficult to answer because of lack of clarity both in the actors' minds and in the theoretical definitions of prestige or power. For example, if power is defined to be a potential (e.g., ability to influence behavior of others), and if this potential is affected by the possession of resources (e.g., money) that can be measured in terms of a metric, it may make very good sense to conceive of power in higher than ordinal terms, even though it may be readily admitted that the actual measurement of relative powers will be difficult. But if power is defined in other terms (e.g., that of a "pecking order"), either by the theorist or by the real-world actors being studied, ordinality may be the highest conceivable level of measurement. Implied throughout this chapter is the argument that it is desirable to attempt to conceptualize our important theoretical variables in such a way that levels of measurement higher than ordinal are at least conceivable.

In a briefer look at the second reason for the need for ordinal measures—the indirectness of measurement—we may simply note that many of the most troublesome issues of attitude or ability measurement stem from the fact that one is attempting to infer (and therefore "measure") postulated properties on the basis of behavioral responses. The responses themselves may be forced into interval scales, as, for example, when one simply sums the positive responses. But without rather strong assumptions concerning the linkages between these indicators and the postulated states, the process of transforming these response scores into measures of the underlying variables becomes problematic. It is well known that the justification for interval or ratio scales based on these research operations requires at least some untestable assumptions and therefore leaves room for debate concerning their legitimacy. Coombs (1953) has pointed out that one of the fundamental problems for the social scientist is whether to impose a certain level of measurement on the data by a priori assumption, treating deviations as "errors," or whether to consider the "errors" as indicators of a more complex underlying reality (e.g., multidimensionality). The issue cannot be resolved by empirical means alone, since the variables of theoretical interest are being measured indirectly in terms of their presumed effects (e.g., behavioral responses).

In many instances indirect measurement and inadequate conceptualization are confounded, with the result that the investigator selects an ordinal measure because he wishes to test a theoretical proposition on a higher level of abstraction than that directly implied by the indicators. For example, he may take GNP per capita as an indicator of "level of industrialization." Although he has obtained a ratio scale on the operational level, and in fact may have a large number of cases with virtually no ties, he may deliberately decide to ignore this information concerning his indicator in order to test a more abstract proposition relating, say, "level of industrialization" to "political alienation." Obviously, without a carefully conceived set of assumptions connecting the indicators with the more abstract constructs, there will be considerable slippage. It might be thought that this slippage can somehow be reduced by converting all variables to ordinal scales and proceeding without the necessity of imposing the more restrictive assumptions required by parametric procedures. This *could* be the case, provided each of the indicators is an exact but unknown monotonic function of its appropriate construct. I am afraid, however, that in many instances the apparently simple resolution of reverting to ordinal measurement merely hides a number of difficult conceptual and substantive problems from view, rather than helps to resolve them.

Finally, we note the third reason for using many ordinal measures: totally inadequate data-collection resources and the necessity of taking shortcuts in the data-collection process. Even though there might be a very clear theoretical definition of a "democratic" or "totalitarian" society, for example, it might be totally impractical to gather the data necessary to obtain good measures for perhaps 100 different societies. Instead, one might have to rely on a small panel of judges to classify societies crudely into one of three or four ordered categories. Furthermore, it may be recognized that such crude categorization may remain necessary for some time to come, or that the variable being measured is not sufficiently important in one's theoretical scheme to justify more accurate measurement. In such instances one may have to resort to ordinal measures even where much stronger measurement is imaginable.

In the next section I shall deal with procedures it is possible to use with ordinal data that are not highly grouped. These techniques may frequently prove workable where one has ten or more levels, though they seem most applicable where there are relatively few ties. In the following section the concern will be with situations in which one has highly grouped data; it will still be necessary, however, to have at least four or five levels for each variable.

Tests with Ungrouped Data

To approach somewhat stronger predictions than are customary with ordinal hypotheses, it is necessary to make assumptions about all the following: (a) the form of the underlying frequency distributions, (b) the distribution of the "error" terms, (c) linearity or nonlinearity, (d) possible peculiar relationships with other variables (e.g., interactions between the independent variables), and (*e*) the nature of measurement errors producing incorrect rankings. To do so might seem highly restrictive, but we must recall that, in effect, certain *implicit* assumptions are being made in any event. For example, one commonly assumes that, at most, measurement errors are random, an assumption that is generally violated whenever crude categorization has been used (Blalock 1970). Since our tests are going to be very weak ones, these assumptions need not be precisely met. For example, if normality of the independent variable *X* is assumed, it will be sufficient that the distribution be roughly symmetrical, unimodel, and clustered toward the center. Similarly, minor deviations from homoscedasticity or random measurement error will create no special difficulties.

Forms of Distribution

Let us assume that we are studying the relationship between *X* and *Y*, both of which have been measured only at the ordinal level. If each variable had been measured as an interval scale, we would assume (i) that the relationship would have been approximately linear; (ii) that the error term in the equation $Y = \alpha + \beta X + \epsilon$ would have had an expected value of zero and a constant variance σ_ϵ^2 for all levels of *X*; (iii) that *X* was not interacting (nonadditively) with other, unmeasured major causes of *Y*; and (iv) that there were only minor random measurement errors producing incorrect rankings in both *X* and *Y*.

It is well known that under these conditions the correlation between *X* (as "correctly" measured) and *Y* depends on the amount of variation in *X*, and we may use this fact to make a series of predictions about the relative magnitudes of, say, tau$_b$ if we subdivide the measured *X* values (measured in ordinal terms). Consider the (*a*) normal, (*b*) rectangular, and (*c*) highly skewed *X* distributions indicated in Figure 15.1. Suppose the *X* values have been correctly ordered, apart from relatively minor random measurement errors. Let us subdivide the individuals into three equal-sized groups (of *n*/3 cases each) by putting the individuals with the lowest *X* scores in group 1 (G_1), the middle third in group 2 (G_2), and the highest third in G_3.

In the normal *X* distribution, the middle third will have scores that

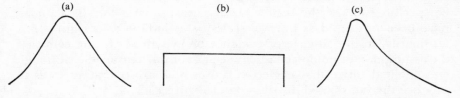

Figure 15.1. Normal, Rectangular, and Positively Skewed Underlying X Distributions.

are much more closely bunched together in terms of their *true* scores, whereas the range of variation on X will be greater (and approximately equal) for G_1 and G_3. Suppose we compute separate taus for the three groups. With the normal distribution we predict that the tau for group 2 (tau$_2$) will be numerically smaller than either tau$_1$ or tau$_3$ but that there will be no significant difference between tau$_1$ and tau$_3$. In contrast, for the rectangular underlying X distribution the three taus will be approximately equal, assuming that the error distributions are completely unrelated to X, and therefore to the method of grouping.

If there is a skewed X distribution of the type indicated in Figure 15.1c it will be difficult to predict the relative magnitudes of tau$_1$ and tau$_2$, but both will be smaller than tau$_3$, assuming a normally distributed error term and a large enough sample to ignore sampling errors. This is because the true X values of the upper third of the cases will be considerably more scattered than those for the lower two-thirds. The decision to cut the X distribution into three parts can of course be modified according to the size of the sample. The sample can be split at the median on X, in which case the prediction is that tau$_2$ will be numerically greater than tau$_1$ for the hypothesized skewed distribution.

It should be explicitly noted that the above predictions are dependent upon the assumptions of homoscedasticity and linearity. If, for example, there is heteroscedasticity such that σ_ϵ^2 is a function of X, the predictions will obviously be thrown off. One of the major advantages of regression theory and the general linear model is that assumptions regarding disturbance terms, measurement errors, and forms of relationships are made explicit, whereas they have tended to remain implicit (or have been thought to be irrelevant) in discussions of ordinal measures of association.

Distribution of Error Terms

Let us again assume a linear relationship between the true X and Y, only minor and random measurement errors with respect to the ordering of X and Y, and zero as the expected value of the residual term ϵ. Furthermore, let us assume that the underlying distribution of X is symmetrical. Now suppose we wish to relax the assumption of homoscedasticity and take the value of σ_ϵ^2 as a function of either X or Y. To be specific, suppose the scatter about a least-squares line (if X and Y have been measured as interval scales) is as indicated in Figure 15.2. Ordinarily, in the absence of evidence or hypotheses to the contrary, the assumption of homoscedasticity seems entirely reasonable, although one might theorize that neglected causes of Y are operating so as to produce the fan-shaped distribution of Figure 15.2.

Once more, since the product-moment correlation between two variables measures the scatter about the least-squares equation relative to

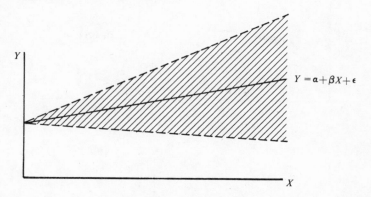

Figure 15.2. Heteroscedastic Disturbance Term for Underlying Relationship between X and Y.

the variation in X, if we dichotomize X at the median and use the same notational convention as before, the assumption of a symmetrical distribution of X scores combines with the presumed pattern of heteroscedasticity to suggest the hypothesis that tau_1 (for the $n/2$ cases with the lowest X scores) will be numerically larger than tau_2. If one assumes that the underlying distribution of X scores is rectangular as well as symmetrical, it might make sense, given a sufficiently large sample, to divide the X scores into three (or more) equal-sized groups and to predict that the numerical values of tau will decrease as one progresses from the lowest X grouping to the highest. If an approximately normal underlying X distribution is assumed, the prediction is that tau_1 will be numerically greater than both tau_2 and tau_3. The relative magnitudes of tau_2 and tau_3 will be indeterminate, since normality implies that tau_3 will be larger than tau_2, whereas the above heteroscedasticity assumption implies that tau_2 will be larger than tau_3.

Linearity versus Nonlinearity

If we assume homoscedasticity, only minor random measurement errors, and a symmetrical frequency distribution of the true X scores, but we are able to anticipate specific forms of nonlinearity, we may again make a series of differential predictions concerning the relative magnitudes of the taus. Let us once more assume that we divide the measured X scores into three groups of equal size, labeling the taus as before. Suppose we are considering the several hypothesized forms of nonlinearity indicated in Figure 15.3. If the underlying X distribution is assumed to be rectangular, the three groups will have approximately equal dispersions with respect to X. If normality is assumed, the middle third (G_2) will have a narrower dispersion on X, which will make definitive predictions concerning tau_2 problematic. The assumption of

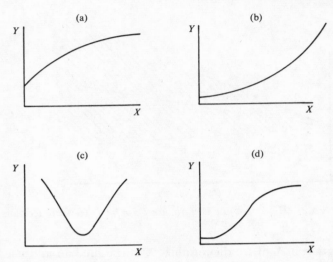

Figure 15.3. Nonlinear Relationships in Underlying Relationship between X *and* Y.

homoscedasticity assures us of approximately the same error-term scatter at all levels of X; therefore, the steeper the slope, the larger the predicted tau. These considerations yield the predictions shown in Table 15.1, which require only brief comment.

With the prediction (a) that the slope of the relationship will decrease toward zero as X increases, as, for example, when we anticipate a "saturation effect," we generally expect the values of tau to decrease as we move to higher levels of X in a rectangular distribution. For the normal X distribution, however, the prediction concerning tau_2 and tau_3 becomes indeterminate, since normality (with linearity) implies that tau_3 is larger than tau_2. We encounter a similar situation with nonlinear relationships of the form of Figure 15.3b, which might have been suggested by a "threshold effect" type of argument—that whenever X is very low there is virtually no relationship with Y. The predictions for the U-shaped curve are self-explanatory. For the S-shaped curve as represented by Figure 15.3d, we would predict the opposite pattern of

Table 15.1

Distribution of X	Form of Nonlinearity			
	Decreasing slope (a)	Increasing slope (b)	U-shape (c)	S-shape (d)
Rectangular	$\tau_1 > \tau_2 > \tau_3 > 0$	$0 < \tau_1 < \tau_2 < \tau_3$	$\tau_1 < 0, \tau_2 \cong 0, \tau_2 > 0$	$\tau_2 > \tau_1, \tau_3 > 0$
Normal	$\tau_1 > \tau_2, \tau_3 > 0$	$0 < \tau_1, \tau_2 < \tau_3$	$\tau_1 < 0, \tau_2 = 0, \tau_3 > 0$	Indeterminate

relationships among the taus implied by the normal-but-linear case; therefore, there are no determinate predictions when underlying normality of X is assumed.

Nonadditive Models

Whenever statistical interactions between X and a second presumed cause (Z) of Y are found in the case of variables measured as interval or ratio scales, it is desirable to formulate an explanatory model of a reasonably simple type. For example, one might try an equation of the form

$$Y = (\alpha_1 + \beta_1 X)(\alpha_2 + \beta_2 Z) = \alpha_1 \alpha_2 + \alpha_2 \beta_1 X + \alpha_1 \beta_2 Z + \beta_1 \beta_2 XZ \ ,$$

which of course contains a cross-product term. It has properly been pointed out by Wilson (1971) that, strictly speaking, with ordinally measured variables such a multiplicative model is not distinguishable from an additive one, since a logarithmic transformation would preserve the ordering with respect to X, Y, and Z, while turning the multiplicative relationship into an additive one. If one's theory implies somewhat stronger than ordinal measurement, however, it is again possible to make relatively weak predictions concerning the tau values.

If X has been measured at the ordinal level, whereas both Y and Z have been measured as interval or ratio scales, one may simply categorize X and use parametric procedures—either covariance analysis or dummy-variable analysis—to study the slopes b_{yz} at varying levels of X. If the theory postulates that Y should increase with both X and Z, but that high levels of both variables should produce unusually high levels of Y, we would expect the slopes b_{yz} to increase with the level of X; and thus a covariance test for interaction can be made.

Let us suppose, however, that all three variables have been measured only at the ordinal level. One may then apply the analysis of covariance analogue suggested by Ploch (this section) to test for interaction. As a supplement to this procedure, we may suggest the following crude test. We assume that within categories of either independent variable the relationships between Y and the other variable are approximately linear, that homoscedasticity holds, and that the underlying frequency distributions of both X and Z are symmetrical. Let us once more divide the total sample into three equal-sized groupings according to the level of the X score. If the underlying distributions are assumed to be normal, it will not be possible to make definitive predictions concerning group 2. But the above multiplicative relationship, with all coefficients assumed positive, implies that the value of tau$_{yz}$ for group 3 will be numerically larger than tau$_{yz}$ for group 1. Similarly, if we categorize the Z variable in the same way, ignoring group 2, then tau$_{xy}$ for group 3 will be numerically larger than tau$_{xy}$ for group 1.

Some Empirical Results

We may test some of the above predictions by using simulated data kindly supplied by Henry T. Reynolds. Real data given at the interval-scale level but analyzed at the ordinal level might also have been used, but the simulated data more closely approximate the specifications of the models. In each case the total sample size is 600, and, to supply a rough indication of the sampling fluctuations involved, there are four independent replications. Obviously, more replications and alternative sample sizes are needed to pin down more precisely any estimates of the sampling errors one might expect to encounter; and analytic or mathematical expressions for standard errors are desirable, but I have been unable to obtain them. For these particular data there are no ties on either X or Y, so that tau_a, tau_b, and gamma are identical.

Results for the linear model involving normal, rectangular, and positively skewed X distributions are given in Tables 15.2A, 15.2B, and 15.2C respectively. In all these cases, the underlying (correct) model is given by the equation $Y = X + \epsilon$, where ϵ is approximately normally distributed with zero mean. The variances of X and ϵ were set so as to produce a moderately high total association between X and Y in each instance. These total associations are given for each replication in the left-hand columns of the subtables.

For the normal X distribution we see from Table 15.2A that tau_2 is always smaller than both tau_1 and tau_3; on the average it is less than

Table 15.2. *Values of Tau for Ungrouped Data*

Replication No.	Total τ	τ_1	τ_2	τ_3	Total τ	τ_1	τ_2	τ_3
	A. Normal X distribution				*B. Rectangular X distribution*			
1	.517	.284	.109	.375	.366	.111	.170	.200
2	.504	.298	.146	.278	.386	.093	.177	.124
3	.474	.225	.054	.272	.418	.184	.188	.112
4	.489	.265	.183	.270	.401	.132	.231	.202
Mean	.496	.268	.123	.299	.393	.130	.192	.159
	C. Skewed (chi-square) X distribution				*D. Nonlinear relationship ($Y = X^3 + \epsilon$)*			
1	.361	.046	.119	.460	.521	.129	.236	.473
2	.370	.063	.076	.383	.486	.128	.123	.464
3	.385	.042	.087	.421	.458	.113	.187	.468
4	.399	.044	.115	.306	.502	.172	.332	.496
Mean	.379	.049	.099	.392	.492	.135	.220	.475

NOTE: $n = 600$; $\tau_a = \tau_b = \gamma = d_{yx}$.

half their numerical values. The values of tau_3, for these data, averaged slightly higher than the values of tau_1, owing to a slight skewness in each of the data sets that may have been a function of minor programming defects or sampling errors in the X variable. From Table 15.2B we see that the three sets of taus are approximately equal, as expected, for the rectangularly distributed X's. There is thus a clear-cut difference between the results shown in Tables 15.2A and 15.2B. For Table 15.2C, X was given a chi-square distribution (with $df = 3$), so that all values of X are positive and the distribution is skewed to the right. We see that values of tau_3 are substantially larger than those of either tau_1 or tau_2, as predicted. Whereas with both normally and rectangularly distributed X's all the tau_i are smaller than the total taus, owing to the restricted variation in X produced by the categorization, tau_3 in this particular skewed model is of approximately the same magnitude as the original tau before grouping.

Table 15.2D gives the results for the nonlinear model $Y = X^3 + \epsilon$, where X values are all positive and both X and ϵ are normally distributed. Since this represents a positive function with an increasing slope, as in Figure 15.3b, we predicted that tau_3 would be greater than either tau_1 or tau_2, with the relationship indeterminate between the latter taus because of the normality of X. We see from the data that the values of tau_3 are consistently and substantially greater than either tau_1 or tau_2. For this particular (rather extreme) nonlinear model, the values of tau_2 are also larger than tau_1 except in one of the four replications. Note the stability of both the original tau and tau_3 across all the replications. Once more, our predictions were confirmed.

Tests with Grouped Data

The procedures discussed in the previous section will not work for highly grouped data for a very simple, practical reason. If, say, X is originally grouped into three to five ordered categories, and if we attempt to subdivide X into three levels in order to obtain G_1, G_2, and G_3, we shall discover that even with five categories, two of the subdivisions will have only two levels and the third will have only one. If we have six ordered categories we can form three groupings each with two levels, but it is extremely unlikely that all three groupings will have approximately the same number of cases, as required by our previous procedure. If we begin with nine or more categories the above grouping procedures might become feasible, provided that the marginal frequencies make it possible to obtain groupings of approximately the same size. Thus, in general, we can only apply these particular procedures in situations in which we have retained a large number of distinct levels of each independent variable. If we use an attitudinal scale involving raw scores of, say, 1-21, with some individuals having each of the possible scores, we can proceed as in the previous section. In this section, however, we shall suppose that we have many fewer levels into which the individuals have been grouped.

One of the thorniest problems we face in dealing with ordinal scales, in the absence of supplementary information or reasonable assumptions concerning the "true" scores, is that of assessing the nature of possible errors that may be introduced in the grouping process. Several studies (Labovitz 1967; Stern 1971; Reynolds 1971) seem to indicate that within very broad limits such grouping decisions may not greatly affect the numerical values of our measures. Perhaps it is more correct to say that, given our relatively low standards of precision and the high percentage of unexplained variance with which we are accustomed to deal, the kinds of differences obtained by various methods of categorization appear to be relatively small. But especially as we begin to assess the relative effects of highly intercorrelated independent variables, and as we turn increasingly to time-series data where changes are often slight relative to measurement errors, we shall need much more precise measures.

The most common convention within both sociology and political science is to convert ordinal data into tables involving no more than three to five categories for each variable. There seem to be several justifications for such a procedure. First, it summarizes the data more conveniently and puts them in visual form, so that the reader may "inspect" the relationship. Second, it reduces the number of very small cells, thereby smoothing out peculiarities that might be attributed to sampling error. Third, it avoids a degree of pretentiousness implying that the data are better than they are and thereby reduces the probability that the reader will be misled by a specious accuracy. But what does one lose by reducing the data to such a degree, or by failing to collect data so as to make possible more refined distinctions? Unfortunately, it is very difficult to give an adequate answer to this kind of question, and this in turn undoubtedly means that the practice will continue until we can learn to ask the right questions and to conduct a sufficient number of methodological studies, with both real and simulated data.

Following a formulation by Coombs (1964), let me provide a very simple illustration of the difficulty. Suppose respondents are asked to pick the one item out of ten that comes closest to their own positions with respect to a certain attitudinal dimension, say, favorableness toward the military establishment. Alternatively, they may be asked to rate themselves on a ten-point scale, or they may be located in one of ten ordered classes by means of a Guttman scaling procedure, or perhaps by latent-structure analysis. Let us assume that there is only a single dimension involved and that information concerning the metric has not been obtained.

As explained by Long and Wilken, Coombs makes the basic assumption that there is an underlying dimension in which a metric distance scale may be embedded, so that each individual can be characterized by a specific though unknown location, as can each item. Suppose that, unknown to us, the "true" item scores are as indicated in Figure 15.4. We make the assumption that each individual will select the item closest to his own position, which may fluctuate from moment to moment or be conceived in terms of a probability distribution. Suppose his true position at the time is at 19. He will thus select the item located at the position 10 on the scale and be placed in category 1. The dashed lines represent the midpoints between the true scores of the items. All persons to the left of the first of these midpoints will (by assumption) select the first item and be placed in category 1. Those who have scores above 20 but less than 35 will select the second item and be placed in category 2, and so forth. Notice that in this example the items have been placed in such a manner that there is much less distance between the more central, or moderate, items than between successive items at either extreme.

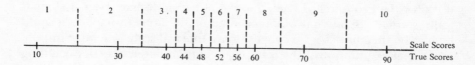

Figure 15.4. Items with True Scores Concentrated toward the Center of Underlying Distribution.

How do we infer information about distances between these true scores, knowing only the items the individuals have selected? The answer is that we cannot do so without further assumptions. Had stronger data-collection methods been used, such as requiring the respondent to rank the items according to his preferences, Coombs's unfolding technique might have been used not only to assess the unidimensionality assumption but also to obtain information that could be used to make inferences concerning the relative magnitudes of the distances between item positions. But given only the instruction "pick one," we must impose further assumptions. We of course have available the frequency distribution of the responses. Perhaps roughly equal numbers of respondents have fallen into each of the ten categories. *If* we are willing to assume an underlying normal distribution, we may expect roughly equal numbers of cases in each of these categories, given the assumed positioning of the items. That is, even though a much wider range of true score positions results in the selection of item 1 than in the selec-

tion of item 5 (which is very close to items 4 and 6), there are relatively
fewer persons in the extreme tail if the distribution is normal. But
perhaps the underlying frequency distribution is rectangular, with just
as many persons in extreme intervals as in central ones. In this case we
expect relatively more individuals in categories 1 and 10, given the assumed positioning of the items. Maybe, however, the items are equally
spaced as indicated in Figure 15.5. Such a spacing, together with a rectangular frequency distribution, can also produce approximately equal
numbers of cases in the ten categories.

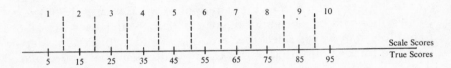

*Figure 15.5. Items with True Scores Equally Distributed along Underlying Dis-
tribution.*

The above points are obvious to anyone with even a superficial acquaintance with the attitude-measurement literature. But the implications for the grouping of one's data do not seem to have been systematically studied. If one has obtained data of the above sort, how should
he handle the analysis? To convert to an interval scale one must impose
additional assumptions, which in part will then determine the resulting
metric. The assumptions of equal spacing and rectangular frequency
distribution justify assigning the numbers 1, 2, 3, $\cdots$, 8, 9, 10 to the
respective categories and then proceeding with parametric statistical
procedures. The assumption of normality, however, implies a very different set of numbers, a set much more similar to that given in our first
hypothetical spacing. A linear correlation coefficient computed between the two sets of scores will undoubtedly be very high by present
standards, but as these standards are raised, the method of scoring may
make a crucial difference, say, in estimating the regression coefficients
for two highly correlated independent variables or in assessing slight
departures from linearity.

It may of course be argued that this is all very foolish, since we can
use ordered categories without worrying about the underlying metric
as long as we are contented with ordinal measures of association. But
this argument takes the particular sample of items used as it is given
and begs the question of what would have happened had a different set
been used. In one sense, the issue may then reduce to one's position
concerning operationism, namely, whether or not one is taking the particular items selected as indicators of an unmeasured variable or as

measures in their own right. In some instances it may be reasonable to argue that only a single measure of, say, a behavioral variable is possible, but here we are particularly concerned with measurements that are either highly indirect or relatively unrefined, in which case a number of alternative indicators become possible.

Had another set of items been used, and had they been located at very different positions on the underlying continuum, the respondents might have fallen into different categories. For example, imagine a distribution of true item positions such that there are four items close together at each extreme, with only two near the center, as indicated in Figure 15.6. Assuming a rectangular frequency distribution of respondents, this results in two central categories' containing most of the cases, with relatively few cases in the extreme categories. This particular configuration may of course be confused with one in which items are approximately equally spaced but the frequency distribution is roughly normal. The important point is that of necessity many persons will fall into categories different from those used in the first instance, as reflected by the resulting ordinal measures.

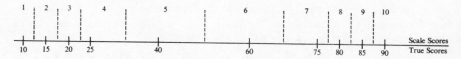

Figure 15.6. Items with True Scores Concentrated toward the Extremes of Underlying Distribution.

Behavior of Ordinal Measures When Categories Are Combined

Suppose we are given only a single set of items and empirical frequencies, as is ordinarily the case, and that we do not wish to commit ourselves on any assumptions that would enable us to infer an underlying metric. Suppose, however, that we wish to know what will happen if we combine our categories into a smaller number, as might be thought necessary for comparing results of different studies, in spite of Reynolds's findings that, in general, collapsing is disadvantageous. How can we expect the various ordinal measures of association to behave under different choices of groupings? Will gamma or tau_b necessarily decrease as categories are combined, or can we at least expect this to happen apart from the vagaries of sampling fluctuations? Can we provide any purely empirical criteria for making grouping decisions?

I strongly suspect that it is *impossible* to answer such questions adequately without the very kinds of assumptions that are required in regression models but are unnecessary in the case of ordinal procedures. The problem appears to be highly complex, but we may tackle a few limited aspects while suggesting a kind of weak test criterion that may be used under special circumstances. Let us first consider the hypothetical data of Table 15.3, which, because they are completely symmetrical in the marginal totals, make it easy to see some of the basic issues involved.

Table 15.3. Grouped Data, Five Levels of X and Y

Y \ X	High		Medium		Low	Total
High	30	20	30	10	10	100
	20	120	100	50	10	300
Medium	30	100	240	100	30	500
	10	50	100	120	20	300
Low	10	10	30	20	30	100
Total	100	300	500	300	100	1,300

Notice that the marginal totals of 100, 300, 500, 300, and 100 for both variables could have been produced by approximately normal frequency distributions and equally spaced items or by a rectangular distribution and unequally spaced items. Conceivably, also, the underlying frequency distribution might have been highly skewed, with items distributed in such a way as to compensate exactly for this skewness. Suppose we now wish to group the categories so as to produce a 3×3 table. We have a number of alternative possibilities even though we restrict the groupings to adjacent categories (assuming that we have been supplied with the correct ordering of the items). The common-sense operation is to preserve the symmetry in both variables and to combine the extreme categories so as to obtain larger numbers of cases in the extreme rows and columns. The result is as shown in Table 15.4A.

But this is certainly not the only possibility. Others are given in Tables 15.4B, 15.4C, and 15.4D. The difference between Tables 15.4B and 15.4C is that, given that the number of concordant pairs exceeds the number of discordant pairs (see results below), the highly skewed marginals in 15.4B are in the same direction, whereas those in 15.4C are in opposite directions. In 15.4D, one of the sets of marginals is symmetrical, whereas the other is highly skewed.

The numerical values of the various tau measures and gamma, as well as those of the numerator $C - D$, representing the actual difference between the numbers of concordant pairs C and discordant pairs D, are given in Table 15.5. As noted below, we can say little about these results that can be expected to hold in general, but we may note a few

Table 15.4. Grouped Data, Collapsed to Various 3 × 3 Tables

Y \ X	High	Medium	Low	Total	High	Medium	Low	Total
		A.				*B.*		
High	190	130	80	400	690	160	50	900
Medium	130	240	130	500	160	120	20	300
Low	80	130	190	400	50	20	30	100
Total	400	500	400	1,300	900	300	100	1,300
		C.				*D.*		
High	80	10	10	100	320	370	210	900
Medium	240	50	10	300	60	100	140	300
Low	580	240	80	900	20	30	50	100
Total	900	300	100	1,300	400	500	400	1,300

facts. As might have been anticipated (though it is not absolutely necessary), the value of $C - D$ decreases as we shift from the 5 × 5 table to the several 3 × 3 tables, though the decrease is surprisingly small in 15.4*A*. This of course means that the same pattern holds for the values of tau_a, which retains the same denominator of $N = \frac{1}{2}n(n - 1)$ regardless of the groupings used. As noted by Quade and Reynolds, the numerical values of tau_a are often quite small in comparison with those of gamma.

Little can be said, in general, about the comparative behaviors of tau_b and tau_c. In the special cases of $k \times k$ tables, in which all columns and all rows contain exactly the same number of cases, it can easily be shown that tau_b and tau_c are identical. As one departs from equal marginals in the $k \times k$ case, tau_c becomes smaller than tau_b. In the more general $r \times c$ case the numerical values of tau_c may be larger than those of tau_b, however, since the denominator of tau_c is $\frac{1}{2}n^2\left[(m - 1)/m\right]$, where m represents the minimum number of rows and columns. If, for example, we hold the number of columns fixed at $c = 3$, an increase in the number of rows above three will generally reduce the number of

Table 15.5. Behavior of Taus and Gamma under Collapsing

Type of table	$C - D$	Tau_a	Tau_b	Tau_c	Gamma
5 × 5 (15.3)	1,485	.18	.24	.22	.32
Symmetrical marginals (15.4A)	1,397	.17	.25	.25	.37
Skewed, same direction (15.4B)	922	.11	.24	.16	.44
Skewed, opposite directions (15.4C)	556	.07	.14	.10	.33
Symmetrical and skewed (15.4D)	998	.12	.21	.18	.38

ties with respect to the row variable and thereby increase the denominator of tau$_b$ without affecting the denominator of tau$_c$.

The interesting comparison is between tau$_b$ and gamma, the two most "respectable" measures. Gamma, of course, must always be greater than tau$_b$ except in the special case of no ties, but in the above example we also notice that the values of gamma jump around considerably, in accordance with the marginal distributions. This undesirable property of gamma is well known, though often ignored in practice. Tau$_b$, in contrast, remains remarkably stable except in 4C, which represents the extreme case of variables whose highly skewed distributions are forced in *opposite* directions.

But can anything more definite be said about the exact behavior of the various measures when the scores have been grouped in these ways? Must one rely on a number of different numerical examples, either with real or contrived data, until practical rules of thumb can be devised? And how can one assess the validity of such rules of thumb? I do not know the answer, but I strongly suspect that *no* very precise predictions can be made (even ruling out sampling error) without an underlying theory concerning the "true" values in the event a metric is available. I shall attempt to justify this position by taking a closer look at the behavior of gamma, the advantage of which is that its denominator is rather simply related to the numerator $C - D$. As a general rule, it seems preferable to use d_{yx}, Wilson's e, tau$_b$, or even tau$_c$ rather than gamma, not only because of the erratic behavior of gamma under alternative groupings but because of its undesirable behavior under partialling, as noted by Reynolds. However, this same erratic behavior affords the possibility of making specific predictions about the magnitude of gamma under different grouping arrangements.

Predicting the Behavior of Gamma

Let us assume that we begin with a $k \times k$ table, though it is not necessary that the numbers of rows and columns be equal. We take the marginal distributions of this table to be fixed and then imagine ourselves collapsing categories in various ways to obtain tables of lesser dimensions. In so doing we will create additional tied pairs, since whenever two (or more) rows or columns are combined, there will be previously untied pairs (from different rows and columns) that will become tied as the rows or columns are collapsed. Suppose we begin with C concordant pairs and D discordant pairs. Let C' and D' represent the number of previously untied concordant and discordant pairs, respectively, that *become* tied in the regrouping process. Then the original value of gamma will be $(C - D)/(C + D)$. Without loss of generality let us suppose that C exceeds D and that we may therefore let $C = KD$, where $K > 1$. We may express gamma as

$$\gamma = \frac{C-D}{C+D} = \frac{(K-1)D}{(K+1)D} = \frac{K-1}{K+1}.$$

Next consider the pairs that originally contribute to C and D but that become tied as the data are regrouped. Among these pairs there is a certain relationship between C' and D' which we may express as $C' = K'D'$, where K' will in general not be the same as K. The new number of concordant pairs will be $C - C'$, and similarly the new number of discordant pairs will be $D - D'$, so that we may write the new gamma as

$$\gamma' = \frac{(C-C')-(D-D')}{(C-C')+(D-D')} = \frac{(K-1)D-(K'-1)D'}{(K+1)D-(K'+1)D'}.$$

It is immediately apparent that if $K = K'$, then

$$\gamma' = \frac{(K-1)(D-D')}{(K+1)(D-D')} = \frac{K-1}{K+1} = \gamma ,$$

so that the two values of gamma are exactly equal. That is, if in the regrouping process we happen to take out exactly the same proportion of concordant and discordant pairs as existed in the data as originally grouped, the value of gamma will not be affected. It is also obvious that if K' happens to be less than unity, the numerator for the regrouped data will be greater than the original value of $C - D$; therefore, even tau$_a$ will be increased. Remember that we are assuming that $C > D$. A value of $K' < 1$ implies that $D' > C'$, a possibility that seems highly unlikely to occur as a result of any kind of reasonable regrouping operation, assuming a large enough sample.

But under what less restrictive conditions would we expect *gamma* to increase numerically under the regrouping? Recall that this is actually what occurred with our hypothetical data. It can easily be shown that this will occur only if $K' < K$, whereas gamma will decrease (assuming it is initially positive) whenever $K' > K$. This can be seen as follows: Suppose $K' > K$. We may then represent K' as $K + \Delta$, where Δ is a positive quantity. Substituting $K + \Delta$ in the equation for γ' we get

$$\gamma' = \frac{(K-1)D-(K+\Delta-1)D'}{(K+1)D-(K+\Delta+1)D'} = \frac{[(K-1)(D-D')]-\Delta D'}{[(K+1)(D-D')]-\Delta D'}.$$

Focusing on the two expressions within brackets, we see that the ratio of these quantities $\gamma = (K - 1)/(K + 1)$ is by assumption positive but less than unity. Since the expression $\Delta D'$ is also positive and is subtracted from the two terms in brackets, and since $\Delta D'$ cannot be so large as to yield a zero or negative denominator, the resulting ratio of numerator and denominator must be less than the ratio of the terms in brackets, that is, the original value of gamma. Hence $\gamma' < \gamma$ if $K' > K$. Similarly, it can be shown that if $K' < K$, then $\gamma' > \gamma$. In other words, whether the new value of gamma will be the same, greater than, or smaller than the original value depends on the ratio of C' and D' compared with that of C and D. This, of course, is not surprising.

It is easy to see why, in general, gamma tends to increase whenever adjacent categories are collapsed, as occurred in Table 15.5 above. If one combines two adjacent X categories one is creating additional ties among previously untied pairs that were relatively close together with respect to X (and presumably Y as well). We anticipate that for these newly tied pairs the difference between C' and D' will be relatively small. Thus $K' < K$, assuming $C > D$, and hence $\gamma' > \gamma$. In effect we are pulling out pairs that were contributing less than their proportionate share to the numerator $C - D$.

We may also make certain additional predictions concerning the behavior of gamma under regrouping, *provided* we are willing to make assumptions about the underlying frequency distributions, homoscedasticity, and linearity or nonlinearity. Our discussion can now be much more brief. First, let us assume homoscedasticity and linearity and only negligible measurement errors that affect the rankings. If the underlying frequency distribution of X is normal, the X distances between the extreme sets of pairs will be greater than the distances between more central pairs. Suppose we begin with a set of X marginals (e.g., 100, 300, 500, 300, 100) such as those given in the hypothetical data of Table 15.3. If we collapse the extreme categories at both ends (which results in the totals 400, 500, 400, as in Table 15.4A), we create additional ties among the extremes, but no additional ties involving the middle category. In collapsing the extreme categories we create a situation in which we cannot make determinate predictions. Were it not for the general tendency for collapsing to increase gamma, we should expect K' to be greater than K (assuming $C > D$), since by creating ties we are pulling out relatively more cases that are far apart in terms of the hypothesized metric, while leaving in the (nontied) pairs closer to the center of the distribution. Because of these opposing tendencies we therefore expect that, for normally distributed X's, collapsing the extreme categories will not greatly affect gamma.

However, if we collapse the categories near the center—a possibility that seldom seems to occur to investigators working with real data—we definitely expect gamma to increase, since we are creating additional ties among pairs that are relatively closely bunched together on the X axis. If we refer to the gamma produced by collapsing near the center as γ_1 and refer to the gamma produced by collapsing the extreme categories as γ_2, we predict that $\gamma_1 > \gamma_2$ and $\gamma_1 > \gamma$, where γ represents the original gamma and where, without loss of generality, we are assuming gamma to be positive. The relative magnitudes of γ_2 and γ cannot be predicted.

In the case of a rectangular X distribution we predict that groupings toward the center and toward the extremes will *both* increase gamma, though we cannot make definite predictions about the relative magnitudes of γ_1 and γ_2 without further assumptions. One difficulty, which we shall encounter in considering actual data, concerns the question whether the Y categories should be similarly collapsed. If we take Y as a (linear) function of X and a disturbance term, and if X has a rectangular distribution, it is highly unlikely that Y will also be rectangular, since the disturbance term is much more likely to be approximately normal than rectangular, and since the distribution of Y is jointly determined by the distributions of X and the disturbance.

With a highly skewed X distribution, we expect different results depending on which end we collapse. With a distribution skewed to the right (as in Fig. 15.1c), collapsing left-hand categories produces a gamma (γ_1) numerically larger than the gamma (γ_2) produced by collapsing right-hand categories. Collapsing to the left creates additional ties among pairs closely bunched with respect to X and thereby gives relatively greater weight to the untied pairs involving X scores much less closely bunched at the right-hand portion of the X axis. When we collapse to the right, however, we again create opposing processes; collapsing generally increases gamma, but in this instance we are producing relatively more ties among pairs that were originally farther apart. Referring to the original value of gamma as γ, and assuming that $\gamma > 0$, we thus predict that $\gamma_1 > \gamma_2$ and $\gamma_1 > \gamma$, but make no prediction concerning the relative sizes of γ_2 and γ.

Similarly, we may check the homoscedasticity assumption. Assuming linearity and a symmetrical X frequency distribution, suppose we again have heteroscedasticity of the form implied by Figure 15.2. With greater scatter at the higher end of the distribution we expect C and D to be closer together at this end, which implies that, if we collapse at the higher end, K' should be considerably less than K, and therefore gamma (γ_1) should be substantially increased. Collapsing at the lower end, however, should either decrease gamma (γ_2) or at least result in a much smaller increase. Our prediction, therefore, is that $\gamma_1 > \gamma_2$, assuming a positive γ for the original relationship.

As a final illustration, suppose the relationship between X and Y is nonlinear, with an increasing slope, as indicated in Figure 15.3b. At the lower end C and D should be closer together, which leads us to predict that $K' < K$ for these pairs, so that collapsing at the lower end should definitely increase gamma. Conversely, collapsing at the upper end should either decrease gamma or produce a much smaller increase. Therefore we predict that $\gamma_1 > \gamma_2$ and $\gamma_1 > \gamma$.

Empirical Results with Grouped Data

With the aid of data supplied by Reynolds, it is possible to test some of the above predictions. The data were computer-generated and conformed to known specifications. In all but one instance the original grouped data were given in the form of 5×5 tables involving two ordinal variables X and Y. These data provide the original values of gamma designated as γ in Table 15.6. The categories were collapsed in various ways, producing γ_1 and γ_2, and in all instances except for the rectangular distribution, the predictions are that $\gamma_1 > \gamma_2$ and $\gamma_1 > \gamma$, with the relationship between γ and γ_2 theoretically indeterminate. The final column in Table 15.6 gives the difference $\gamma_1 - \gamma_2$, which indicates the order of magnitude of the effect of collapsing the data in various ways. Except in the 10×10 original table (for normal X's), the collapsing in each instance involved a reduction of the number of X categories from five to three, and the Y categories either remained unchanged or were also reduced to three. The sample sizes for the normal linear and normal nonlinear models were 700 each, whereas 1,000 cases each were used for the rectangular and skewed distributions.

Table 15.6. Values of Gamma for Grouped Data

Model	Dimensions of Table		Gamma Values			
	Original	Collapsed	γ	γ_1	γ_2	$\gamma_1 - \gamma_2$
Rectangular X ($n = 1000$)						
Collapse X, Y	5×5	3×3	.62	.77	.66	.11
Collapse X only	5×5	3×5		.70	.65	.05
Normal X (5×5)($n = 700$)						
Collapse X, Y	5×5	3×3	.76	.91	.76	.15
Collapse X only	5×5	3×5		.89	.76	.13
Normal X (10×10)($n = 700$)						
Collapse X, Y	10×10	$5 \times 5, 4 \times 4$	.64	.85	.69	.16
Skewed X (chi square)($n = 1000$)						
Collapse X, Y	5×5	3×3	.67	.97	.66	.31
Collapse X only	5×5	3×5		.97	.67	.30
Nonlinear ($Y = X^3 + \epsilon$)($n = 700$)						
Collapse X, Y	5×5	3×3	.58	.75	.56	.19
Collapse X only	5×5	3×5		.65	.57	.08

The results for the rectangular distribution are perhaps the most difficult to explain. The independent variable X was given a rectangular distribution, whereas Y was constructed as a linear function of X plus a disturbance term with a normal distribution. Therefore Y was symmetrical, but neither normal nor rectangular. The original five categories of X were collapsed into three by first combining the three middle categories (yielding γ_1) and then by combining the two extreme categories on either side of the middle category (yielding γ_2). As expected, both γ_1 and γ_2 were numerically larger than γ, but we also note that when Y, too, was collapsed (in the same fashion as X), γ_1 was considerably greater than γ_2—probably because, since the disturbance term was normally distributed, collapsing Y toward the center tended to give relatively greater weight to the extreme values of Y, which were dominated by the rectangularly distributed X component rather than the normally distributed disturbance term. In contrast, where we retained all five levels of Y the difference between γ_1 and γ_2 was much smaller, and we suspect that this difference would have been even smaller had we begun with as many as eight or ten categories for Y.

Rectangular frequency distributions are of course exceedingly rare in sociology. More usually, interest centers on either normal distributions or unimodal skewed distributions. With normal frequency distributions, reported for both 5×5 and 10×10 tables, not only was X given a normal distribution, but Y was taken as a linear function of X plus an independent normally distributed disturbance term, which gave Y a normal distribution as well. For the 5×5 data it can be seen that it made virtually no difference whether we collapsed Y as well as X, or retained all five levels of Y. For γ_1, the middle three categories were collapsed, whereas the extreme categories were collapsed to yield γ_2. Results were exactly as expected. By coincidence, the values of γ and γ_2 were almost exactly equal, except to the third decimal. Basically the same pattern occurred in the case of the original 10×10 table, where we first collapsed the middle six categories of both X and Y to yield a 5×5 table and γ_1. Returning to the original data, we then collapsed the four extreme categories at both ends to produce a 4×4 table and γ_2. Here, however, $\gamma_2 > \gamma$. To determine the relative effects of the rectangular and normal distributions, it is most meaningful to compare the 5×5 tables collapsing X only.

For the skewed model, X was given a chi-square distribution (with $df = 3$), and thereby skewed to the right as in Figure 15.1c; Y was taken as a linear function of X and a normally distributed disturbance term; and results of collapsing both X and Y and X only were compared. It can be seen that γ_1, obtained by collapsing the three left-hand columns, was almost unity and was substantially greater than either γ or γ_2, which resulted from collapsing the three right-hand columns closest to the long tail of the skewed distribution. In this instance, collapsing both X and Y produced almost the same results as collapsing X only.

Finally, the particular nonlinear model for which data were constructed involved the equation $Y = X^3 + \epsilon$, where X was given only positive values, and where both X and ϵ were normally distributed. Therefore Y was an increasing function of X with an increasing slope, as indicated in Figure 15.3*b*. When both X and Y were similarly collapsed, the results were very striking and as expected, whereas the pattern was less pronounced when only X was collapsed. Here, γ_1 was produced by collapsing the three left-hand categories, with additional ties produced among pairs relatively close to the origin where the slope of the curve was less steep. Similarly, γ_2 was obtained by collapsing the three right-hand categories containing pairs nearer the steeper portion of the curve. Once more, γ and γ_2 were approximately equal.

These results basically support our argument, though it can be seen that there are certain ambiguities concerning the decision whether or not to collapse Y as well as X. Such a decision must depend upon one's assumptions concerning the distribution of the disturbance term, assumptions seldom made explicit by users of ordinal measures of association. Unless such disturbance terms are thought to be dominated by one or two omitted variables with unusual distributions, a very reasonable assumption is that they are normally distributed and that they may be *added* (rather than, say, multipled) to whatever deterministic equation is being postulated. That assumption is practically always made with parametric models, and, in the absence of specific arguments to the contrary, it seems entirely reasonable for the kind of approach advocated in this chapter.

Concluding Remarks

It has been noted at several points that the proposed tests are very weak ones, involving only predictions about the relative magnitudes of ordinal measures of association. When we add to this the fact that differences between the measures are not likely to be large, that they will be subject to sampling fluctuations, and that departures from linearity, homoscedasticity, or normality may not be very great in most practical applications, it should be readily apparent that these tests will only be useful in providing general hints and hypotheses for more refined studies. Additionally, there may be *several* complications (e.g., heteroscedasticity combined with nonlinearity) that may make it much more difficult to make definitive predictions.

For all these reasons it will be advisable to rely on multiple tests whenever possible. For example, if an independent variable X can be related to several distinct dependent variables that are only weakly intercorrelated, additional checks will be possible. For illustrative purposes, suppose that one is in doubt concerning two possibilities, the first involving a potential nonlinearity in the relationship between X and Y, and the second entailing a skewed frequency distribution in X. By using a second dependent variable assumed to be linearly related to X, one might be in a position to choose between these two alternatives. Clearly, the more dependent variables one can find, the less likely that any two competing alternatives will account equally well for all patterns of relationships among the ordinal measures.

In instances in which the results of multiple weak tests of the sort considered here warrant proceeding with reasonably strong assumptions concerning forms of underlying distributions, linearity or nonlinearity, and the like, it seems reasonable to proceed with parametric analytic tools *as supplements to* standard ordinal techniques. For example, if the gammas for alternative categorizations using as many as three distinct dependent variables all yield results similar to those given in Table 15.5 in the case of the assumed normal distribution of X and linear relationships with the Y_i, the X categories might be scored as though the true distribution were actually normal. If this is possible with respect to each of the remaining ordinal variables in the theoretical system, parametric simultaneous-equation procedures might be used in an exploratory fashion. Or, for recursive models, the parametric results could be compared with those obtained by means of partial tau_b values. It is important to emphasize that, unless both parametric and nonparametric procedures are used in analyzing data, it will be exceedingly difficult to accumulate evidence regarding the relative merits of these different approaches in instances in which measurement has been very crude.

Finally, if data analyses are to be more effectively integrated with social science theories, the latter must be made more specific with respect to predictions that imply more than an ordinal level of measurement. There is no reason, for example, why qualitative propositions linking X to Y cannot be refined so as to specify approximate forms of relationships other than linear ones, or joint effects other than additive ones. Similarly, if a theorist is able to identify a reasonable number of the variables affecting an X distribution, it may be possible to predict the approximate form of the frequency distribution. For example, the presumption that there are a very large number of weakly intercorrelated causes of prejudice or other attitudinal variables can be expected to produce an approximately normal frequency distribution. If in some subpopulation this distribution is expected to be truncated—as, for example, persons with low prejudice unlikely to join the Ku Klux Klan, or those with low abilities unlikely to be admitted to college—a skewed distribution for this subpopulation could be predicted.

The more specific one can be about the causal processes that have generated a particular set of population data, the greater the number of weak predictions that can be made for ordinal data. While it may be true, as Wilson (1971) argues, that ordinal measures based on *pairs* of individuals cannot be directly used to evaluate causal theories pertaining to individual cases, it is possible to use these theories to make specific predictions based on the known behavior of their parametric counterparts. Methodological studies involving simulated data may then shed sufficient light on the empirical behavior of the ordinal coefficients to close the gap between the theoretical formulations, on the one hand, and our data analyses on the other. Once more it should be emphasized, however, that improvements in data-collection procedures will be far more important, in the long run, than the kinds of weak predictions that must be made whenever inadequate attention has been given to measurement problems at the data-collection stage.

References

Blalock, H. M.
1964. *Causal Inferences in Nonexperimental Research.* Chapel Hill: University of North Carolina Press.
1970. "A Causal Approach to Nonrandom Measurement Errors." *American Political Science Review* 64 (December): 1099-1111.
Caplow, Theodore
1956. "A Theory of Coalitions in the Triad." *American Sociological Review* 21 (August): 489-93.
Coombs, Clyde H.
1953. "Theory and Methods of Social Measurement." In L. Festinger and D. Katz, eds., *Research Methods in the Behavioral Sciences.* New York: Dryden.
1964. *A Theory of Data.* New York: Wiley.
Gamson, William A.
1961. "A Theory of Coalition Formation." *American Sociological Review* 26 (June): 373-82.
Hawkes, Roland K.
1971. "The Multivariate Analysis of Ordinal Variables." *American Journal of Sociology* 76 (March): 908-26.
Labovitz, Sanford
1967. "Some Observations on Measurement and Statistics." *Social Forces* 46 (December): 151-60.
Leik, Robert K., and Walter R. Gove
1969. "The Conception and Measurement of Asymmetric Monotonic Relationships in Sociology." *American Journal of Sociology* 74 (May): 696-709.
1971. "Integrated Approach to Measuring Association." In H. L. Costner, ed., *Sociological Methodology, 1971.* chap. 10. San Francisco: Jossey-Bass.
Reynolds, Henry T.
1971. "Making Causal Inferences with Ordinal Data." Institute for Research in Social Sciences, Working Papers in Methodology, no. 5. Chapel Hill: University of North Carolina.
Somers, Robert H.
1962. "A New Asymmetric Measure of Association for Ordinal Variables." *American Sociological Review* 27 (December): 799-811.
Stern, Maxine Springer
1971. "The Effects of Grouping on the Correlation Coefficient." Paper presented at the sixty-sixth Annual American Sociological Association Meetings, Denver, 1971.
Wilson, Thomas P.
1971. "Critique of Ordinal Variables." *Social Forces* 49 (March): 432-44.

Subject Index

Name Index